Yamada-kun and the Seven Witches

12

Miki Yoshikawa

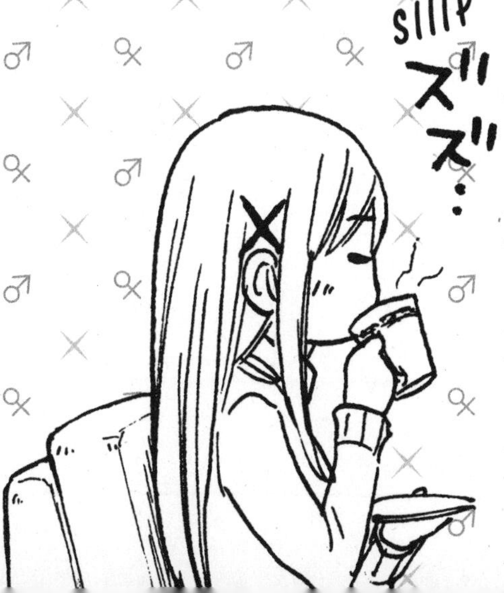
SIIIP
ズズ…

Ryu Yamada

A second-year at Suzaku High School and part of the Supernatural Studies Club. He has happily taken the position of secretary to the president of the Student Council. He's known as the "Copy Guy" and possesses the ability to copy the power of whichever witch he kisses. He loves Shiraishi and Yakisoba bread.

Urara Shiraishi

A second-year at Suzaku High School and president of the Supernatural Studies Club. A coolheaded girl who's always studying. Formerly known as the "Switch Witch." Despite being ultra-cute and a top-notch student, she's dating Yamada for some odd reason.

Toranosuke Miyamura

A second-year at Suzaku High School and president of the Student Council. He's sharp-witted and is the most popular kid in school. He seems to like teasing and playing around with Yamada.

Nene Odagiri

A second-year at Suzaku High School and clerk for the Student Council. She always acts arrogant, but doesn't seem to actually be a bad person. She likes Yamada. Why?!

Shinichi Tamaki

A second-year at Suzaku High School and treasurer for the Student Council. He's known as the "Capture Guy" and steals the power of the witch whom he kisses. He pretends to be an elite, but he's really just lonely. His hobby is reading light novels.

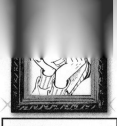

Miyabi Itou

A second-year at Suzaku High School and part of the Supernatural Studies Club. She's the only member of the club who's into the occult. She's an idiot but is surprisingly popular with boys.

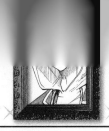

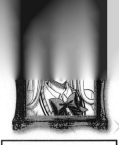

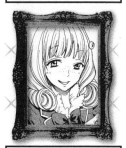

Rika Saionji

A third-year at Suzaku High School and the former seventh witch. She's an abnormal person who does things like never wearing panties.

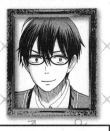

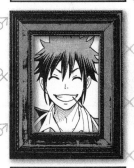

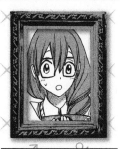

Meiko Otsuka

A second-year at Suzaku High School and the former "Thought Witch." A shy girl who is a member of the Manga Studies Club.

Jin Kurosaki

A first-year at Suzaku High School and one of the vice-presidents of the Student Council. He's always expressionless, so his nickname is "Assassin." He has a pretty bad attitude, but is totally obedient to Miyamura, whom he idolizes.

Haruma Yamazaki

A third-year at Suzaku High School and the crafty, former president of the Student Council. Before becoming the Student Council president, he was a member of the Supernatural Studies Club, but he had his memories erased by Rika. He now has his memories back and is enjoying his everyday life.

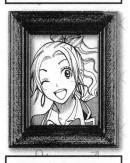

Maria Sarushima

A second-year at Suzaku High School and the former "Prediction Witch." She used to live abroad and greets people with kisses.

Midori Arisugawa

A first-year at Suzaku High School and one of the vice-presidents of the Student Council. She's a girl with an easy-going attitude, and is a bit dimwitted. Her motto is "live life with ease." Her chest is HUGE!

Kentaro Tsubaki

A second-year at Suzaku High School and part of the Supernatural Studies Club. He's skillful and used to live abroad. When he feels lonely or sad, he fries up some tempura to soothe his heart.

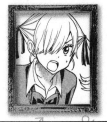

Noa Takigawa

A first-year at Suzaku High School and the former "Retrocognition Witch." A little rascal who is infatuated with Yamada.

CONTENTS

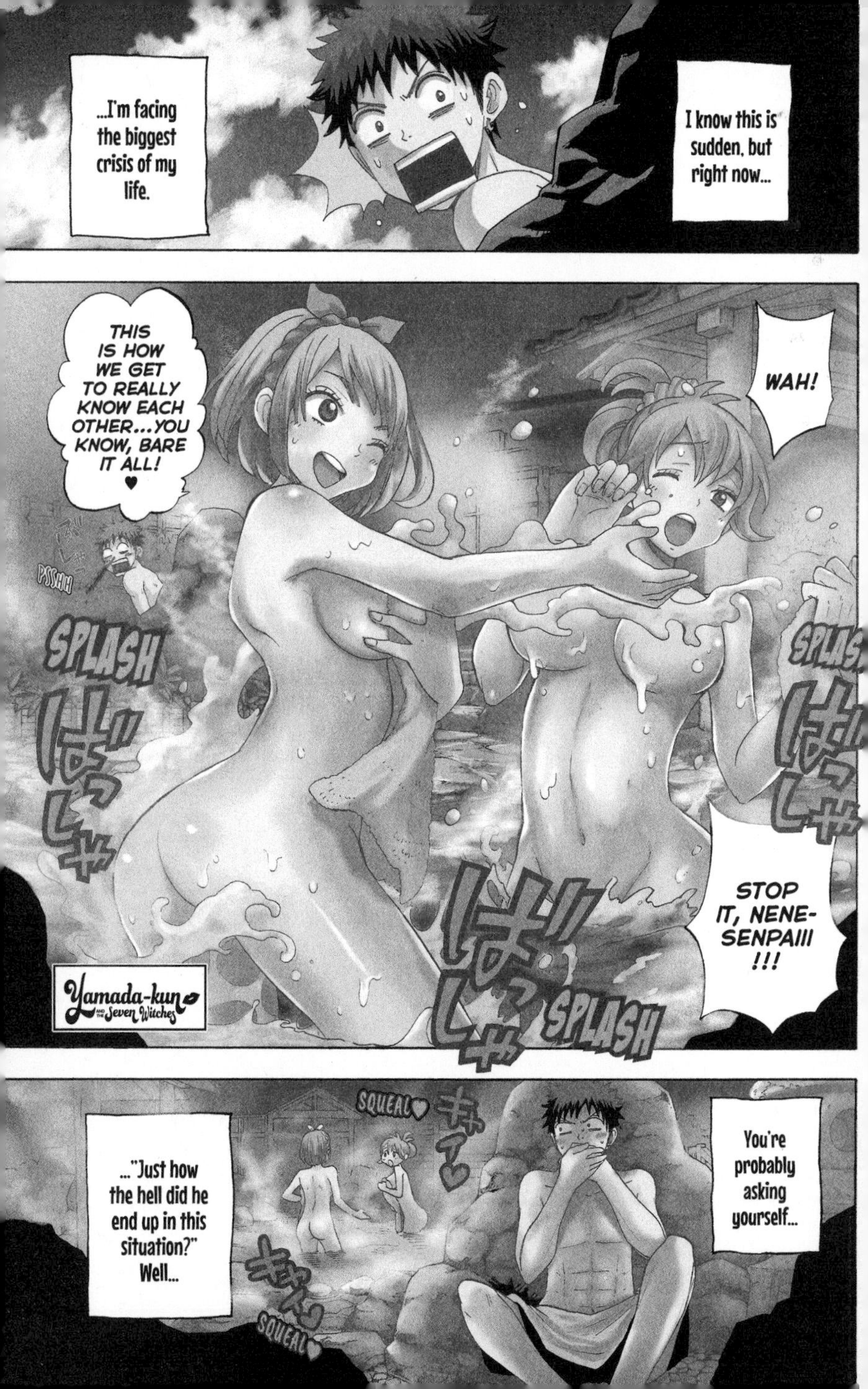

I know this is sudden, but right now...
...I'm facing the biggest crisis of my life.
WAH!
SPLASH
ばっしゃ
STOP IT, NENE-SENPAIII !!!
ばっしゃ
SPLASH
THIS IS HOW WE GET TO REALLY KNOW EACH OTHER...YOU KNOW, BARE IT ALL! ♥
PSSHH
SPLASH
ばっしゃ
Yamada-kun and the Seven Witches
You're probably asking yourself...
SQUEAL♥
キャ♥
..."Just how the hell did he end up in this situation?" Well...
キャ
SQUEAL♥

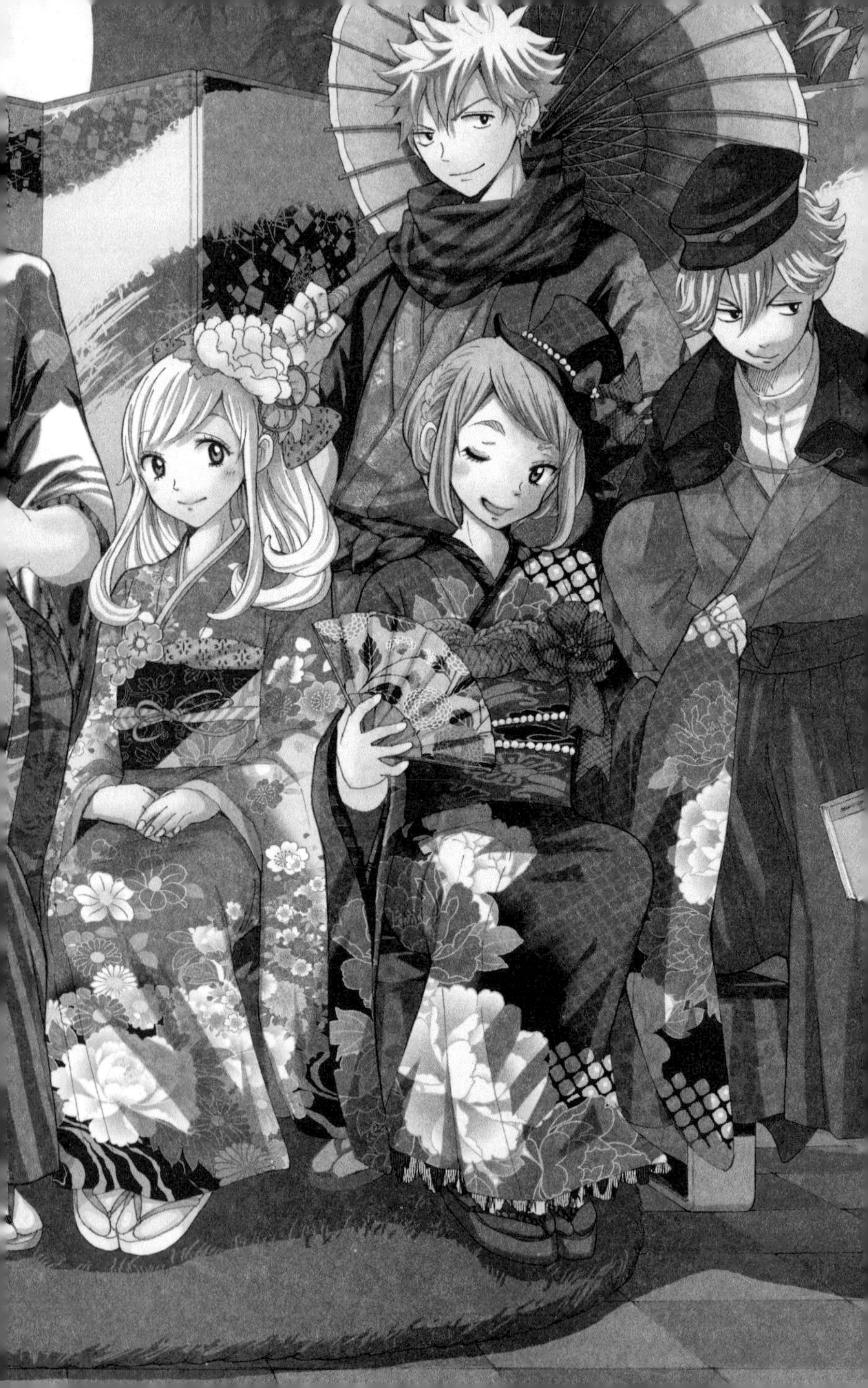

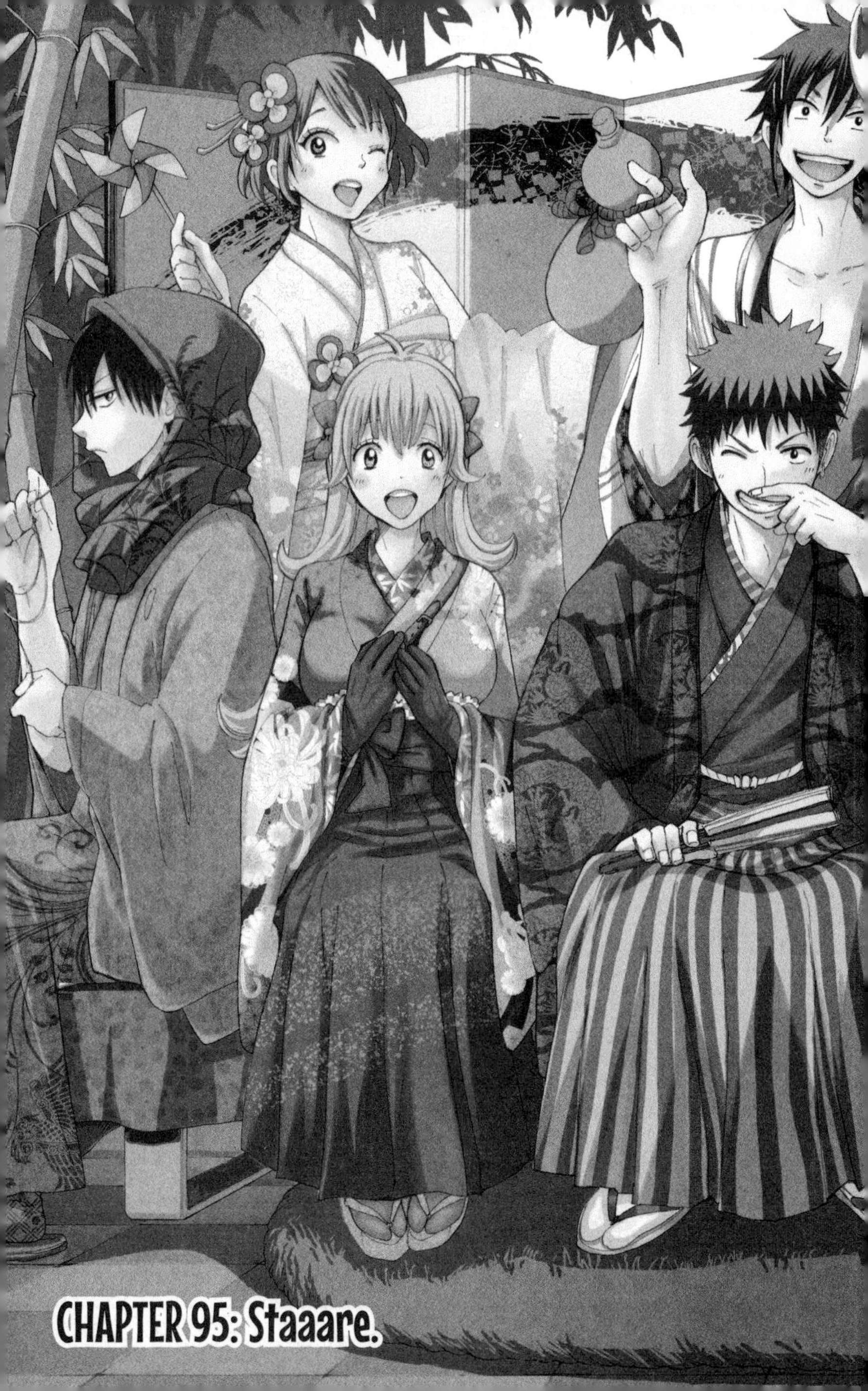

CHAPTER 95: Staaare.

Yamada-kun
AND THE
Seven Witches

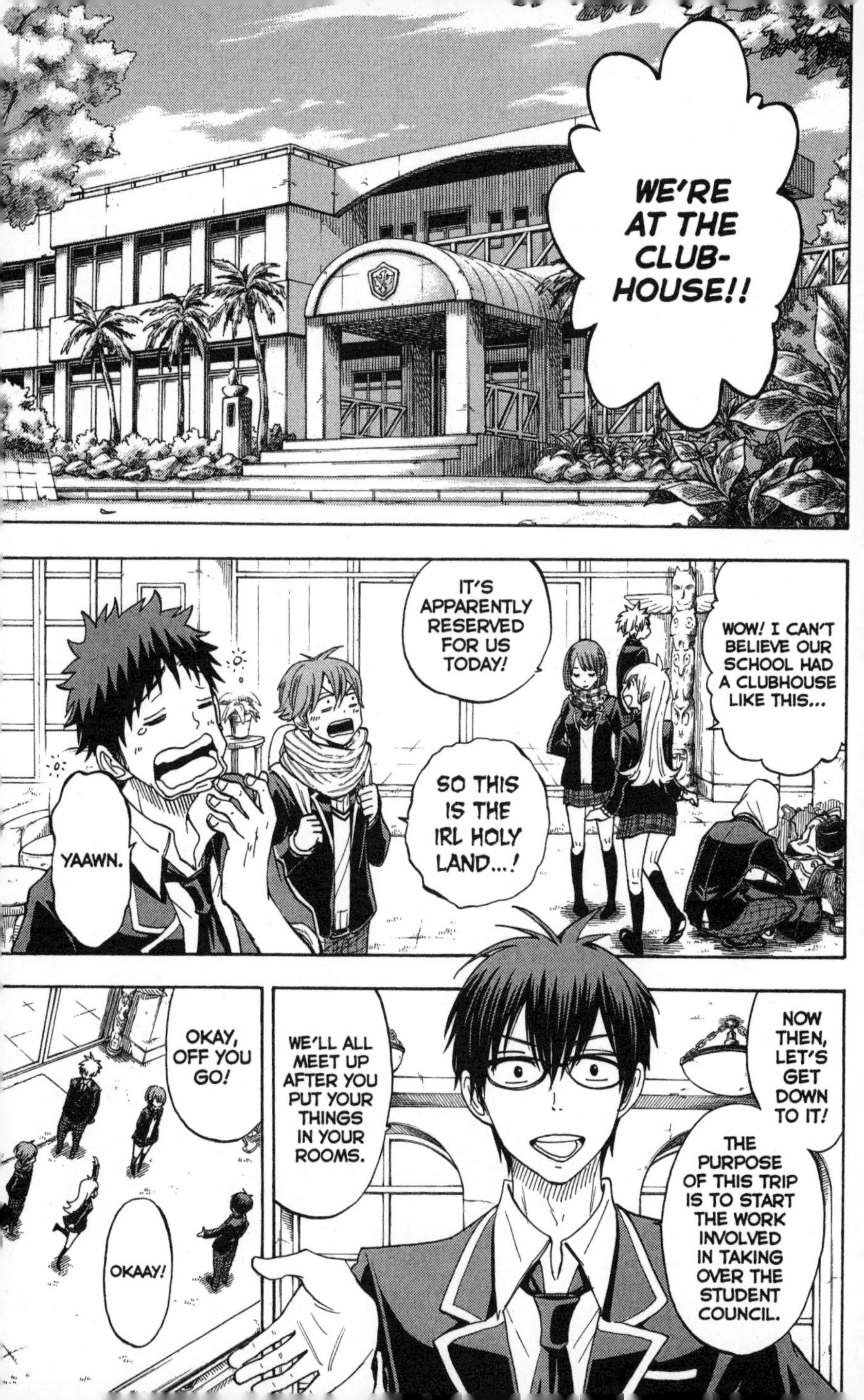
WE'RE AT THE CLUB-HOUSE!!
WOW! I CAN'T BELIEVE OUR SCHOOL HAD A CLUBHOUSE LIKE THIS...
IT'S APPARENTLY RESERVED FOR US TODAY!
SO THIS IS THE IRL HOLY LAND...!
YAAWN.
NOW THEN, LET'S GET DOWN TO IT!
THE PURPOSE OF THIS TRIP IS TO START THE WORK INVOLVED IN TAKING OVER THE STUDENT COUNCIL.
WE'LL ALL MEET UP AFTER YOU PUT YOUR THINGS IN YOUR ROOMS.
OKAY, OFF YOU GO!
OKAAY!

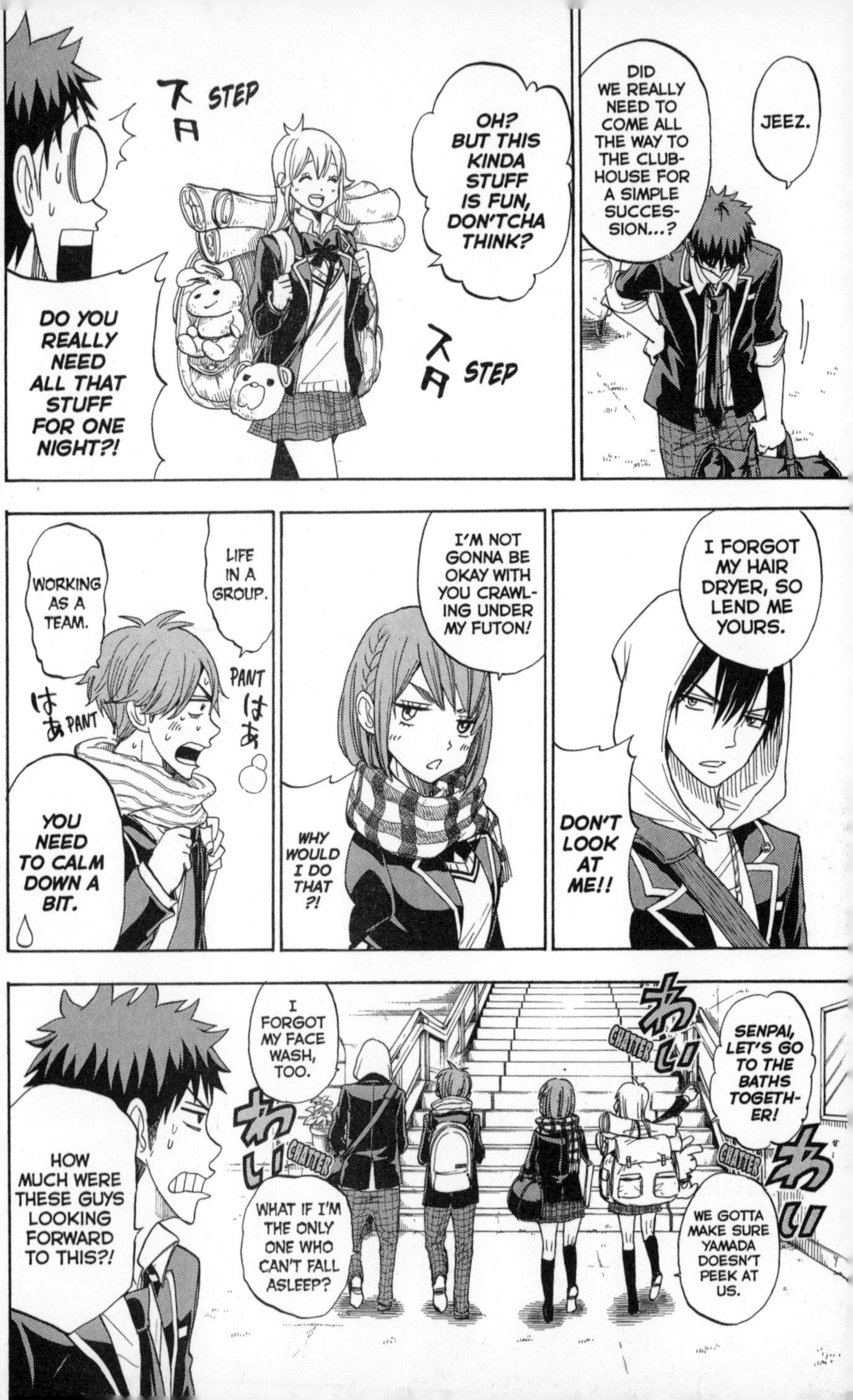
JEEZ.
DID WE REALLY NEED TO COME ALL THE WAY TO THE CLUB-HOUSE FOR A SIMPLE SUCCES-SION...?
OH? BUT THIS KINDA STUFF IS FUN, DON'TCHA THINK?
STEP
STEP
DO YOU REALLY NEED ALL THAT STUFF FOR ONE NIGHT?!
I FORGOT MY HAIR DRYER, SO LEND ME YOURS.
DON'T LOOK AT ME!!
I'M NOT GONNA BE OKAY WITH YOU CRAWL-ING UNDER MY FUTON!
WHY WOULD I DO THAT?!
LIFE IN A GROUP.
WORKING AS A TEAM.
PANT
PANT
YOU NEED TO CALM DOWN A BIT.
SENPAI, LET'S GO TO THE BATHS TOGETH-ER!
CHATTER
WE GOTTA MAKE SURE YAMADA DOESN'T PEEK AT US.
CHATTER
I FORGOT MY FACE WASH, TOO.
WHAT IF I'M THE ONLY ONE WHO CAN'T FALL ASLEEP?
CHATTER
HOW MUCH WERE THESE GUYS LOOKING FORWARD TO THIS?!

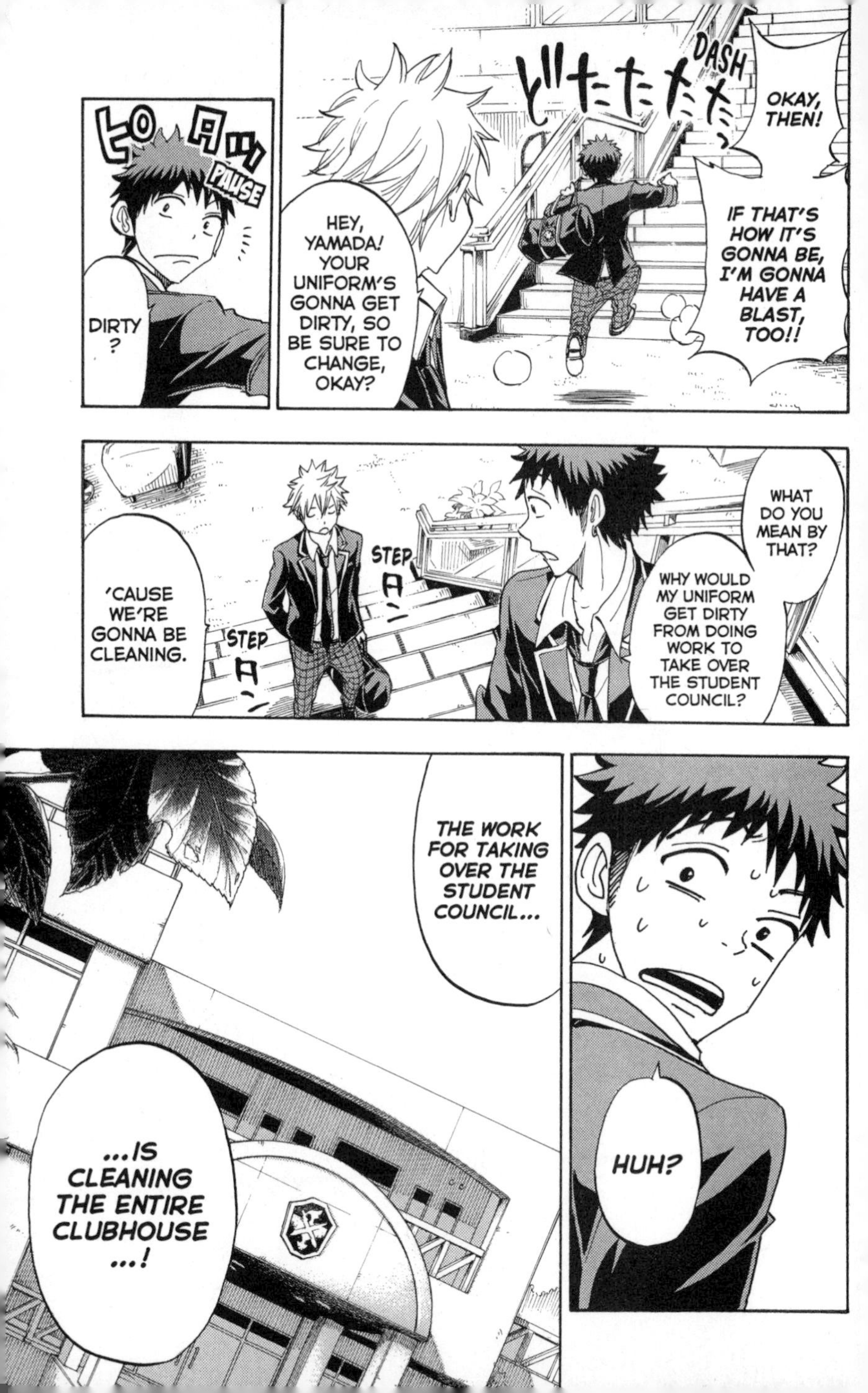
DASH
OKAY, THEN!
IF THAT'S HOW IT'S GONNA BE, I'M GONNA HAVE A BLAST, TOO!!
HEY, YAMADA! YOUR UNIFORM'S GONNA GET DIRTY, SO BE SURE TO CHANGE, OKAY?
PAUSE
DIRTY?
WHAT DO YOU MEAN BY THAT?
WHY WOULD MY UNIFORM GET DIRTY FROM DOING WORK TO TAKE OVER THE STUDENT COUNCIL?
STEP
STEP
'CAUSE WE'RE GONNA BE CLEANING.
HUH?
THE WORK FOR TAKING OVER THE STUDENT COUNCIL...
...IS CLEANING THE ENTIRE CLUBHOUSE ...!

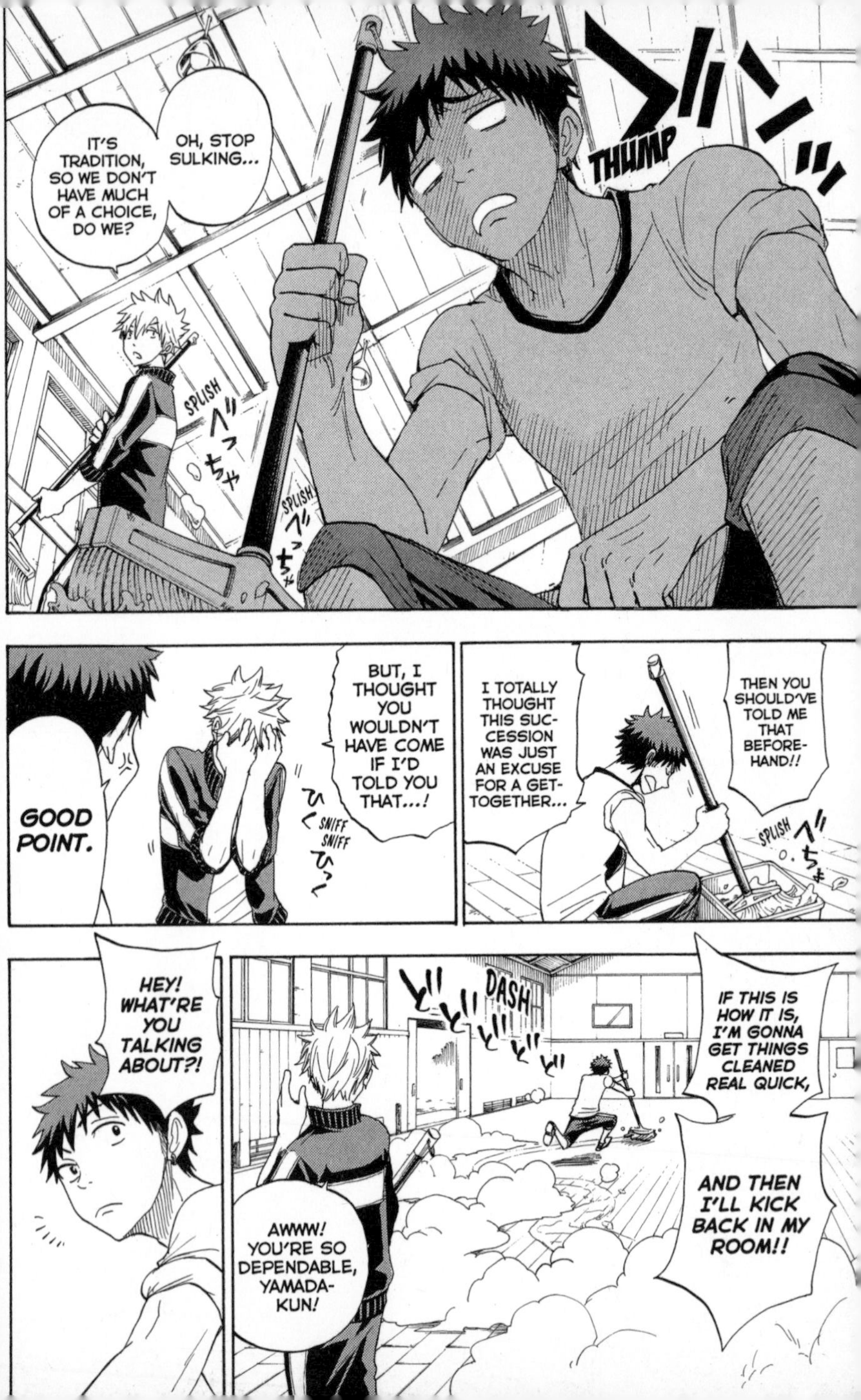

THUMP
OH, STOP SULKING...
IT'S TRADITION, SO WE DON'T HAVE MUCH OF A CHOICE, DO WE?
SPLISH
SPLISH
THEN YOU SHOULD'VE TOLD ME THAT BEFORE-HAND!!
I TOTALLY THOUGHT THIS SUC-CESSION WAS JUST AN EXCUSE FOR A GET-TOGETHER...
SPLISH
BUT, I THOUGHT YOU WOULDN'T HAVE COME IF I'D TOLD YOU THAT...!
SNIFF SNIFF
GOOD POINT.
IF THIS IS HOW IT IS, I'M GONNA GET THINGS CLEANED REAL QUICK,
AND THEN I'LL KICK BACK IN MY ROOM!!
DASH
AWWW! YOU'RE SO DEPENDABLE, YAMADA-KUN!
HEY! WHAT'RE YOU TALKING ABOUT?!

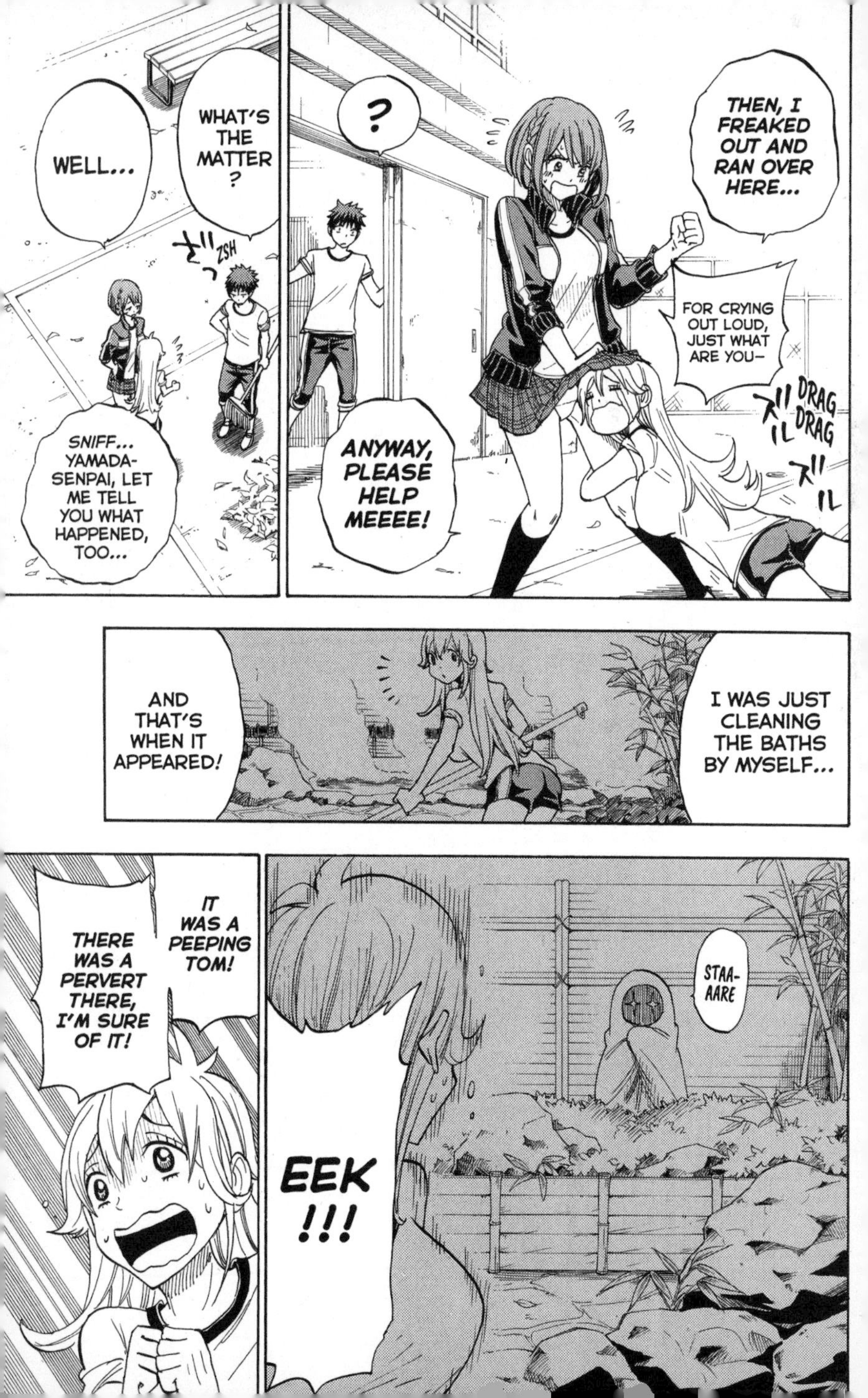
THEN, I FREAKED OUT AND RAN OVER HERE...
?
FOR CRYING OUT LOUD, JUST WHAT ARE YOU–
DRAG DRAG
ANYWAY, PLEASE HELP MEEEE!
WHAT'S THE MATTER?
WELL...
ZSH
SNIFF... YAMADA-SENPAI, LET ME TELL YOU WHAT HAPPENED, TOO...
I WAS JUST CLEANING THE BATHS BY MYSELF...
AND THAT'S WHEN IT APPEARED!
STAA-AARE
EEK!!!
IT WAS A PEEPING TOM!
THERE WAS A PERVERT THERE, I'M SURE OF IT!

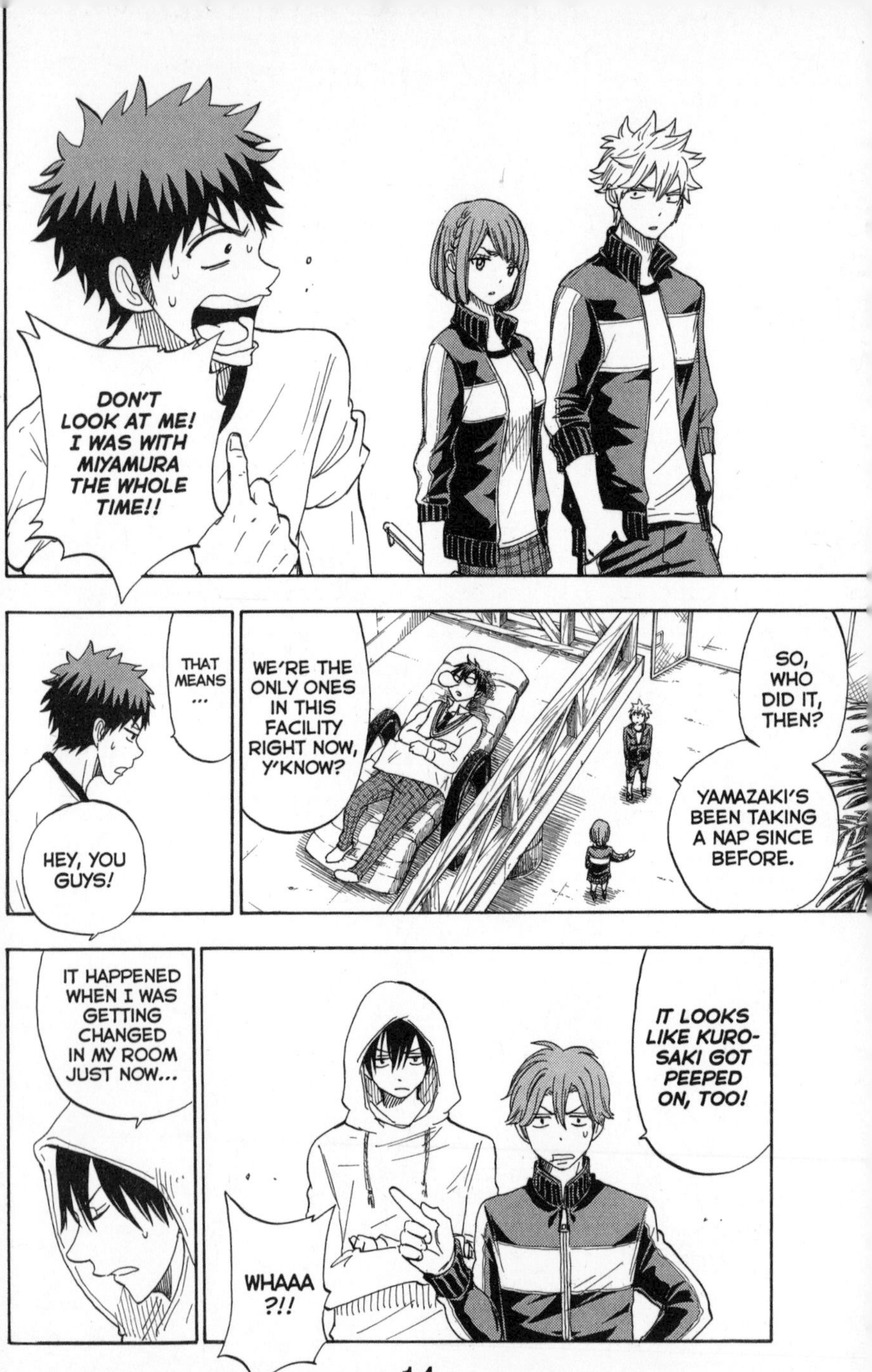
DON'T LOOK AT ME! I WAS WITH MIYAMURA THE WHOLE TIME!!
SO, WHO DID IT, THEN?
YAMAZAKI'S BEEN TAKING A NAP SINCE BEFORE.
WE'RE THE ONLY ONES IN THIS FACILITY RIGHT NOW, Y'KNOW?
THAT MEANS ...
HEY, YOU GUYS!
IT LOOKS LIKE KURO-SAKI GOT PEEPED ON, TOO!
WHAAA ?!!
IT HAPPENED WHEN I WAS GETTING CHANGED IN MY ROOM JUST NOW...

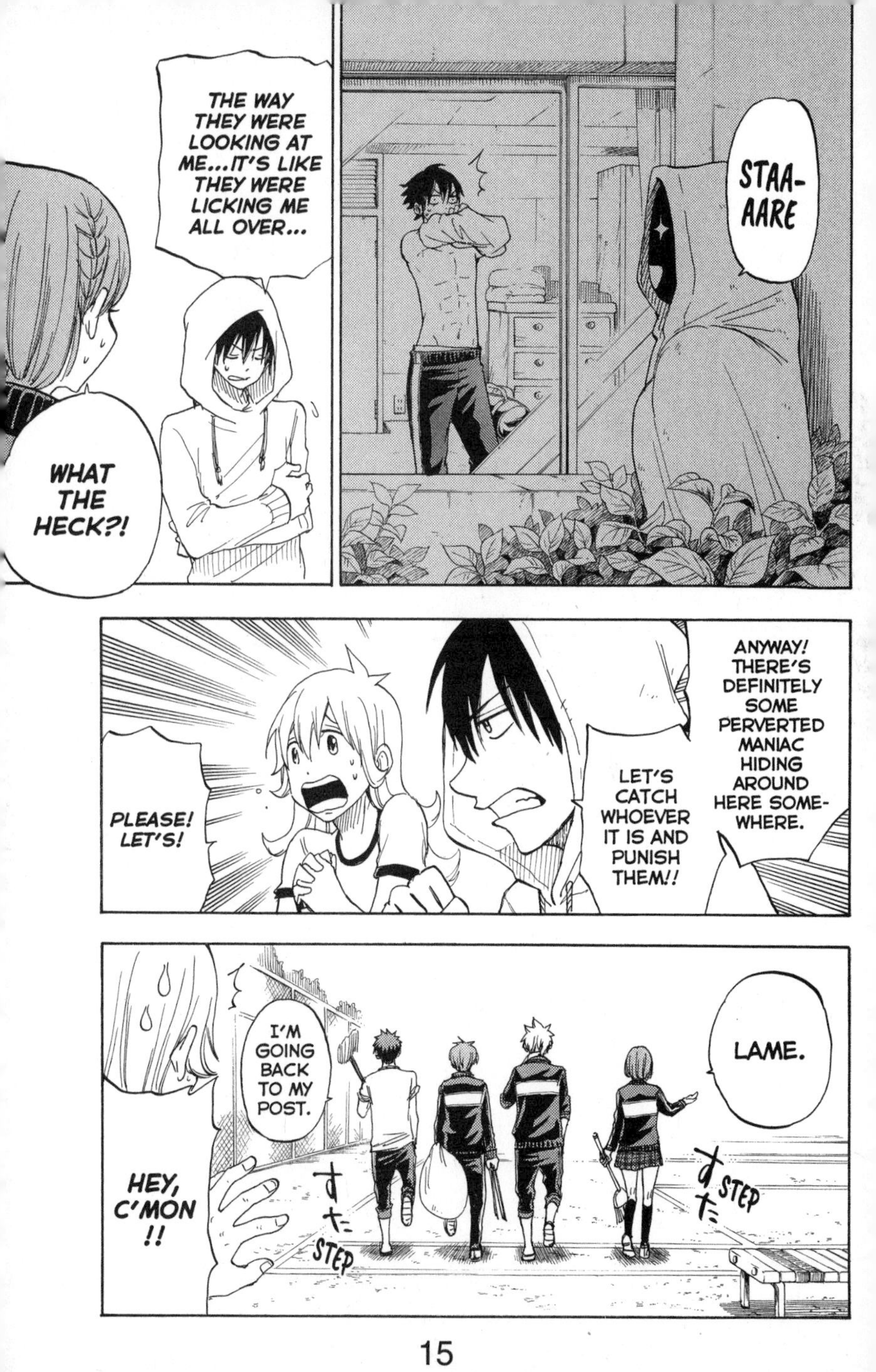
STAA-AARE
THE WAY THEY WERE LOOKING AT ME...IT'S LIKE THEY WERE LICKING ME ALL OVER...
WHAT THE HECK?!
ANYWAY! THERE'S DEFINITELY SOME PERVERTED MANIAC HIDING AROUND HERE SOMEWHERE.
LET'S CATCH WHOEVER IT IS AND PUNISH THEM!!
PLEASE! LET'S!
LAME.
すた STEP
I'M GOING BACK TO MY POST.
HEY, C'MON!!
すた STEP

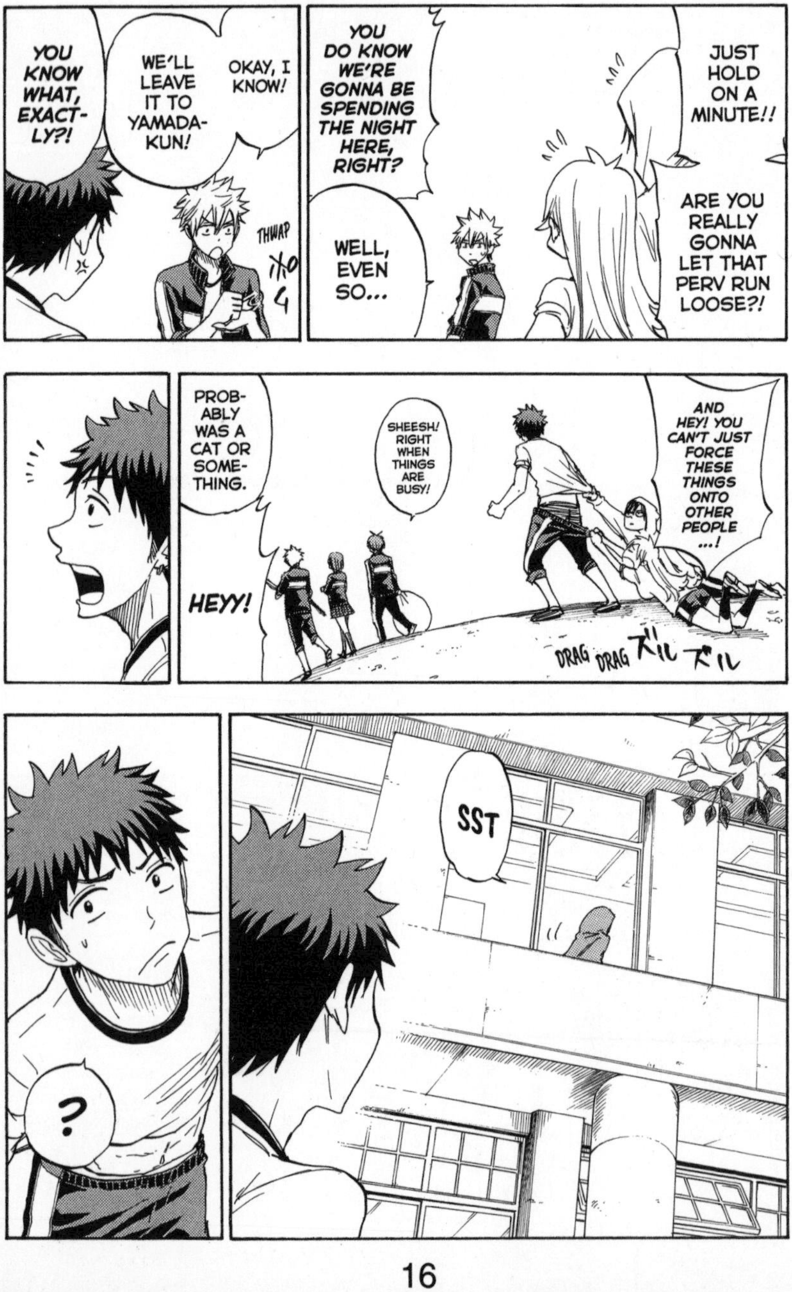
JUST HOLD ON A MINUTE!!
ARE YOU REALLY GONNA LET THAT PERV RUN LOOSE?!
YOU DO KNOW WE'RE GONNA BE SPENDING THE NIGHT HERE, RIGHT?
WELL, EVEN SO...
OKAY, I KNOW!
WE'LL LEAVE IT TO YAMADA-KUN!
YOU KNOW WHAT, EXACTLY?!
THWAP
AND HEY! YOU CAN'T JUST FORCE THESE THINGS ONTO OTHER PEOPLE ...!
SHEESH! RIGHT WHEN THINGS ARE BUSY!
PROBABLY WAS A CAT OR SOMETHING.
HEYY!
DRAG DRAG
SST
?

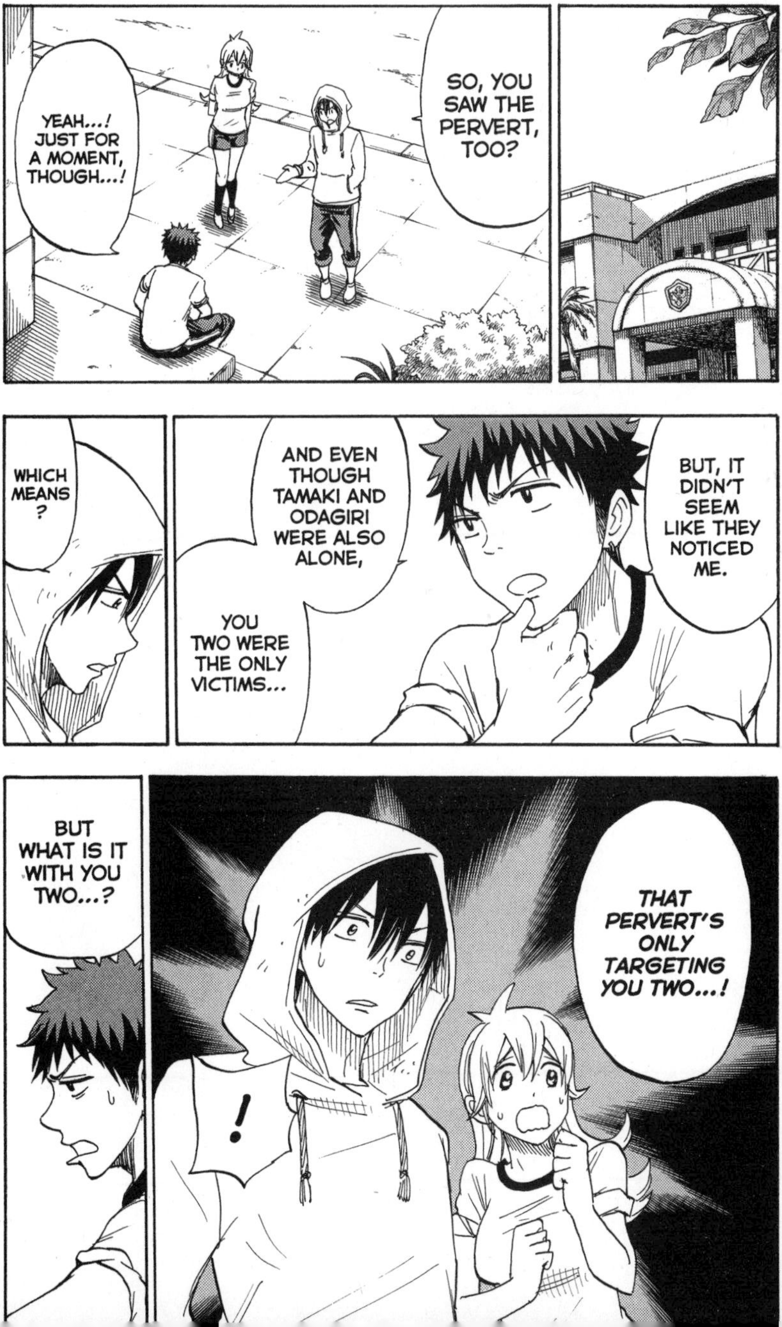
SO, YOU SAW THE PERVERT, TOO?
YEAH...! JUST FOR A MOMENT, THOUGH...!
BUT, IT DIDN'T SEEM LIKE THEY NOTICED ME.
AND EVEN THOUGH TAMAKI AND ODAGIRI WERE ALSO ALONE,
YOU TWO WERE THE ONLY VICTIMS...
WHICH MEANS ?
THAT PERVERT'S ONLY TARGETING YOU TWO...!
!
BUT WHAT IS IT WITH YOU TWO...?

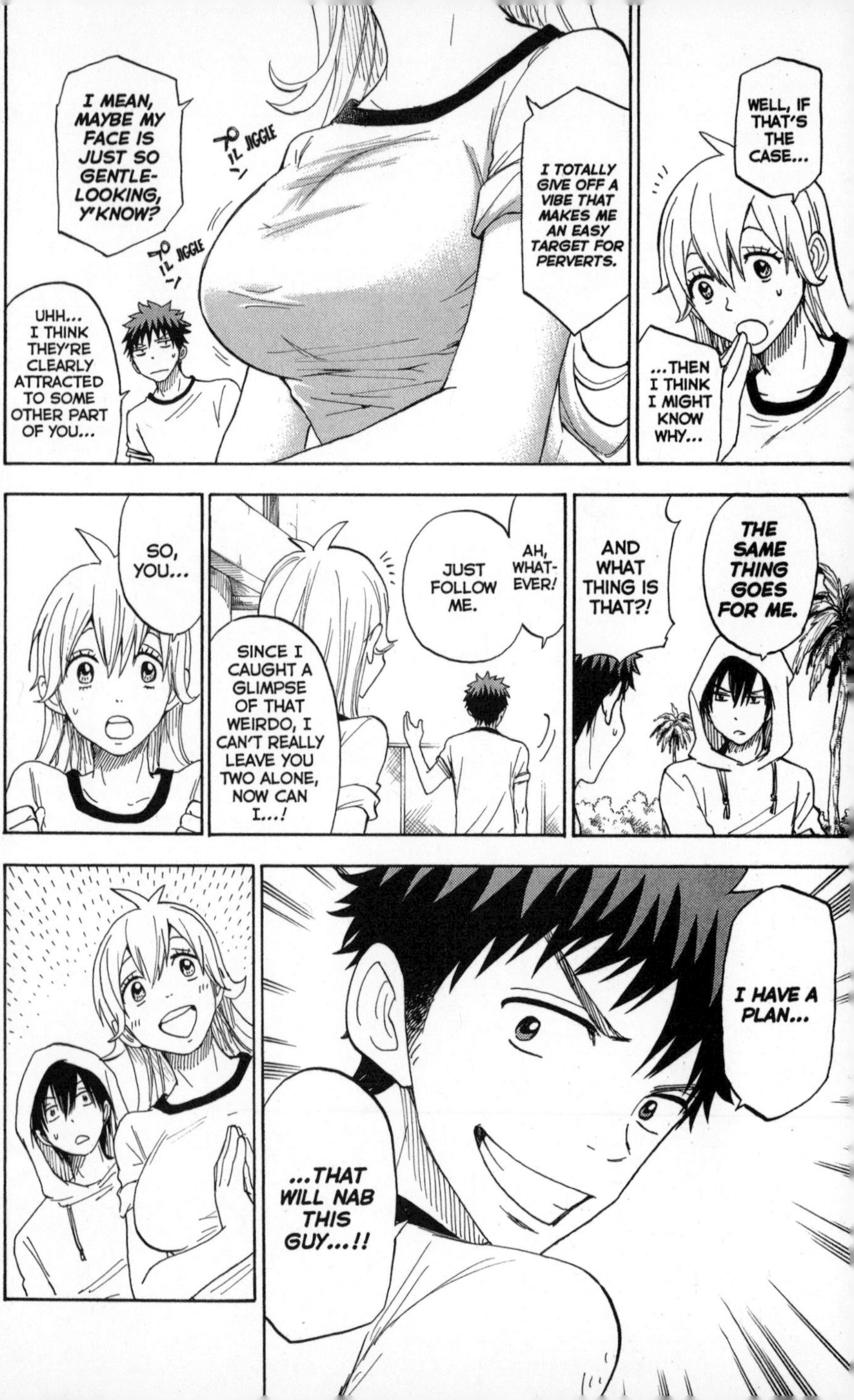
WELL, IF THAT'S THE CASE...
...THEN I THINK I MIGHT KNOW WHY...
I TOTALLY GIVE OFF A VIBE THAT MAKES ME AN EASY TARGET FOR PERVERTS.
I MEAN, MAYBE MY FACE IS JUST SO GENTLE-LOOKING, Y'KNOW?
JIGGLE
JIGGLE
UHH... I THINK THEY'RE CLEARLY ATTRACTED TO SOME OTHER PART OF YOU...
THE SAME THING GOES FOR ME.
AND WHAT THING IS THAT?!
AH, WHATEVER!
JUST FOLLOW ME.
SINCE I CAUGHT A GLIMPSE OF THAT WEIRDO, I CAN'T REALLY LEAVE YOU TWO ALONE, NOW CAN I...!
SO, YOU...
I HAVE A PLAN...
...THAT WILL NAB THIS GUY...!!

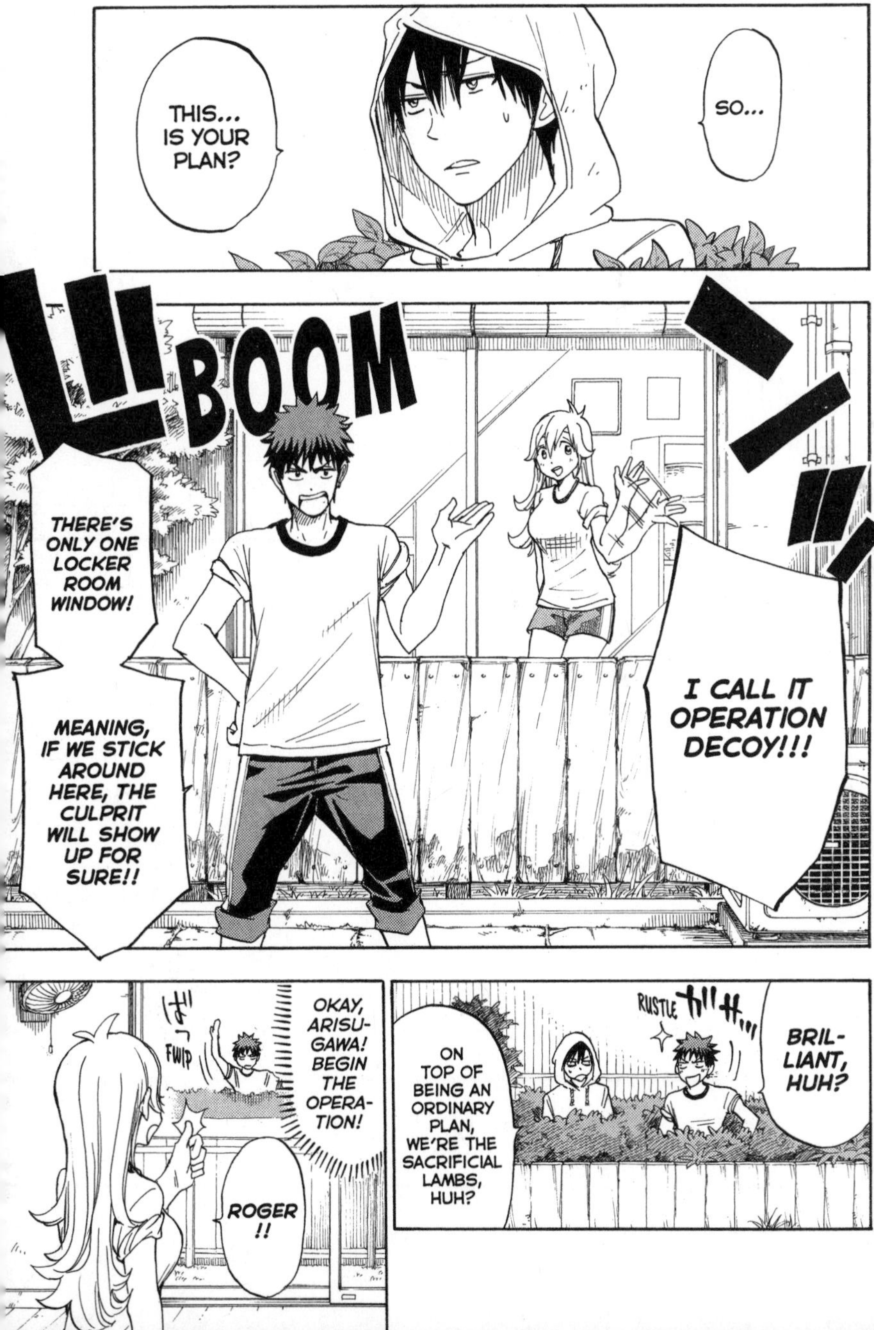
SO...
THIS... IS YOUR PLAN?
BOOM
THERE'S ONLY ONE LOCKER ROOM WINDOW!
MEANING, IF WE STICK AROUND HERE, THE CULPRIT WILL SHOW UP FOR SURE!!
I CALL IT OPERATION DECOY!!!
RUSTLE
BRIL-LIANT, HUH?
ON TOP OF BEING AN ORDINARY PLAN, WE'RE THE SACRIFICIAL LAMBS, HUH?
OKAY, ARISU-GAWA! BEGIN THE OPERA-TION!
FWIP
ROGER!!

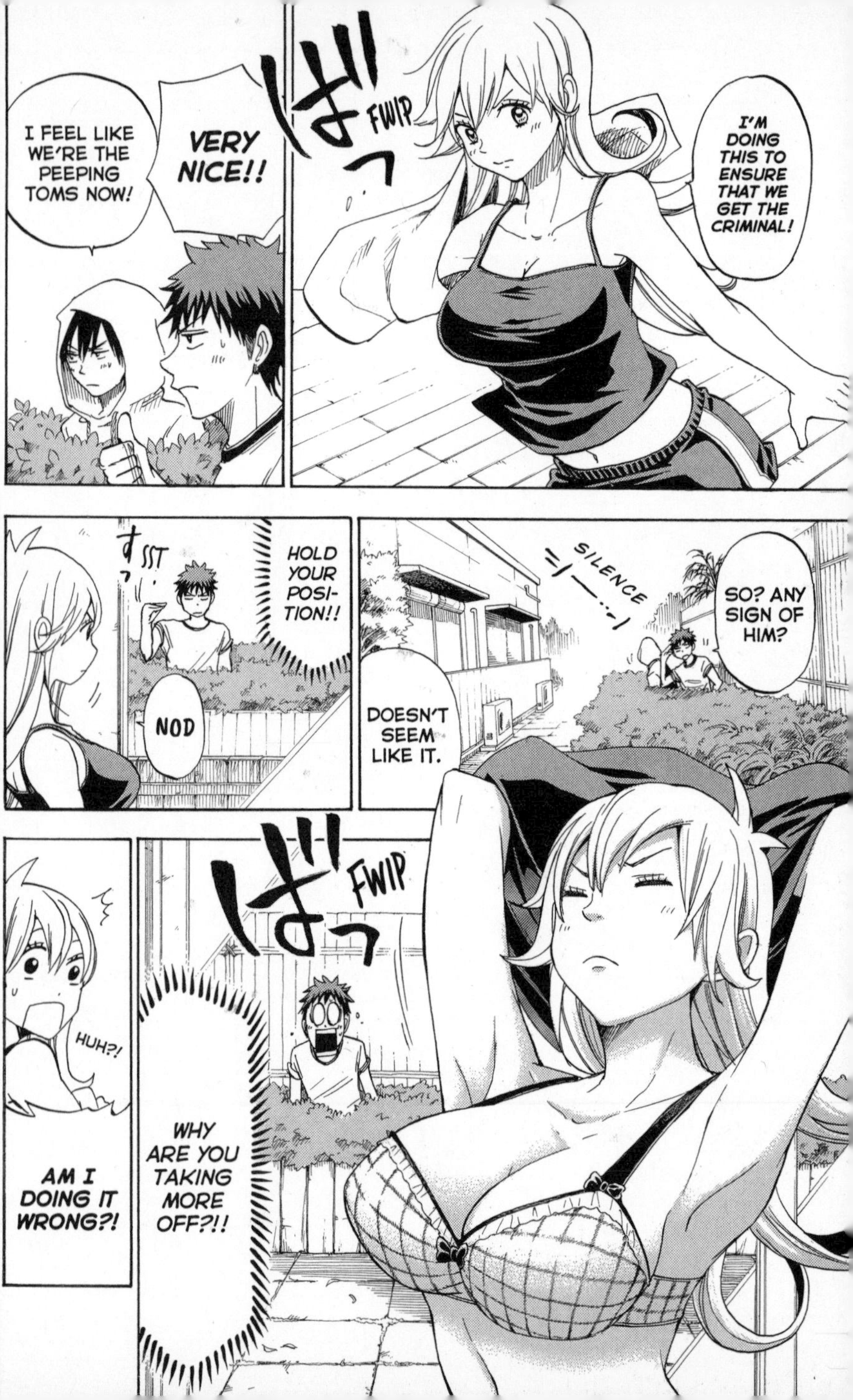
I'M DOING THIS TO ENSURE THAT WE GET THE CRIMINAL!
ばっ FWIP
VERY NICE!!
I FEEL LIKE WE'RE THE PEEPING TOMS NOW!
SO? ANY SIGN OF HIM?
SILENCE
DOESN'T SEEM LIKE IT.
HOLD YOUR POSI-TION!!
すっ SST
NOD
ばっ FWIP
WHY ARE YOU TAKING MORE OFF?!!
HUH?!
AM I DOING IT WRONG?!

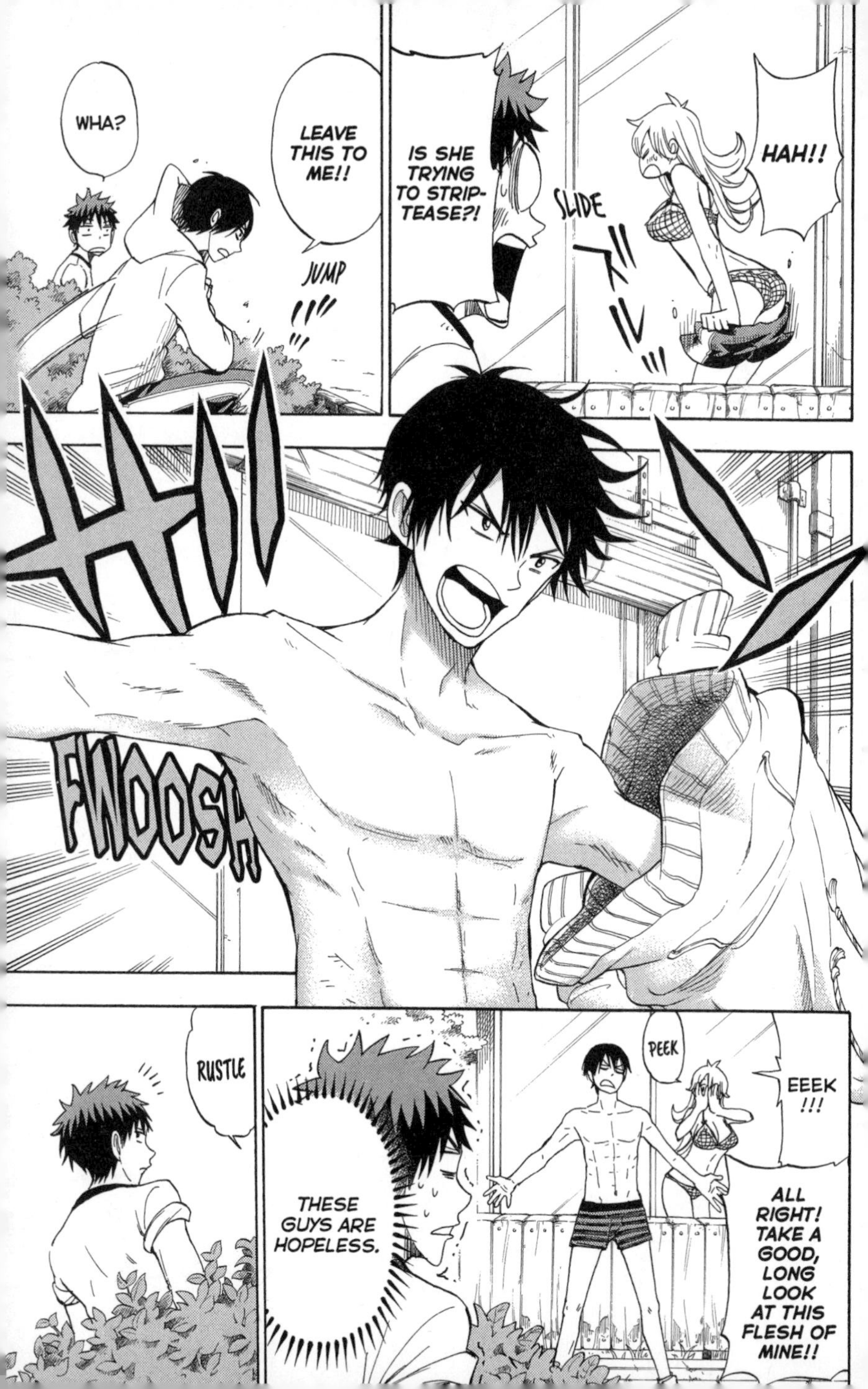
HAH!!
SLIDE
IS SHE TRYING TO STRIP-TEASE?!
LEAVE THIS TO ME!!
JUMP
WHA?
FWOOSH
EEEK!!!
PEEK
ALL RIGHT! TAKE A GOOD, LONG LOOK AT THIS FLESH OF MINE!!
THESE GUYS ARE HOPELESS.
RUSTLE

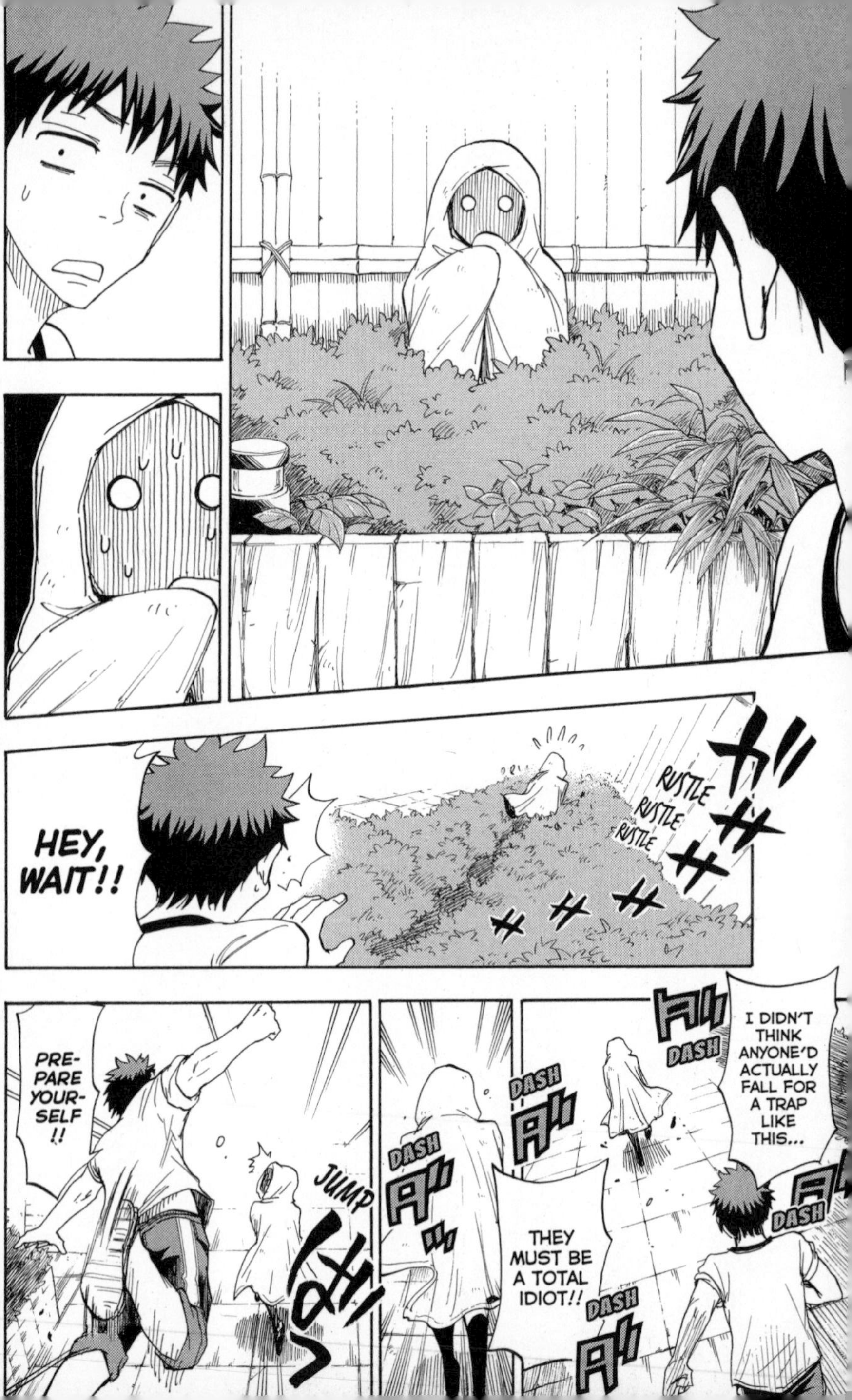

HEY, WAIT!!
RUSTLE
RUSTLE
RUSTLE
I DIDN'T THINK ANYONE'D ACTUALLY FALL FOR A TRAP LIKE THIS...
DASH
DASH
DASH
THEY MUST BE A TOTAL IDIOT!!
DASH
DASH
PRE-PARE YOUR-SELF!!
JUMP

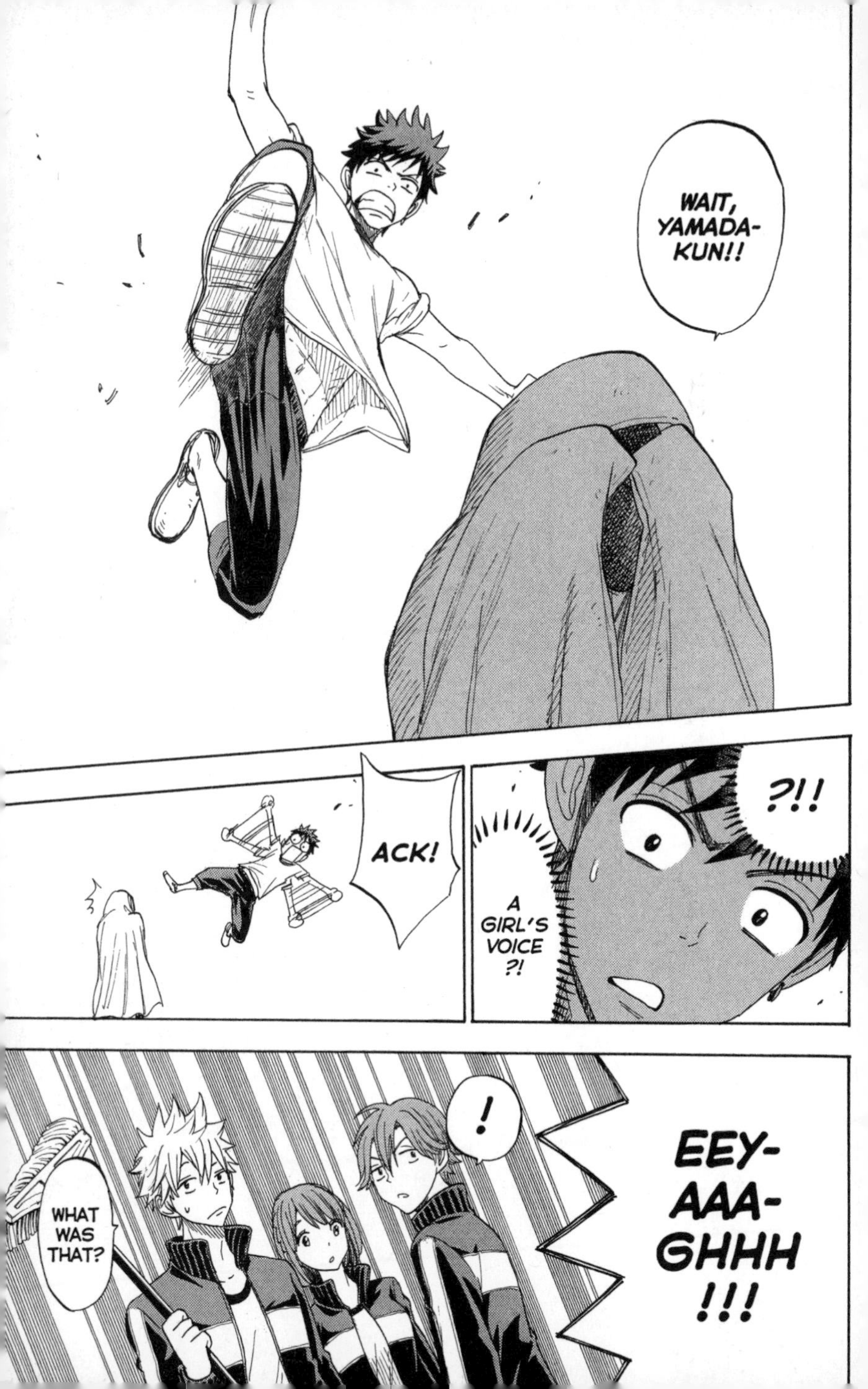
WAIT, YAMADA-KUN!!
?!!
A GIRL'S VOICE ?!
ACK!
EEY-AAA-GHHH !!!
!
WHAT WAS THAT?

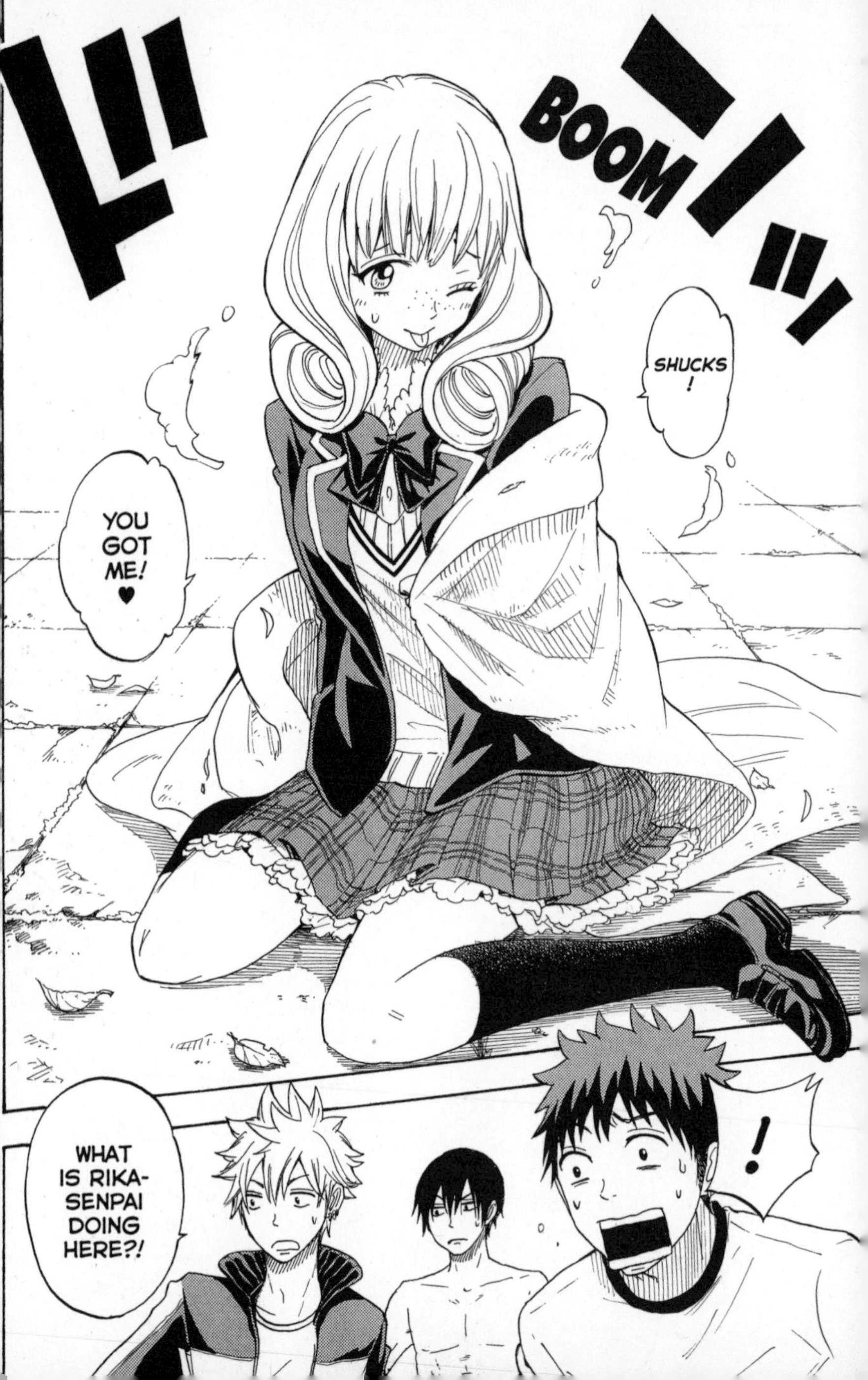
BOOM
SHUCKS!
YOU GOT ME! ♥
!
WHAT IS RIKA-SENPAI DOING HERE?!

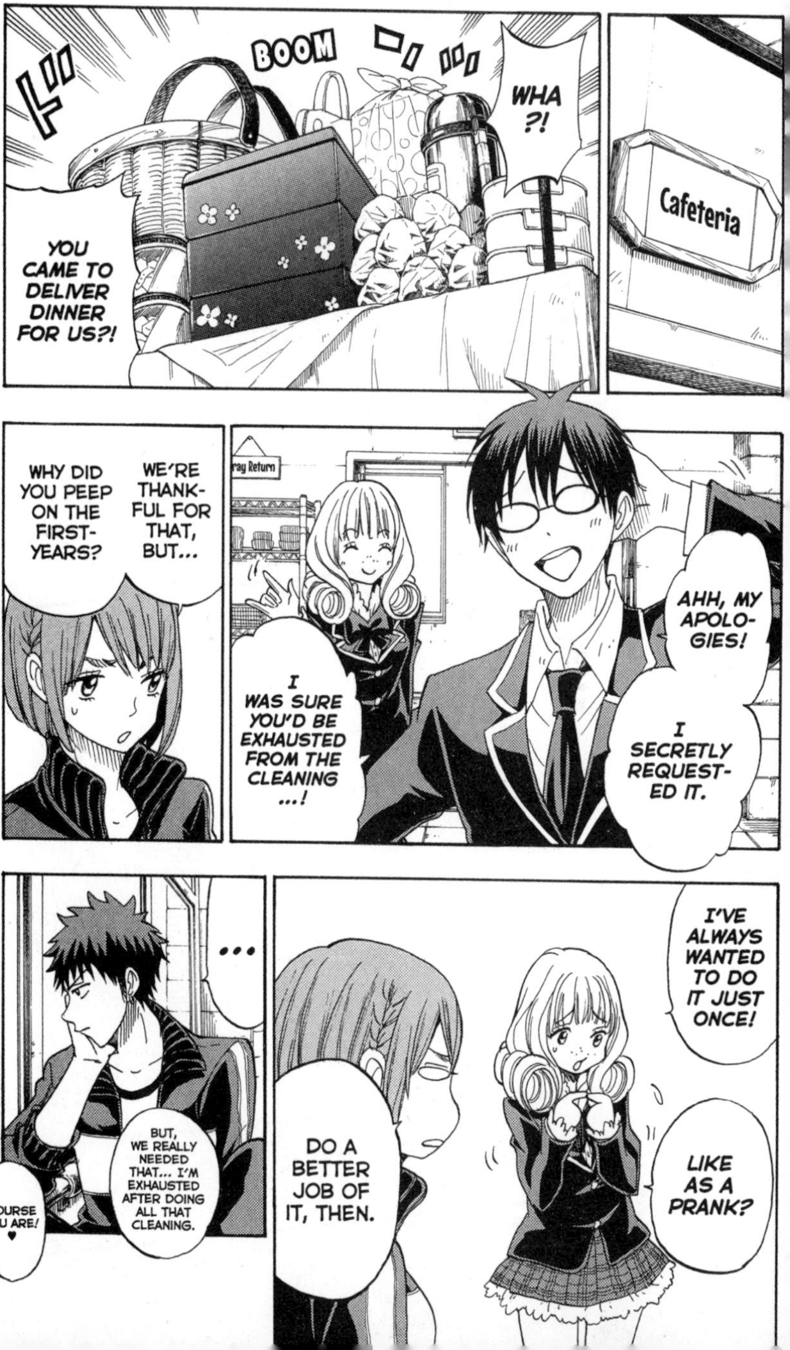
Cafeteria
WHA?!
BOOM
YOU CAME TO DELIVER DINNER FOR US?!
AHH, MY APOLOGIES!
I SECRETLY REQUESTED IT.
ray Return
I WAS SURE YOU'D BE EXHAUSTED FROM THE CLEANING...!
WE'RE THANKFUL FOR THAT, BUT...
WHY DID YOU PEEP ON THE FIRST-YEARS?
I'VE ALWAYS WANTED TO DO IT JUST ONCE!
LIKE AS A PRANK?
DO A BETTER JOB OF IT, THEN.
...
BUT, WE REALLY NEEDED THAT... I'M EXHAUSTED AFTER DOING ALL THAT CLEANING.
COURSE YOU ARE! ♥

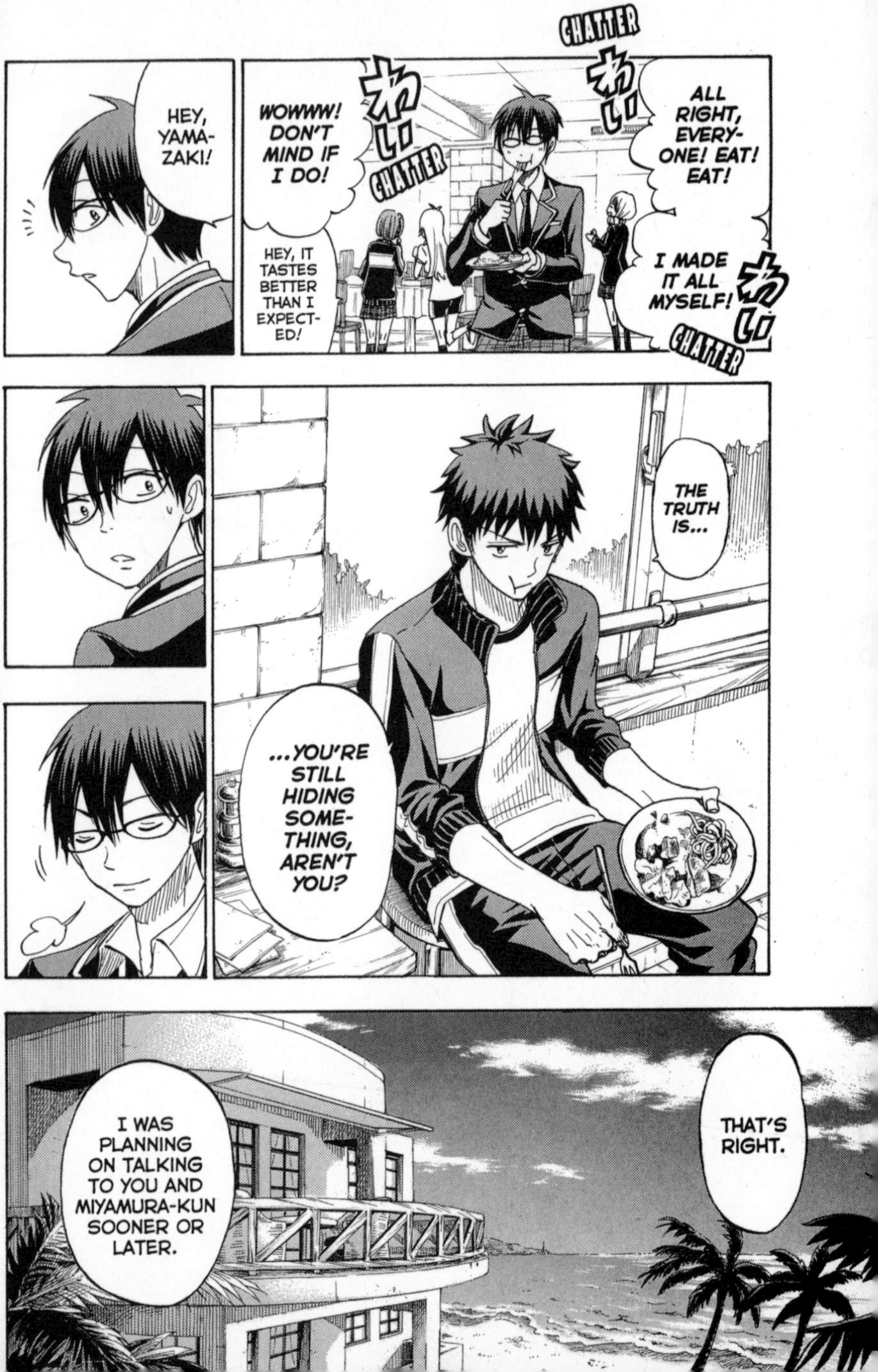
CHATTER
わい
ALL RIGHT, EVERYONE! EAT! EAT!
I MADE IT ALL MYSELF!
わい
CHATTER
わい
WOWWW! DON'T MIND IF I DO!
CHATTER
HEY, IT TASTES BETTER THAN I EXPECTED!
HEY, YAMAZAKI!
THE TRUTH IS...
...YOU'RE STILL HIDING SOMETHING, AREN'T YOU?
THAT'S RIGHT.
I WAS PLANNING ON TALKING TO YOU AND MIYAMURA-KUN SOONER OR LATER.

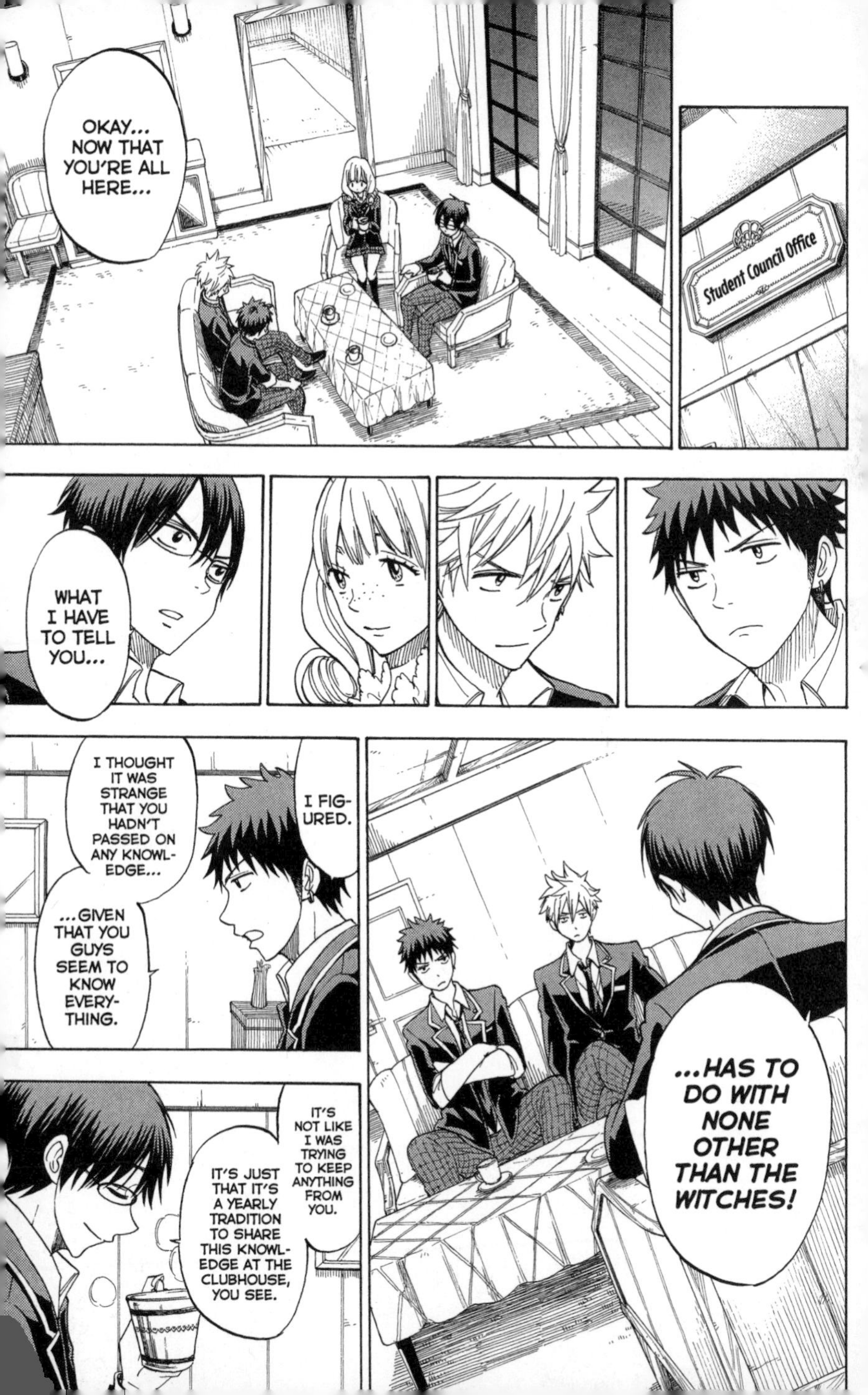
Student Council Office
OKAY... NOW THAT YOU'RE ALL HERE...
WHAT I HAVE TO TELL YOU...
...HAS TO DO WITH NONE OTHER THAN THE WITCHES!
I FIG-URED.
I THOUGHT IT WAS STRANGE THAT YOU HADN'T PASSED ON ANY KNOWL-EDGE...
...GIVEN THAT YOU GUYS SEEM TO KNOW EVERY-THING.
IT'S NOT LIKE I WAS TRYING TO KEEP ANYTHING FROM YOU.
IT'S JUST THAT IT'S A YEARLY TRADITION TO SHARE THIS KNOWL-EDGE AT THE CLUBHOUSE, YOU SEE.

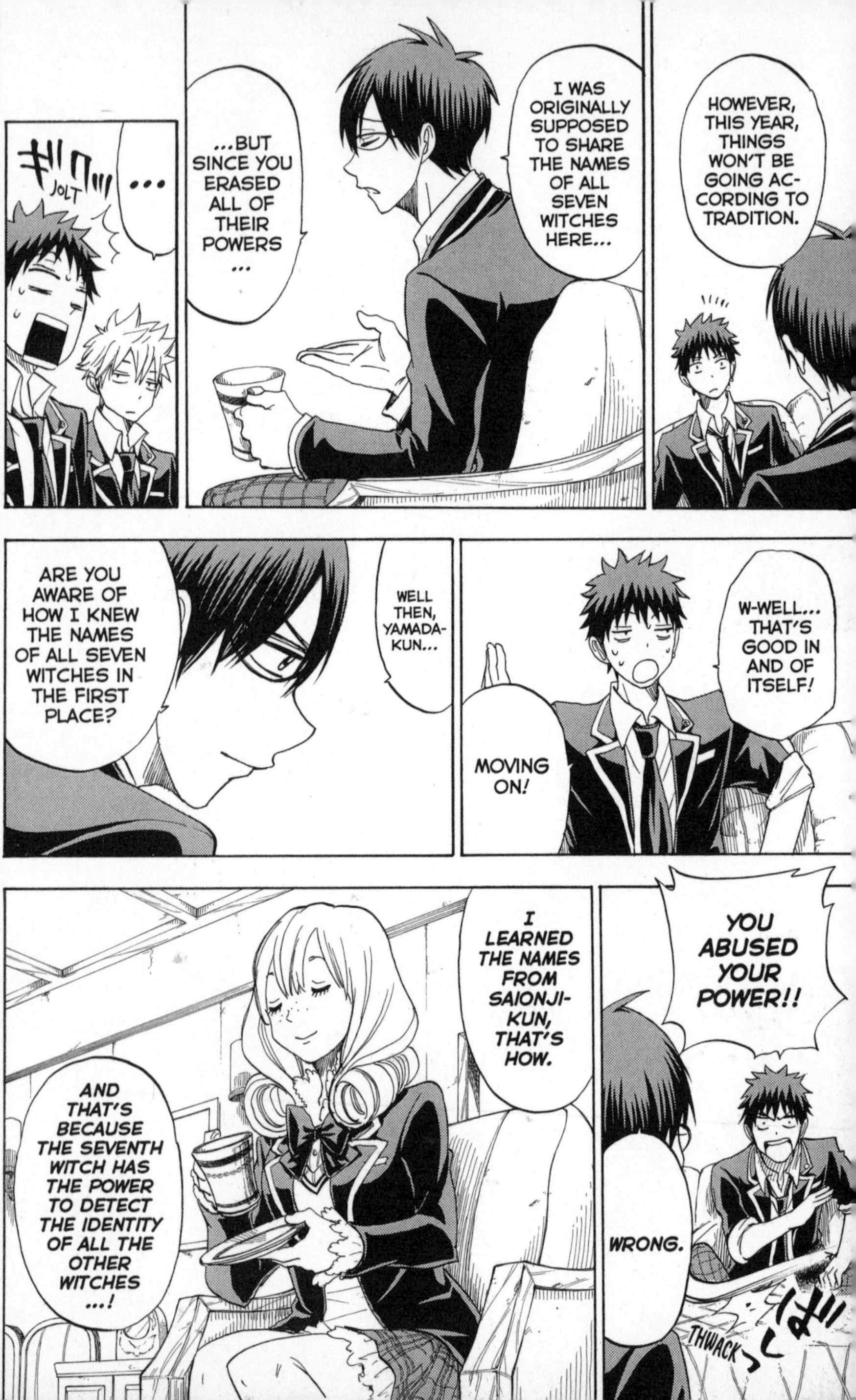
HOWEVER, THIS YEAR, THINGS WON'T BE GOING ACCORDING TO TRADITION.
I WAS ORIGINALLY SUPPOSED TO SHARE THE NAMES OF ALL SEVEN WITCHES HERE...
...BUT SINCE YOU ERASED ALL OF THEIR POWERS...
...
ギクッ
JOLT
W-WELL... THAT'S GOOD IN AND OF ITSELF!
MOVING ON!
WELL THEN, YAMADA-KUN...
ARE YOU AWARE OF HOW I KNEW THE NAMES OF ALL SEVEN WITCHES IN THE FIRST PLACE?
YOU ABUSED YOUR POWER!!
WRONG.
THWACK
I LEARNED THE NAMES FROM SAIONJI-KUN, THAT'S HOW.
AND THAT'S BECAUSE THE SEVENTH WITCH HAS THE POWER TO DETECT THE IDENTITY OF ALL THE OTHER WITCHES...!

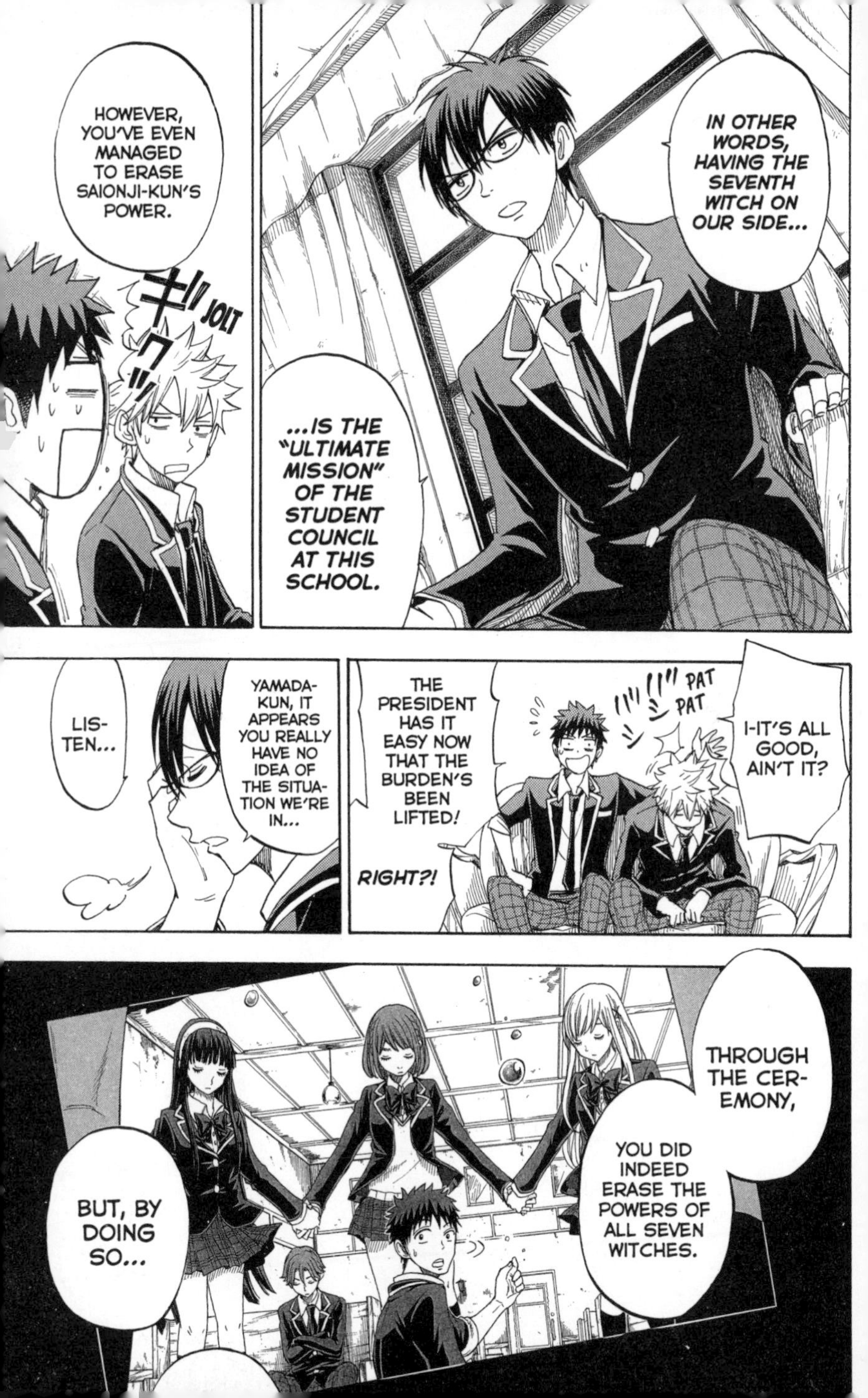
IN OTHER WORDS, HAVING THE SEVENTH WITCH ON OUR SIDE...
...IS THE "ULTIMATE MISSION" OF THE STUDENT COUNCIL AT THIS SCHOOL.
HOWEVER, YOU'VE EVEN MANAGED TO ERASE SAIONJI-KUN'S POWER.
JOLT
I-IT'S ALL GOOD, AIN'T IT?
PAT PAT
THE PRESIDENT HAS IT EASY NOW THAT THE BURDEN'S BEEN LIFTED!
RIGHT?!
YAMADA-KUN, IT APPEARS YOU REALLY HAVE NO IDEA OF THE SITUATION WE'RE IN...
LIS-TEN...
THROUGH THE CER-EMONY,
YOU DID INDEED ERASE THE POWERS OF ALL SEVEN WITCHES.
BUT, BY DOING SO...

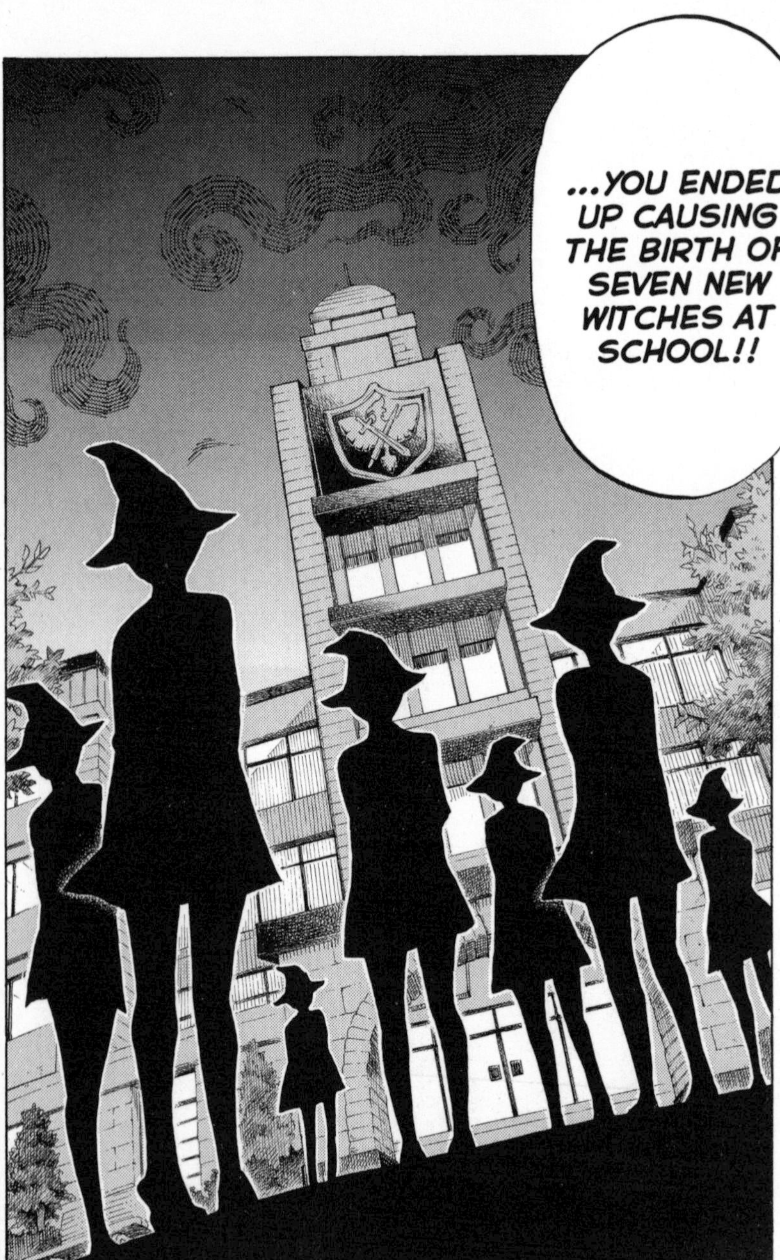
...YOU ENDED UP CAUSING THE BIRTH OF SEVEN NEW WITCHES AT SCHOOL!!

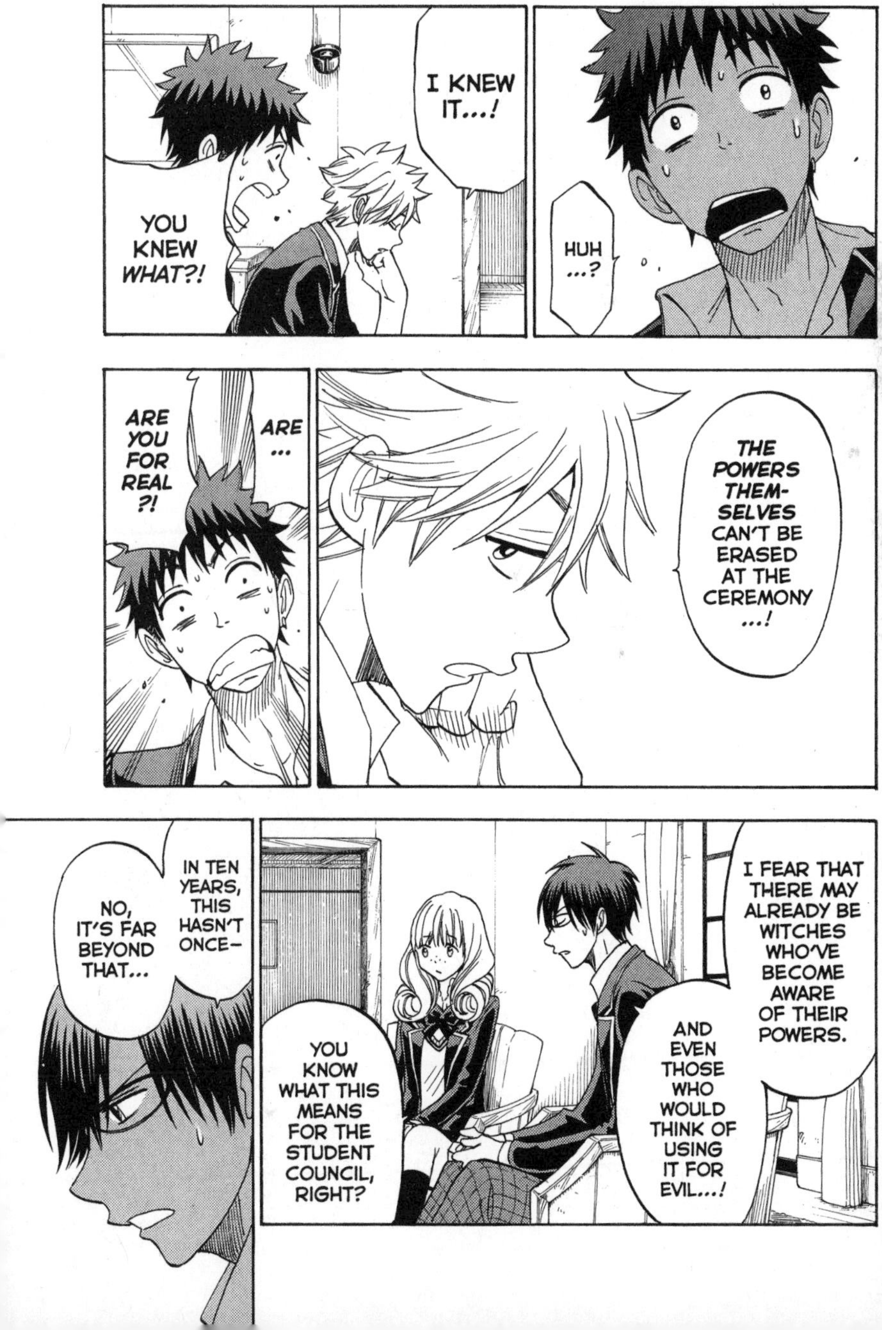
HUH ...?
I KNEW IT...!
YOU KNEW WHAT?!
THE POWERS THEMSELVES CAN'T BE ERASED AT THE CEREMONY...!
ARE ...
ARE YOU FOR REAL ?!
I FEAR THAT THERE MAY ALREADY BE WITCHES WHO'VE BECOME AWARE OF THEIR POWERS.
AND EVEN THOSE WHO WOULD THINK OF USING IT FOR EVIL...!
YOU KNOW WHAT THIS MEANS FOR THE STUDENT COUNCIL, RIGHT?
IN TEN YEARS, THIS HASN'T ONCE—
NO, IT'S FAR BEYOND THAT...

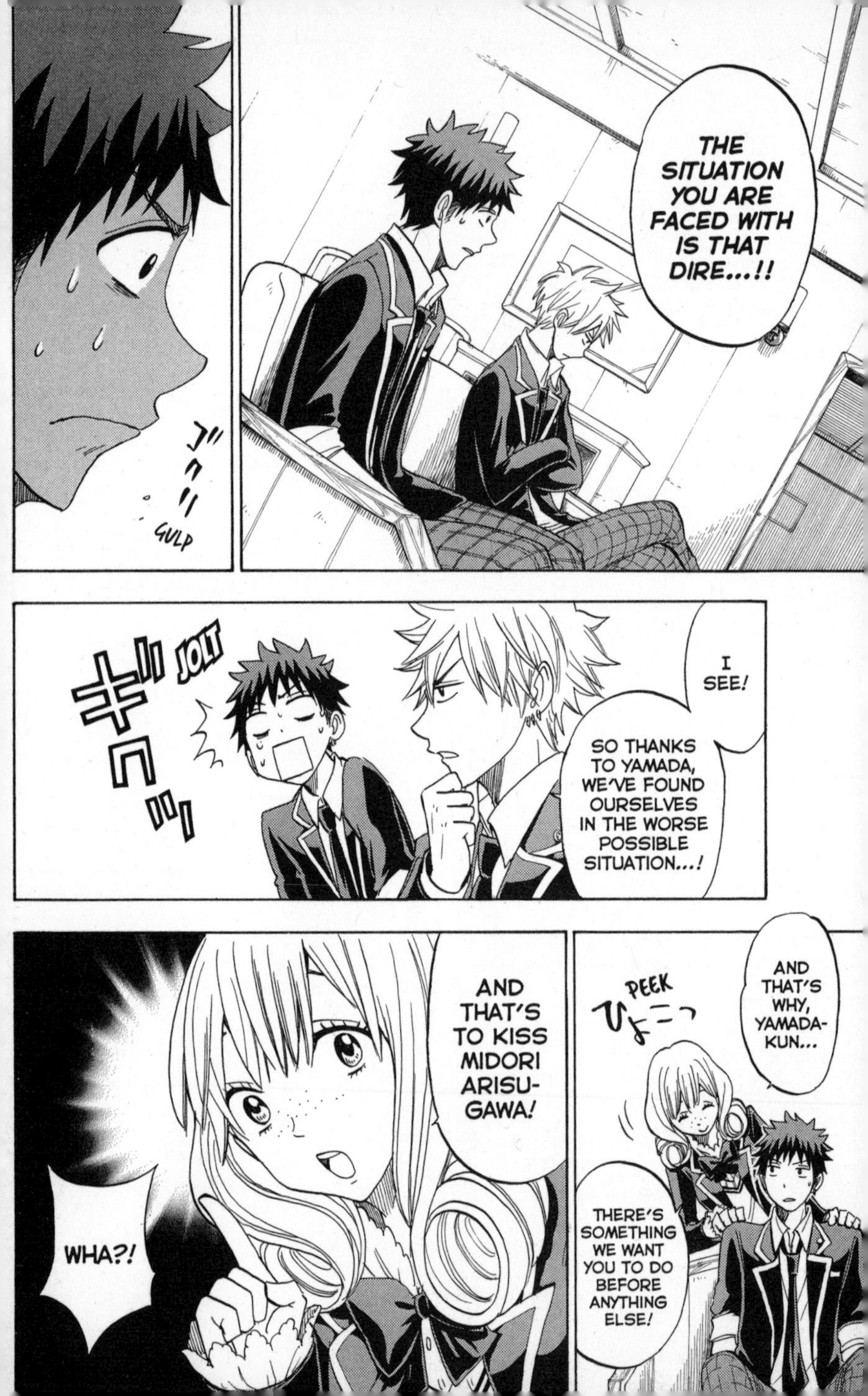
THE SITUATION YOU ARE FACED WITH IS THAT DIRE...!!
GULP
I SEE!
SO THANKS TO YAMADA, WE'VE FOUND OURSELVES IN THE WORSE POSSIBLE SITUATION...!
JOLT
AND THAT'S WHY, YAMADA-KUN...
PEEK
THERE'S SOMETHING WE WANT YOU TO DO BEFORE ANYTHING ELSE!
AND THAT'S TO KISS MIDORI ARISU-GAWA!
WHA?!

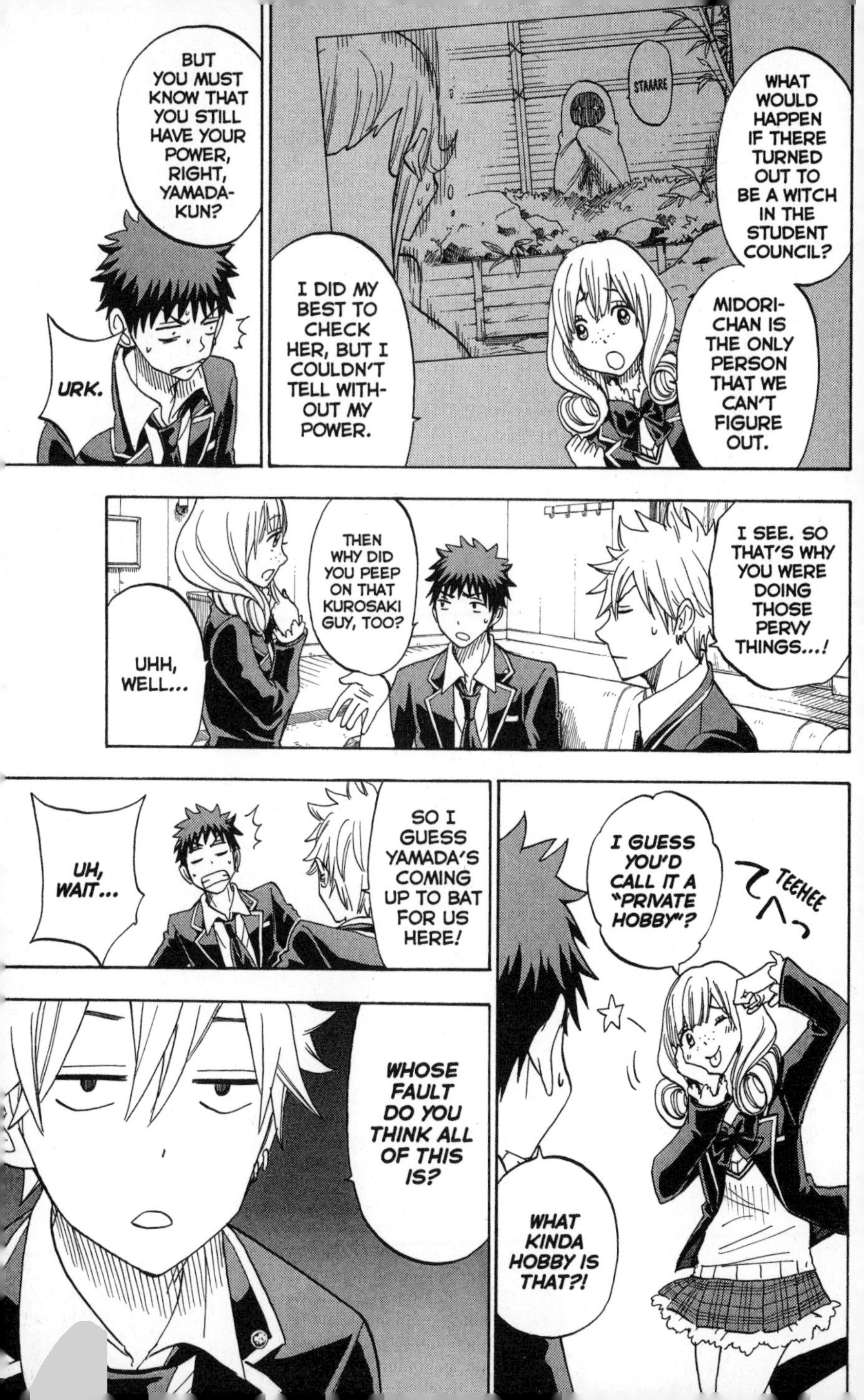

WHAT WOULD HAPPEN IF THERE TURNED OUT TO BE A WITCH IN THE STUDENT COUNCIL?
STAAARE
MIDORI-CHAN IS THE ONLY PERSON THAT WE CAN'T FIGURE OUT.
I DID MY BEST TO CHECK HER, BUT I COULDN'T TELL WITH-OUT MY POWER.
BUT YOU MUST KNOW THAT YOU STILL HAVE YOUR POWER, RIGHT, YAMADA-KUN?
URK.
I SEE. SO THAT'S WHY YOU WERE DOING THOSE PERVY THINGS...!
THEN WHY DID YOU PEEP ON THAT KUROSAKI GUY, TOO?
UHH, WELL...
I GUESS YOU'D CALL IT A "PRIVATE HOBBY"?
TEEHEE
WHAT KINDA HOBBY IS THAT?!
SO I GUESS YAMADA'S COMING UP TO BAT FOR US HERE!
UH, WAIT...
WHOSE FAULT DO YOU THINK ALL OF THIS IS?

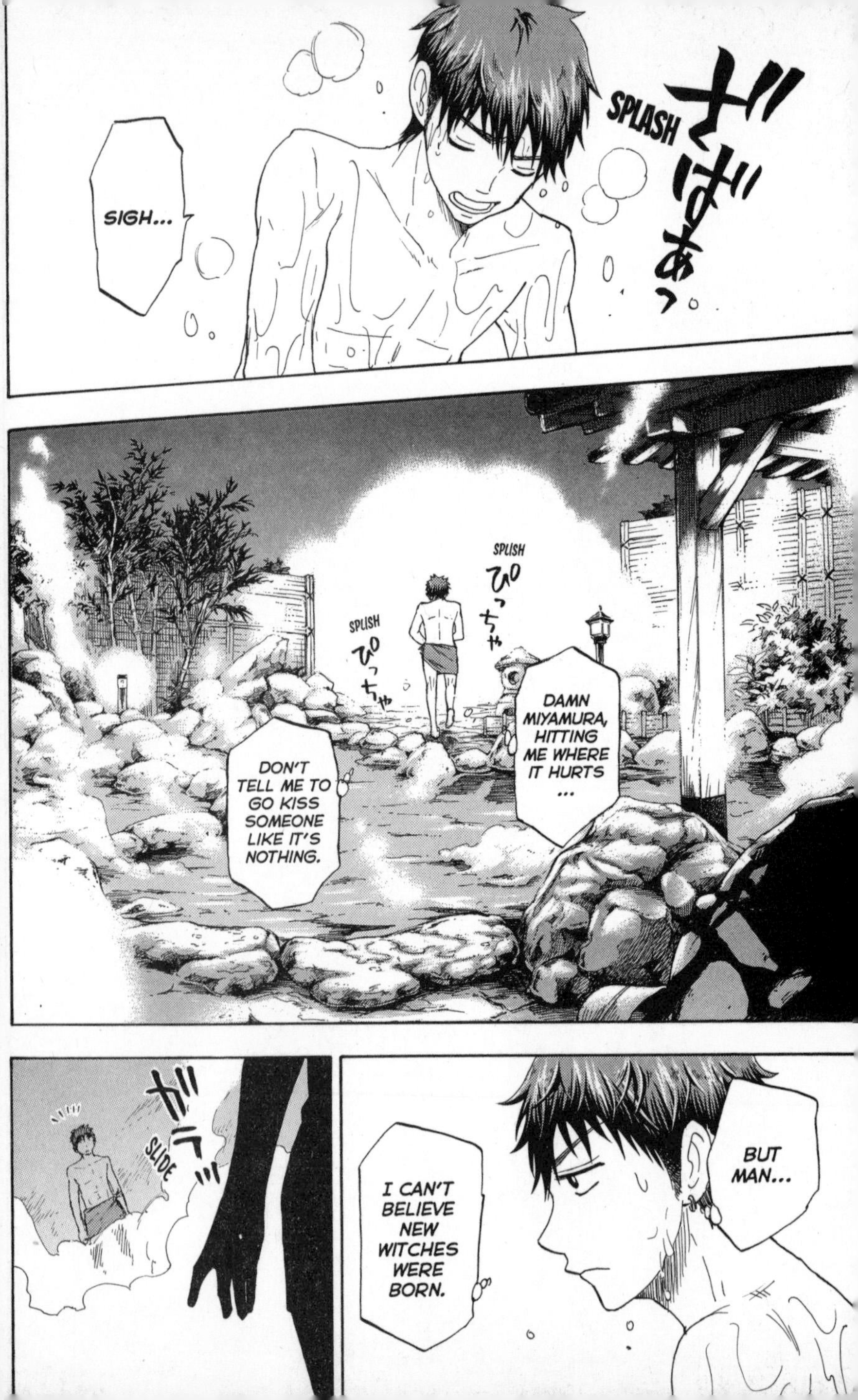

SPLASH
ざばあっ
SIGH...
SPLISH
ぴっちゃ
SPLISH
ぴっちゃ
DAMN MIYAMURA, HITTING ME WHERE IT HURTS...
DON'T TELL ME TO GO KISS SOMEONE LIKE IT'S NOTHING.
BUT MAN...
I CAN'T BELIEVE NEW WITCHES WERE BORN.
SLIDE
ガラッ

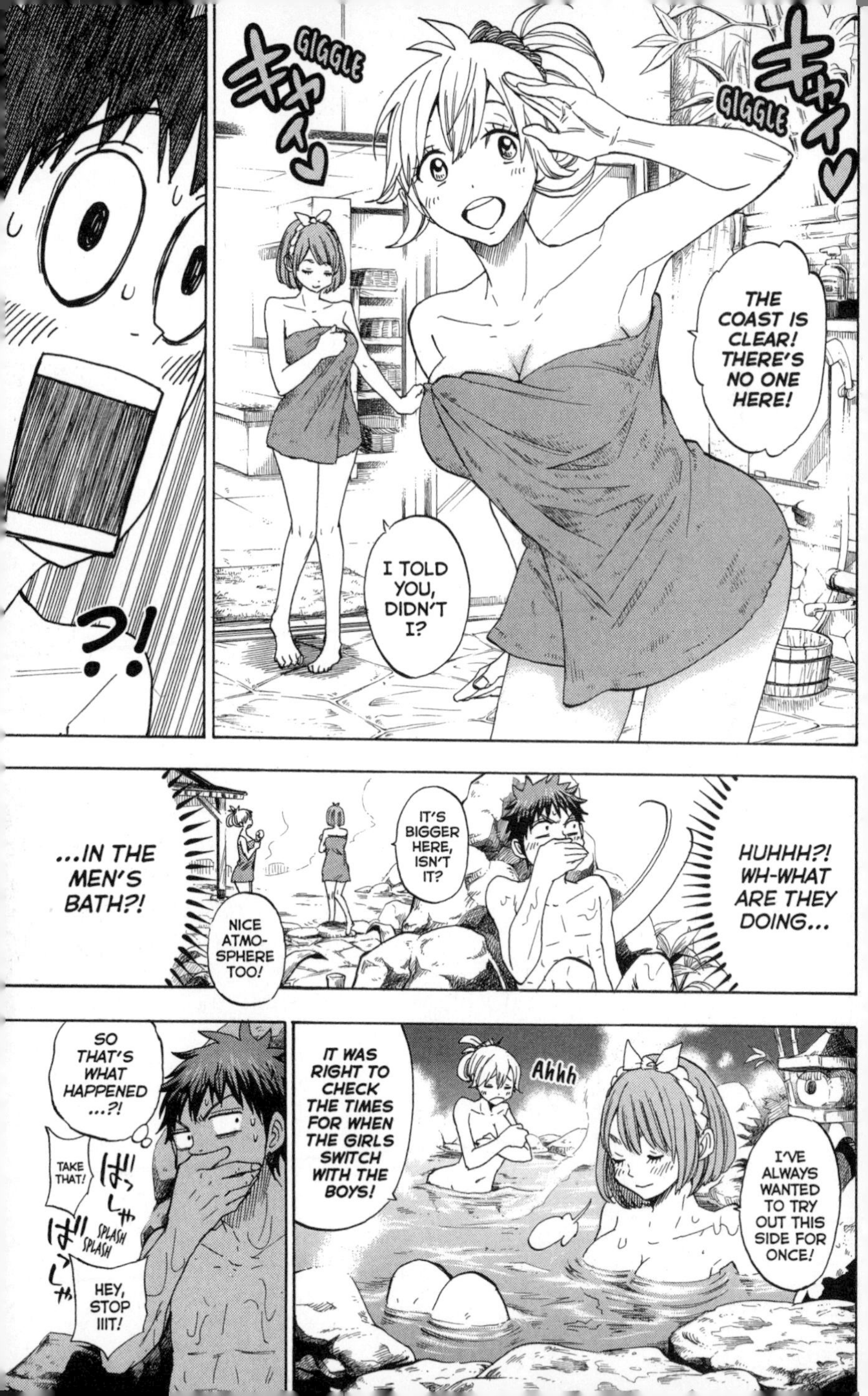
キャイ♥
GIGGLE
キャイ♥
GIGGLE
THE COAST IS CLEAR! THERE'S NO ONE HERE!
I TOLD YOU, DIDN'T I?
?!
HUHHH?! WH-WHAT ARE THEY DOING...
IT'S BIGGER HERE, ISN'T IT?
NICE ATMOSPHERE TOO!
...IN THE MEN'S BATH?!
I'VE ALWAYS WANTED TO TRY OUT THIS SIDE FOR ONCE!
Ahhh
IT WAS RIGHT TO CHECK THE TIMES FOR WHEN THE GIRLS SWITCH WITH THE BOYS!
SO THAT'S WHAT HAPPENED...?!
TAKE THAT!
ぱっしゃ
SPLASH
ぱっしゃ
SPLASH
HEY, STOP IIIT!

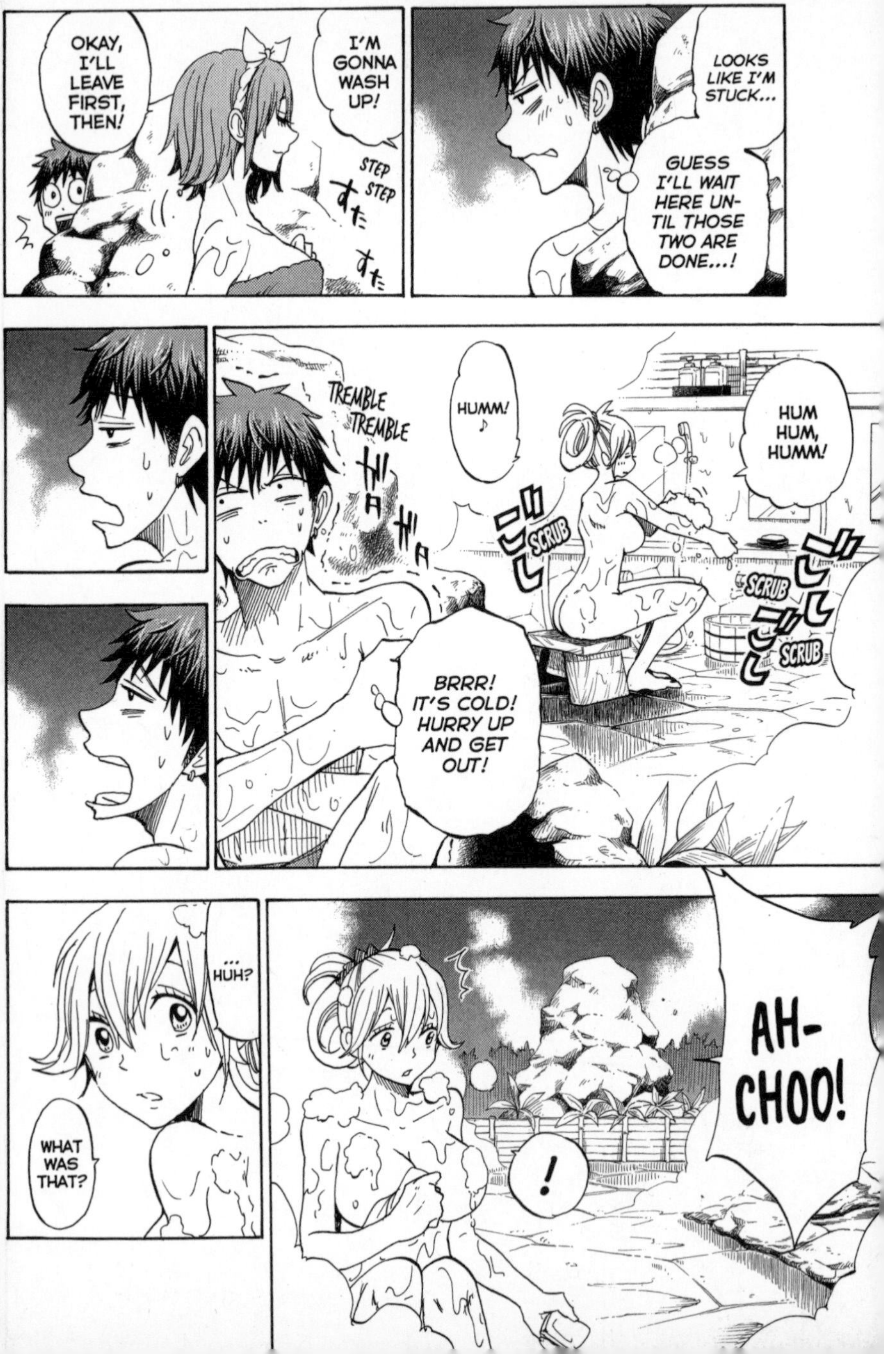
LOOKS LIKE I'M STUCK...
GUESS I'LL WAIT HERE UNTIL THOSE TWO ARE DONE...!
I'M GONNA WASH UP!
STEP STEP
すた すた
OKAY, I'LL LEAVE FIRST, THEN!
HUM HUM, HUMM!
SCRUB
SCRUB
HUMM! ♪
SCRUB
TREMBLE TREMBLE
BRRR! IT'S COLD! HURRY UP AND GET OUT!
AH-CHOO!
!
...HUH?
WHAT WAS THAT?

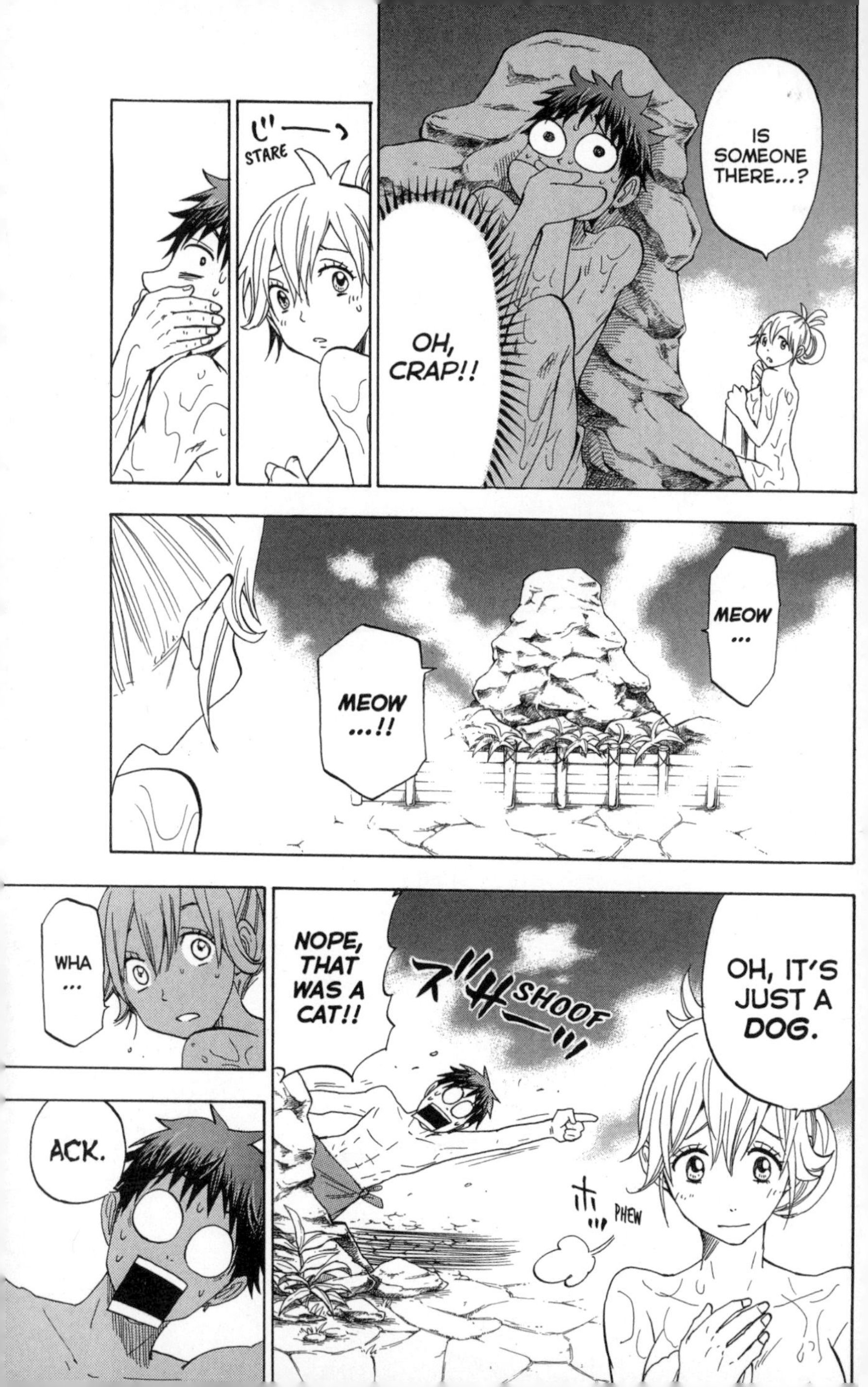

IS SOMEONE THERE...?
OH, CRAP!!
じーっ
STARE
MEOW ...
MEOW ...!!
OH, IT'S JUST A DOG.
スッサーッ
SHOOF
NOPE, THAT WAS A CAT!!
ホッ
PHEW
WHA ...
ACK.

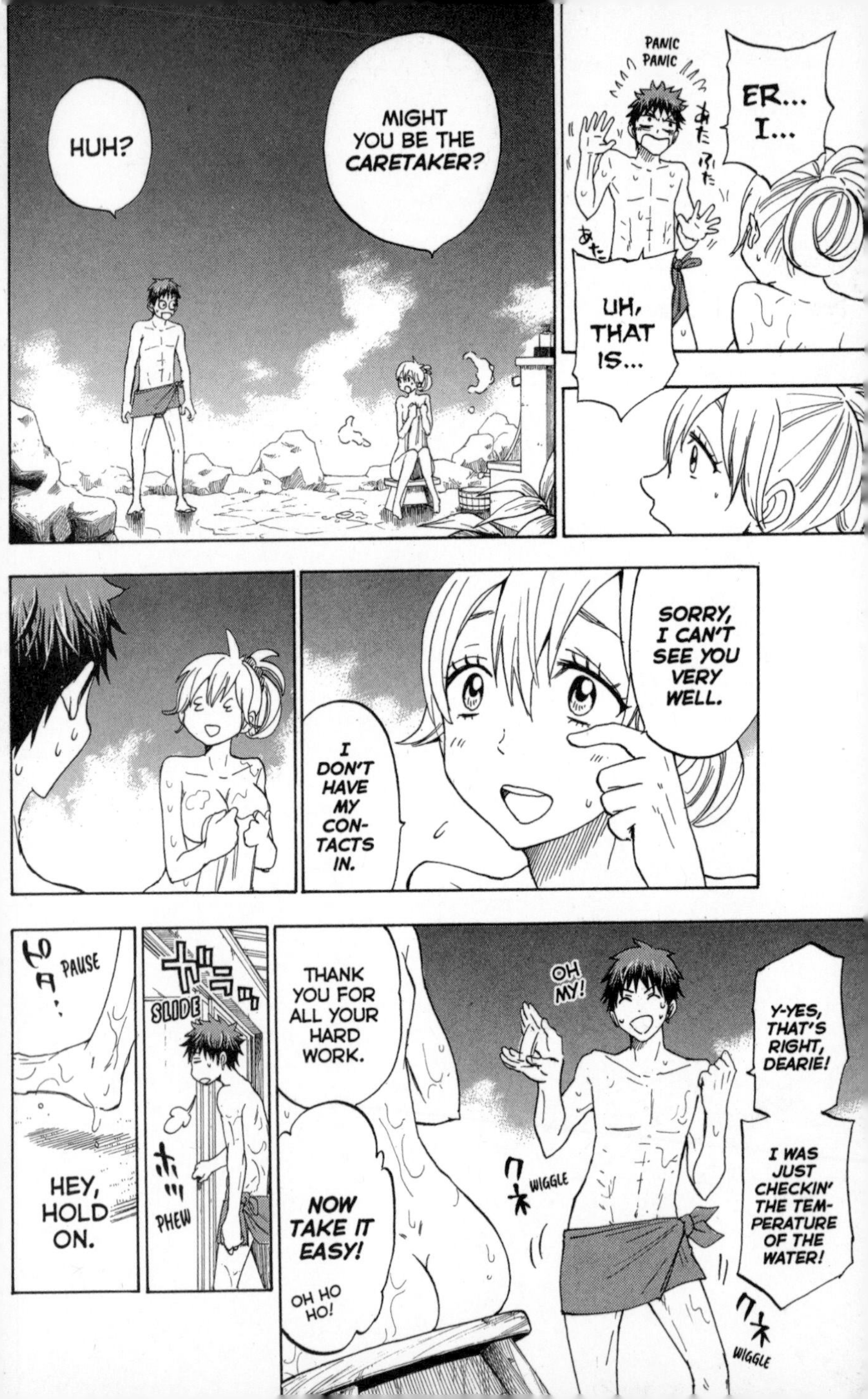
PANIC PANIC
あたふた
ER... I...
UH, THAT IS...
MIGHT YOU BE THE CARETAKER?
HUH?
SORRY, I CAN'T SEE YOU VERY WELL.
I DON'T HAVE MY CONTACTS IN.
Y-YES, THAT'S RIGHT, DEARIE!
OH MY!
I WAS JUST CHECKIN' THE TEMPERATURE OF THE WATER!
WIGGLE
WIGGLE
THANK YOU FOR ALL YOUR HARD WORK.
NOW TAKE IT EASY!
OH HO HO!
SLIDE
PHEW
PAUSE
HEY, HOLD ON.

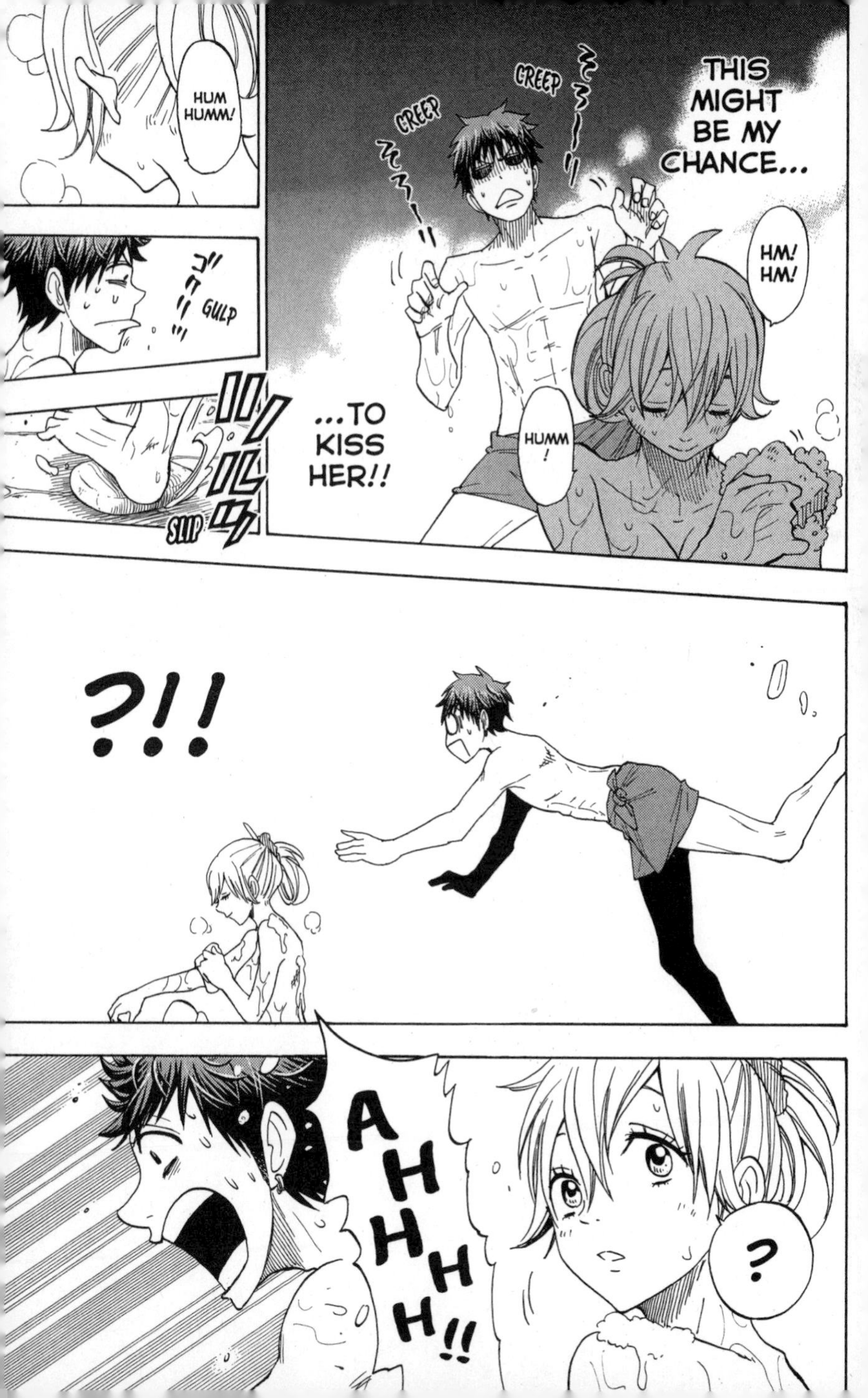
THIS MIGHT BE MY CHANCE...
CREEP
CREEP
HM! HM!
...TO KISS HER!!
HUMM!
HUM HUMM!
GULP
SLIP
?!!
AHHHH!!
?

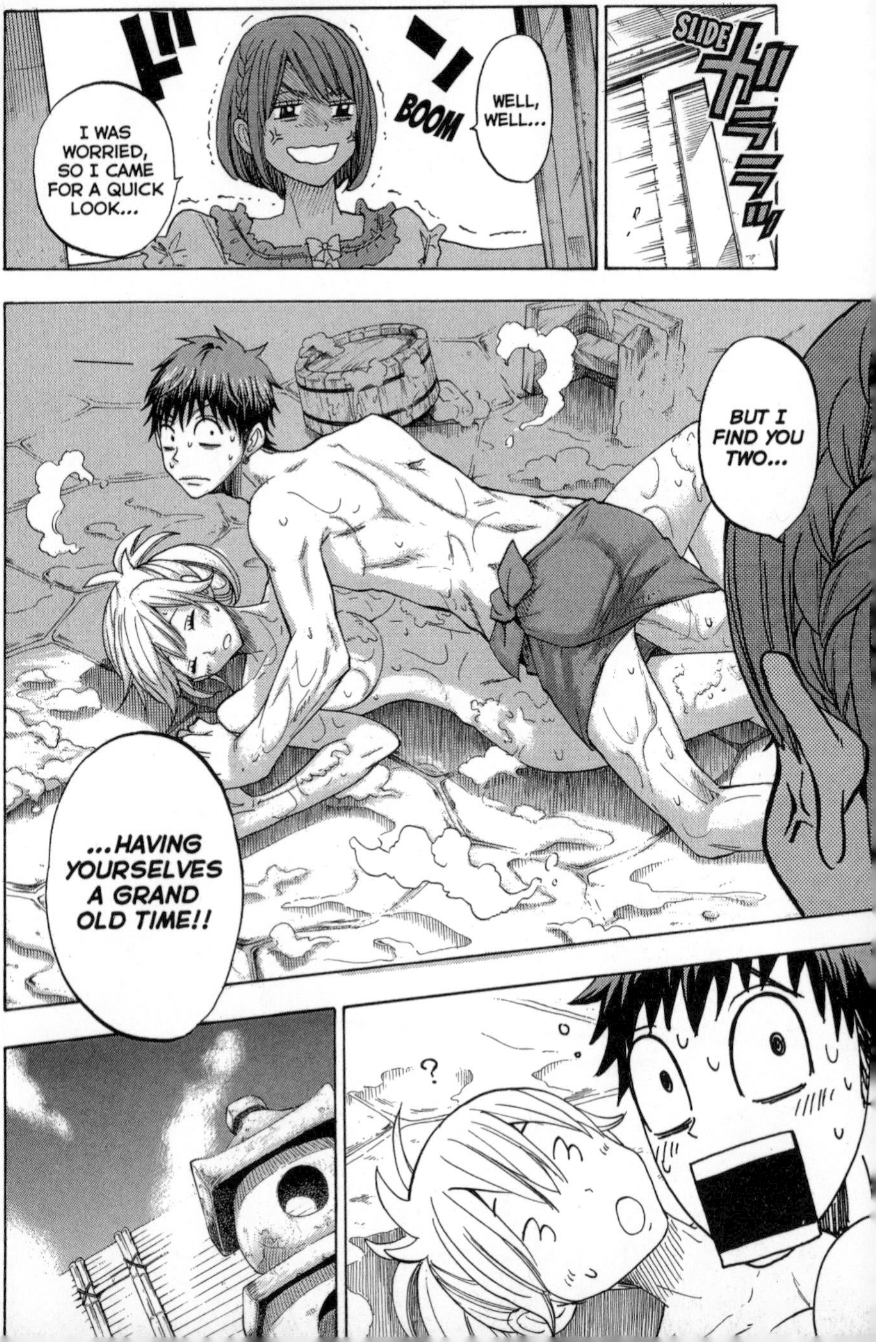
SLIDE
ガラララッ
WELL, WELL...
ドーン
BOOM
I WAS WORRIED, SO I CAME FOR A QUICK LOOK...
BUT I FIND YOU TWO...
...HAVING YOURSELVES A GRAND OLD TIME!!
?

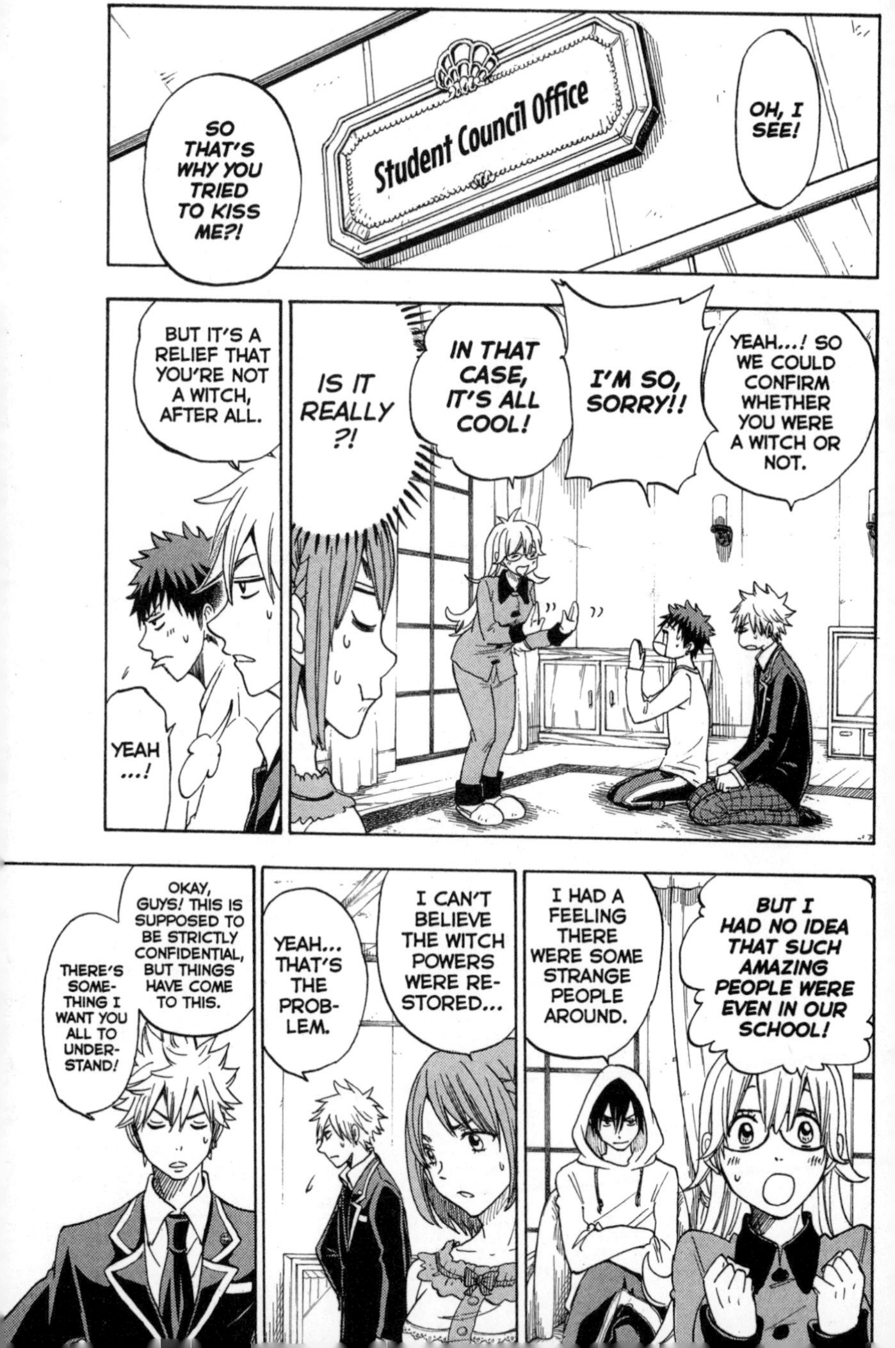
Student Council Office
OH, I SEE!
SO THAT'S WHY YOU TRIED TO KISS ME?!
YEAH...! SO WE COULD CONFIRM WHETHER YOU WERE A WITCH OR NOT.
I'M SO, SORRY!!
IN THAT CASE, IT'S ALL COOL!
IS IT REALLY ?!
BUT IT'S A RELIEF THAT YOU'RE NOT A WITCH, AFTER ALL.
YEAH ...!
BUT I HAD NO IDEA THAT SUCH AMAZING PEOPLE WERE EVEN IN OUR SCHOOL!
I HAD A FEELING THERE WERE SOME STRANGE PEOPLE AROUND.
I CAN'T BELIEVE THE WITCH POWERS WERE RE-STORED...
YEAH... THAT'S THE PROB-LEM.
OKAY, GUYS! THIS IS SUPPOSED TO BE STRICTLY CONFIDENTIAL, BUT THINGS HAVE COME TO THIS.
THERE'S SOME-THING I WANT YOU ALL TO UNDER-STAND!

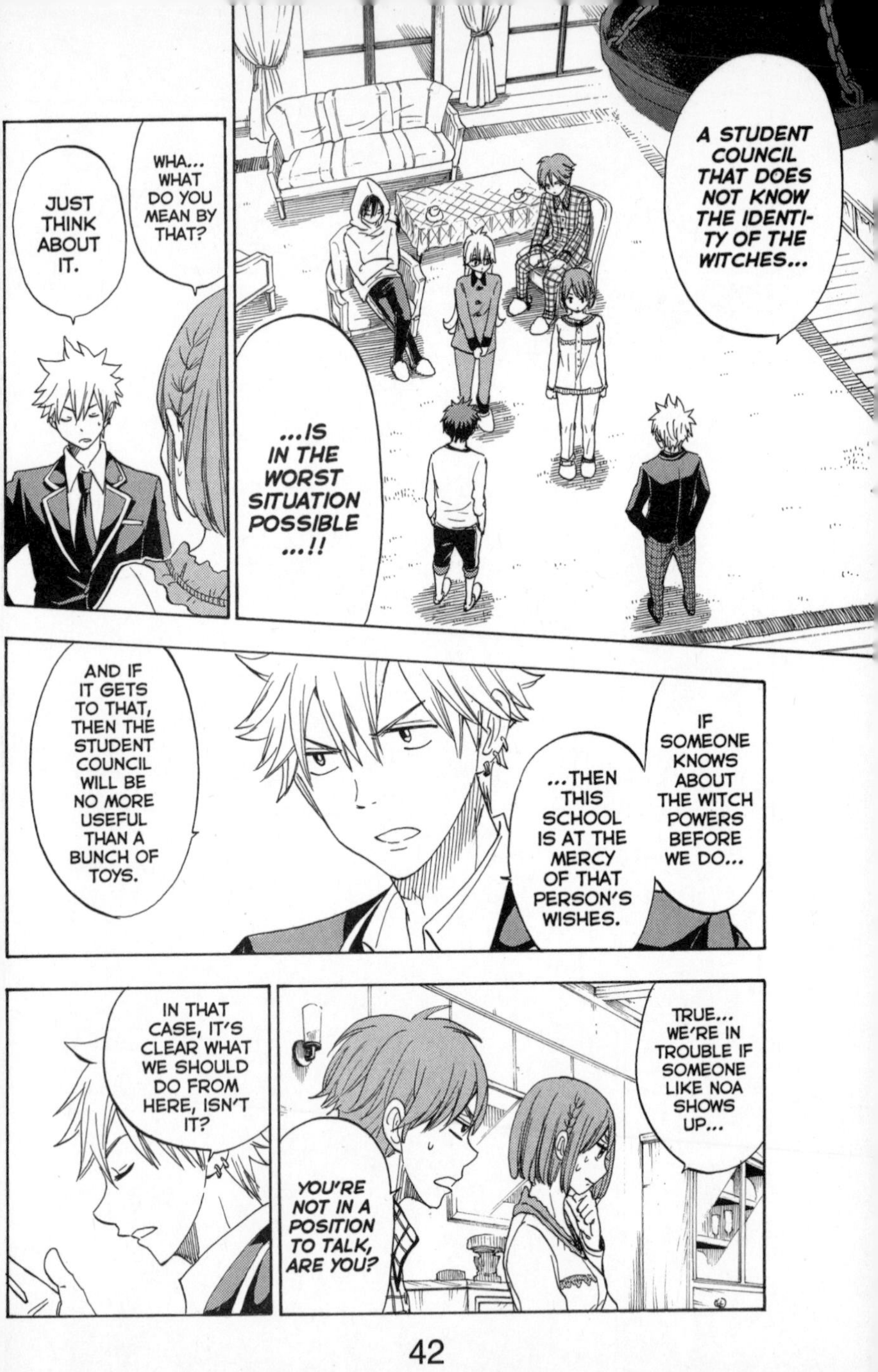
A STUDENT COUNCIL THAT DOES NOT KNOW THE IDENTITY OF THE WITCHES...
...IS IN THE WORST SITUATION POSSIBLE ...!!
WHA... WHAT DO YOU MEAN BY THAT?
JUST THINK ABOUT IT.
IF SOMEONE KNOWS ABOUT THE WITCH POWERS BEFORE WE DO...
...THEN THIS SCHOOL IS AT THE MERCY OF THAT PERSON'S WISHES.
AND IF IT GETS TO THAT, THEN THE STUDENT COUNCIL WILL BE NO MORE USEFUL THAN A BUNCH OF TOYS.
TRUE... WE'RE IN TROUBLE IF SOMEONE LIKE NOA SHOWS UP...
YOU'RE NOT IN A POSITION TO TALK, ARE YOU?
IN THAT CASE, IT'S CLEAR WHAT WE SHOULD DO FROM HERE, ISN'T IT?

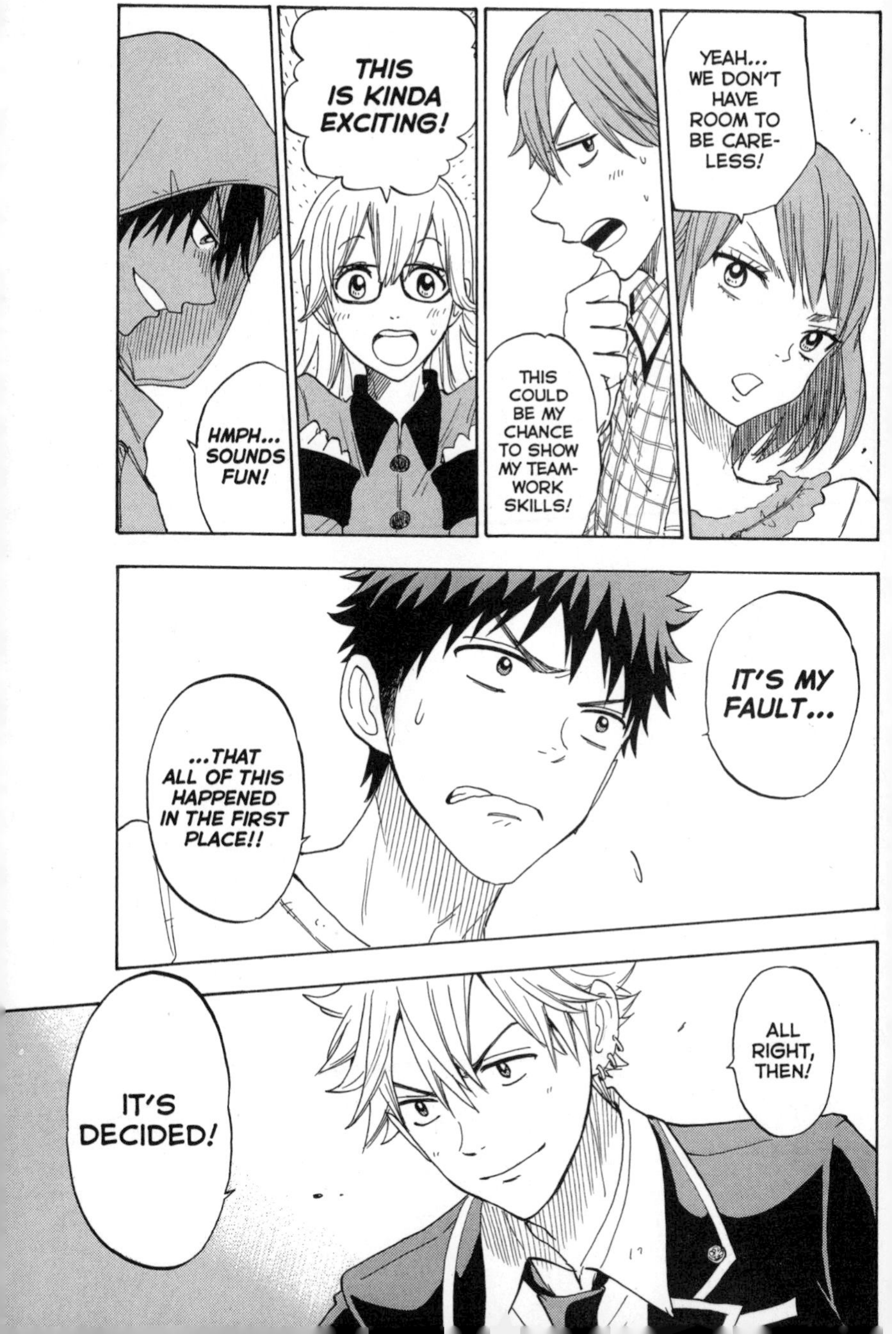
YEAH... WE DON'T HAVE ROOM TO BE CARE-LESS!
THIS COULD BE MY CHANCE TO SHOW MY TEAM-WORK SKILLS!
THIS IS KINDA EXCITING!
HMPH... SOUNDS FUN!
IT'S MY FAULT...
...THAT ALL OF THIS HAPPENED IN THE FIRST PLACE!!
ALL RIGHT, THEN!
IT'S DECIDED!

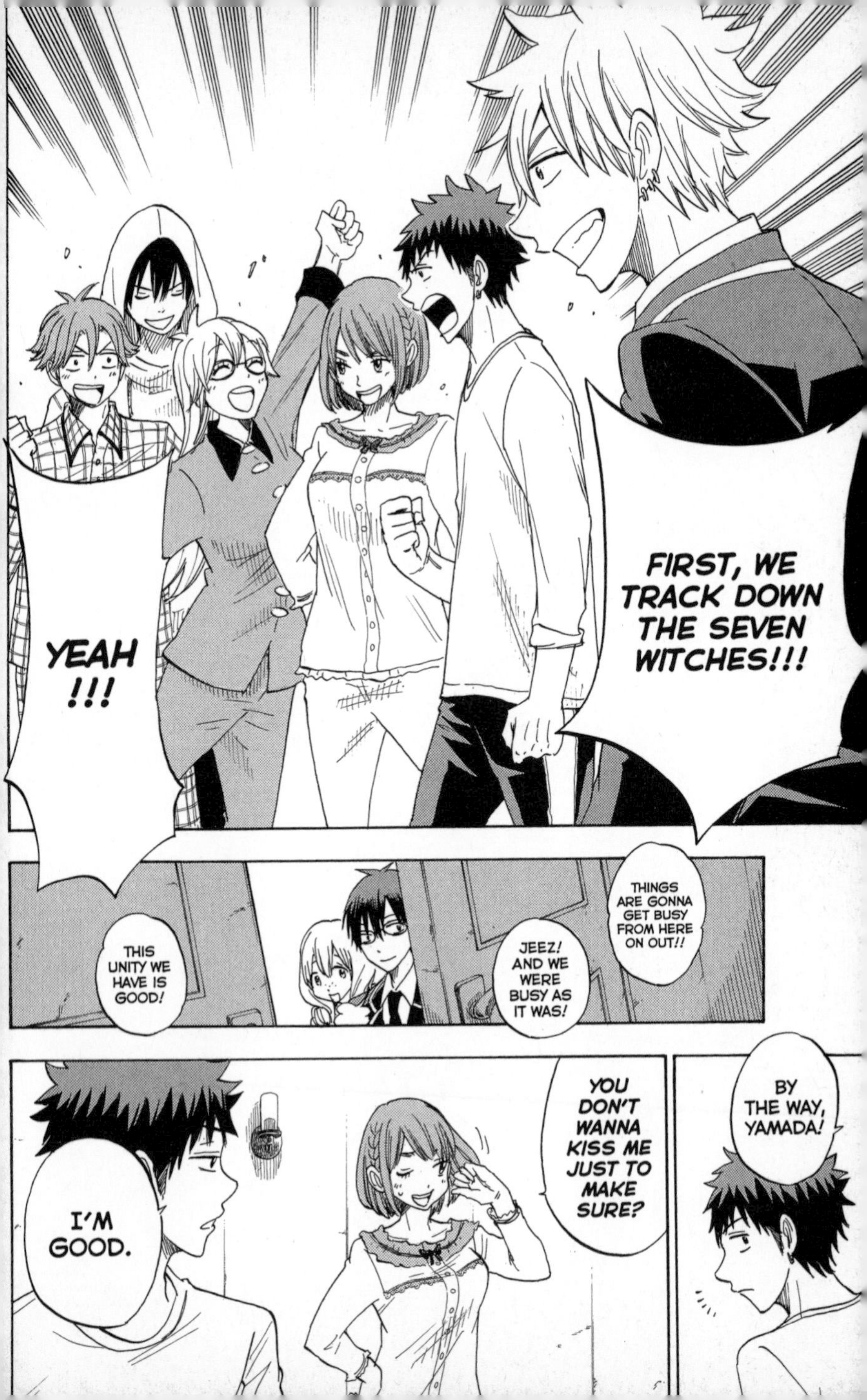
FIRST, WE TRACK DOWN THE SEVEN WITCHES!!!
YEAH!!!
THINGS ARE GONNA GET BUSY FROM HERE ON OUT!!
JEEZ! AND WE WERE BUSY AS IT WAS!
THIS UNITY WE HAVE IS GOOD!
BY THE WAY, YAMADA!
YOU DON'T WANNA KISS ME JUST TO MAKE SURE?
I'M GOOD.

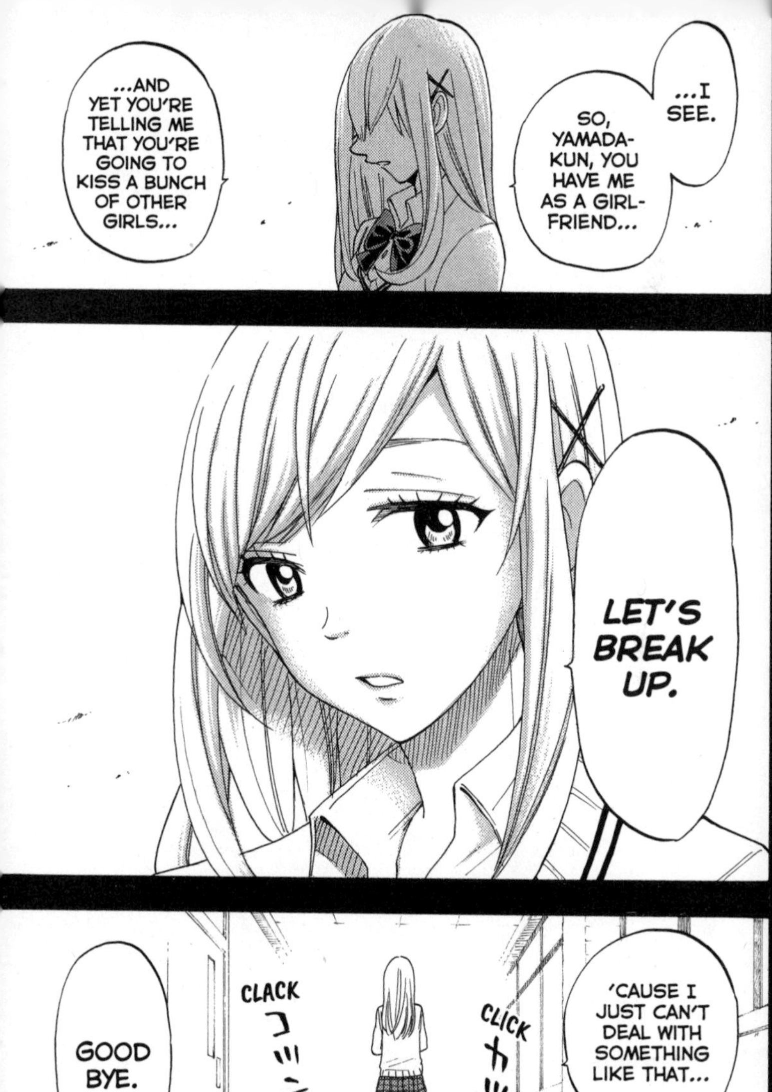
...I SEE.
SO, YAMADA-KUN, YOU HAVE ME AS A GIRL-FRIEND...
...AND YET YOU'RE TELLING ME THAT YOU'RE GOING TO KISS A BUNCH OF OTHER GIRLS...
LET'S BREAK UP.
'CAUSE I JUST CAN'T DEAL WITH SOMETHING LIKE THAT...
CLICK
CLACK
GOOD BYE.

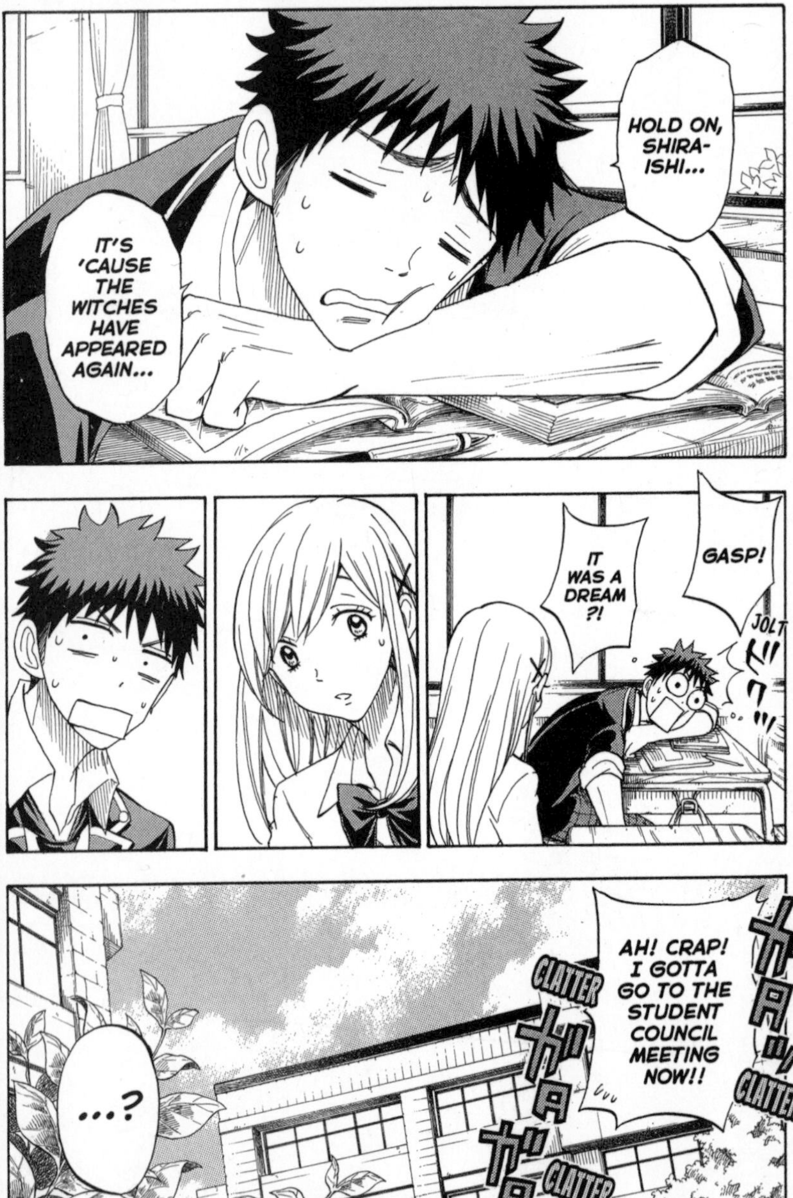
HOLD ON, SHIRA-ISHI...
IT'S 'CAUSE THE WITCHES HAVE APPEARED AGAIN...
GASP!
IT WAS A DREAM ?!
JOLT
CLATTER
AH! CRAP! I GOTTA GO TO THE STUDENT COUNCIL MEETING NOW!!
CLATTER
CLATTER
...?

CHAPTER 96: Like a ninja.

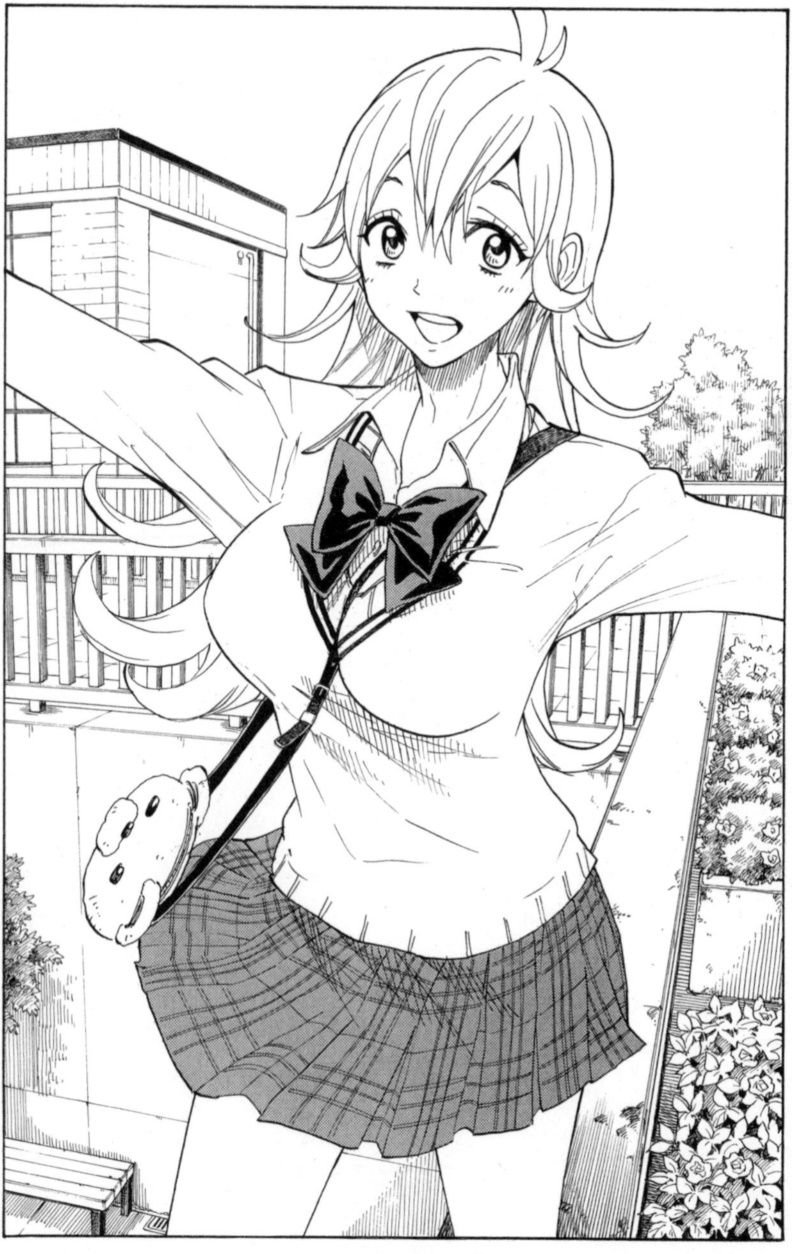

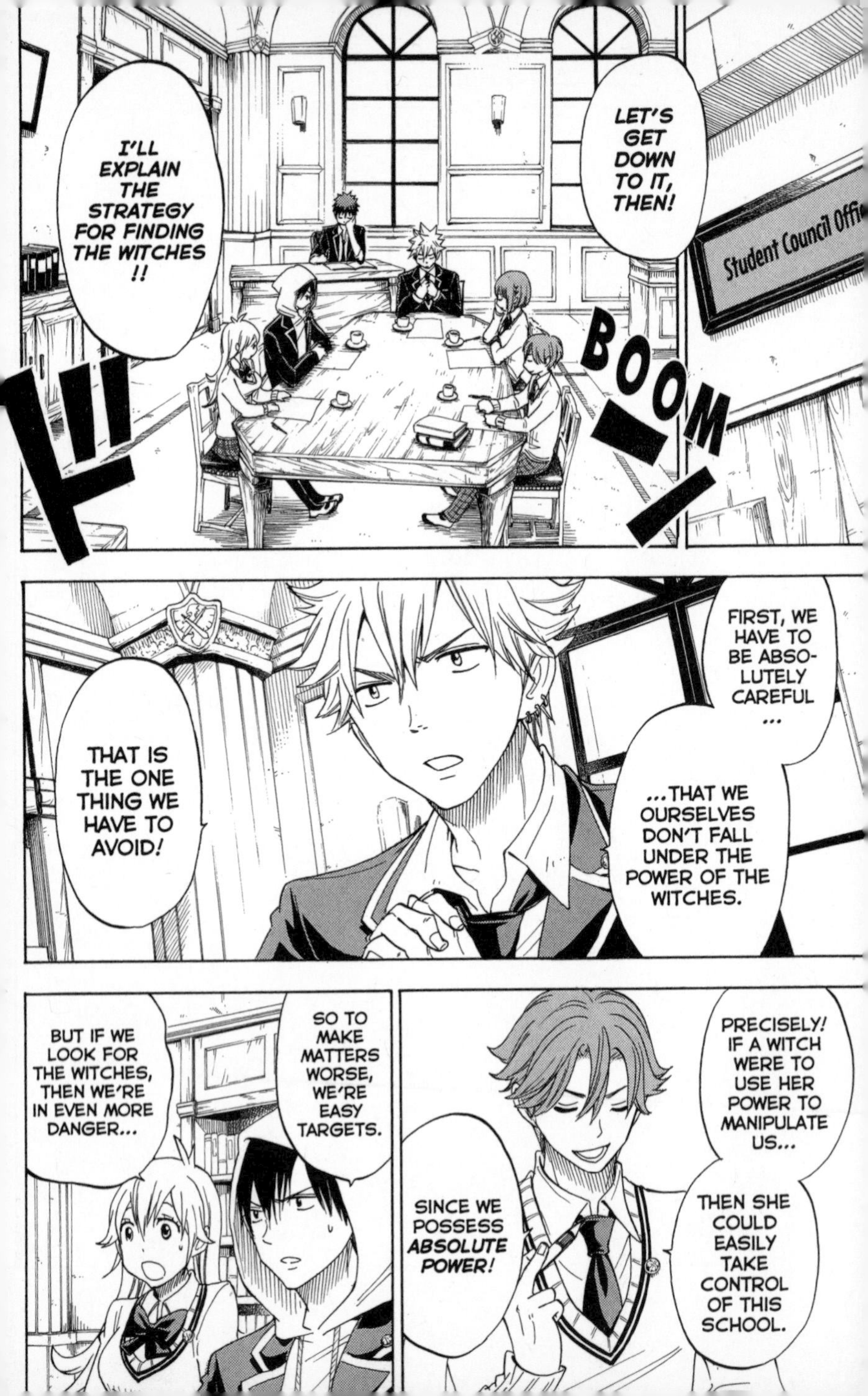
LET'S GET DOWN TO IT, THEN!
Student Council Offi
BOOM
I'LL EXPLAIN THE STRATEGY FOR FINDING THE WITCHES!!
FIRST, WE HAVE TO BE ABSOLUTELY CAREFUL...
...THAT WE OURSELVES DON'T FALL UNDER THE POWER OF THE WITCHES.
THAT IS THE ONE THING WE HAVE TO AVOID!
PRECISELY! IF A WITCH WERE TO USE HER POWER TO MANIPULATE US...
THEN SHE COULD EASILY TAKE CONTROL OF THIS SCHOOL.
SINCE WE POSSESS ABSOLUTE POWER!
SO TO MAKE MATTERS WORSE, WE'RE EASY TARGETS.
BUT IF WE LOOK FOR THE WITCHES, THEN WE'RE IN EVEN MORE DANGER...

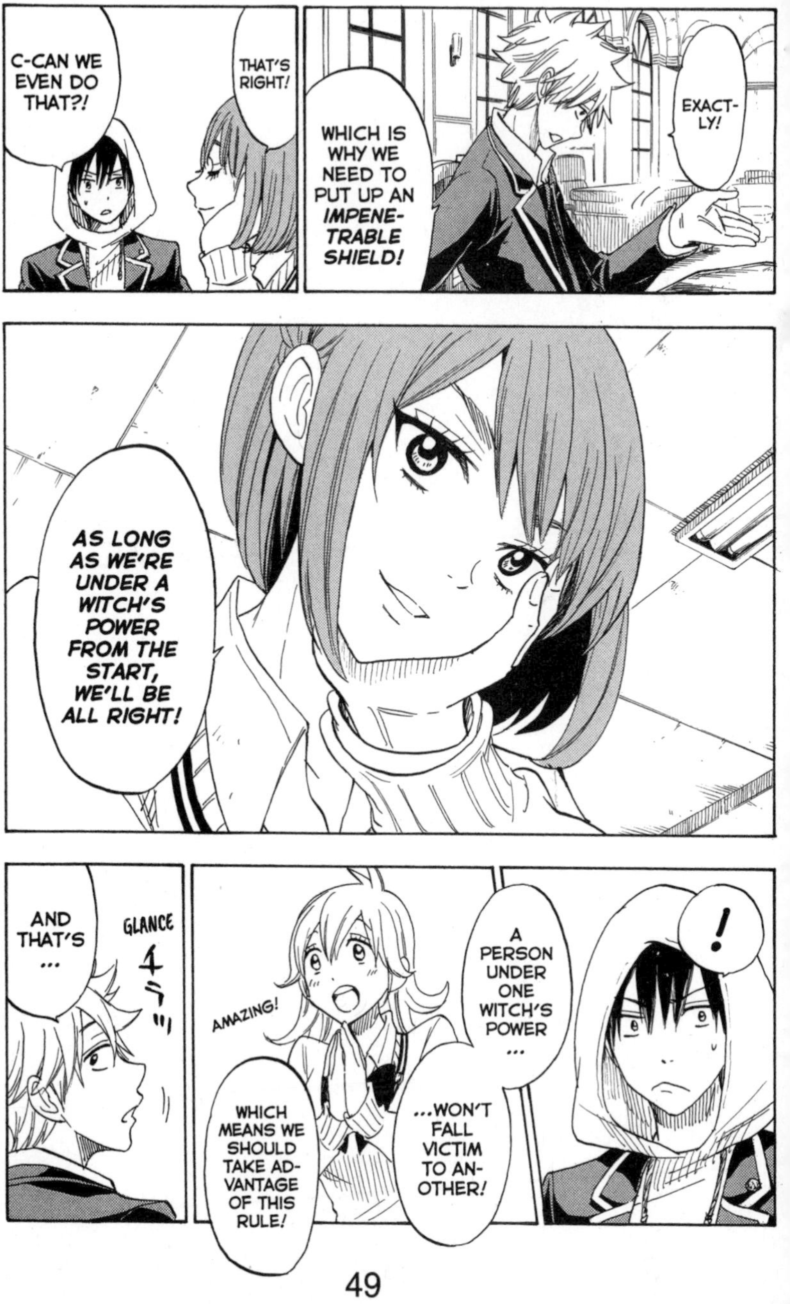
EXACTLY!
WHICH IS WHY WE NEED TO PUT UP AN IMPENETRABLE SHIELD!
THAT'S RIGHT!
C-CAN WE EVEN DO THAT?!
AS LONG AS WE'RE UNDER A WITCH'S POWER FROM THE START, WE'LL BE ALL RIGHT!
!
A PERSON UNDER ONE WITCH'S POWER ...
...WON'T FALL VICTIM TO ANOTHER!
AMAZING!
WHICH MEANS WE SHOULD TAKE ADVANTAGE OF THIS RULE!
GLANCE
AND THAT'S ...

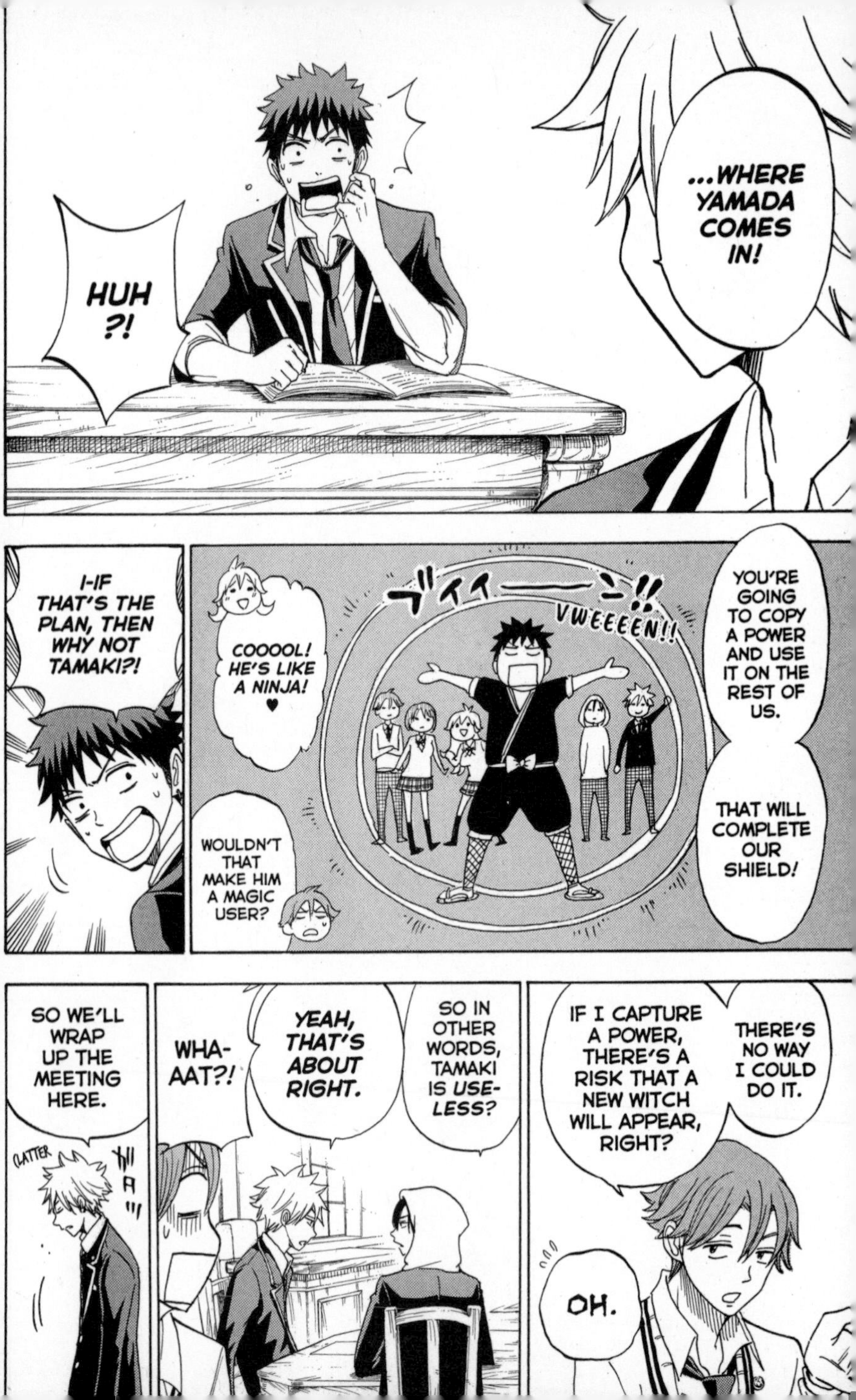
...WHERE YAMADA COMES IN!
HUH?!
YOU'RE GOING TO COPY A POWER AND USE IT ON THE REST OF US.
THAT WILL COMPLETE OUR SHIELD!
VWEEEEEN!!
COOOOL! HE'S LIKE A NINJA! ♥
WOULDN'T THAT MAKE HIM A MAGIC USER?
I-IF THAT'S THE PLAN, THEN WHY NOT TAMAKI?!
THERE'S NO WAY I COULD DO IT.
IF I CAPTURE A POWER, THERE'S A RISK THAT A NEW WITCH WILL APPEAR, RIGHT?
OH.
SO IN OTHER WORDS, TAMAKI IS USE-LESS?
YEAH, THAT'S ABOUT RIGHT.
WHA-AAT?!
SO WE'LL WRAP UP THE MEETING HERE.
CLATTER

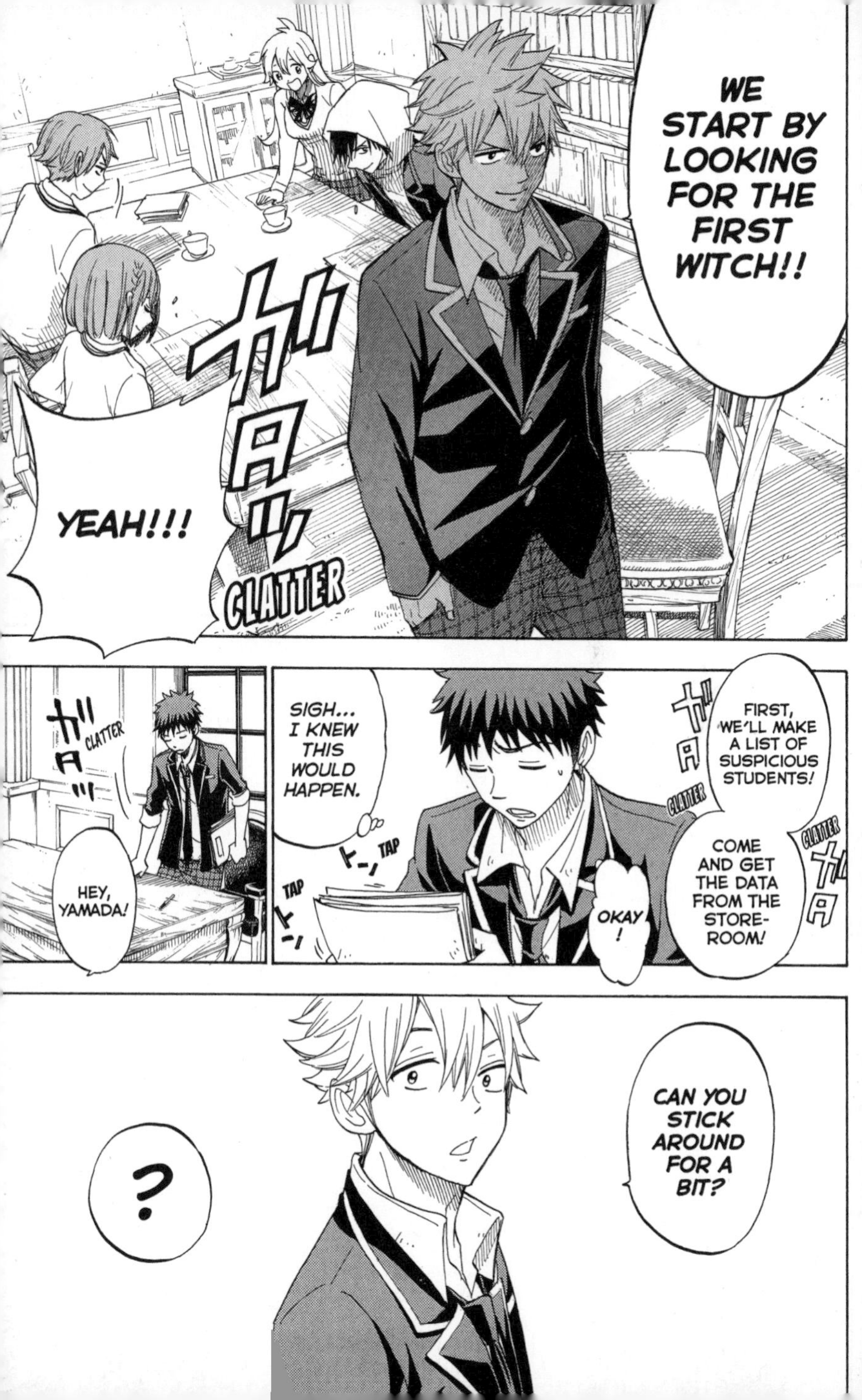
WE START BY LOOKING FOR THE FIRST WITCH!!
YEAH!!!
CLATTER
FIRST, WE'LL MAKE A LIST OF SUSPICIOUS STUDENTS!
CLATTER
COME AND GET THE DATA FROM THE STORE-ROOM!
CLATTER
OKAY!
SIGH... I KNEW THIS WOULD HAPPEN.
TAP
TAP
CLATTER
HEY, YAMADA!
CAN YOU STICK AROUND FOR A BIT?
?

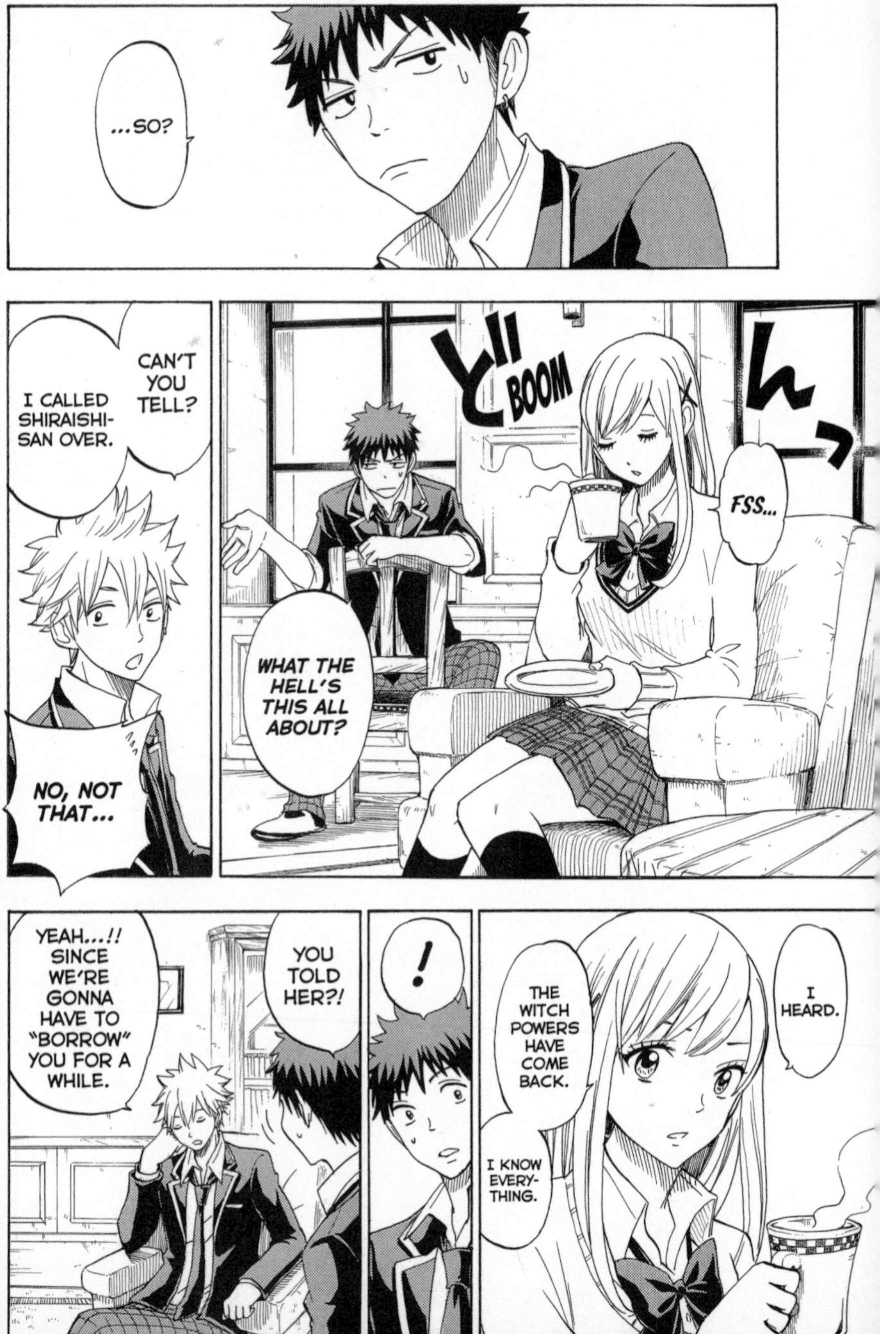
...SO?
FSS...
BOOM
WHAT THE HELL'S THIS ALL ABOUT?
CAN'T YOU TELL?
I CALLED SHIRAISHI-SAN OVER.
NO, NOT THAT...
I HEARD.
THE WITCH POWERS HAVE COME BACK.
I KNOW EVERY-THING.
!
YOU TOLD HER?!
YEAH...!! SINCE WE'RE GONNA HAVE TO "BORROW" YOU FOR A WHILE.

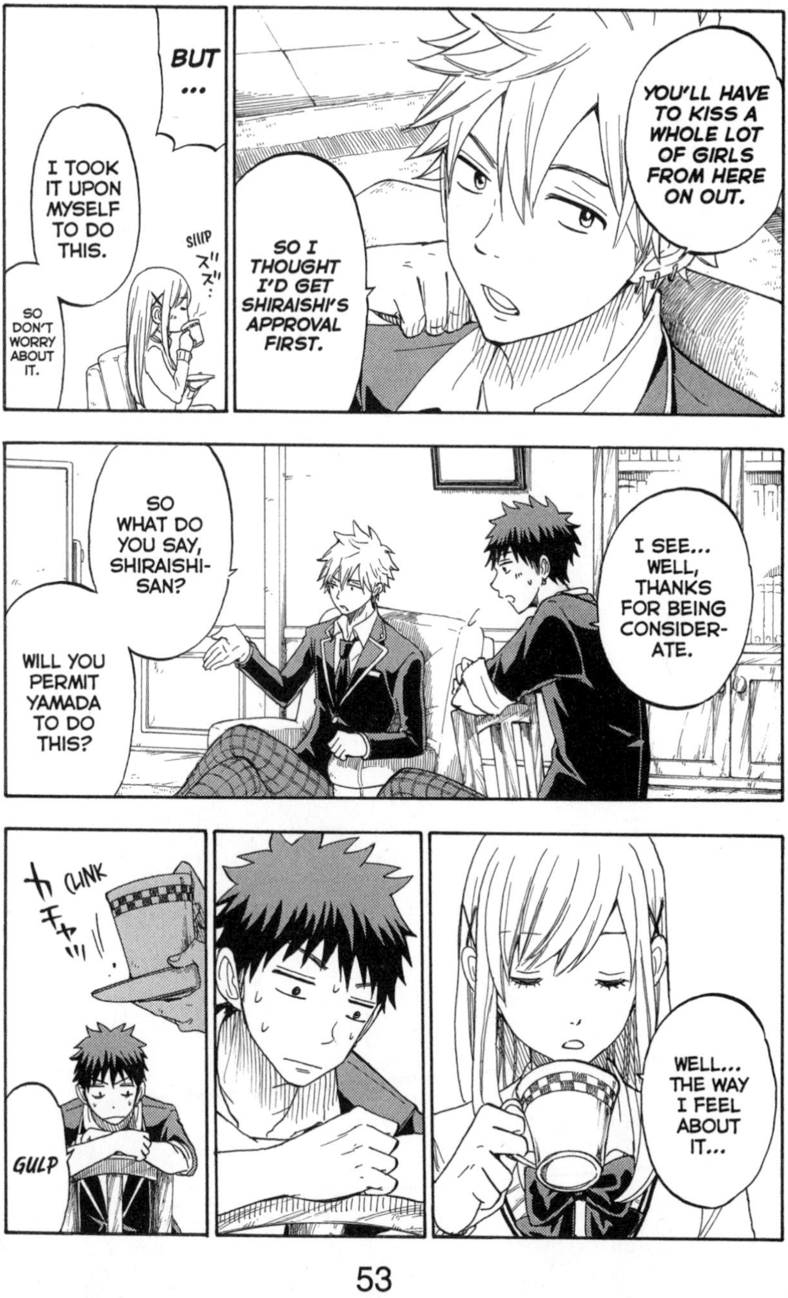
YOU'LL HAVE TO KISS A WHOLE LOT OF GIRLS FROM HERE ON OUT.
SO I THOUGHT I'D GET SHIRAISHI'S APPROVAL FIRST.
BUT...
I TOOK IT UPON MYSELF TO DO THIS.
SIIIP
ズズ‥
SO DON'T WORRY ABOUT IT.
I SEE... WELL, THANKS FOR BEING CONSIDER-ATE.
SO WHAT DO YOU SAY, SHIRAISHI-SAN?
WILL YOU PERMIT YAMADA TO DO THIS?
WELL... THE WAY I FEEL ABOUT IT...
カチャッ
CLINK
GULP

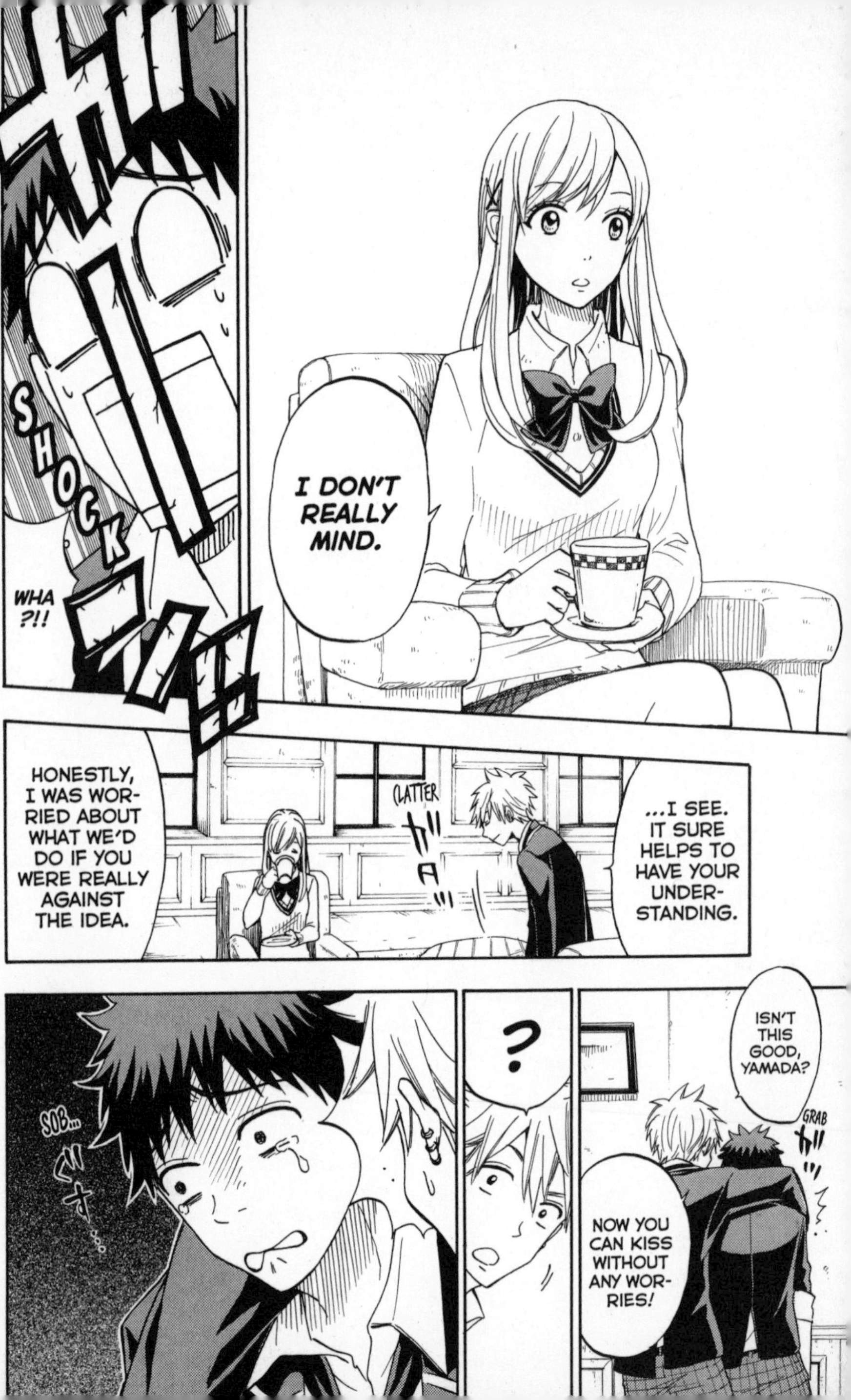
I DON'T REALLY MIND.
SHOCK
WHA?!!
...I SEE. IT SURE HELPS TO HAVE YOUR UNDER-STANDING.
CLATTER
HONESTLY, I WAS WOR-RIED ABOUT WHAT WE'D DO IF YOU WERE REALLY AGAINST THE IDEA.
ISN'T THIS GOOD, YAMADA?
GRAB
NOW YOU CAN KISS WITHOUT ANY WOR-RIES!
?
SOB...

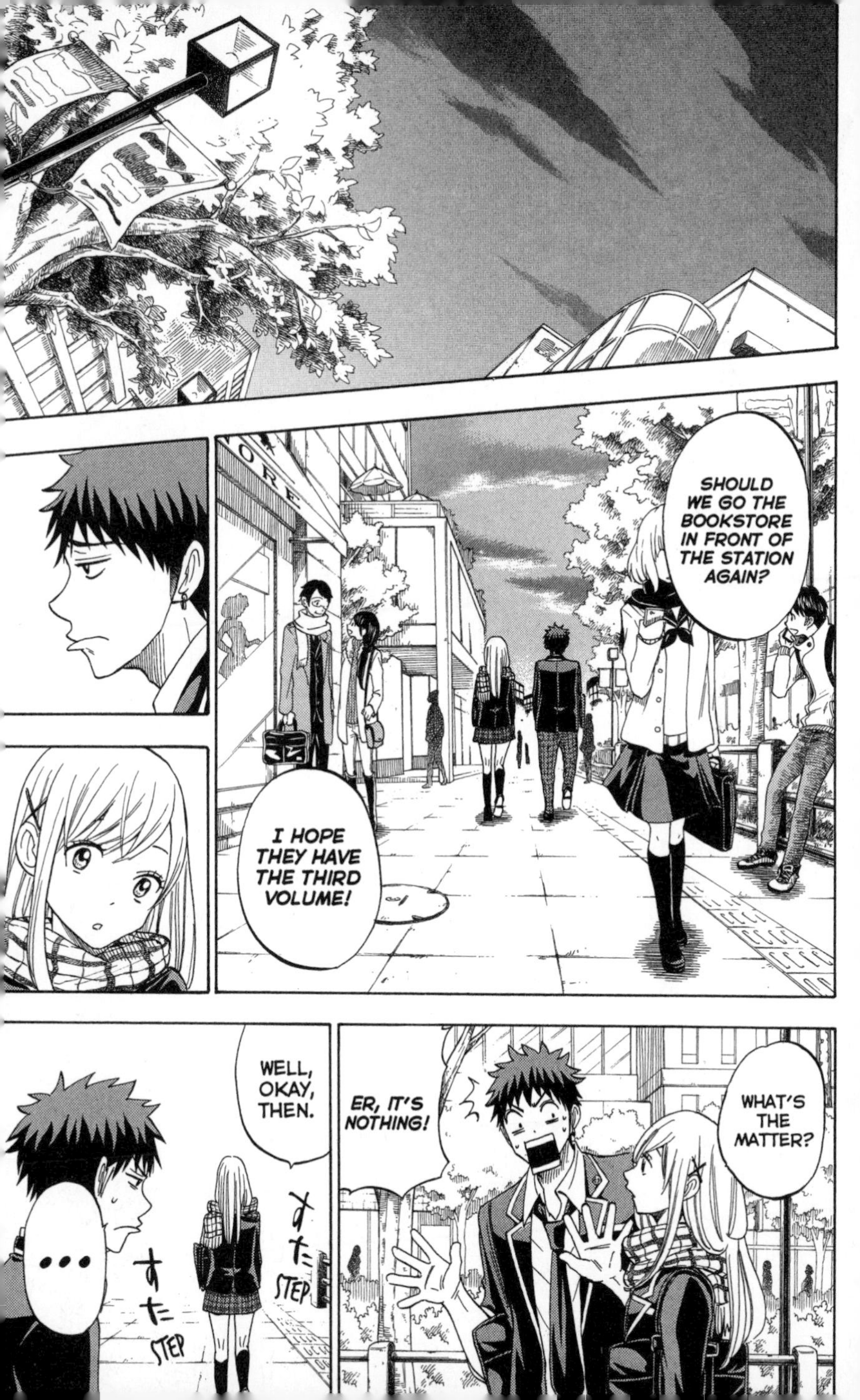
SHOULD WE GO THE BOOKSTORE IN FRONT OF THE STATION AGAIN?
I HOPE THEY HAVE THE THIRD VOLUME!
WHAT'S THE MATTER?
ER, IT'S NOTHING!
WELL, OKAY, THEN.
すた STEP
...
すた STEP

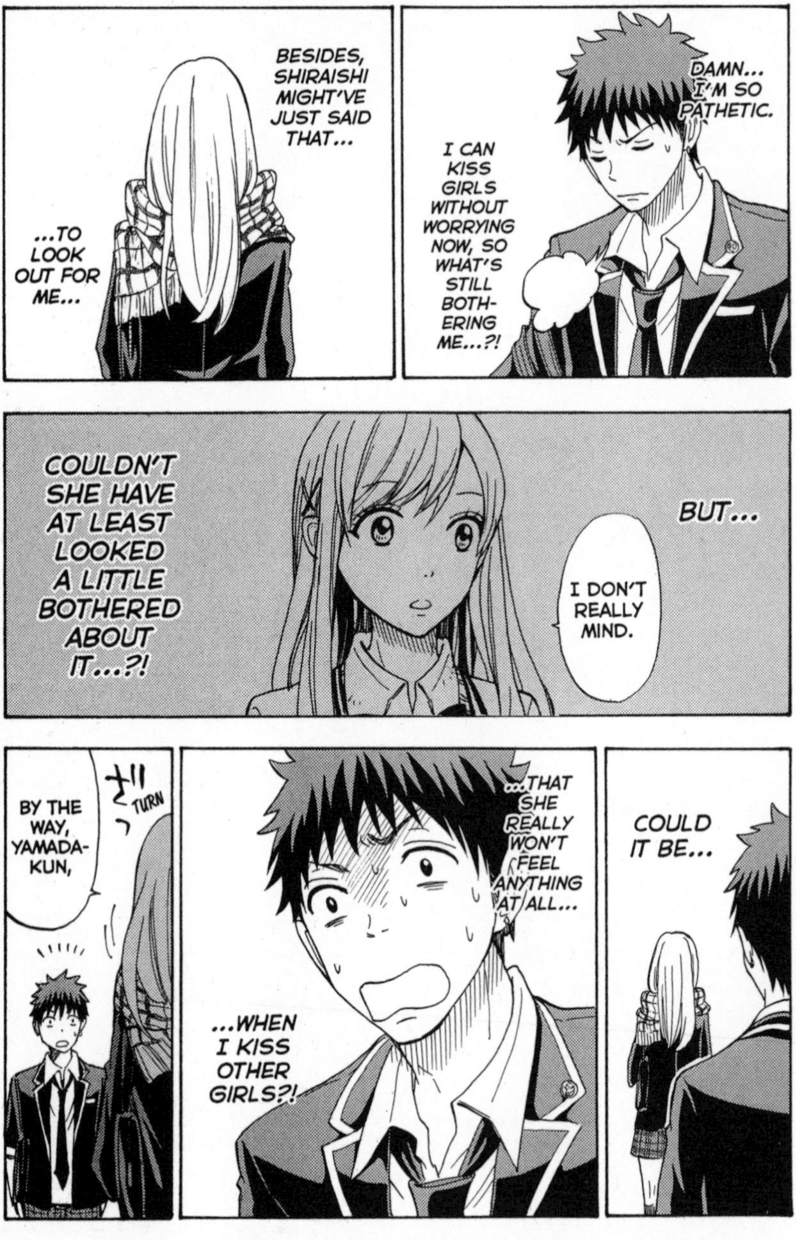
DAMN... I'M SO PATHETIC.
I CAN KISS GIRLS WITHOUT WORRYING NOW, SO WHAT'S STILL BOTHERING ME...?!
BESIDES, SHIRAISHI MIGHT'VE JUST SAID THAT...
...TO LOOK OUT FOR ME...
BUT...
I DON'T REALLY MIND.
COULDN'T SHE HAVE AT LEAST LOOKED A LITTLE BOTHERED ABOUT IT...?!
COULD IT BE...
...THAT SHE REALLY WON'T FEEL ANYTHING AT ALL...
...WHEN I KISS OTHER GIRLS?!
TURN
BY THE WAY, YAMADA-KUN,

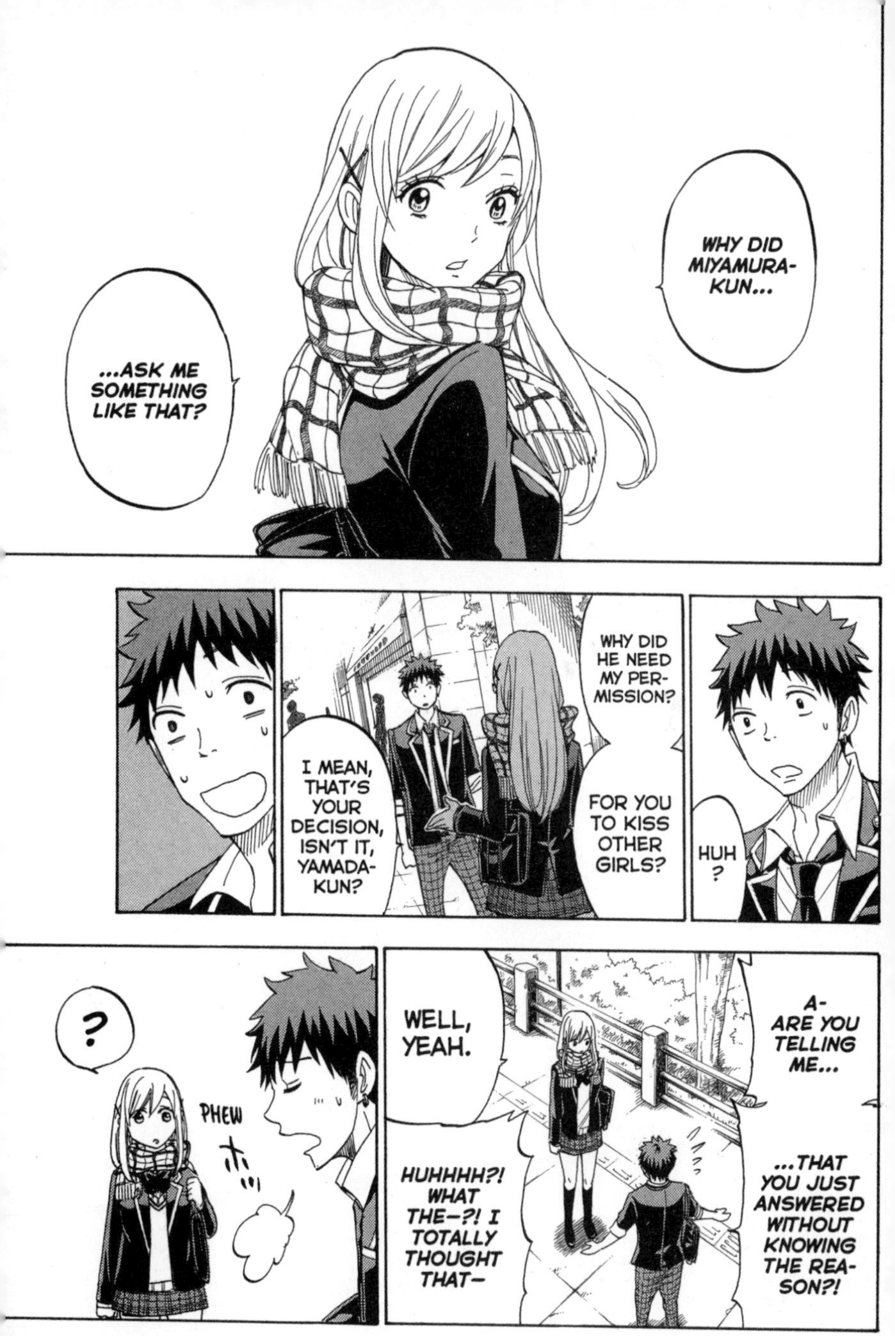
WHY DID MIYAMURA-KUN...
...ASK ME SOMETHING LIKE THAT?
HUH?
WHY DID HE NEED MY PER-MISSION?
FOR YOU TO KISS OTHER GIRLS?
I MEAN, THAT'S YOUR DECISION, ISN'T IT, YAMADA-KUN?
A- ARE YOU TELLING ME...
...THAT YOU JUST ANSWERED WITHOUT KNOWING THE REA-SON?!
WELL, YEAH.
HUHHHH?! WHAT THE—?! I TOTALLY THOUGHT THAT—
PHEW
?

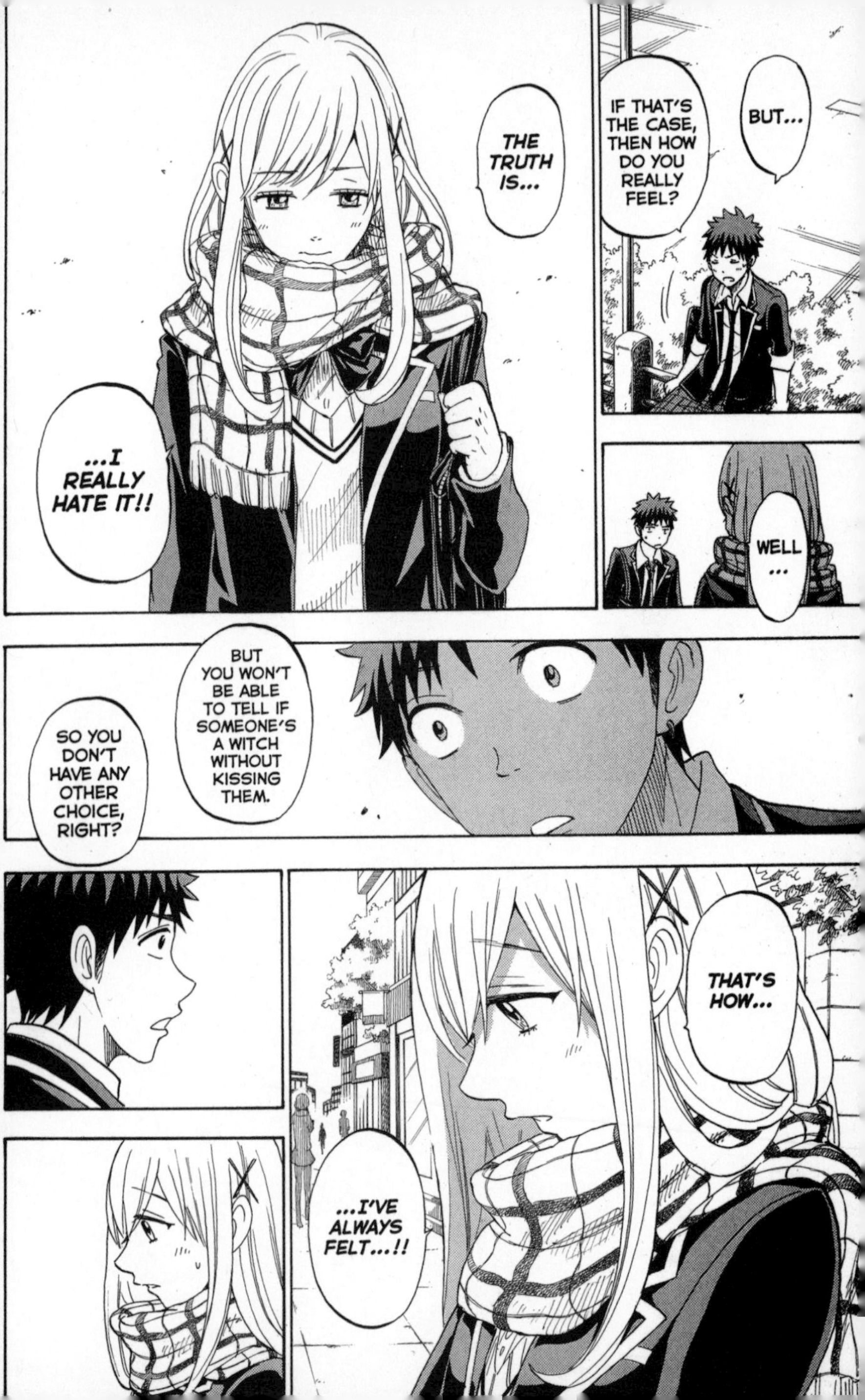
BUT...
IF THAT'S THE CASE, THEN HOW DO YOU REALLY FEEL?
WELL...
THE TRUTH IS...
...I REALLY HATE IT!!
BUT YOU WON'T BE ABLE TO TELL IF SOMEONE'S A WITCH WITHOUT KISSING THEM.
SO YOU DON'T HAVE ANY OTHER CHOICE, RIGHT?
THAT'S HOW...
...I'VE ALWAYS FELT...!!

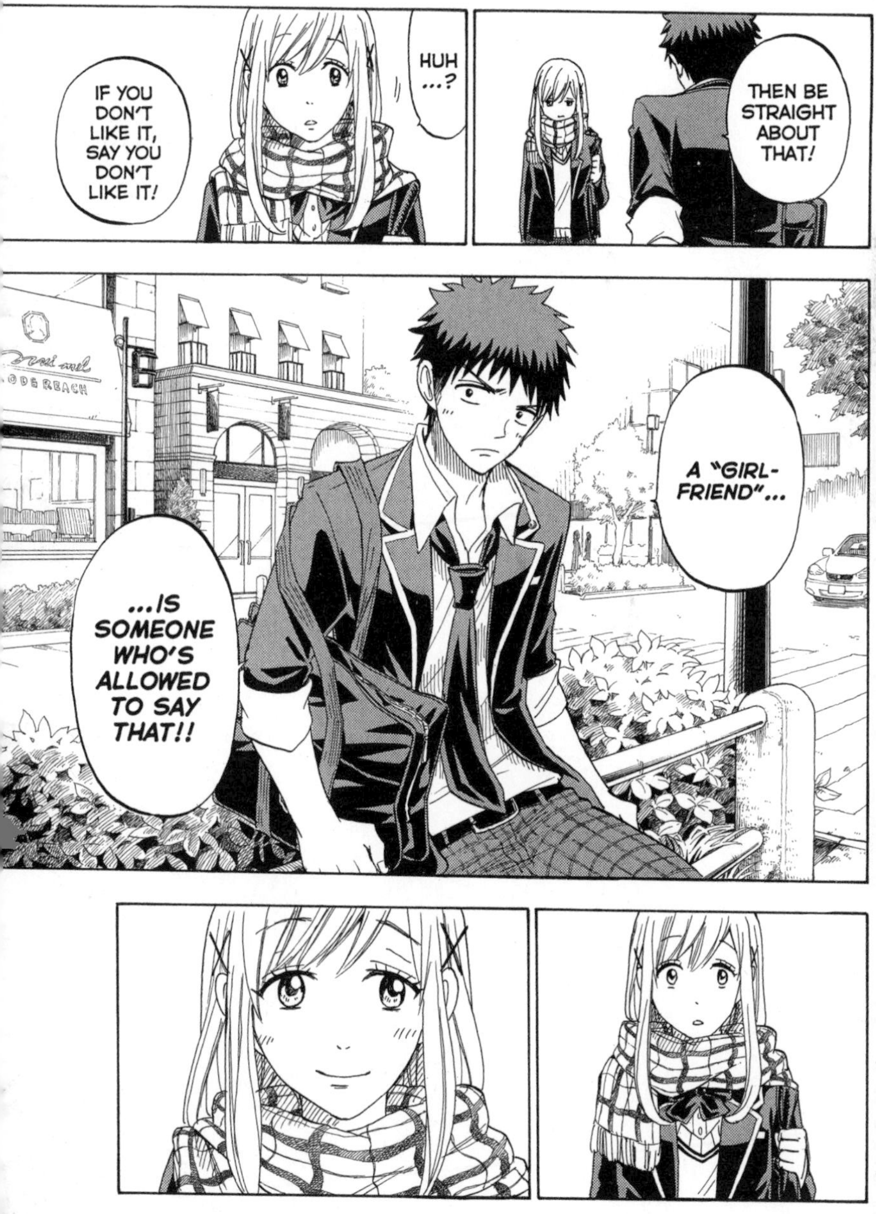
THEN BE STRAIGHT ABOUT THAT!
HUH ...?
IF YOU DON'T LIKE IT, SAY YOU DON'T LIKE IT!
A "GIRL-FRIEND"...
...IS SOMEONE WHO'S ALLOWED TO SAY THAT!!

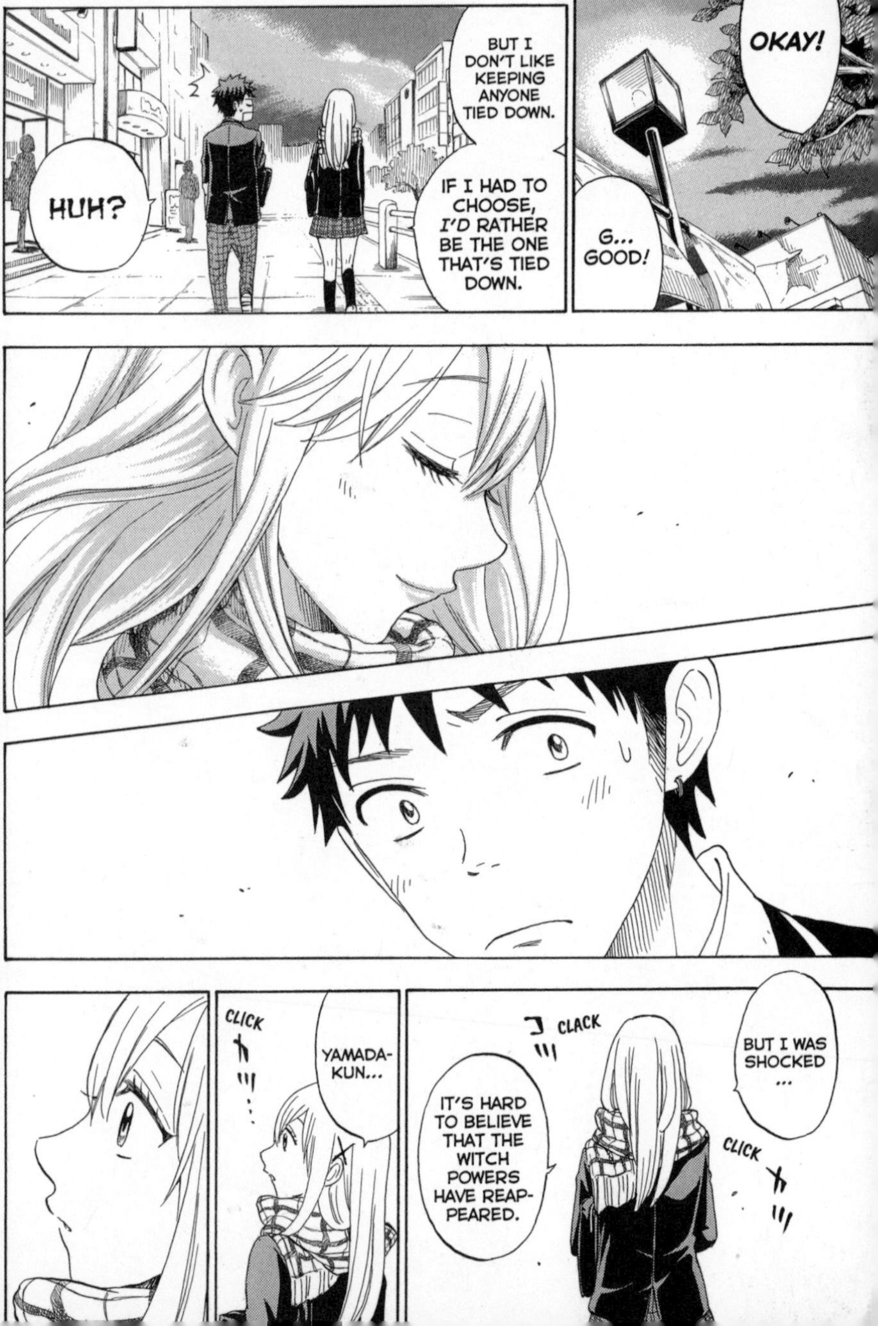
OKAY!
G... GOOD!
BUT I DON'T LIKE KEEPING ANYONE TIED DOWN.
IF I HAD TO CHOOSE, *I'D* RATHER BE THE ONE THAT'S TIED DOWN.
HUH?
BUT I WAS SHOCKED ...
CLACK
CLICK
IT'S HARD TO BELIEVE THAT THE WITCH POWERS HAVE REAP-PEARED.
YAMADA-KUN...
CLICK

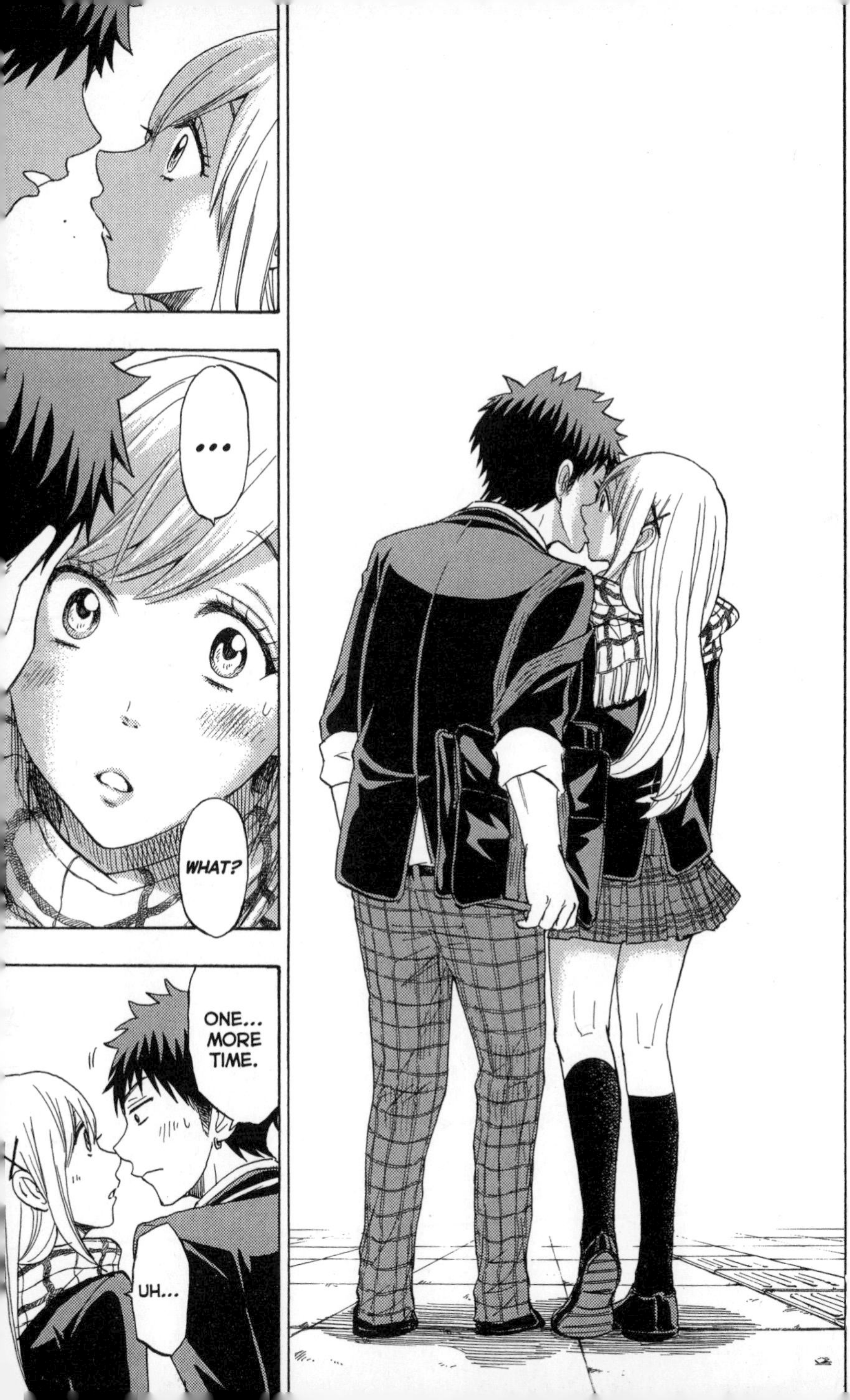
...
WHAT?
ONE... MORE TIME.
UH...

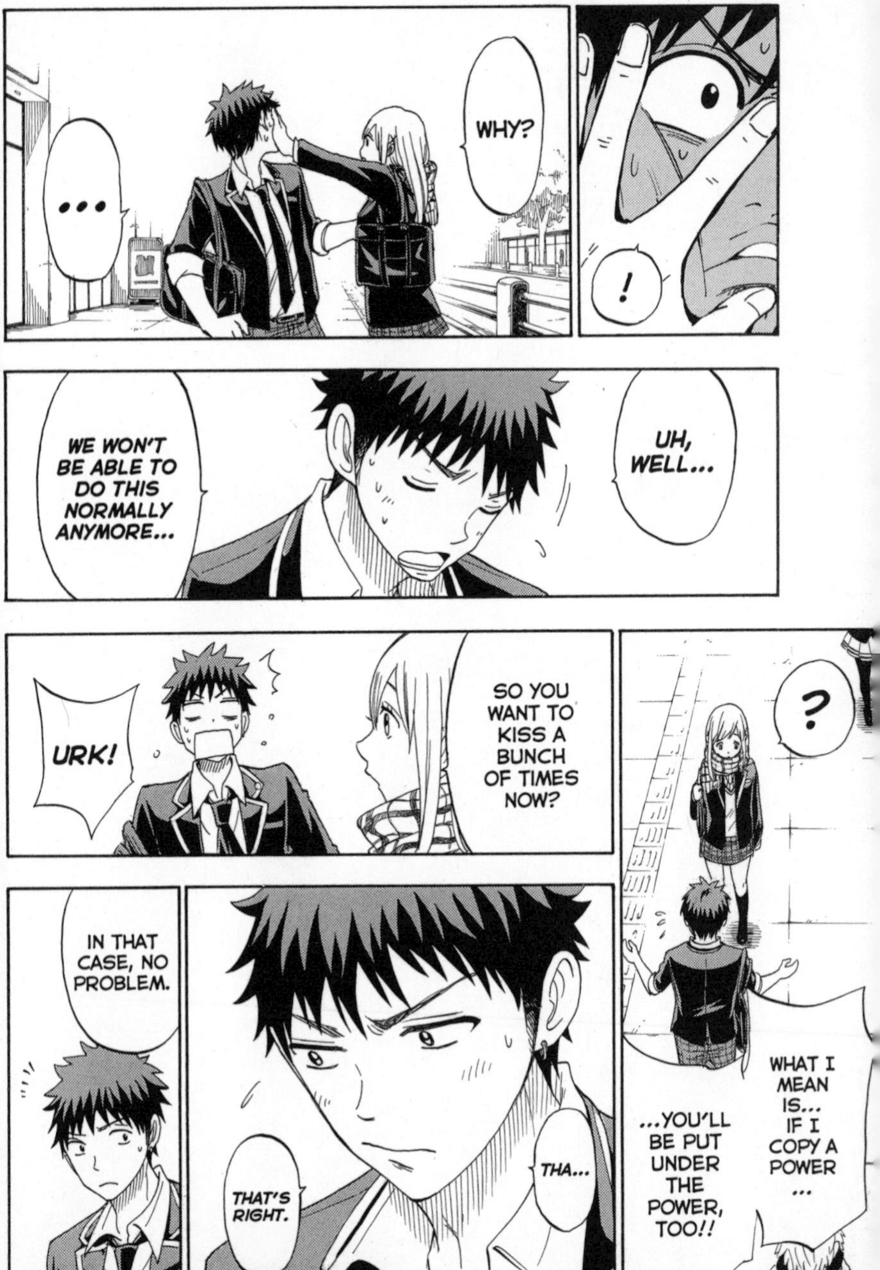
!
WHY?
...
UH, WELL...
WE WON'T BE ABLE TO DO THIS NORMALLY ANYMORE...
?
WHAT I MEAN IS... IF I COPY A POWER ...
...YOU'LL BE PUT UNDER THE POWER, TOO!!
SO YOU WANT TO KISS A BUNCH OF TIMES NOW?
URK!
THA...
THAT'S RIGHT.
IN THAT CASE, NO PROBLEM.

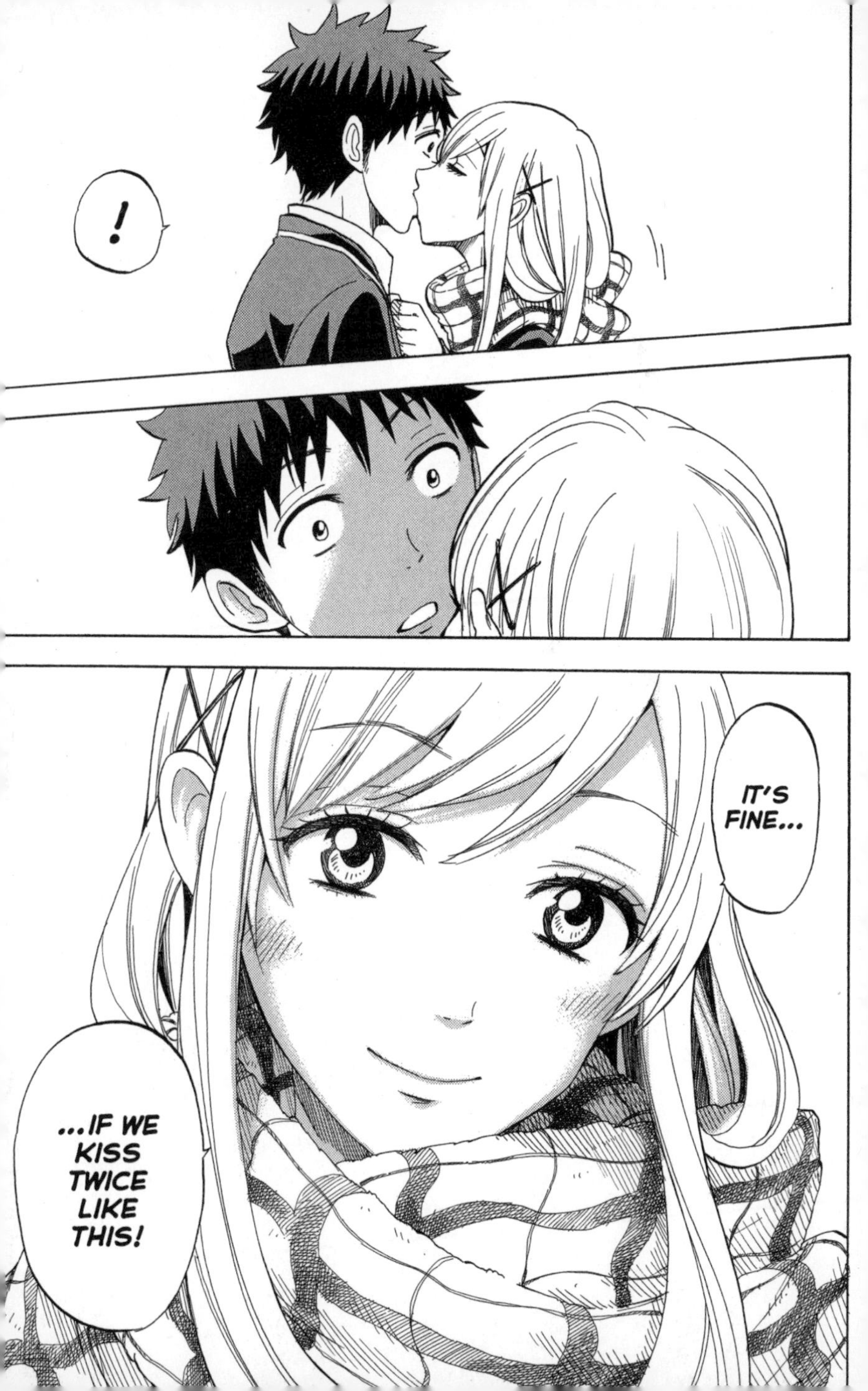
!
IT'S FINE...
...IF WE KISS TWICE LIKE THIS!

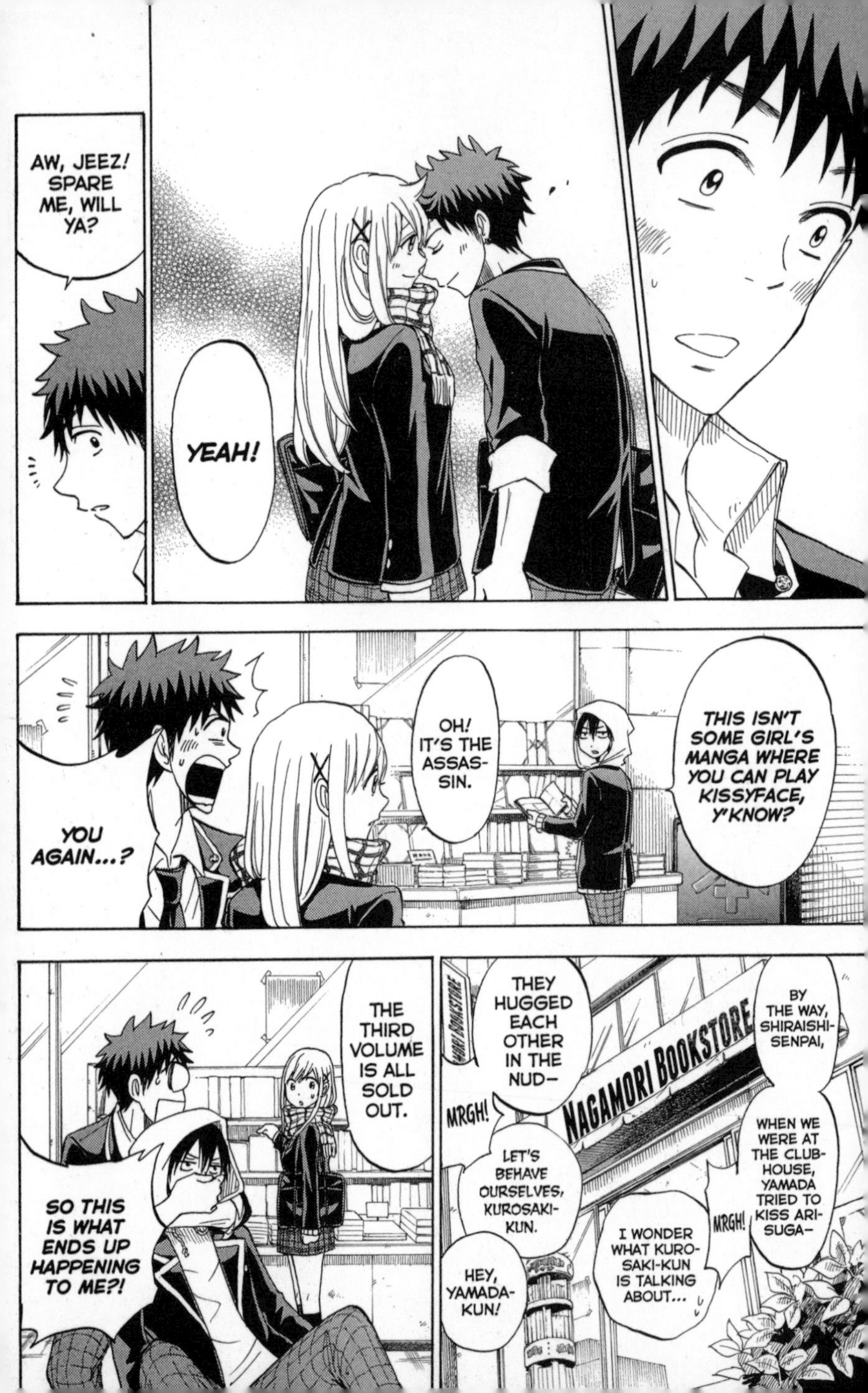
YEAH!
AW, JEEZ! SPARE ME, WILL YA?
THIS ISN'T SOME GIRL'S MANGA WHERE YOU CAN PLAY KISSYFACE, Y'KNOW?
OH! IT'S THE ASSAS-SIN.
YOU AGAIN...?
BY THE WAY, SHIRAISHI-SENPAI,
WHEN WE WERE AT THE CLUB-HOUSE, YAMADA TRIED TO KISS ARI-SUGA–
MRGH!
NAGAMORI BOOKSTORE
THEY HUGGED EACH OTHER IN THE NUD–
MRGH!
I WONDER WHAT KURO-SAKI-KUN IS TALKING ABOUT...
LET'S BEHAVE OURSELVES, KUROSAKI-KUN.
HEY, YAMADA-KUN!
THE THIRD VOLUME IS ALL SOLD OUT.
SO THIS IS WHAT ENDS UP HAPPENING TO ME?!

CHAPTER 97: Susshi.

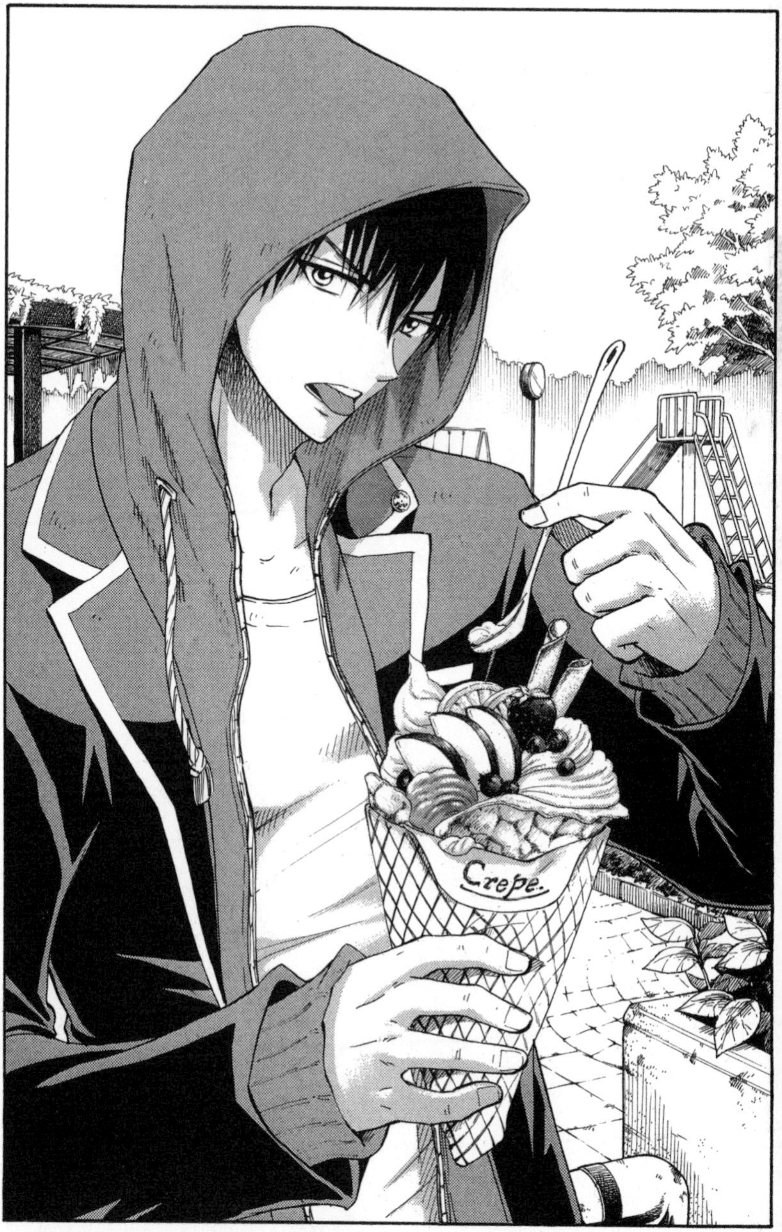
Crepe.

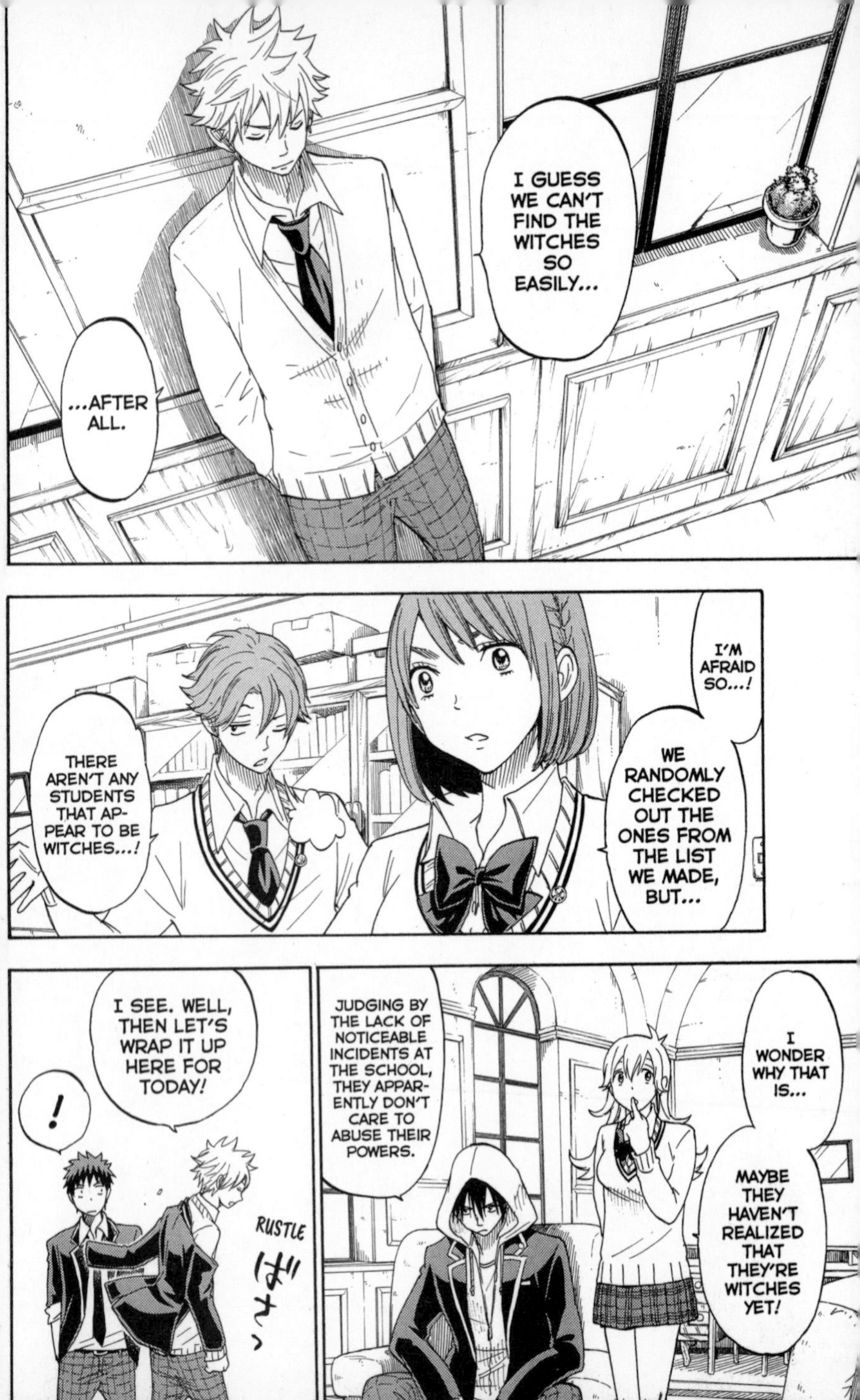
I GUESS WE CAN'T FIND THE WITCHES SO EASILY...
...AFTER ALL.
I'M AFRAID SO...!
WE RANDOMLY CHECKED OUT THE ONES FROM THE LIST WE MADE, BUT...
THERE AREN'T ANY STUDENTS THAT APPEAR TO BE WITCHES...!
I WONDER WHY THAT IS...
MAYBE THEY HAVEN'T REALIZED THAT THEY'RE WITCHES YET!
JUDGING BY THE LACK OF NOTICEABLE INCIDENTS AT THE SCHOOL, THEY APPARENTLY DON'T CARE TO ABUSE THEIR POWERS.
I SEE. WELL, THEN LET'S WRAP IT UP HERE FOR TODAY!
!
RUSTLE
ばさっ

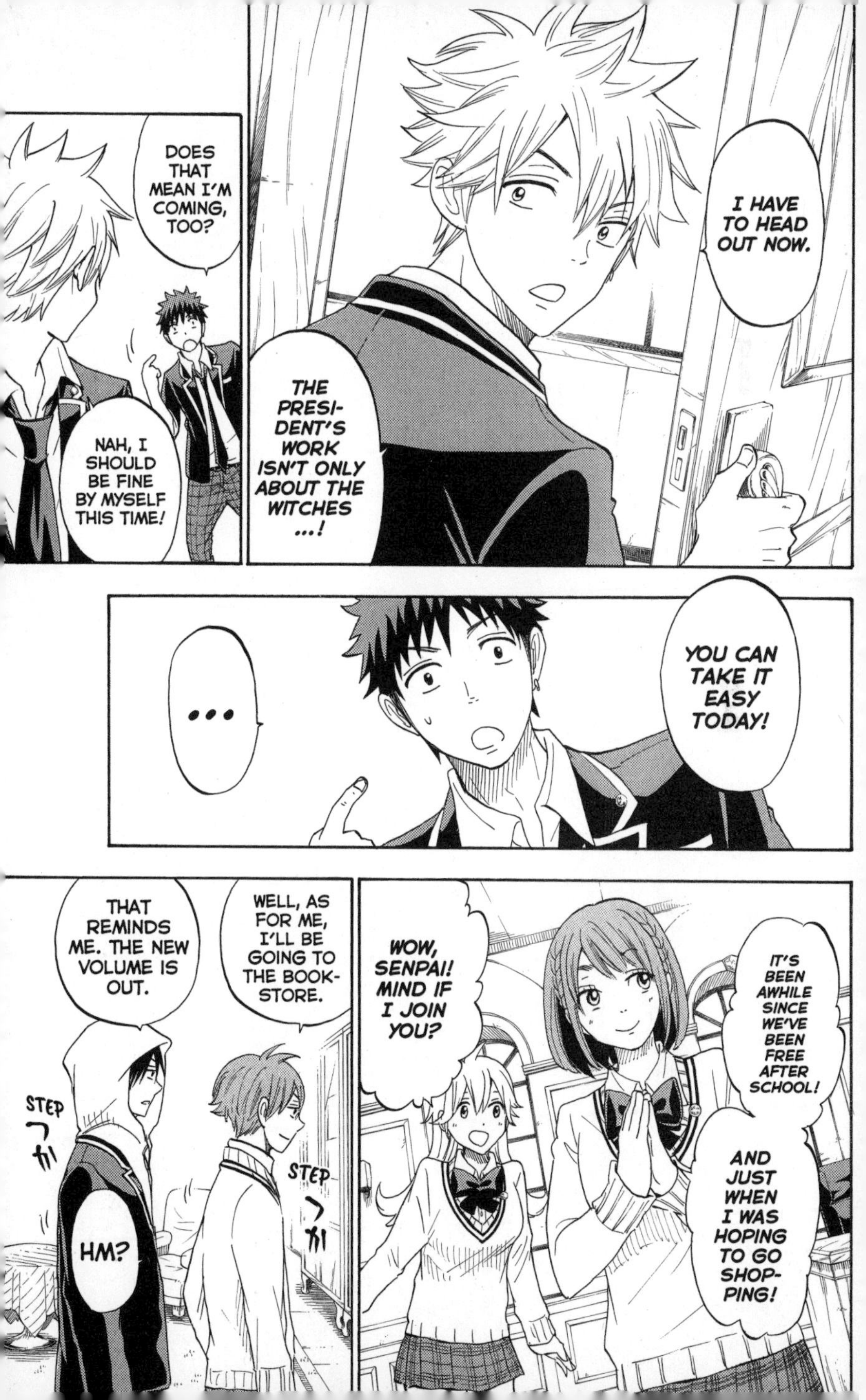
I HAVE TO HEAD OUT NOW.
THE PRESIDENT'S WORK ISN'T ONLY ABOUT THE WITCHES ...!
DOES THAT MEAN I'M COMING, TOO?
NAH, I SHOULD BE FINE BY MYSELF THIS TIME!
YOU CAN TAKE IT EASY TODAY!
...
IT'S BEEN AWHILE SINCE WE'VE BEEN FREE AFTER SCHOOL!
AND JUST WHEN I WAS HOPING TO GO SHOPPING!
WOW, SENPAI! MIND IF I JOIN YOU?
WELL, AS FOR ME, I'LL BE GOING TO THE BOOKSTORE.
STEP
THAT REMINDS ME. THE NEW VOLUME IS OUT.
STEP
HM?

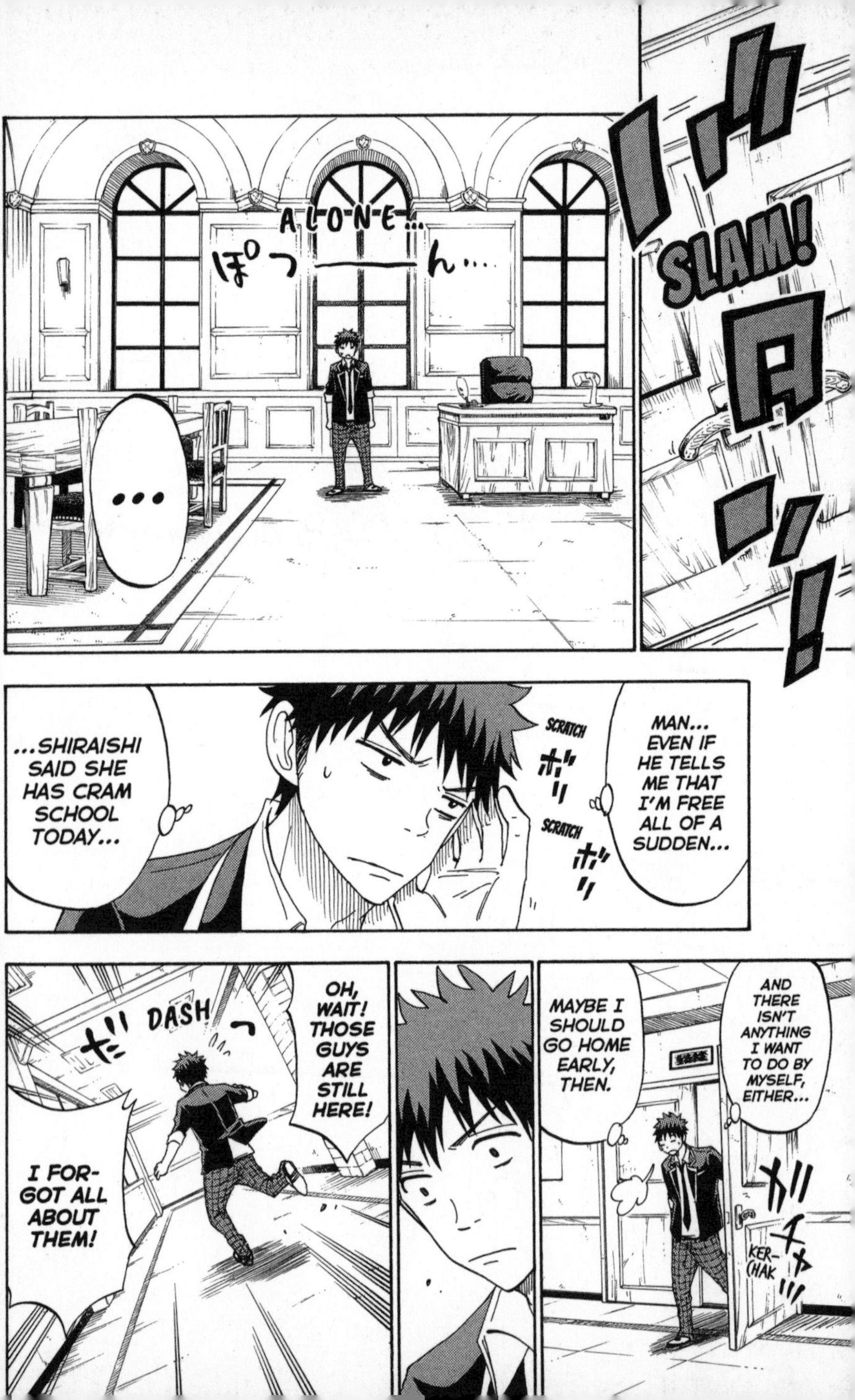
SLAM!
ALONE...
ぽつ――ん…
...
MAN... EVEN IF HE TELLS ME THAT I'M FREE ALL OF A SUDDEN...
SCRATCH
ボリ
SCRATCH
ボリ
...SHIRAISHI SAID SHE HAS CRAM SCHOOL TODAY...
AND THERE ISN'T ANYTHING I WANT TO DO BY MYSELF, EITHER...
MAYBE I SHOULD GO HOME EARLY, THEN.
ガチャ
KER-CHAK
OH, WAIT! THOSE GUYS ARE STILL HERE!
ダッ
DASH
I FOR-GOT ALL ABOUT THEM!

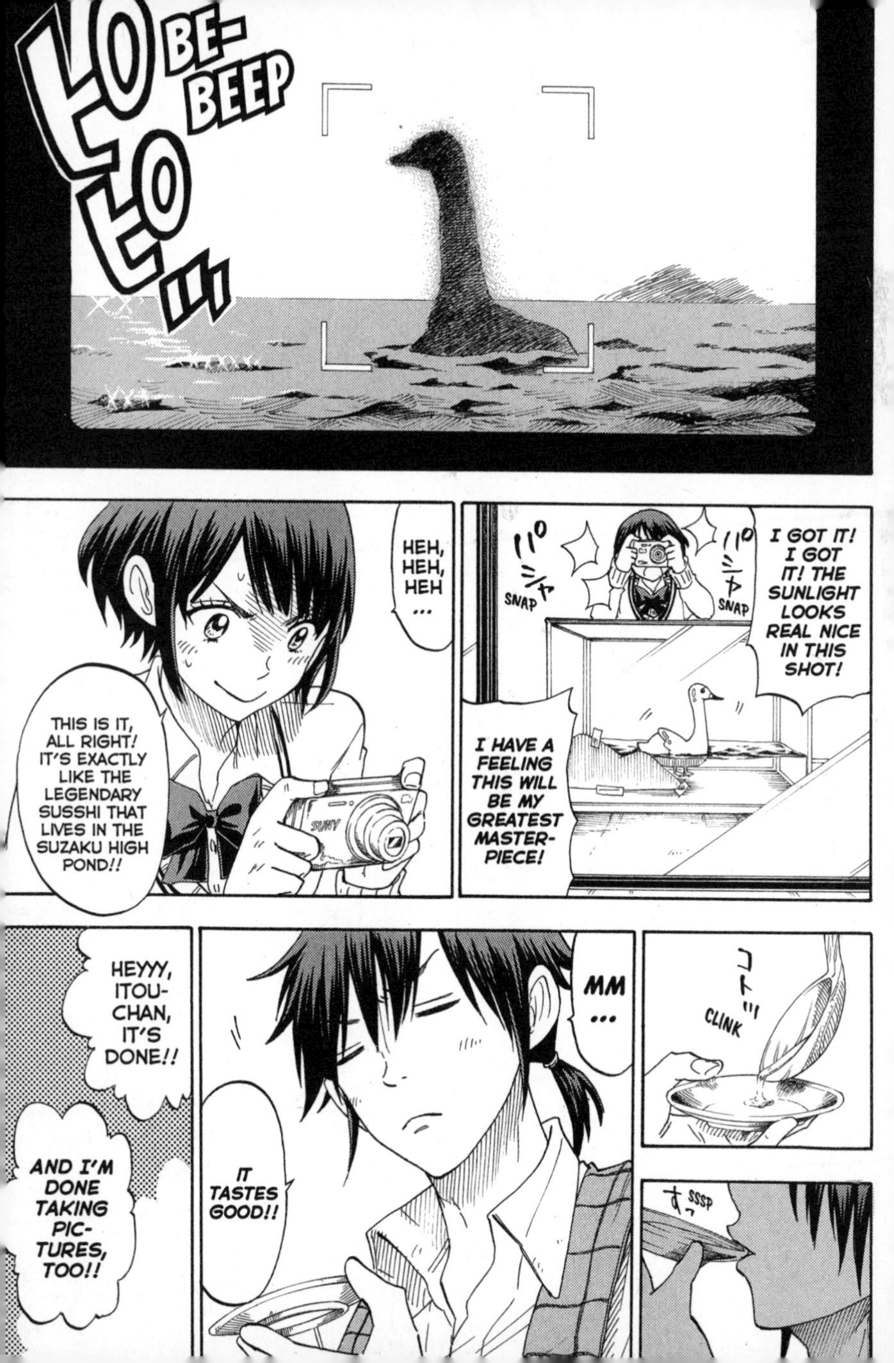
ピロピロッ
BE-BEEP
パシャ
SNAP
パシャ
SNAP
I GOT IT! I GOT IT! THE SUNLIGHT LOOKS REAL NICE IN THIS SHOT!
I HAVE A FEELING THIS WILL BE MY GREATEST MASTER-PIECE!
HEH, HEH, HEH...
THIS IS IT, ALL RIGHT! IT'S EXACTLY LIKE THE LEGENDARY SUSSHI THAT LIVES IN THE SUZAKU HIGH POND!!
SUNY
コトッ
CLINK
すっ
SSSP
MM...
IT TASTES GOOD!!
HEYYY, ITOU-CHAN, IT'S DONE!!
AND I'M DONE TAKING PIC-TURES, TOO!!

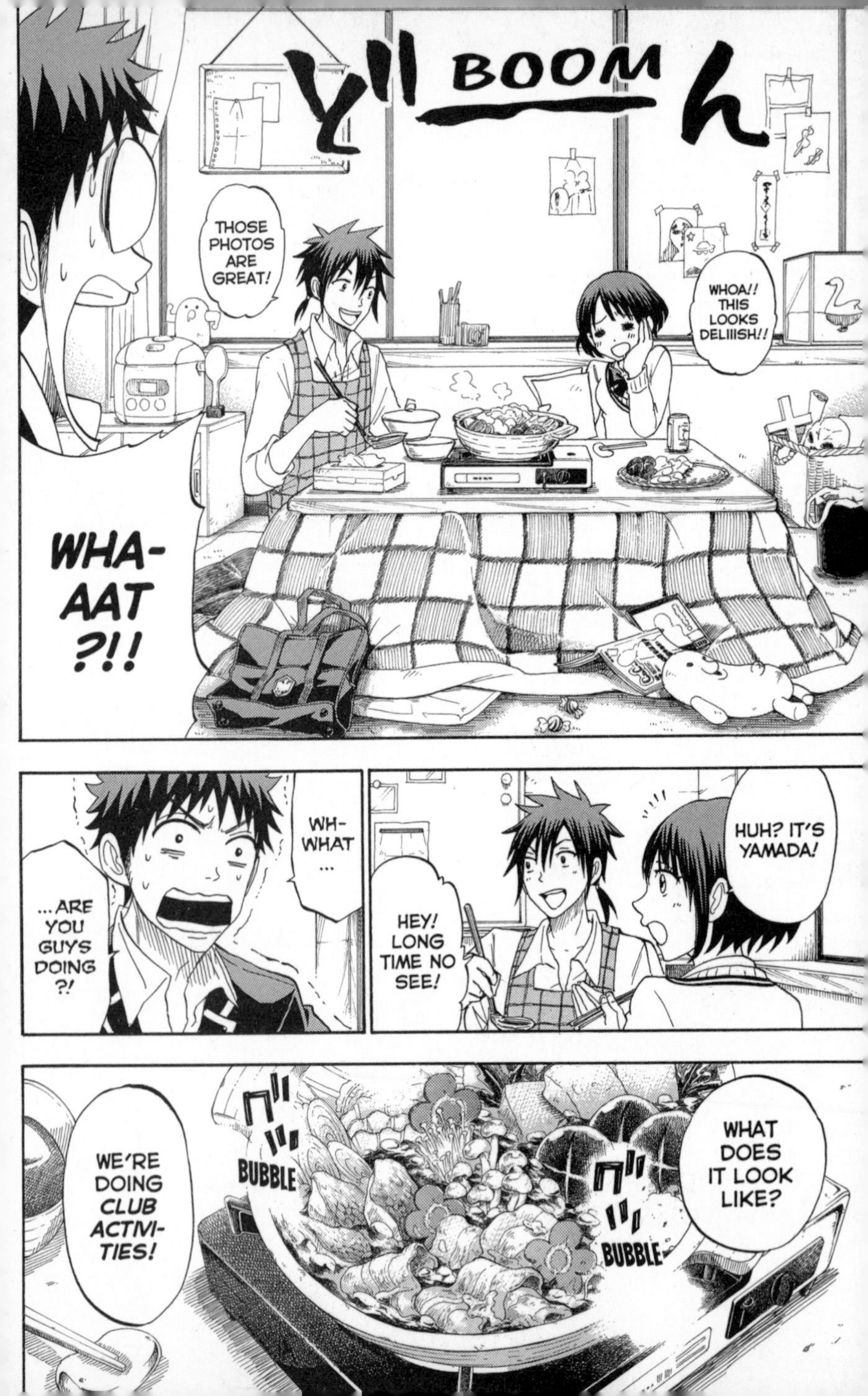
BOOM
WHOA!! THIS LOOKS DELIIISH!!
THOSE PHOTOS ARE GREAT!
WHA-AAT?!!
HUH? IT'S YAMADA!
HEY! LONG TIME NO SEE!
WH-WHAT ...
...ARE YOU GUYS DOING ?!
WHAT DOES IT LOOK LIKE?
BUBBLE
BUBBLE
WE'RE DOING CLUB ACTIVITIES!

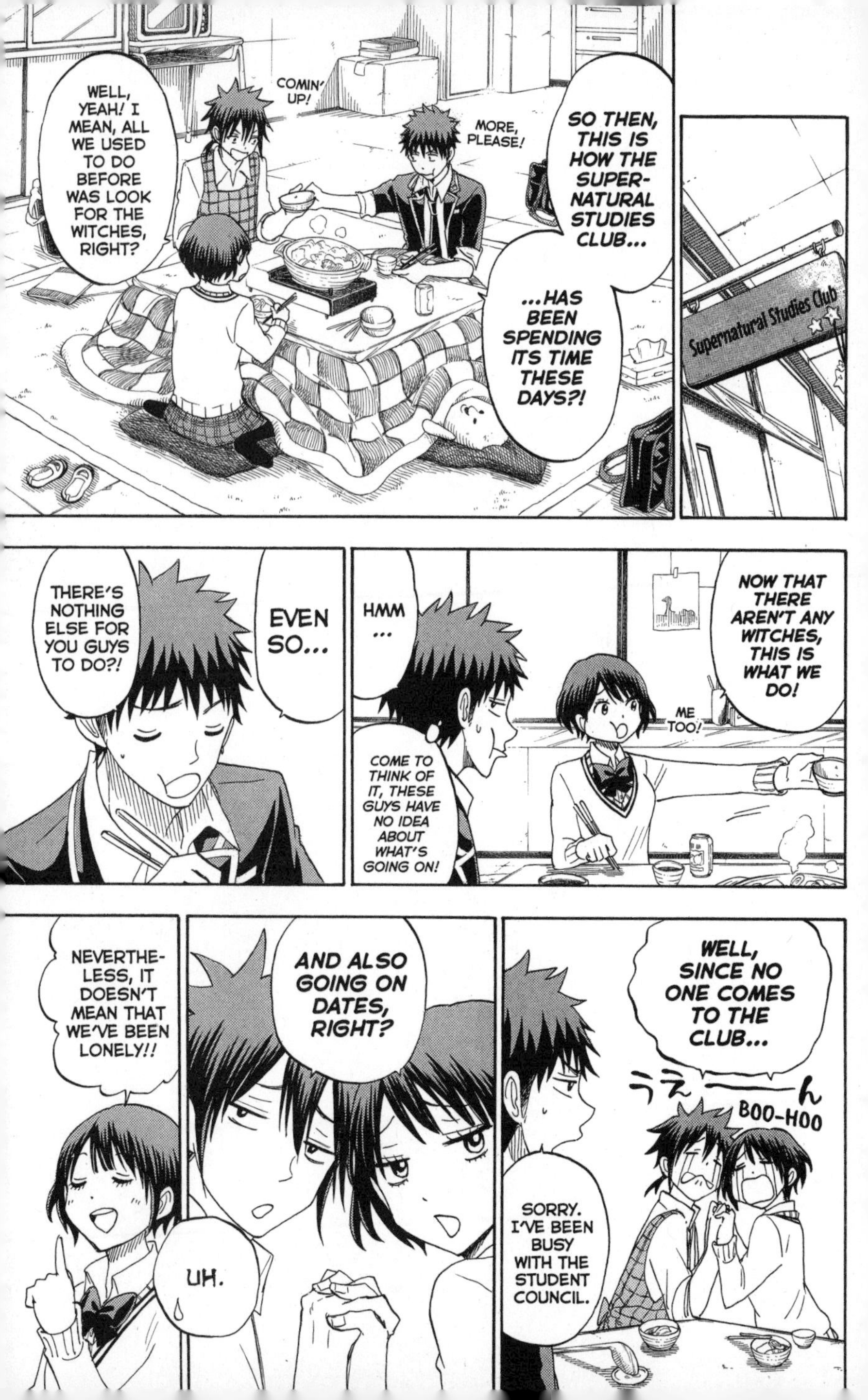
Supernatural Studies Club
SO THEN, THIS IS HOW THE SUPER-NATURAL STUDIES CLUB...
...HAS BEEN SPENDING ITS TIME THESE DAYS?!
MORE, PLEASE!
COMIN' UP!
WELL, YEAH! I MEAN, ALL WE USED TO DO BEFORE WAS LOOK FOR THE WITCHES, RIGHT?
NOW THAT THERE AREN'T ANY WITCHES, THIS IS WHAT WE DO!
ME TOO!
HMM ...
COME TO THINK OF IT, THESE GUYS HAVE NO IDEA ABOUT WHAT'S GOING ON!
EVEN SO...
THERE'S NOTHING ELSE FOR YOU GUYS TO DO?!
WELL, SINCE NO ONE COMES TO THE CLUB...
うえーーん
BOO-HOO
SORRY. I'VE BEEN BUSY WITH THE STUDENT COUNCIL.
AND ALSO GOING ON DATES, RIGHT?
UH.
NEVERTHE-LESS, IT DOESN'T MEAN THAT WE'VE BEEN LONELY!!

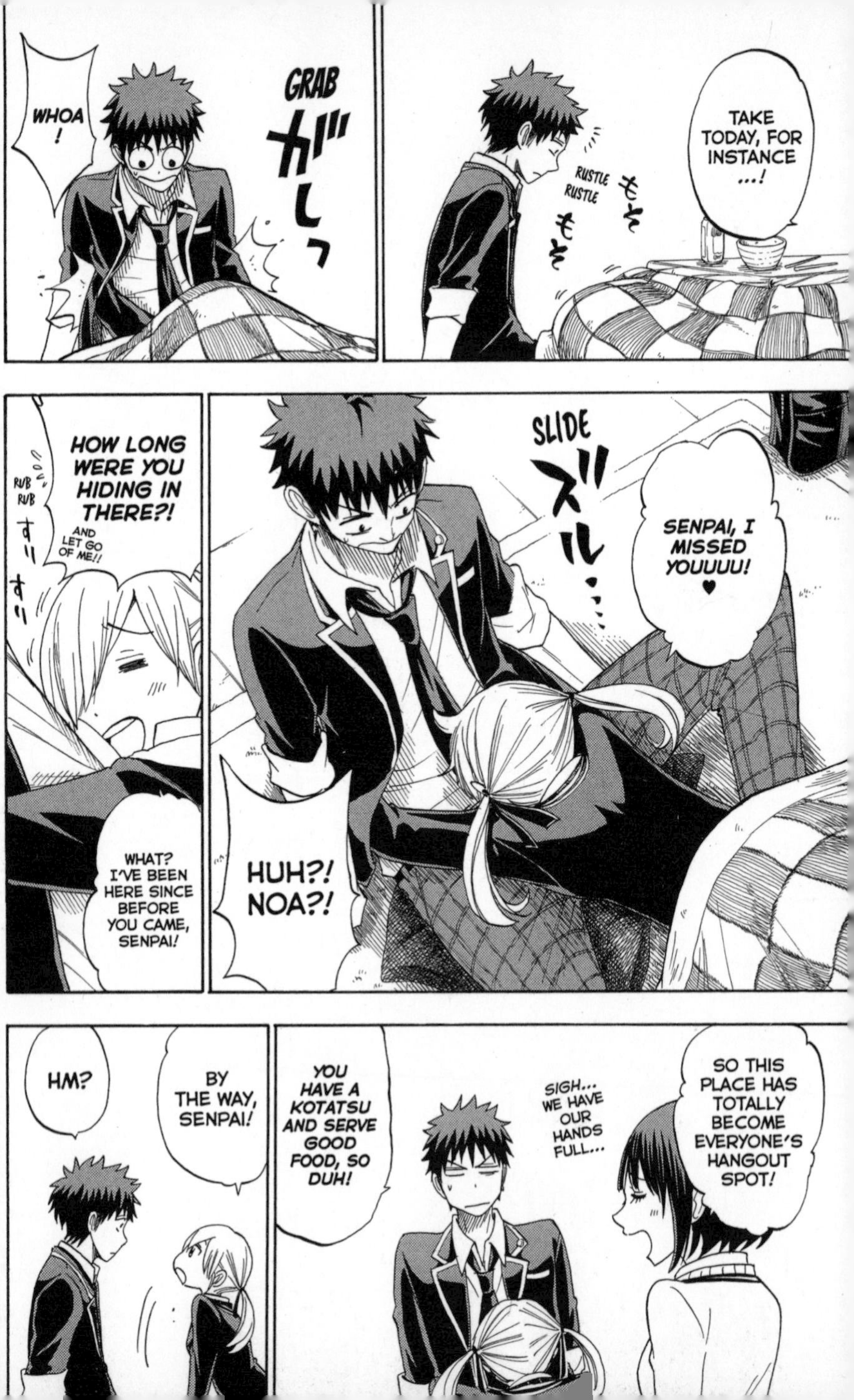
TAKE TODAY, FOR INSTANCE ...!
RUSTLE RUSTLE
もそもそ
GRAB
がしっ
WHOA!
SENPAI, I MISSED YOUUUU! ♥
SLIDE
ズル…
HUH?! NOA?!
HOW LONG WERE YOU HIDING IN THERE?!
AND LET GO OF ME!!
RUB RUB
すりすり
WHAT? I'VE BEEN HERE SINCE BEFORE YOU CAME, SENPAI!
SO THIS PLACE HAS TOTALLY BECOME EVERYONE'S HANGOUT SPOT!
SIGH... WE HAVE OUR HANDS FULL...
YOU HAVE A KOTATSU AND SERVE GOOD FOOD, SO DUH!
BY THE WAY, SENPAI!
HM?

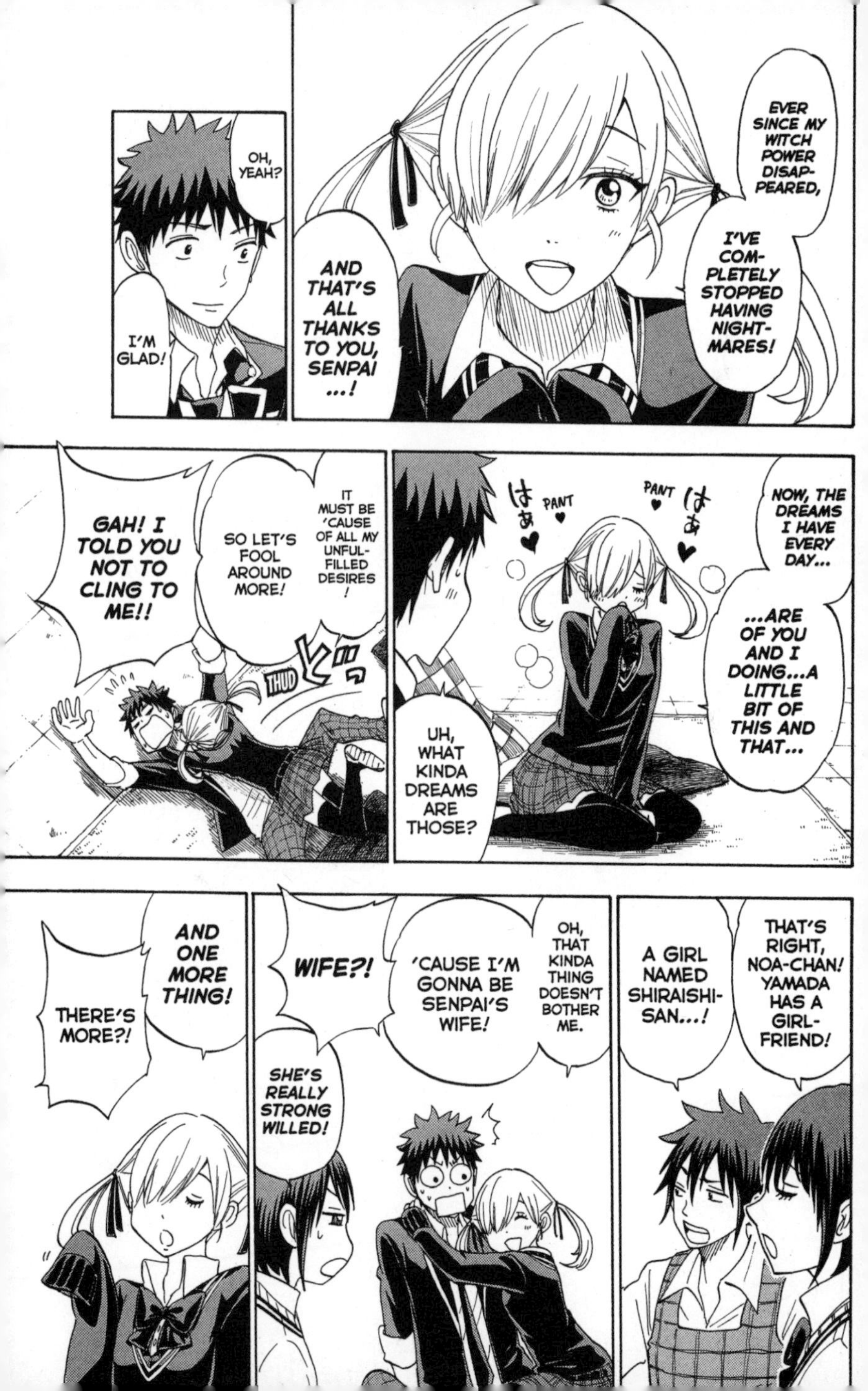
EVER SINCE MY WITCH POWER DISAPPEARED,
I'VE COMPLETELY STOPPED HAVING NIGHTMARES!
AND THAT'S ALL THANKS TO YOU, SENPAI...!
OH, YEAH?
I'M GLAD!
NOW, THE DREAMS I HAVE EVERY DAY...
...ARE OF YOU AND I DOING...A LITTLE BIT OF THIS AND THAT...
はぁ PANT ♥ はぁ PANT ♥
UH, WHAT KINDA DREAMS ARE THOSE?
IT MUST BE 'CAUSE OF ALL MY UNFULFILLED DESIRES!
SO LET'S FOOL AROUND MORE!
GAH! I TOLD YOU NOT TO CLING TO ME!!
THUD どっ
THAT'S RIGHT, NOA-CHAN! YAMADA HAS A GIRLFRIEND!
A GIRL NAMED SHIRAISHI-SAN...!
OH, THAT KINDA THING DOESN'T BOTHER ME.
'CAUSE I'M GONNA BE SENPAI'S WIFE!
WIFE?!
SHE'S REALLY STRONG WILLED!
AND ONE MORE THING!
THERE'S MORE?!

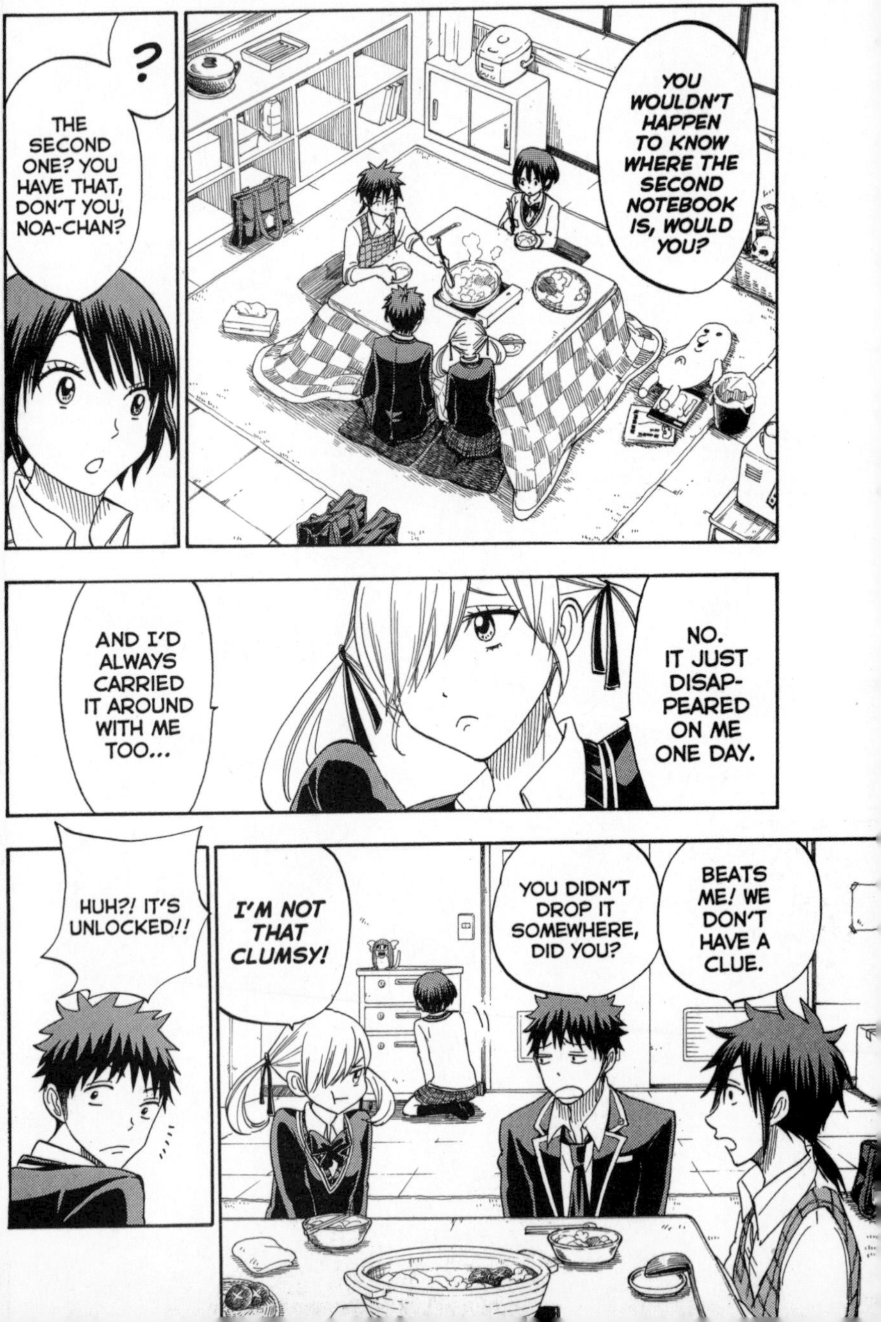
YOU WOULDN'T HAPPEN TO KNOW WHERE THE SECOND NOTEBOOK IS, WOULD YOU?
?
THE SECOND ONE? YOU HAVE THAT, DON'T YOU, NOA-CHAN?
NO. IT JUST DISAP-PEARED ON ME ONE DAY.
AND I'D ALWAYS CARRIED IT AROUND WITH ME TOO...
BEATS ME! WE DON'T HAVE A CLUE.
YOU DIDN'T DROP IT SOMEWHERE, DID YOU?
I'M NOT THAT CLUMSY!
HUH?! IT'S UNLOCKED!!

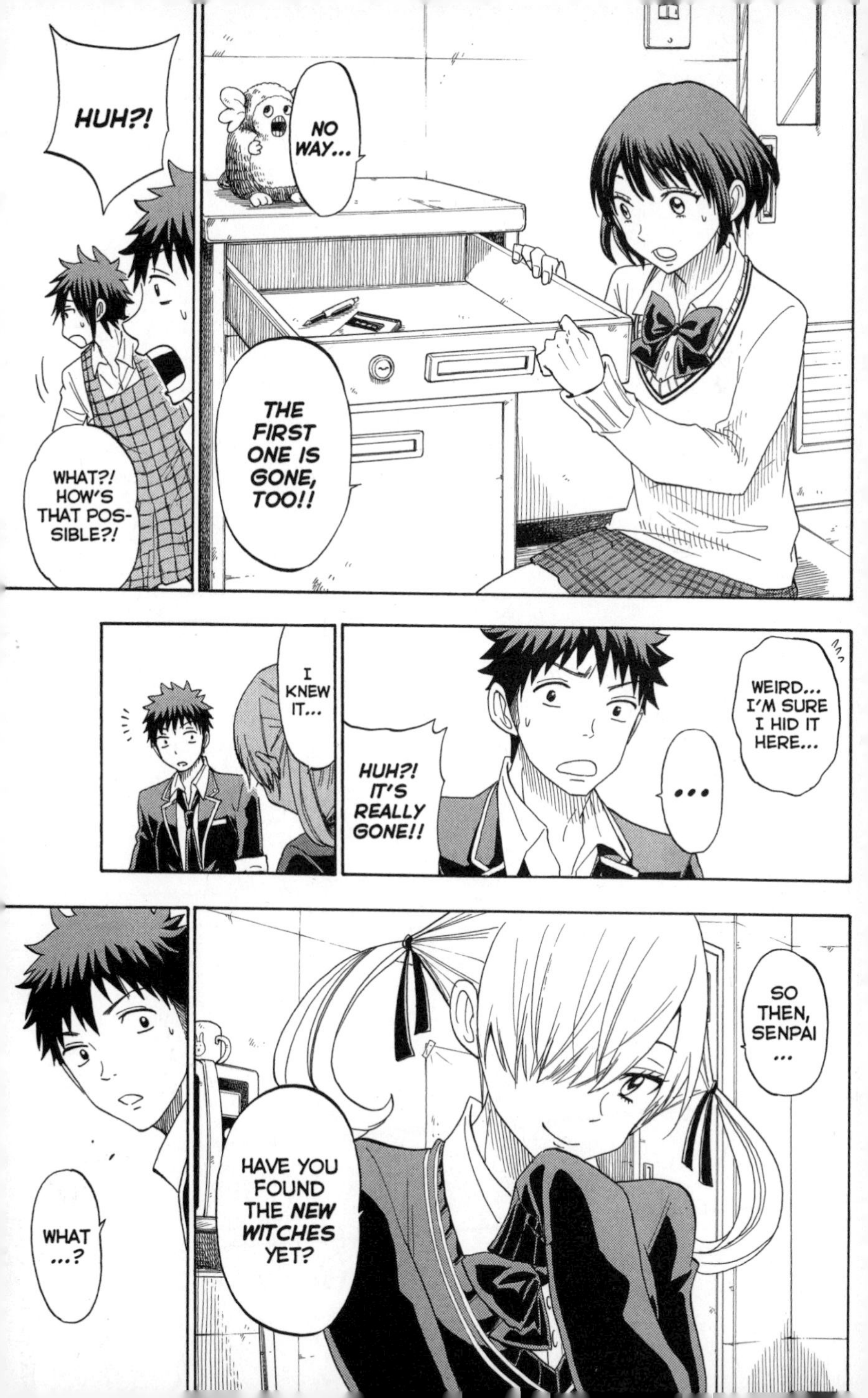
NO WAY...
THE FIRST ONE IS GONE, TOO!!
HUH?!
WHAT?! HOW'S THAT POS-SIBLE?!
WEIRD... I'M SURE I HID IT HERE...
...
HUH?! IT'S REALLY GONE!!
I KNEW IT...
SO THEN, SENPAI...
HAVE YOU FOUND THE *NEW WITCHES* YET?
WHAT...?

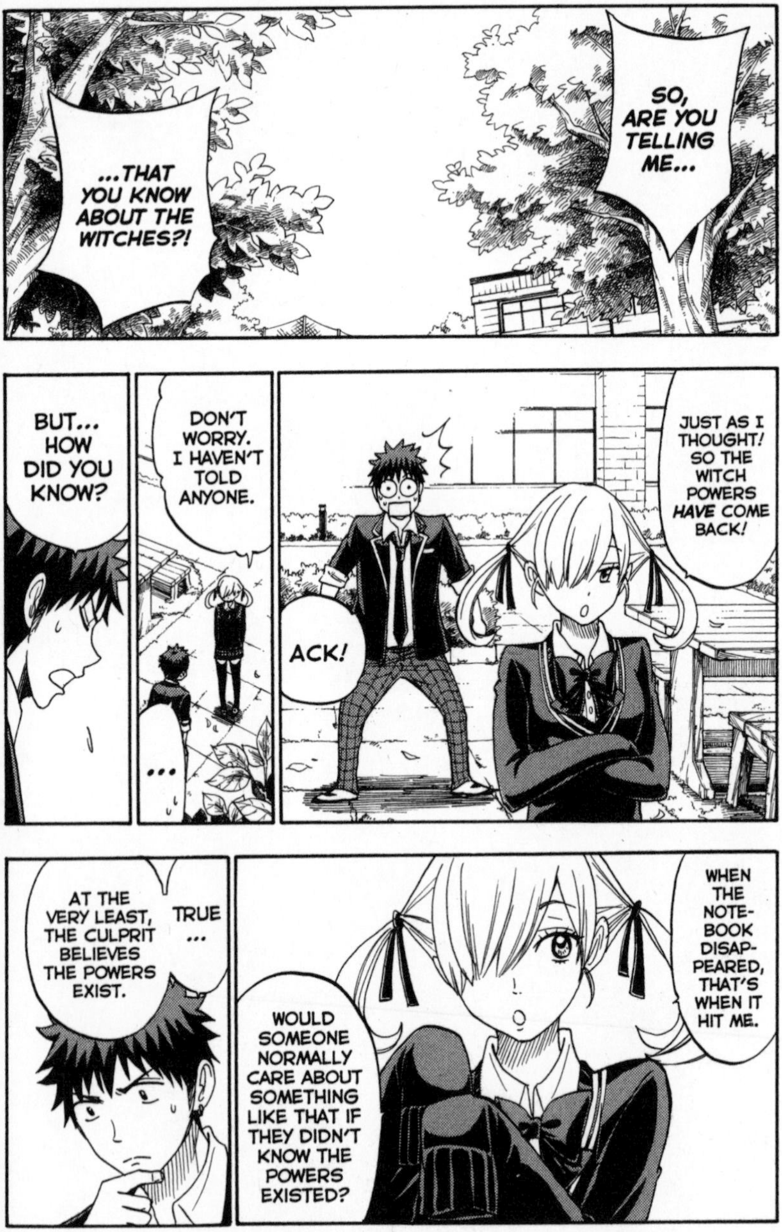
SO, ARE YOU TELLING ME...
...THAT YOU KNOW ABOUT THE WITCHES?!
JUST AS I THOUGHT! SO THE WITCH POWERS *HAVE* COME BACK!
ACK!
DON'T WORRY. I HAVEN'T TOLD ANYONE.
...
BUT... HOW DID YOU KNOW?
WHEN THE NOTE-BOOK DISAP-PEARED, THAT'S WHEN IT HIT ME.
WOULD SOMEONE NORMALLY CARE ABOUT SOMETHING LIKE THAT IF THEY DIDN'T KNOW THE POWERS EXISTED?
TRUE...
AT THE VERY LEAST, THE CULPRIT BELIEVES THE POWERS EXIST.

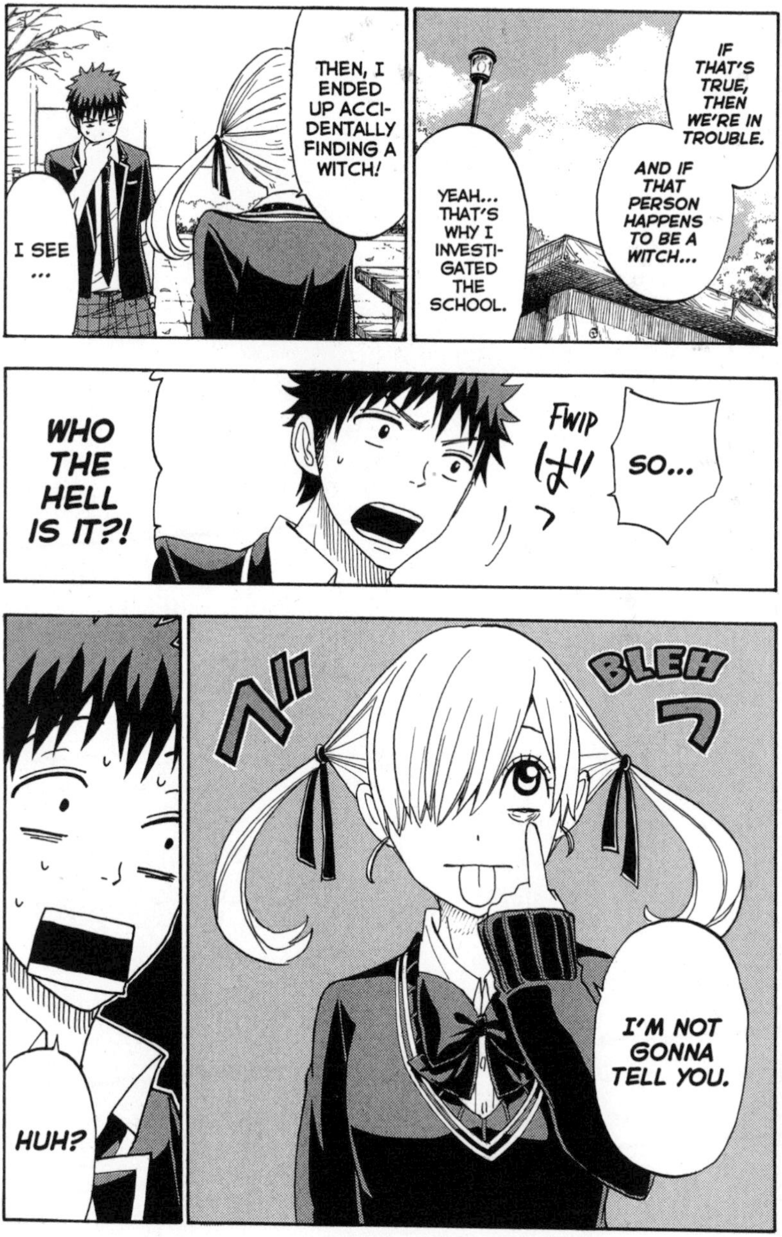
IF THAT'S TRUE, THEN WE'RE IN TROUBLE.
AND IF THAT PERSON HAPPENS TO BE A WITCH...
YEAH... THAT'S WHY I INVESTIGATED THE SCHOOL.
THEN, I ENDED UP ACCIDENTALLY FINDING A WITCH!
I SEE ...
SO...
FWIP
WHO THE HELL IS IT?!
BLEH
I'M NOT GONNA TELL YOU.
HUH?

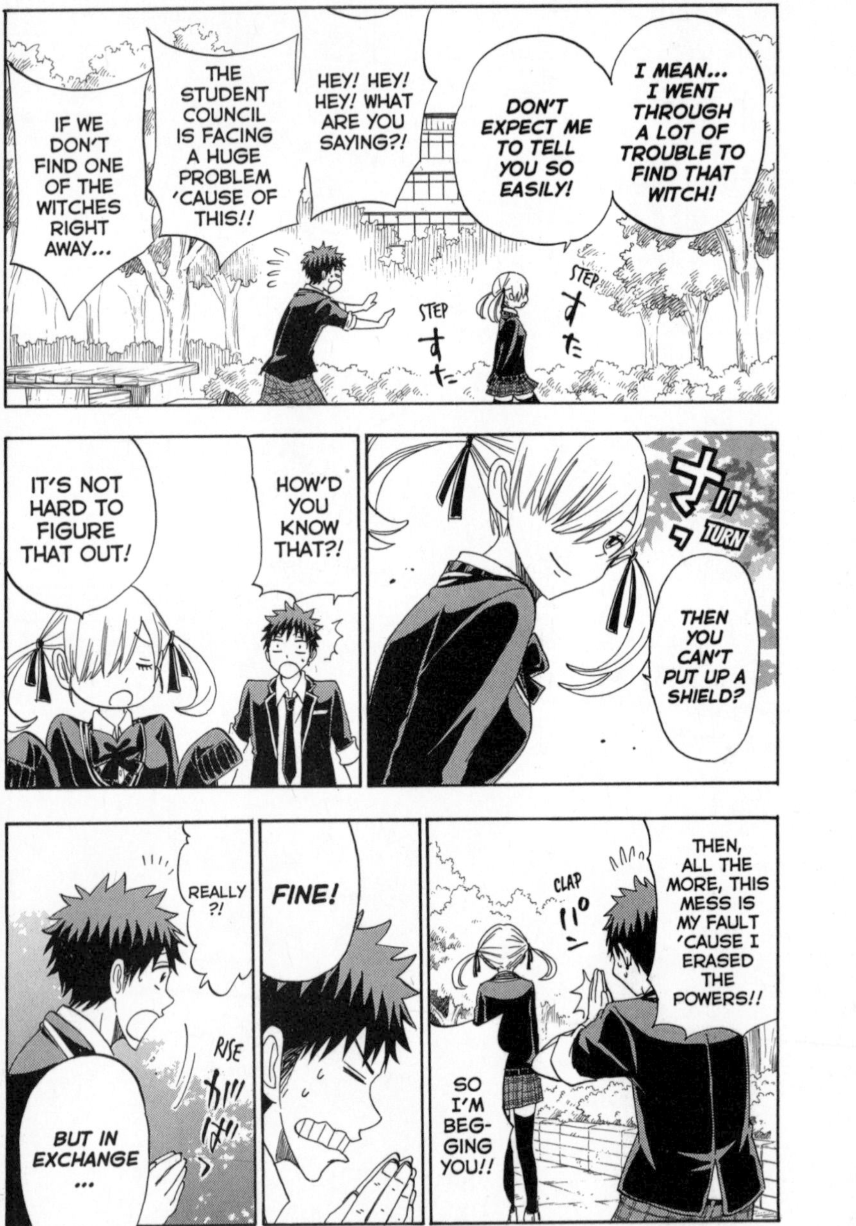
I MEAN... I WENT THROUGH A LOT OF TROUBLE TO FIND THAT WITCH!
DON'T EXPECT ME TO TELL YOU SO EASILY!
STEP
STEP
HEY! HEY! HEY! WHAT ARE YOU SAYING?!
THE STUDENT COUNCIL IS FACING A HUGE PROBLEM 'CAUSE OF THIS!!
IF WE DON'T FIND ONE OF THE WITCHES RIGHT AWAY...
TURN
THEN YOU CAN'T PUT UP A SHIELD?
HOW'D YOU KNOW THAT?!
IT'S NOT HARD TO FIGURE THAT OUT!
THEN, ALL THE MORE, THIS MESS IS MY FAULT 'CAUSE I ERASED THE POWERS!!
CLAP
SO I'M BEG-GING YOU!!
FINE!
REALLY?!
RISE
BUT IN EXCHANGE ...

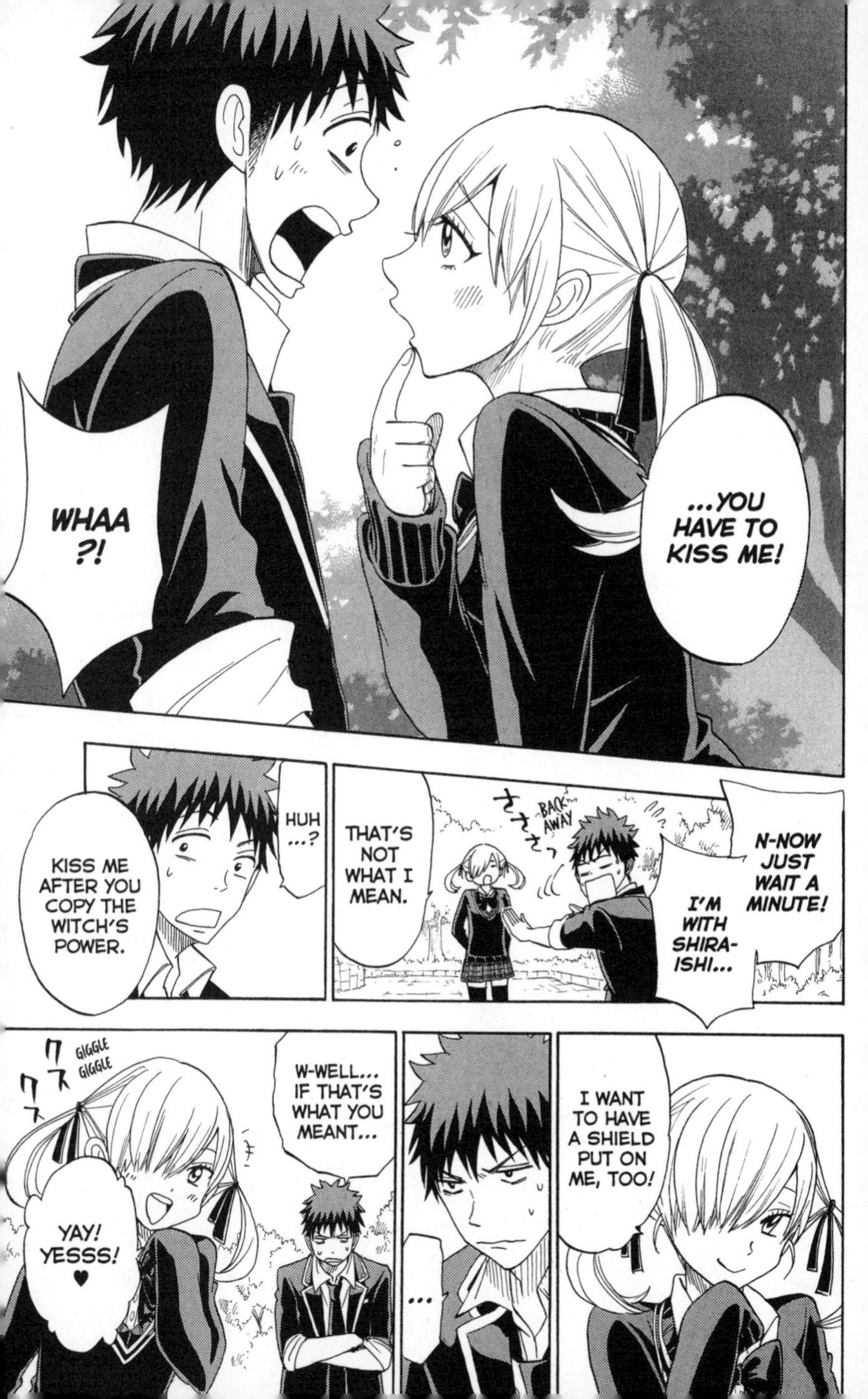
...YOU HAVE TO KISS ME!
WHAA ?!
N-NOW JUST WAIT A MINUTE!
I'M WITH SHIRA-ISHI...
BACK AWAY
THAT'S NOT WHAT I MEAN.
HUH ...?
KISS ME AFTER YOU COPY THE WITCH'S POWER.
I WANT TO HAVE A SHIELD PUT ON ME, TOO!
...
W-WELL... IF THAT'S WHAT YOU MEANT...
GIGGLE GIGGLE
YAY! YESSS! ♥

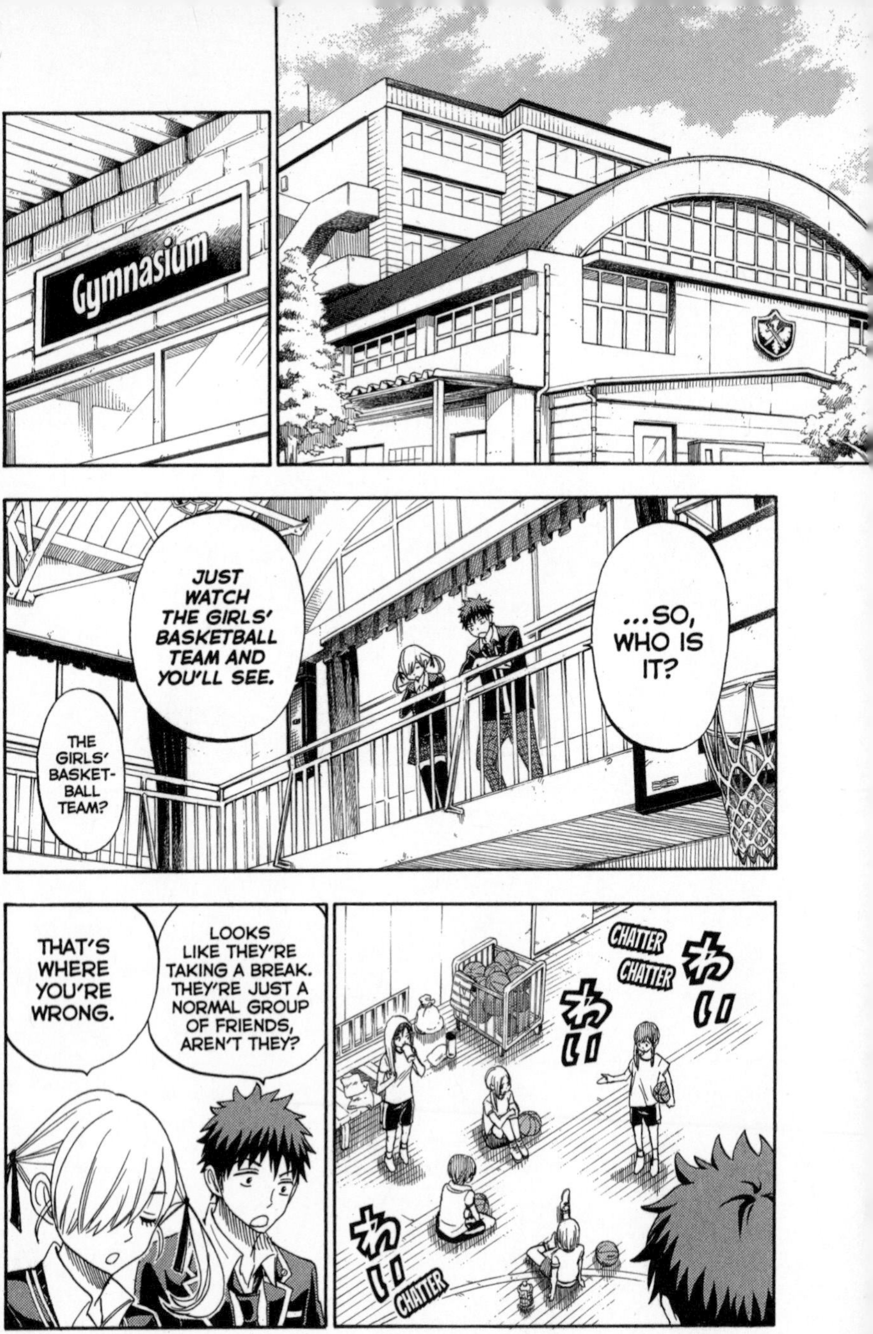
Gymnasium
...SO, WHO IS IT?
JUST WATCH THE GIRLS' BASKETBALL TEAM AND YOU'LL SEE.
THE GIRLS' BASKET-BALL TEAM?
CHATTER CHATTER
わい
わい
わい
CHATTER
LOOKS LIKE THEY'RE TAKING A BREAK. THEY'RE JUST A NORMAL GROUP OF FRIENDS, AREN'T THEY?
THAT'S WHERE YOU'RE WRONG.

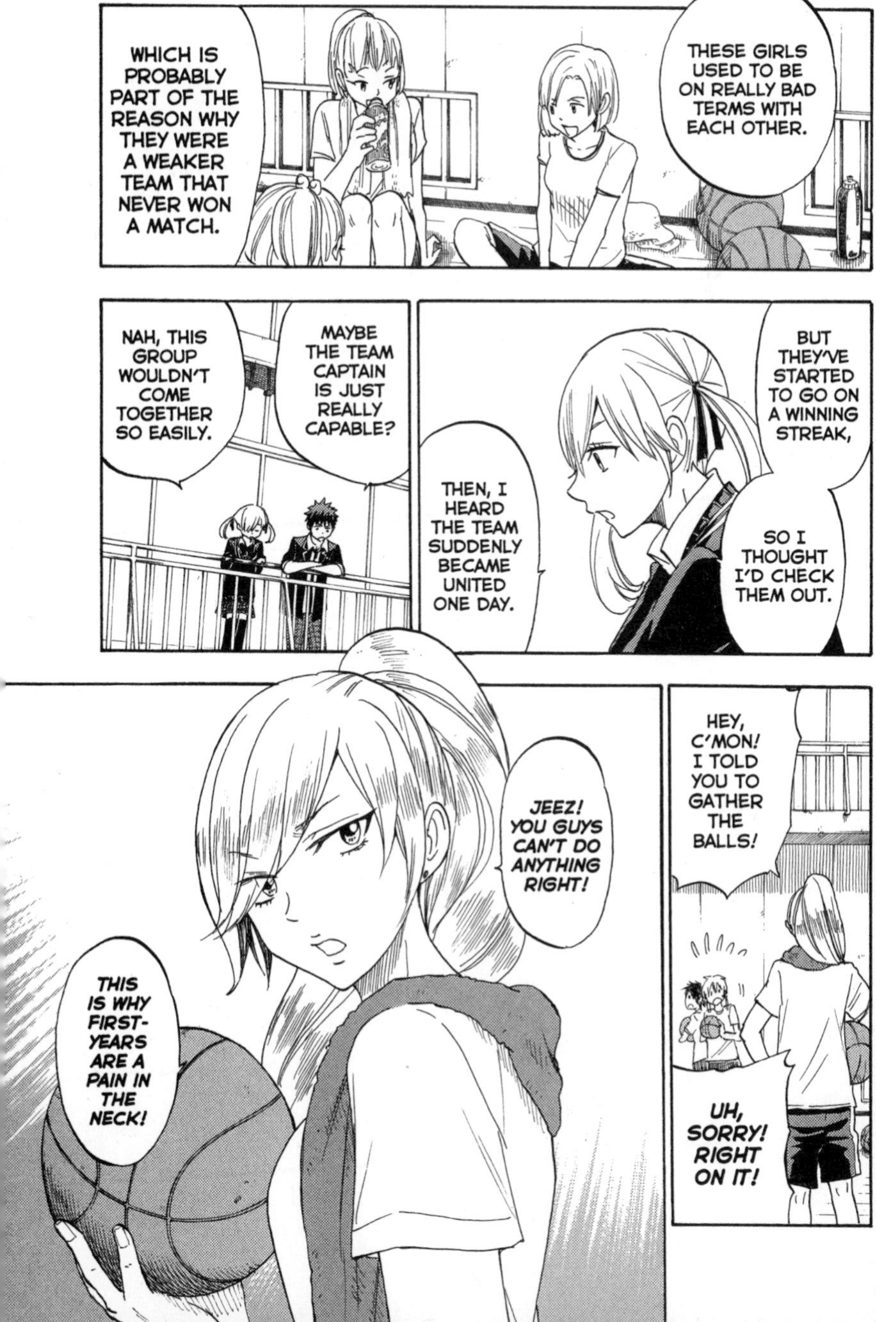
THESE GIRLS USED TO BE ON REALLY BAD TERMS WITH EACH OTHER.
WHICH IS PROBABLY PART OF THE REASON WHY THEY WERE A WEAKER TEAM THAT NEVER WON A MATCH.
BUT THEY'VE STARTED TO GO ON A WINNING STREAK,
SO I THOUGHT I'D CHECK THEM OUT.
THEN, I HEARD THE TEAM SUDDENLY BECAME UNITED ONE DAY.
MAYBE THE TEAM CAPTAIN IS JUST REALLY CAPABLE?
NAH, THIS GROUP WOULDN'T COME TOGETHER SO EASILY.
HEY, C'MON! I TOLD YOU TO GATHER THE BALLS!
UH, SORRY! RIGHT ON IT!
JEEZ! YOU GUYS CAN'T DO ANYTHING RIGHT!
THIS IS WHY FIRST-YEARS ARE A PAIN IN THE NECK!

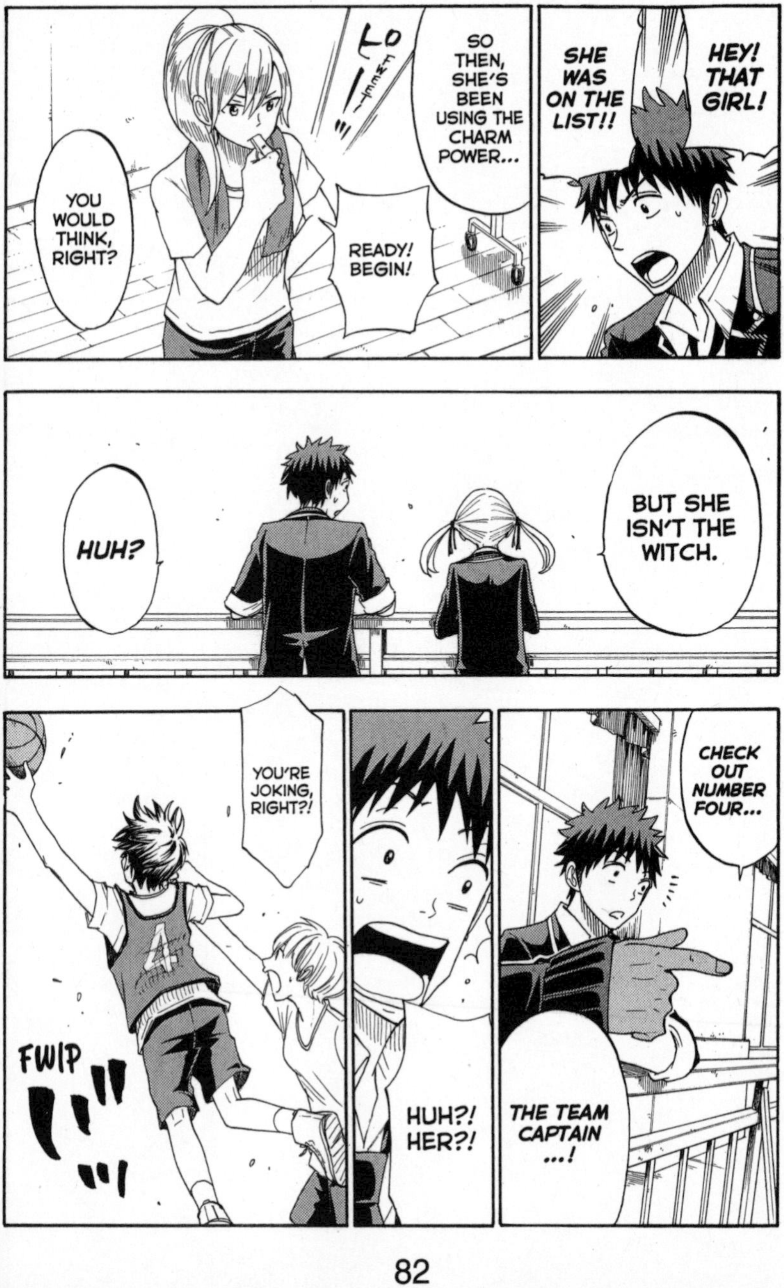
HEY! THAT GIRL!
SHE WAS ON THE LIST!!
SO THEN, SHE'S BEEN USING THE CHARM POWER...
TWEET
READY! BEGIN!
YOU WOULD THINK, RIGHT?
BUT SHE ISN'T THE WITCH.
HUH?
CHECK OUT NUMBER FOUR...
THE TEAM CAPTAIN ...!
HUH?! HER?!
YOU'RE JOKING, RIGHT?!
FWIP

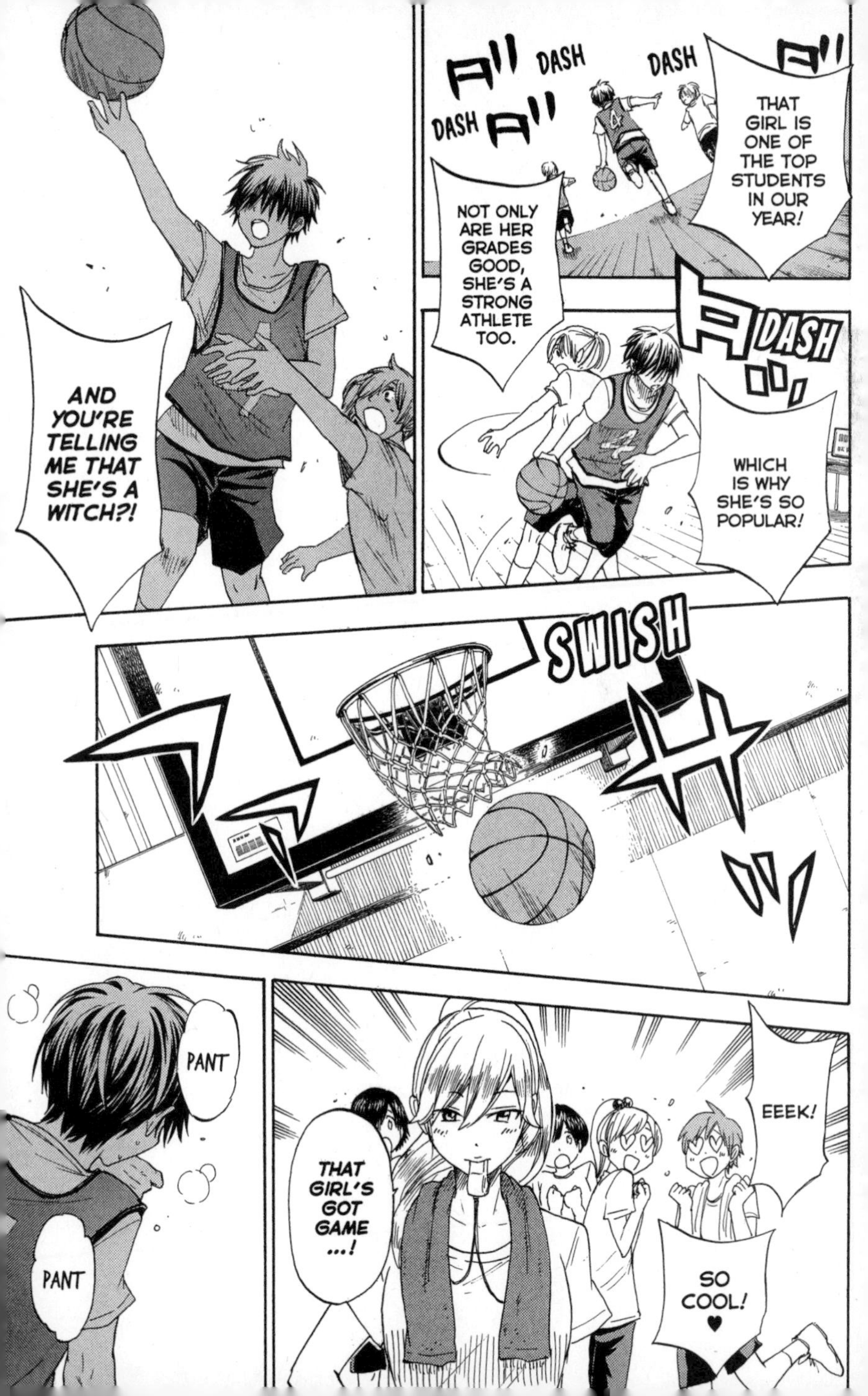

DASH
DASH
DASH
THAT GIRL IS ONE OF THE TOP STUDENTS IN OUR YEAR!
NOT ONLY ARE HER GRADES GOOD, SHE'S A STRONG ATHLETE TOO.
DASH
WHICH IS WHY SHE'S SO POPULAR!
AND YOU'RE TELLING ME THAT SHE'S A WITCH?!
SWISH
EEEK!
SO COOL! ♥
THAT GIRL'S GOT GAME ...!
PANT
PANT

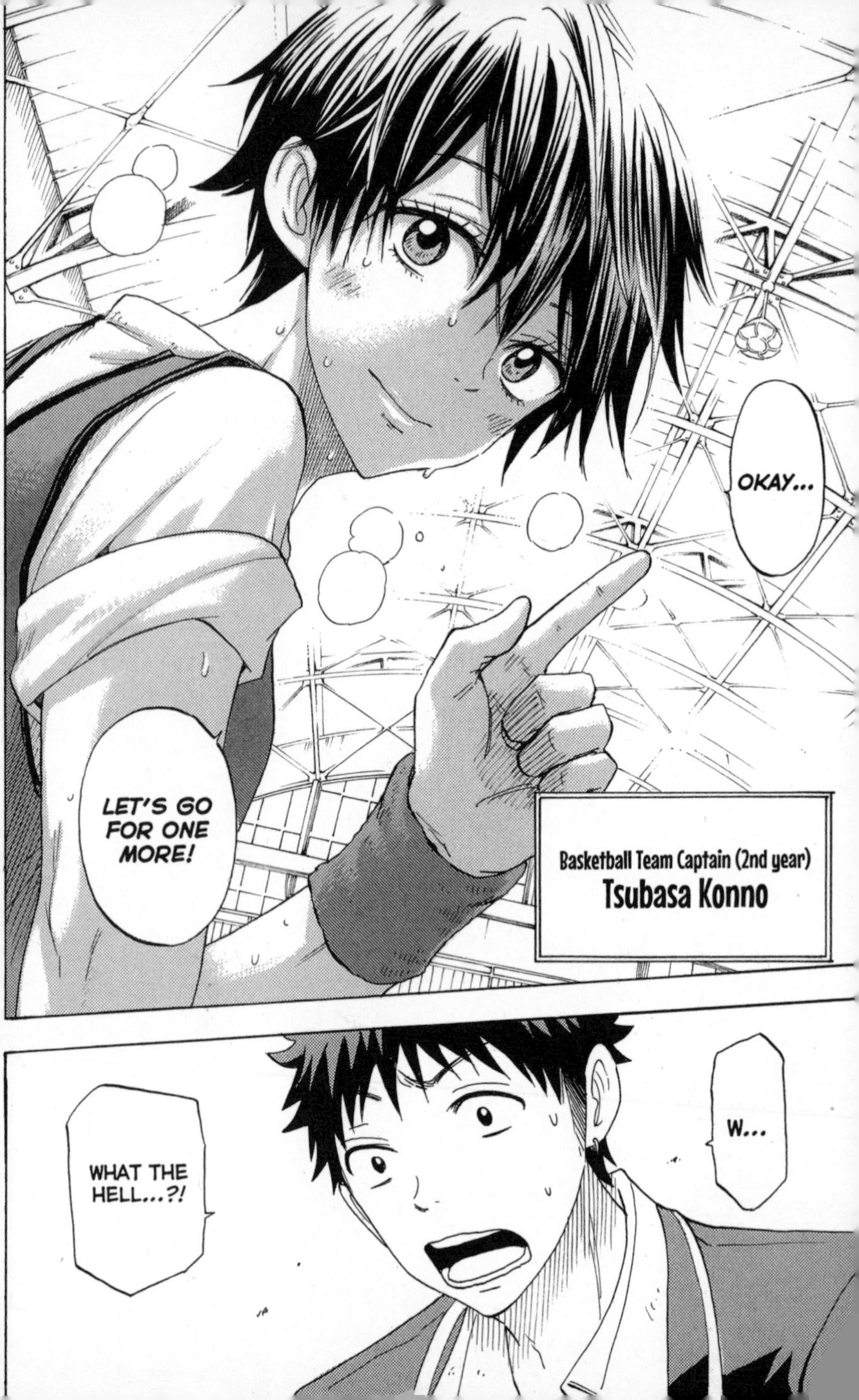
OKAY...
LET'S GO FOR ONE MORE!
Basketball Team Captain (2nd year)
Tsubasa Konno
W...
WHAT THE HELL...?!

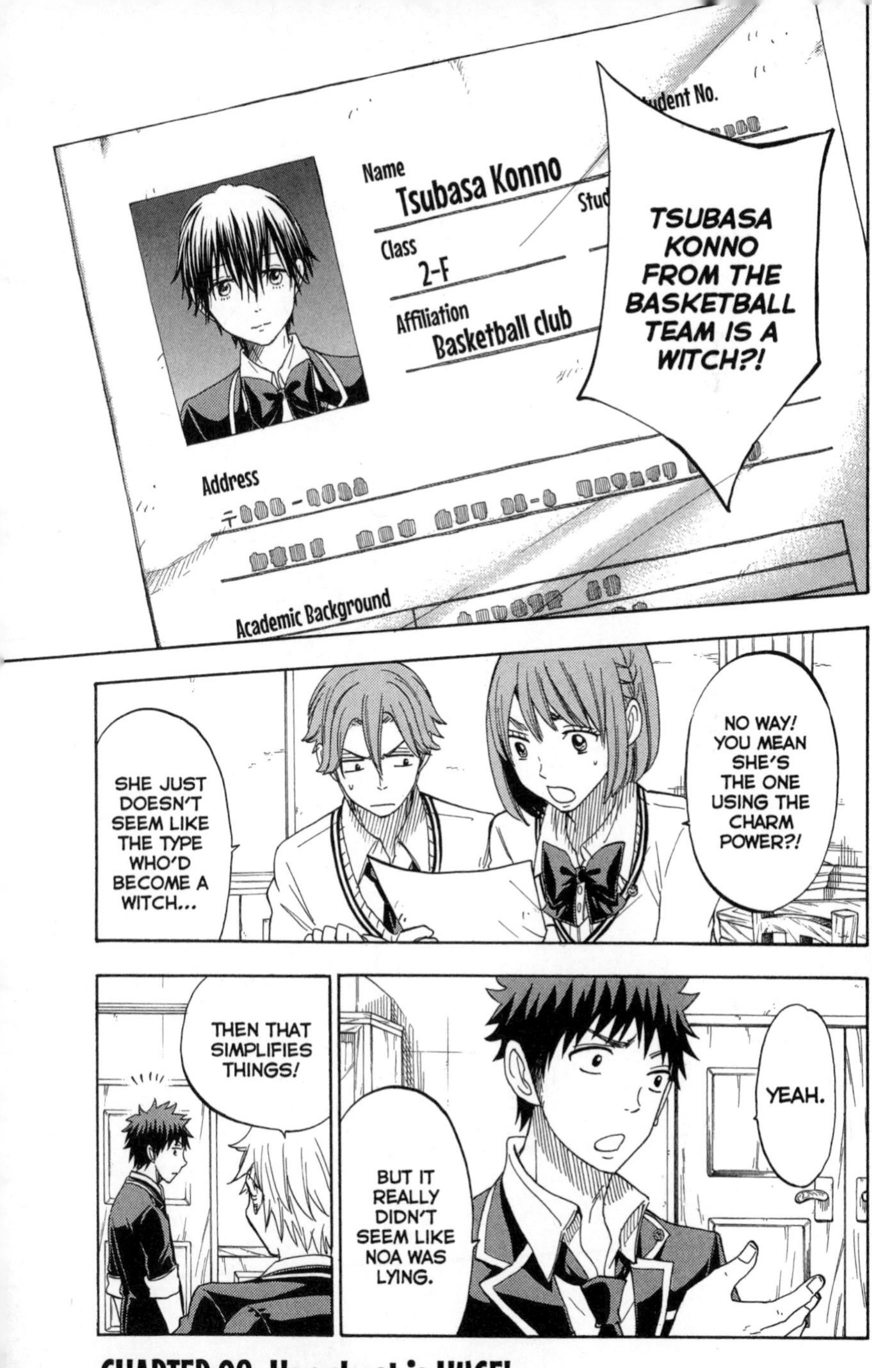
Name
Tsubasa Konno
Class
2-F
Affiliation
Basketball club
Address
Academic Background
TSUBASA KONNO FROM THE BASKETBALL TEAM IS A WITCH?!
NO WAY! YOU MEAN SHE'S THE ONE USING THE CHARM POWER?!
SHE JUST DOESN'T SEEM LIKE THE TYPE WHO'D BECOME A WITCH...
YEAH.
BUT IT REALLY DIDN'T SEEM LIKE NOA WAS LYING.
THEN THAT SIMPLIFIES THINGS!

CHAPTER 98: Her chest is HUGE!

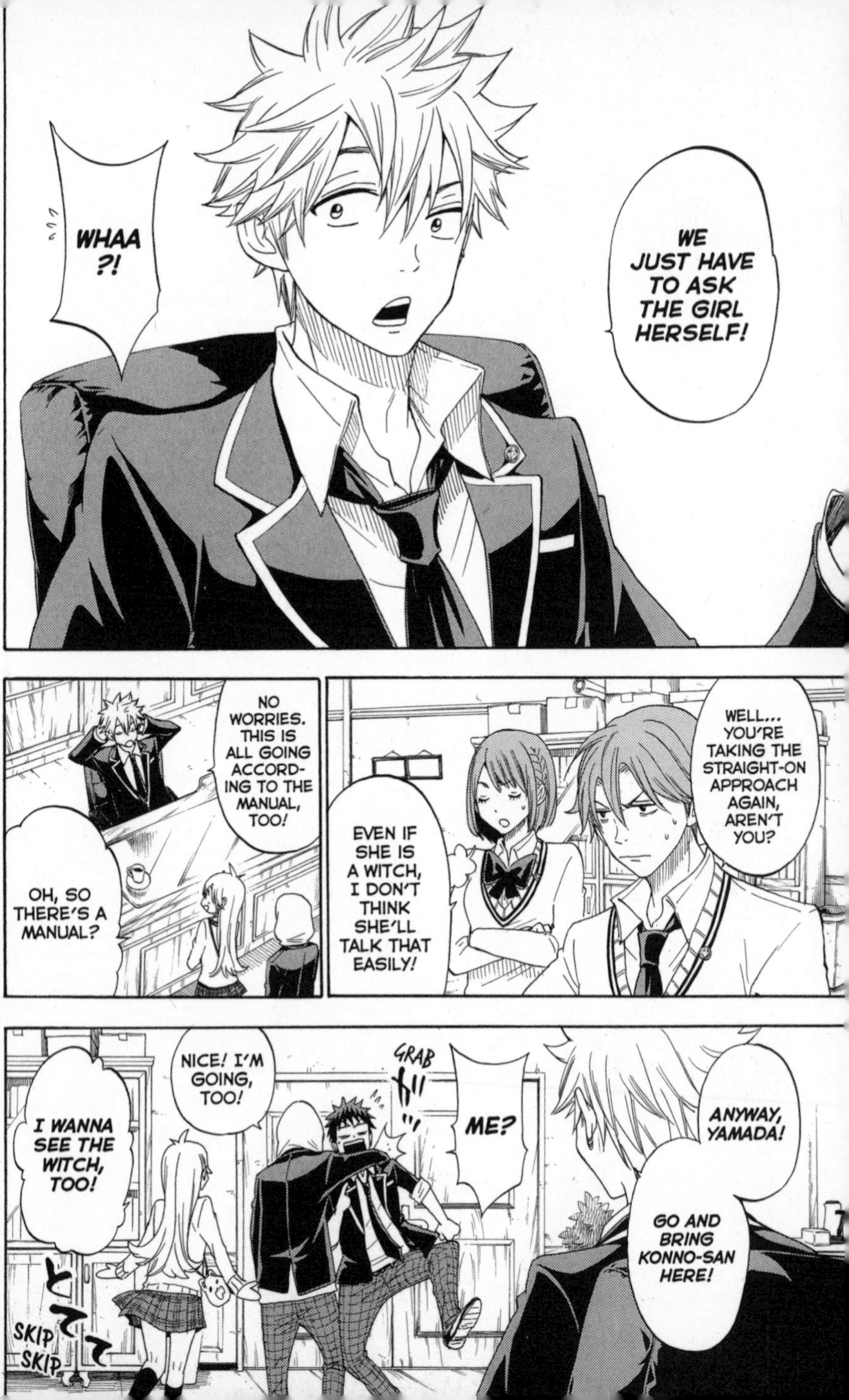
WE JUST HAVE TO ASK THE GIRL HERSELF!
WHAA ?!
WELL... YOU'RE TAKING THE STRAIGHT-ON APPROACH AGAIN, AREN'T YOU?
EVEN IF SHE IS A WITCH, I DON'T THINK SHE'LL TALK THAT EASILY!
NO WORRIES. THIS IS ALL GOING ACCORDING TO THE MANUAL, TOO!
OH, SO THERE'S A MANUAL?
ANYWAY, YAMADA!
GO AND BRING KONNO-SAN HERE!
ME?
GRAB
NICE! I'M GOING, TOO!
I WANNA SEE THE WITCH, TOO!
SKIP SKIP

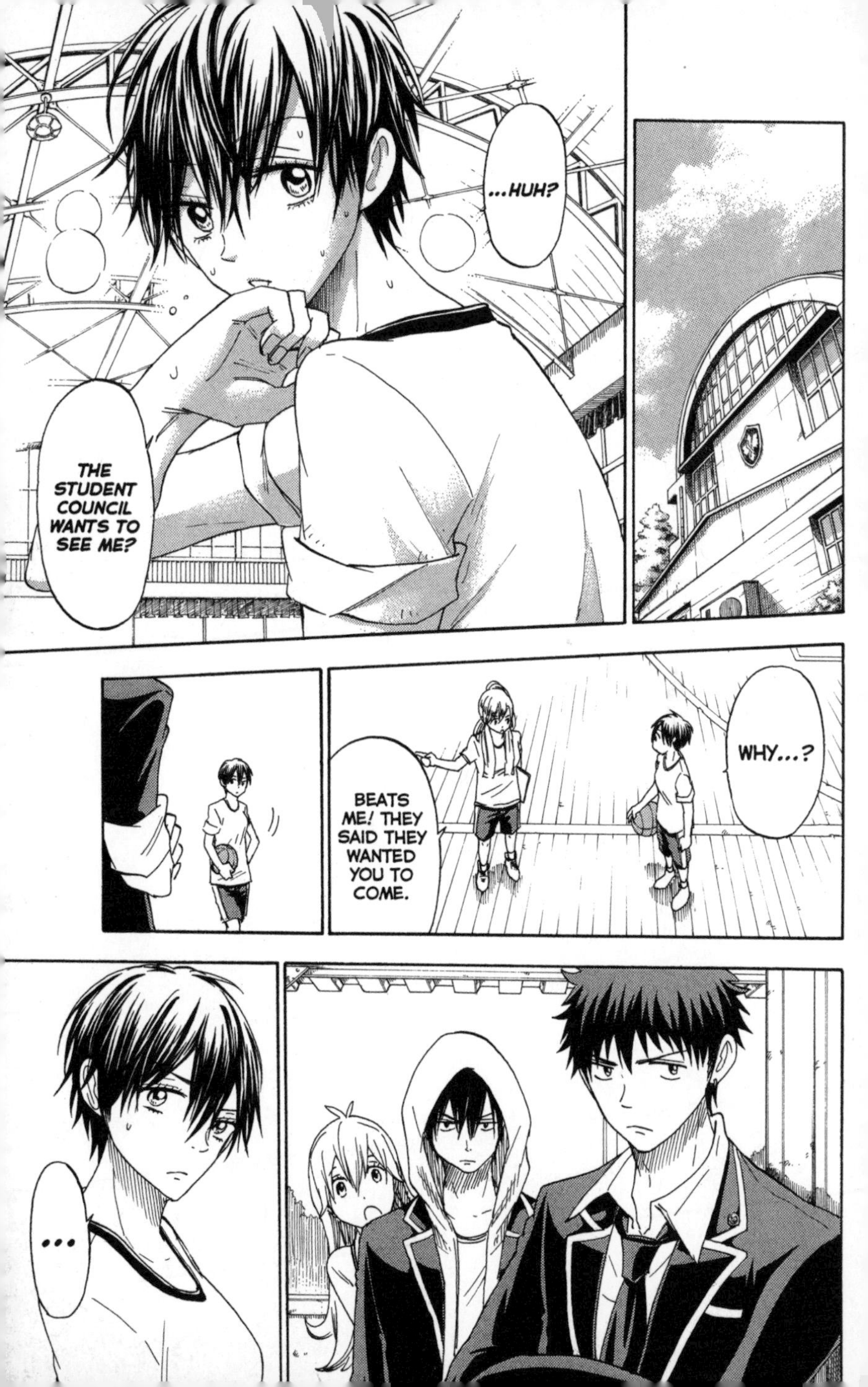
...HUH?
THE STUDENT COUNCIL WANTS TO SEE ME?
WHY...?
BEATS ME! THEY SAID THEY WANTED YOU TO COME.
...

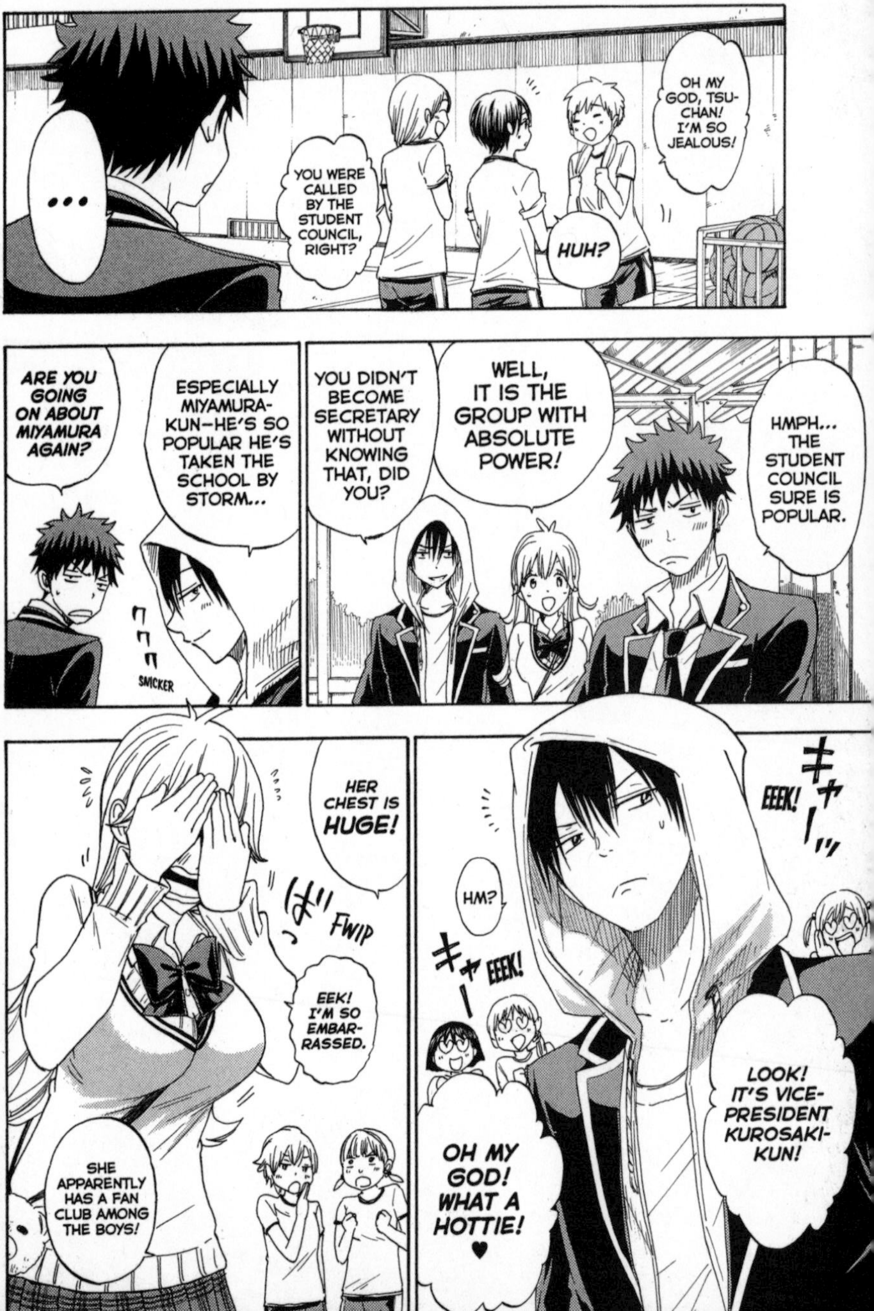
OH MY GOD, TSU-CHAN! I'M SO JEALOUS!
HUH?
YOU WERE CALLED BY THE STUDENT COUNCIL, RIGHT?
...
HMPH... THE STUDENT COUNCIL SURE IS POPULAR.
WELL, IT IS THE GROUP WITH ABSOLUTE POWER!
YOU DIDN'T BECOME SECRETARY WITHOUT KNOWING THAT, DID YOU?
ESPECIALLY MIYAMURA-KUN—HE'S SO POPULAR HE'S TAKEN THE SCHOOL BY STORM...
ククク
SNICKER
ARE YOU GOING ON ABOUT MIYAMURA AGAIN?
キャーッ
EEEK!
HM?
キャー
EEEK!
LOOK! IT'S VICE-PRESIDENT KUROSAKI-KUN!
OH MY GOD! WHAT A HOTTIE! ♥
HER CHEST IS HUGE!
ばっ
FWIP
EEK! I'M SO EMBARRASSED.
SHE APPARENTLY HAS A FAN CLUB AMONG THE BOYS!

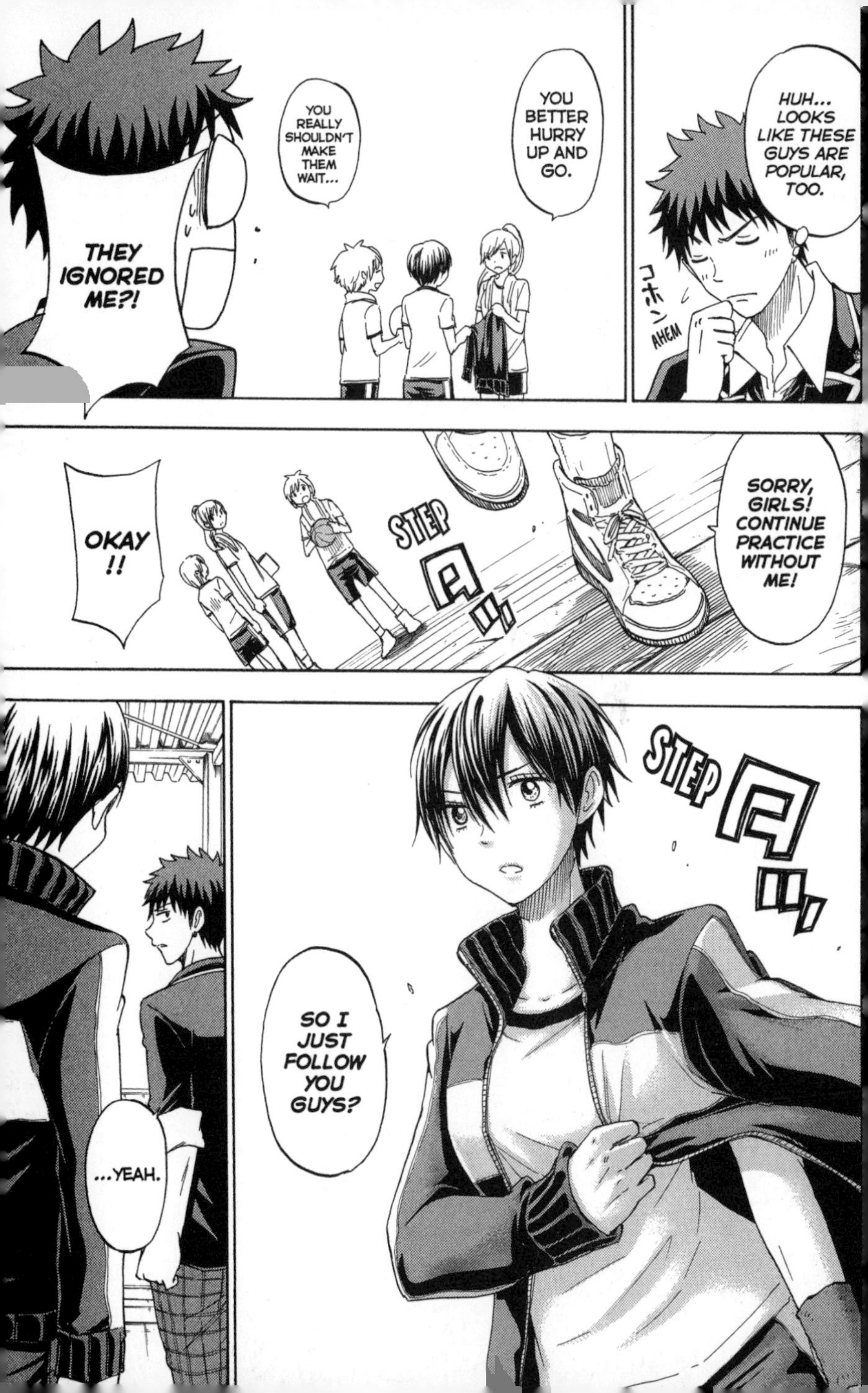
HUH... LOOKS LIKE THESE GUYS ARE POPULAR, TOO.
コホン
AHEM
YOU BETTER HURRY UP AND GO.
YOU REALLY SHOULDN'T MAKE THEM WAIT...
THEY IGNORED ME?!
SORRY, GIRLS! CONTINUE PRACTICE WITHOUT ME!
STEP
OKAY!!
STEP
SO I JUST FOLLOW YOU GUYS?
...YEAH.

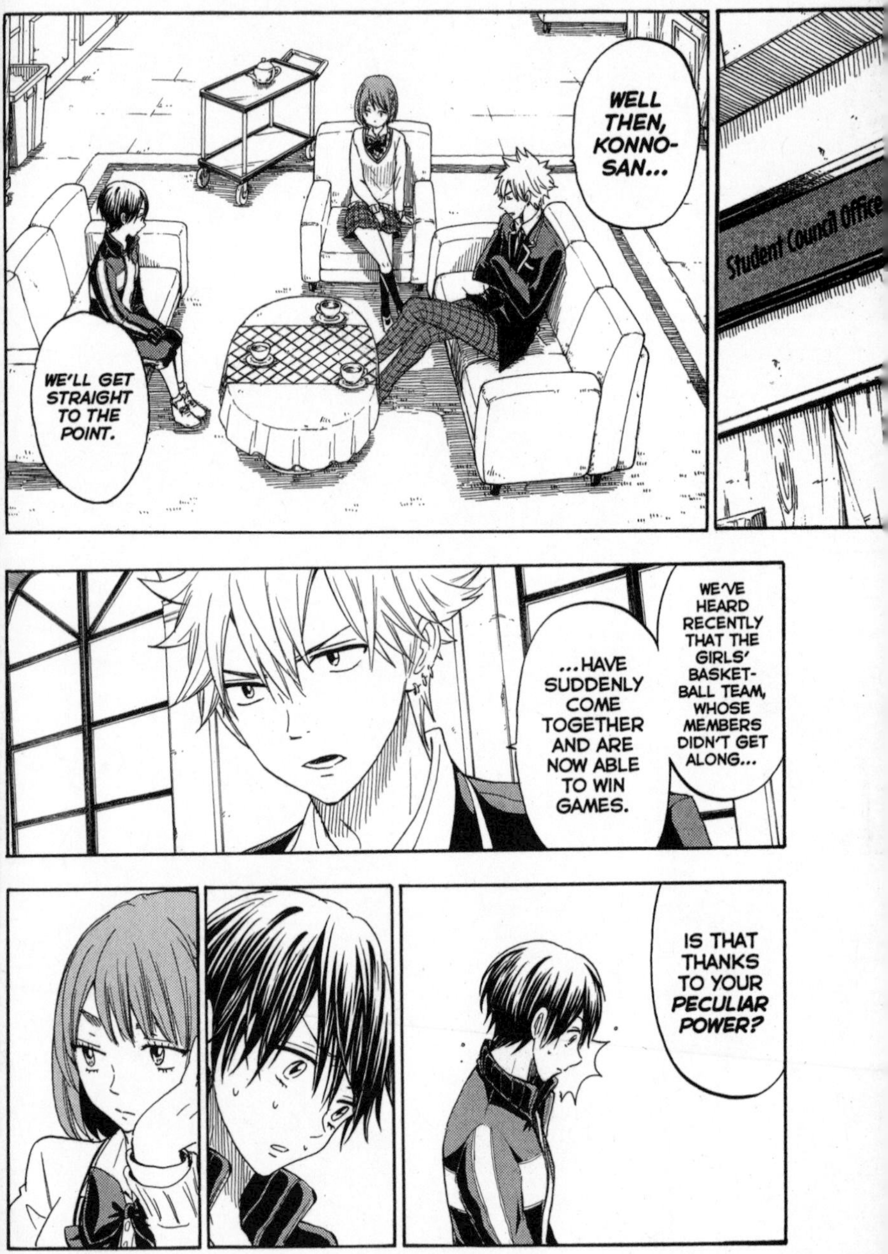
Student Council Office
WELL THEN, KONNO-SAN...
WE'LL GET STRAIGHT TO THE POINT.
WE'VE HEARD RECENTLY THAT THE GIRLS' BASKET-BALL TEAM, WHOSE MEMBERS DIDN'T GET ALONG...
...HAVE SUDDENLY COME TOGETHER AND ARE NOW ABLE TO WIN GAMES.
IS THAT THANKS TO YOUR *PECULIAR POWER?*

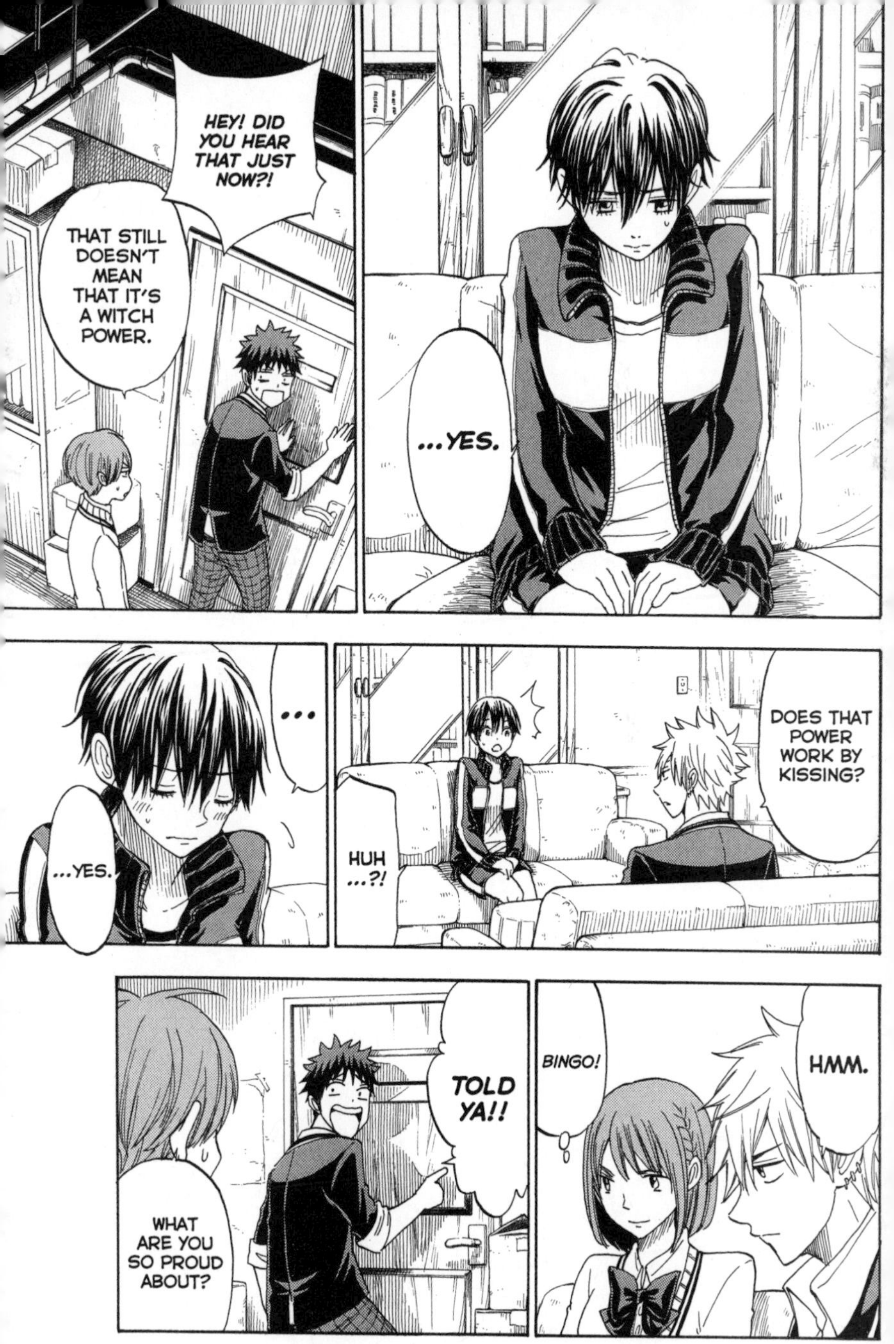
...YES.
HEY! DID YOU HEAR THAT JUST NOW?!
THAT STILL DOESN'T MEAN THAT IT'S A WITCH POWER.
DOES THAT POWER WORK BY KISSING?
HUH ...?!
...
...YES.
HMM.
BINGO!
TOLD YA!!
WHAT ARE YOU SO PROUD ABOUT?

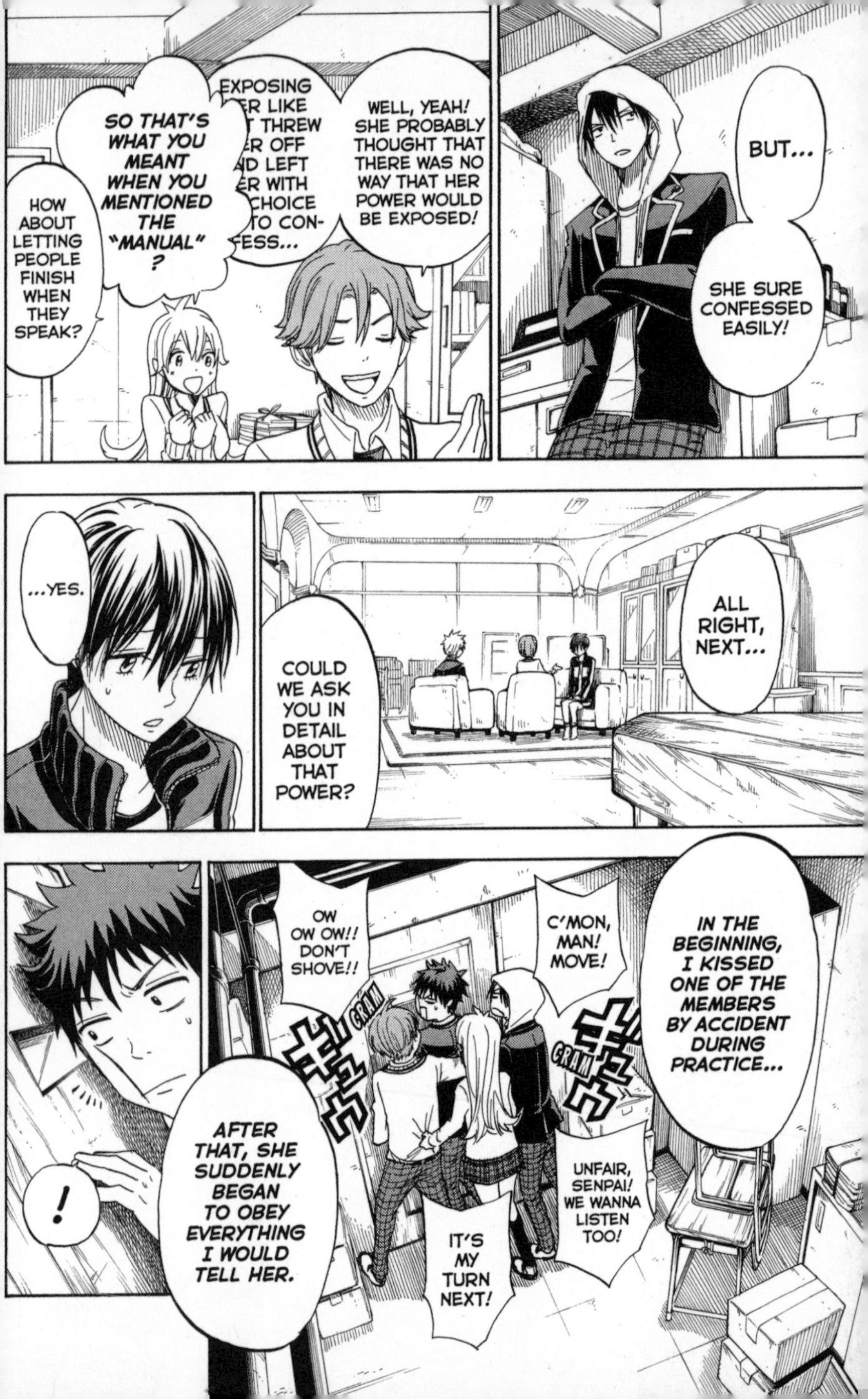
BUT...
SHE SURE CONFESSED EASILY!
WELL, YEAH! SHE PROBABLY THOUGHT THAT THERE WAS NO WAY THAT HER POWER WOULD BE EXPOSED!
EXPOSING ER LIKE T THREW ER OFF ND LEFT ER WITH CHOICE TO CON-FESS...
SO THAT'S WHAT YOU MEANT WHEN YOU MENTIONED THE "MANUAL"?
HOW ABOUT LETTING PEOPLE FINISH WHEN THEY SPEAK?
ALL RIGHT, NEXT...
COULD WE ASK YOU IN DETAIL ABOUT THAT POWER?
...YES.
IN THE BEGINNING, I KISSED ONE OF THE MEMBERS BY ACCIDENT DURING PRACTICE...
C'MON, MAN! MOVE!
OW OW OW!! DON'T SHOVE!!
CRAM
CRAM
UNFAIR, SENPAI! WE WANNA LISTEN TOO!
IT'S MY TURN NEXT!
AFTER THAT, SHE SUDDENLY BEGAN TO OBEY EVERYTHING I WOULD TELL HER.
!

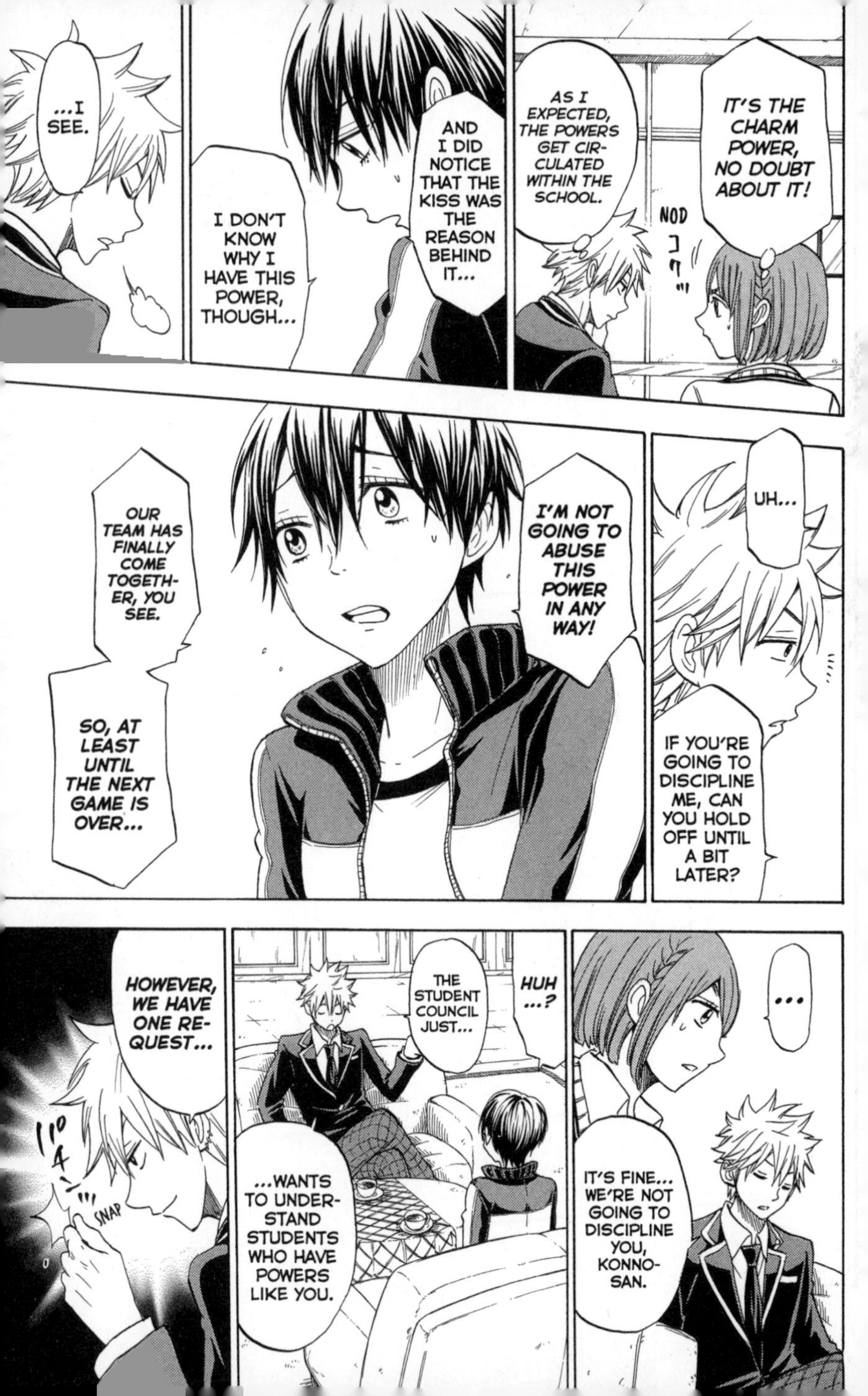
IT'S THE CHARM POWER, NO DOUBT ABOUT IT!
AS I EXPECTED, THE POWERS GET CIR-CULATED WITHIN THE SCHOOL.
NOD
AND I DID NOTICE THAT THE KISS WAS THE REASON BEHIND IT...
I DON'T KNOW WHY I HAVE THIS POWER, THOUGH...
...I SEE.
UH...
IF YOU'RE GOING TO DISCIPLINE ME, CAN YOU HOLD OFF UNTIL A BIT LATER?
I'M NOT GOING TO ABUSE THIS POWER IN ANY WAY!
OUR TEAM HAS FINALLY COME TOGETH-ER, YOU SEE.
SO, AT LEAST UNTIL THE NEXT GAME IS OVER...
...
IT'S FINE... WE'RE NOT GOING TO DISCIPLINE YOU, KONNO-SAN.
HUH...?
THE STUDENT COUNCIL JUST...
...WANTS TO UNDER-STAND STUDENTS WHO HAVE POWERS LIKE YOU.
HOWEVER, WE HAVE ONE RE-QUEST...
SNAP

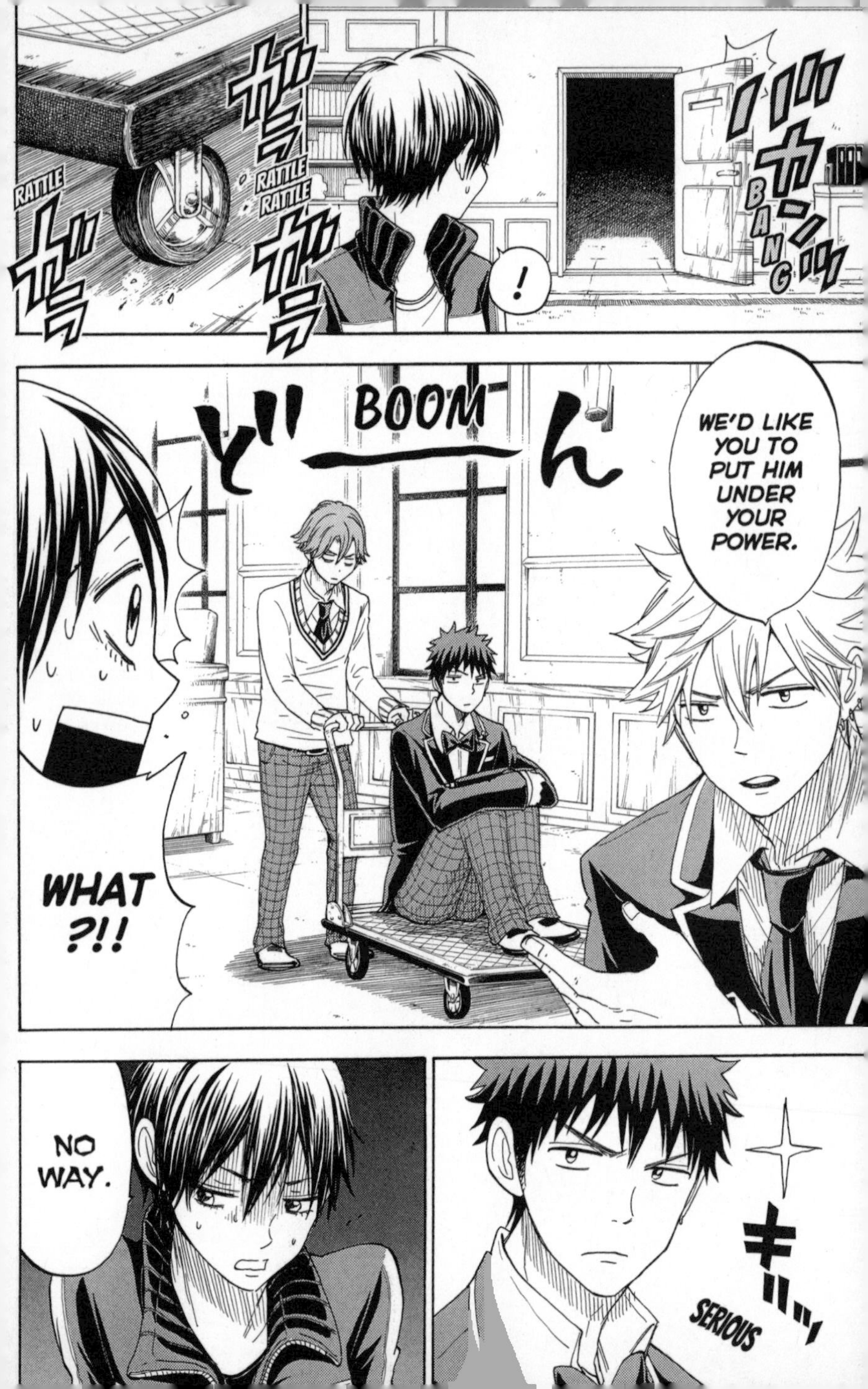
BANG
!
RATTLE RATTLE
RATTLE
WE'D LIKE YOU TO PUT HIM UNDER YOUR POWER.
BOOM
WHAT ?!!
SERIOUS
NO WAY.

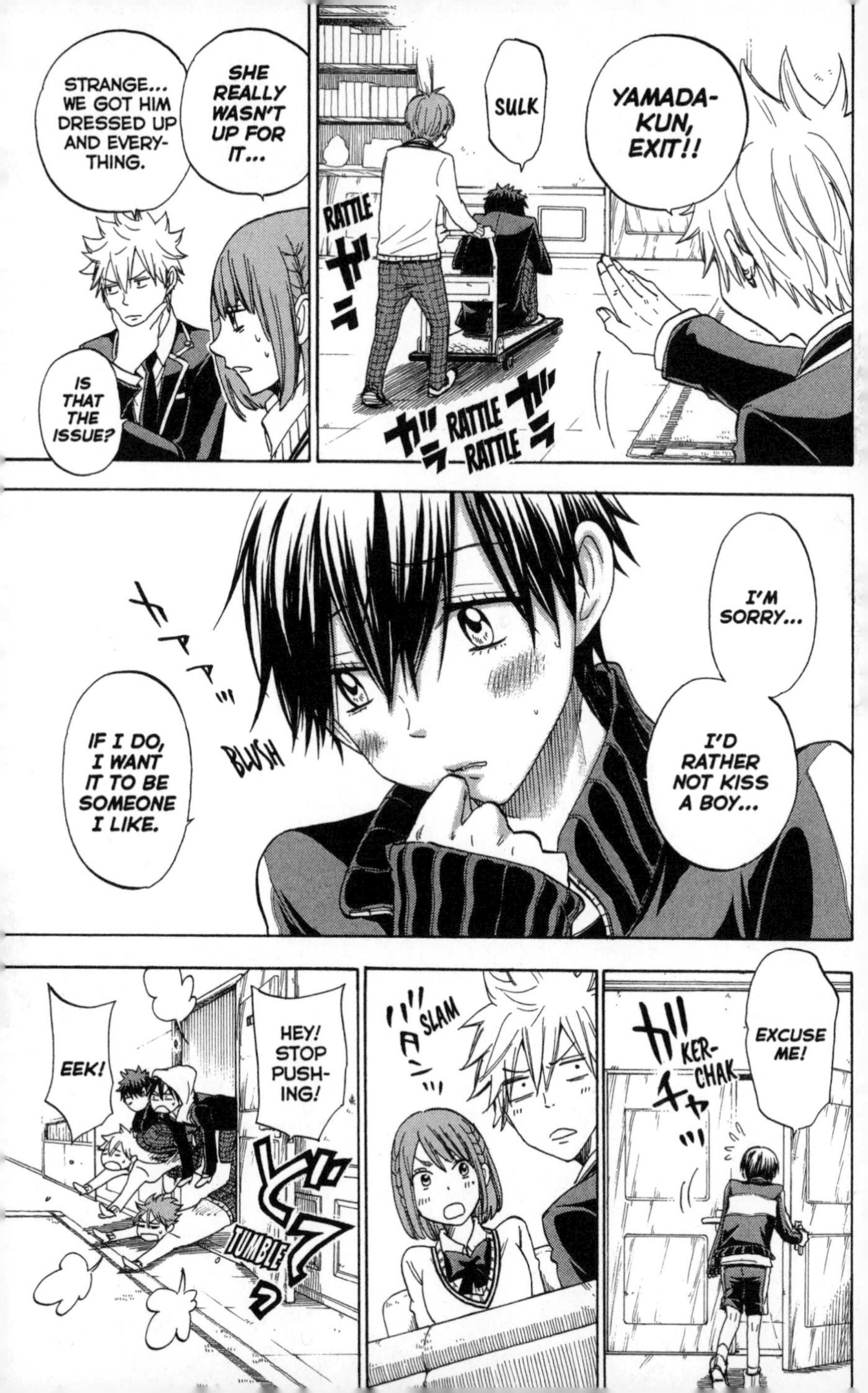
YAMADA-KUN, EXIT!!
SULK
RATTLE
RATTLE RATTLE
SHE REALLY WASN'T UP FOR IT...
STRANGE... WE GOT HIM DRESSED UP AND EVERY-THING.
IS THAT THE ISSUE?
I'M SORRY...
I'D RATHER NOT KISS A BOY...
IF I DO, I WANT IT TO BE SOMEONE I LIKE.
BLUSH
EXCUSE ME!
KER-CHAK
SLAM
HEY! STOP PUSH-ING!
EEK!
TUMBLE

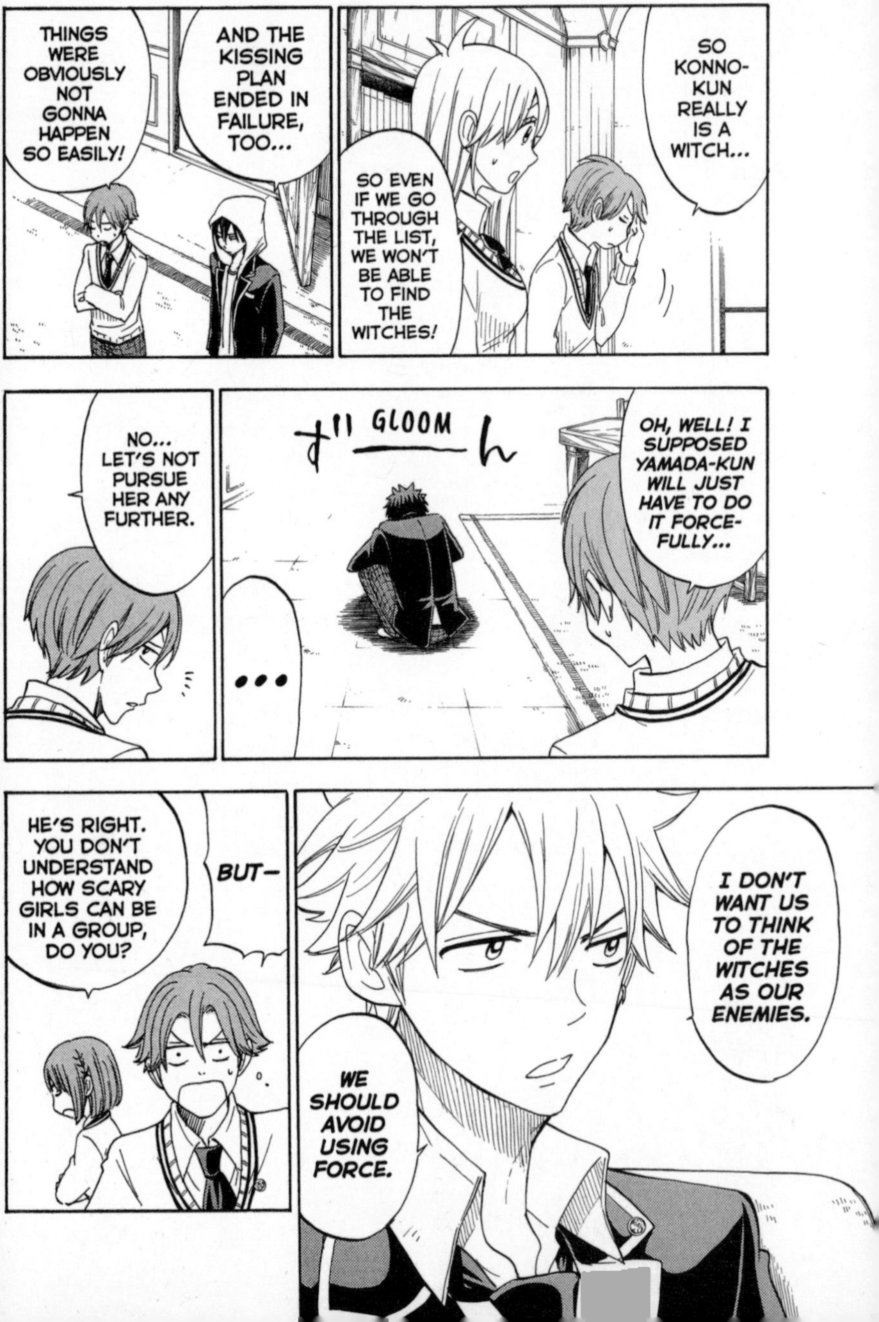
SO KONNO-KUN REALLY IS A WITCH...
SO EVEN IF WE GO THROUGH THE LIST, WE WON'T BE ABLE TO FIND THE WITCHES!
AND THE KISSING PLAN ENDED IN FAILURE, TOO...
THINGS WERE OBVIOUSLY NOT GONNA HAPPEN SO EASILY!
OH, WELL! I SUPPOSED YAMADA-KUN WILL JUST HAVE TO DO IT FORCEFULLY...
ず—ん GLOOM
...
NO... LET'S NOT PURSUE HER ANY FURTHER.
I DON'T WANT US TO THINK OF THE WITCHES AS OUR ENEMIES.
WE SHOULD AVOID USING FORCE.
BUT—
HE'S RIGHT. YOU DON'T UNDERSTAND HOW SCARY GIRLS CAN BE IN A GROUP, DO YOU?

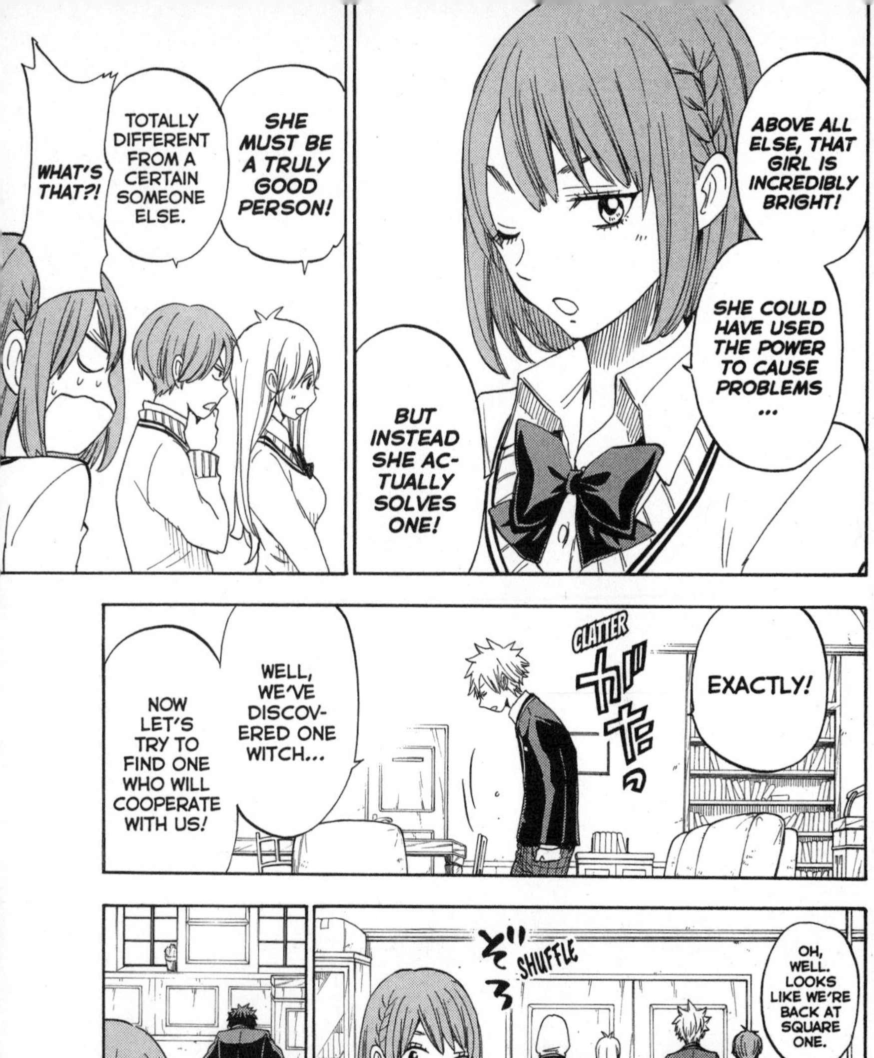
ABOVE ALL ELSE, THAT GIRL IS INCREDIBLY BRIGHT!
SHE COULD HAVE USED THE POWER TO CAUSE PROBLEMS ...
BUT INSTEAD SHE ACTUALLY SOLVES ONE!
SHE MUST BE A TRULY GOOD PERSON!
TOTALLY DIFFERENT FROM A CERTAIN SOMEONE ELSE.
WHAT'S THAT?!
EXACTLY!
CLATTER
WELL, WE'VE DISCOVERED ONE WITCH...
NOW LET'S TRY TO FIND ONE WHO WILL COOPERATE WITH US!
OH, WELL. LOOKS LIKE WE'RE BACK AT SQUARE ONE.
SHUFFLE
SHUFFLE
IT'S NOT LIKE THAT AT ALL.
!
...

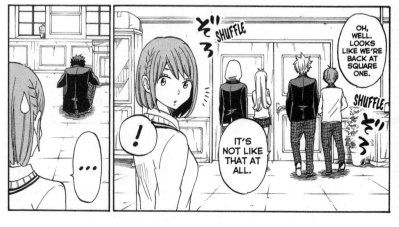

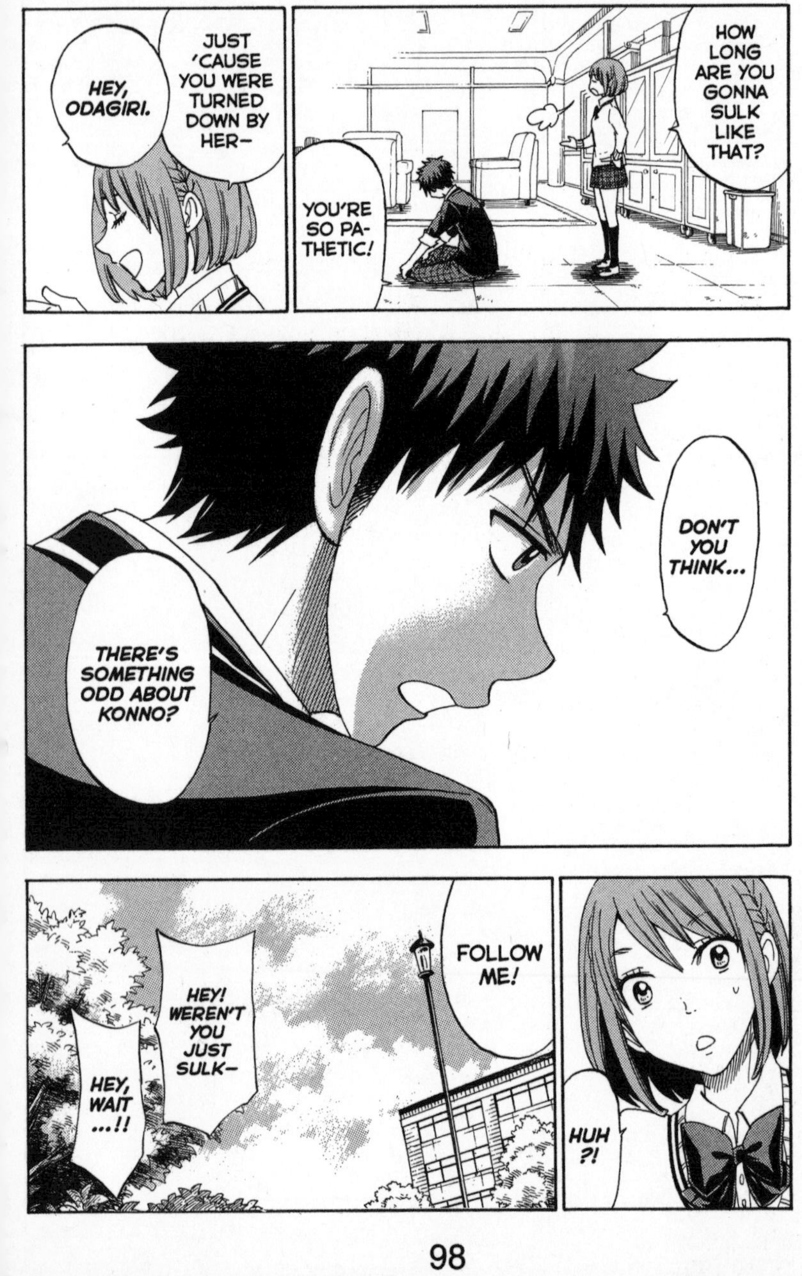
HOW LONG ARE YOU GONNA SULK LIKE THAT?
YOU'RE SO PA-THETIC!
JUST 'CAUSE YOU WERE TURNED DOWN BY HER–
HEY, ODAGIRI.
DON'T YOU THINK...
THERE'S SOMETHING ODD ABOUT KONNO?
HUH ?!
FOLLOW ME!
HEY! WEREN'T YOU JUST SULK–
HEY, WAIT ...!!

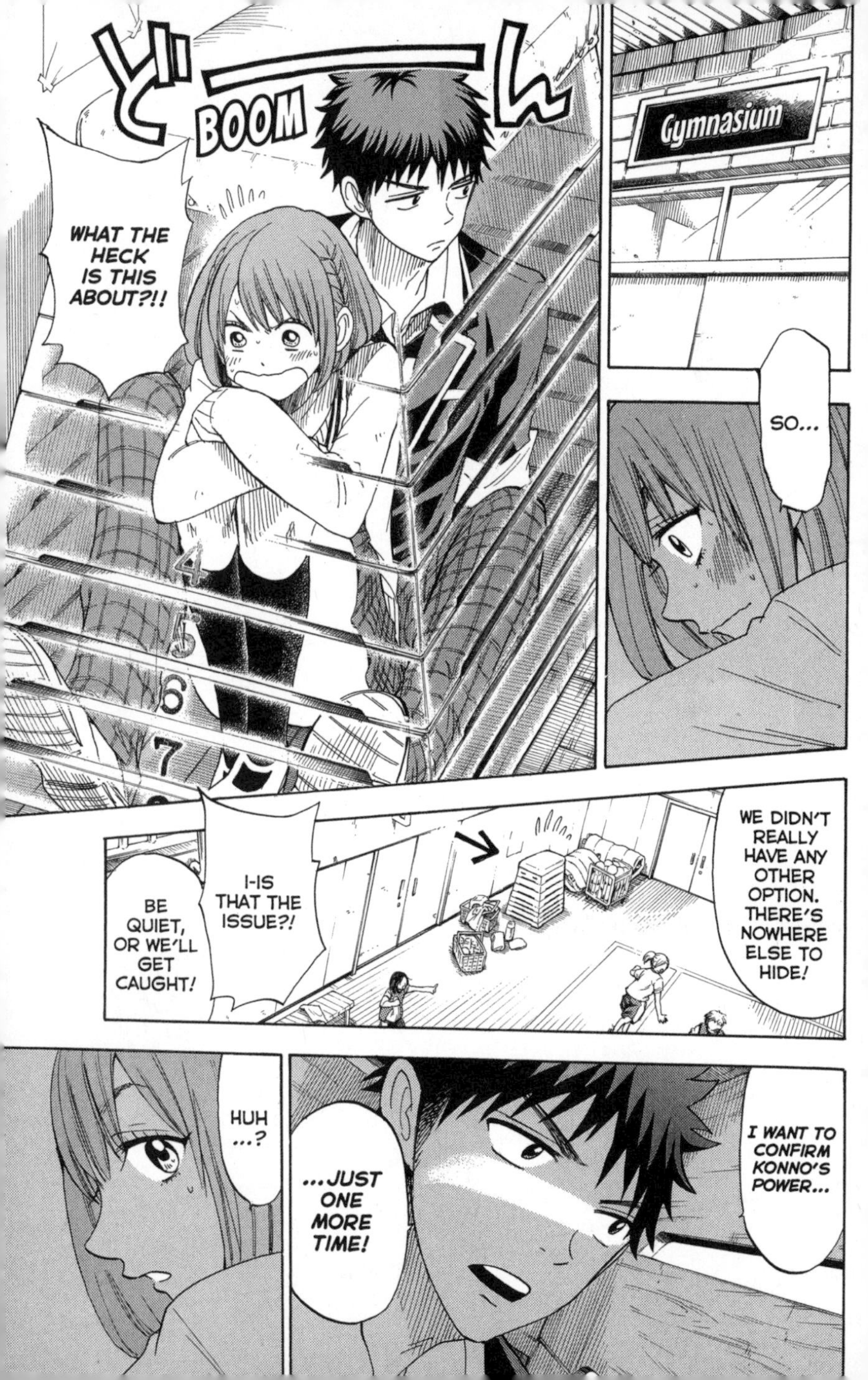
Gymnasium
SO...
どーーーん
BOOM
WHAT THE HECK IS THIS ABOUT?!!
WE DIDN'T REALLY HAVE ANY OTHER OPTION. THERE'S NOWHERE ELSE TO HIDE!
I-IS THAT THE ISSUE?!
BE QUIET, OR WE'LL GET CAUGHT!
I WANT TO CONFIRM KONNO'S POWER...
...JUST ONE MORE TIME!
HUH ...?

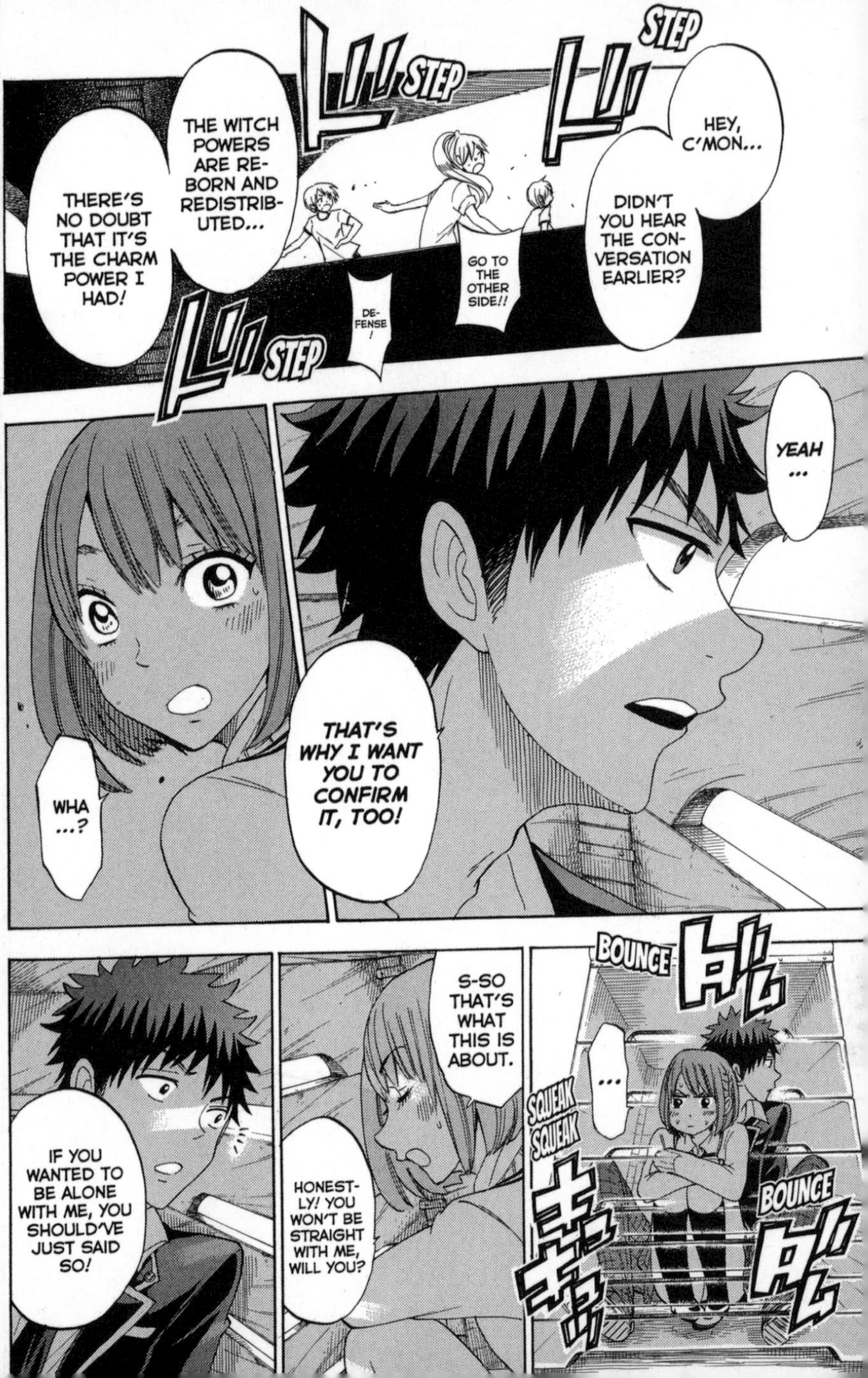
STEP
HEY, C'MON...
DIDN'T YOU HEAR THE CON-VERSATION EARLIER?
STEP
GO TO THE OTHER SIDE!!
DE-FENSE!
THE WITCH POWERS ARE RE-BORN AND REDISTRIB-UTED...
THERE'S NO DOUBT THAT IT'S THE CHARM POWER I HAD!
STEP
YEAH ...
THAT'S WHY I WANT YOU TO CONFIRM IT, TOO!
WHA ...?
BOUNCE
...
SQUEAK SQUEAK
BOUNCE
S-SO THAT'S WHAT THIS IS ABOUT.
HONEST-LY! YOU WON'T BE STRAIGHT WITH ME, WILL YOU?
IF YOU WANTED TO BE ALONE WITH ME, YOU SHOULD'VE JUST SAID SO!

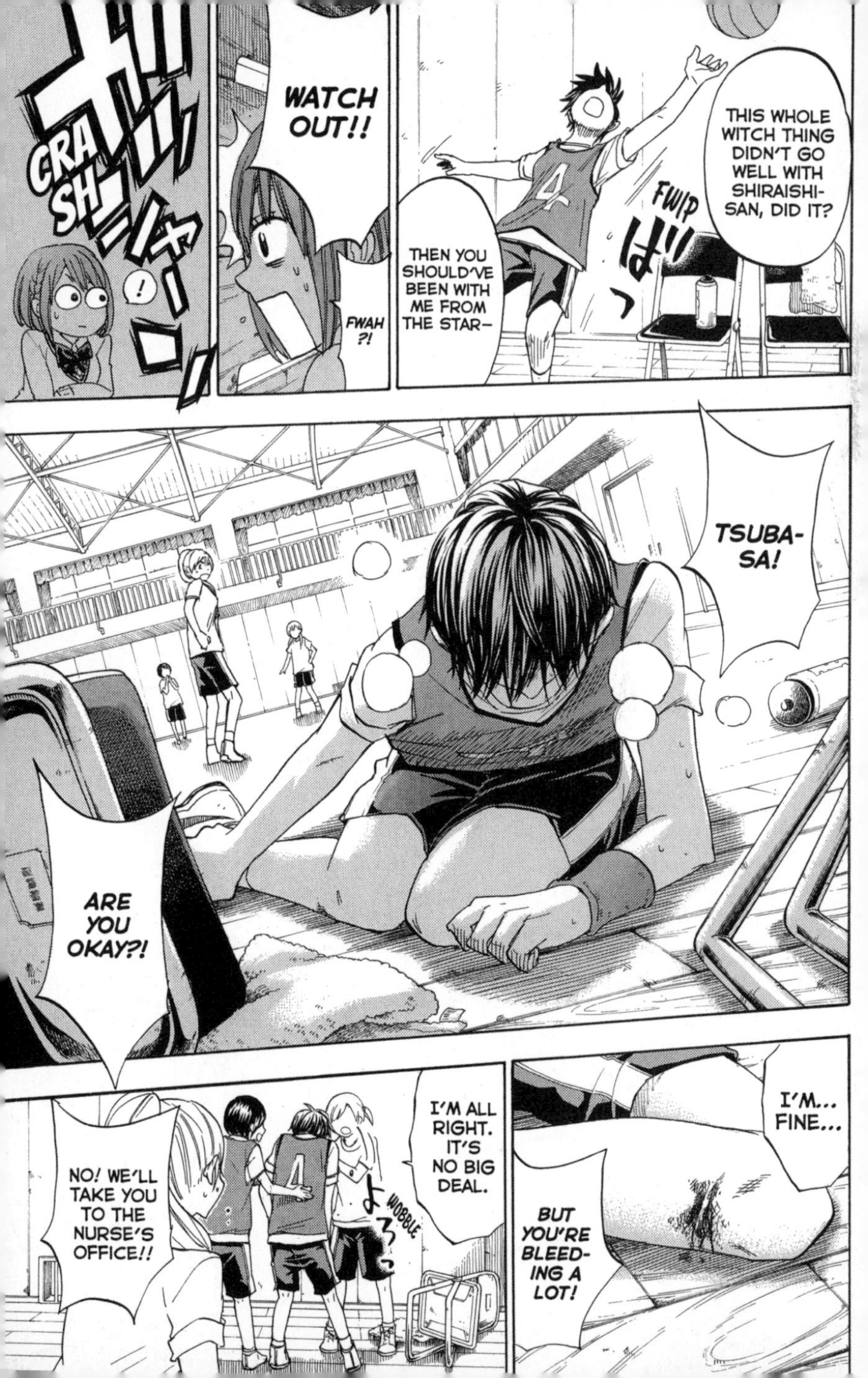

THIS WHOLE WITCH THING DIDN'T GO WELL WITH SHIRAISHI-SAN, DID IT?
FWIP
THEN YOU SHOULD'VE BEEN WITH ME FROM THE STAR–
WATCH OUT!!
FWAH ?!
CRASH
!
TSUBA-SA!
ARE YOU OKAY?!
I'M... FINE...
BUT YOU'RE BLEED-ING A LOT!
I'M ALL RIGHT. IT'S NO BIG DEAL.
WOBBLE
NO! WE'LL TAKE YOU TO THE NURSE'S OFFICE!!

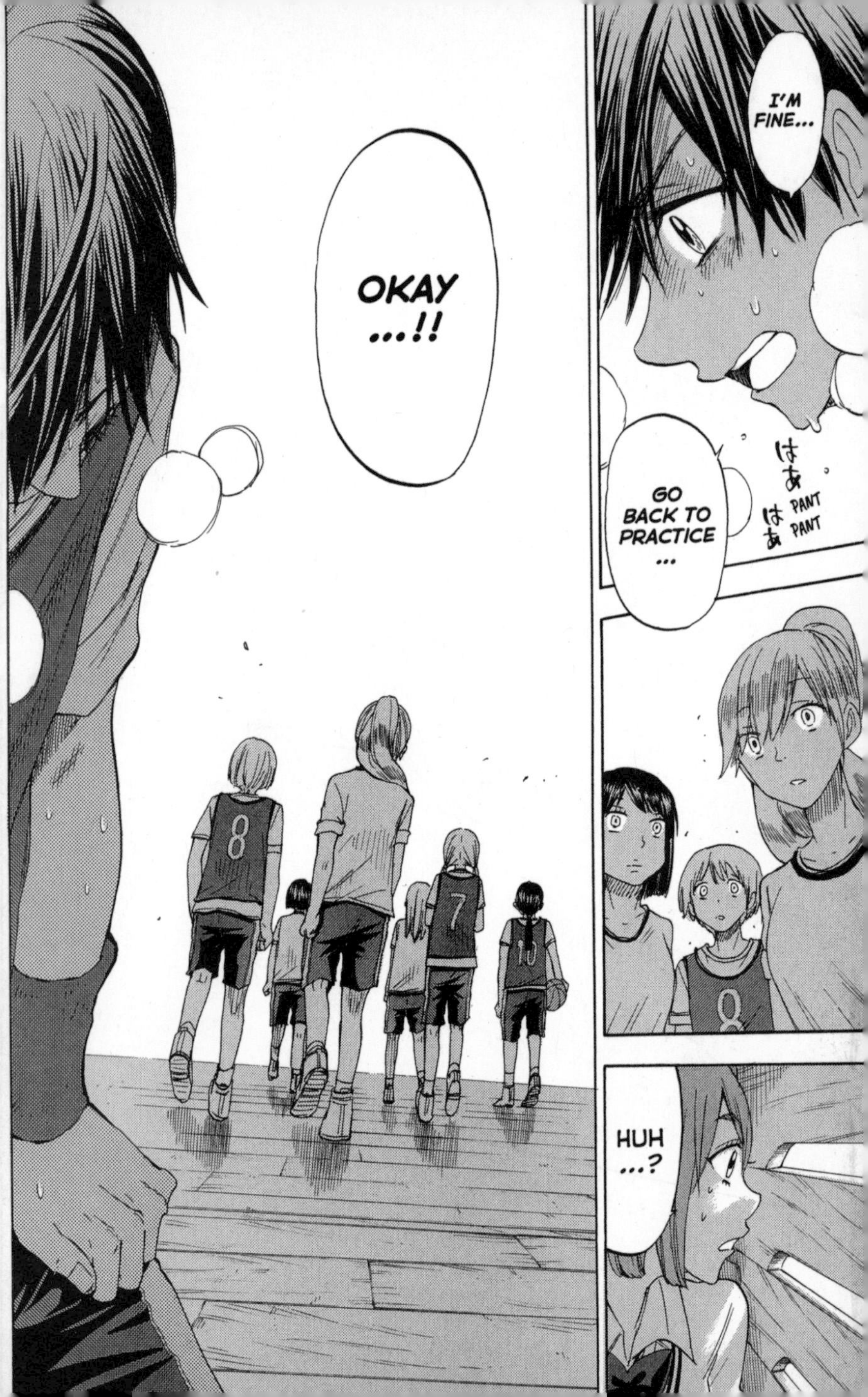
I'M FINE...
はあ はあ
PANT PANT
GO BACK TO PRACTICE ...
HUH ...?
OKAY ...!!

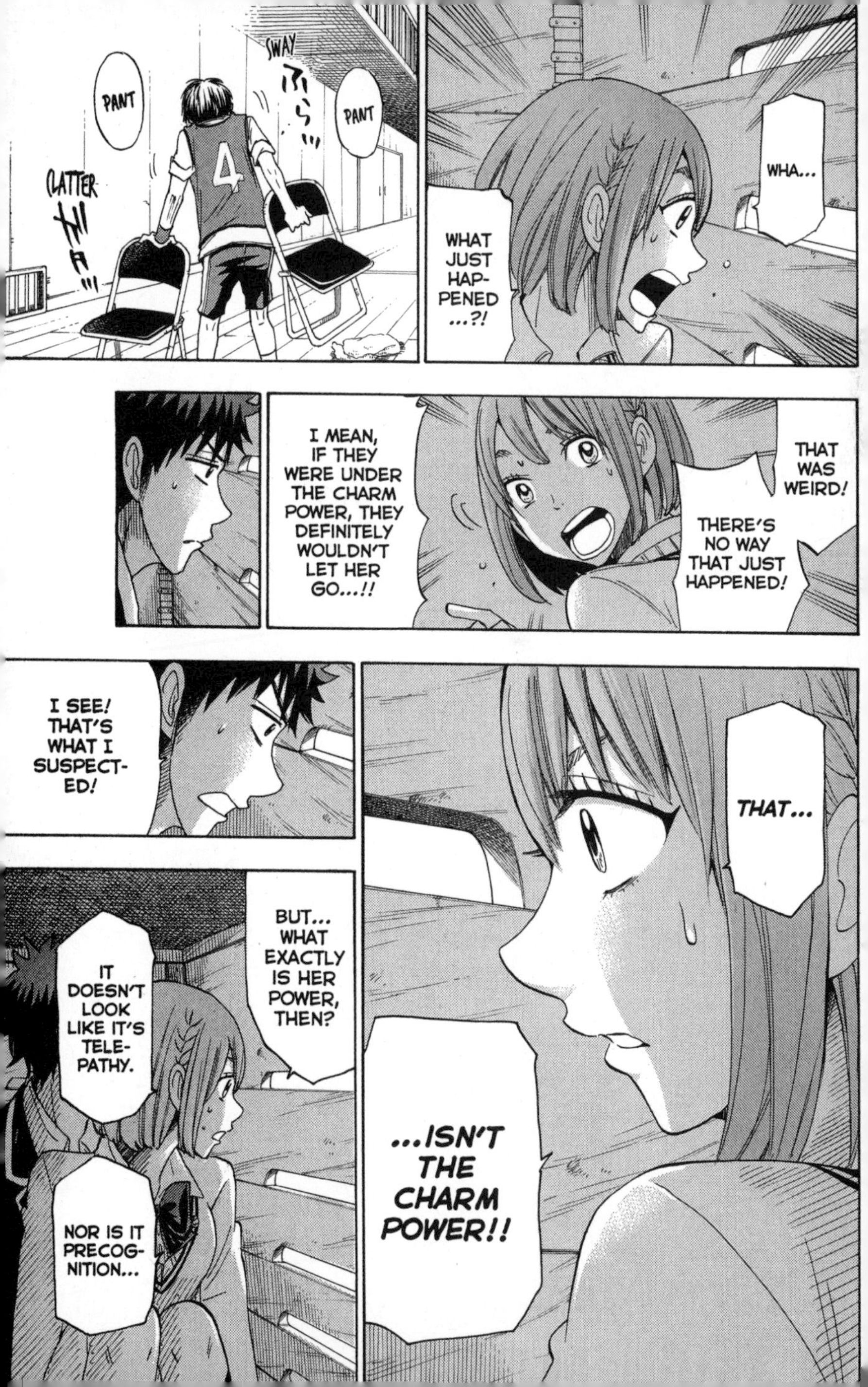
WHA...
WHAT JUST HAPPENED...?!
PANT
SWAY
ふら
PANT
CLATTER
ガタ
THAT WAS WEIRD!
THERE'S NO WAY THAT JUST HAPPENED!
I MEAN, IF THEY WERE UNDER THE CHARM POWER, THEY DEFINITELY WOULDN'T LET HER GO...!!
THAT...
...ISN'T THE CHARM POWER!!
I SEE! THAT'S WHAT I SUSPECTED!
BUT... WHAT EXACTLY IS HER POWER, THEN?
IT DOESN'T LOOK LIKE IT'S TELEPATHY.
NOR IS IT PRECOGNITION...

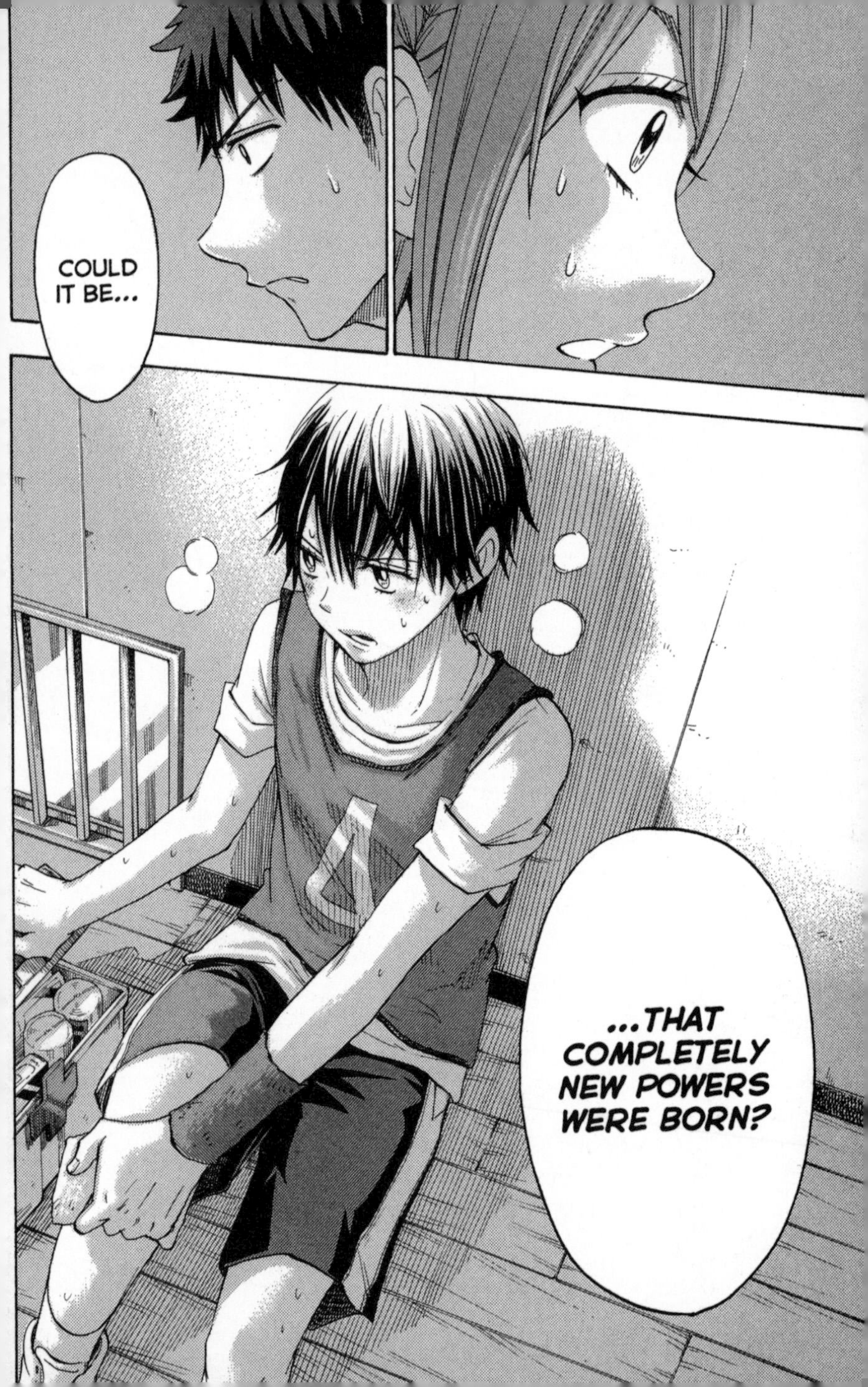
COULD IT BE...
...THAT COMPLETELY NEW POWERS WERE BORN?

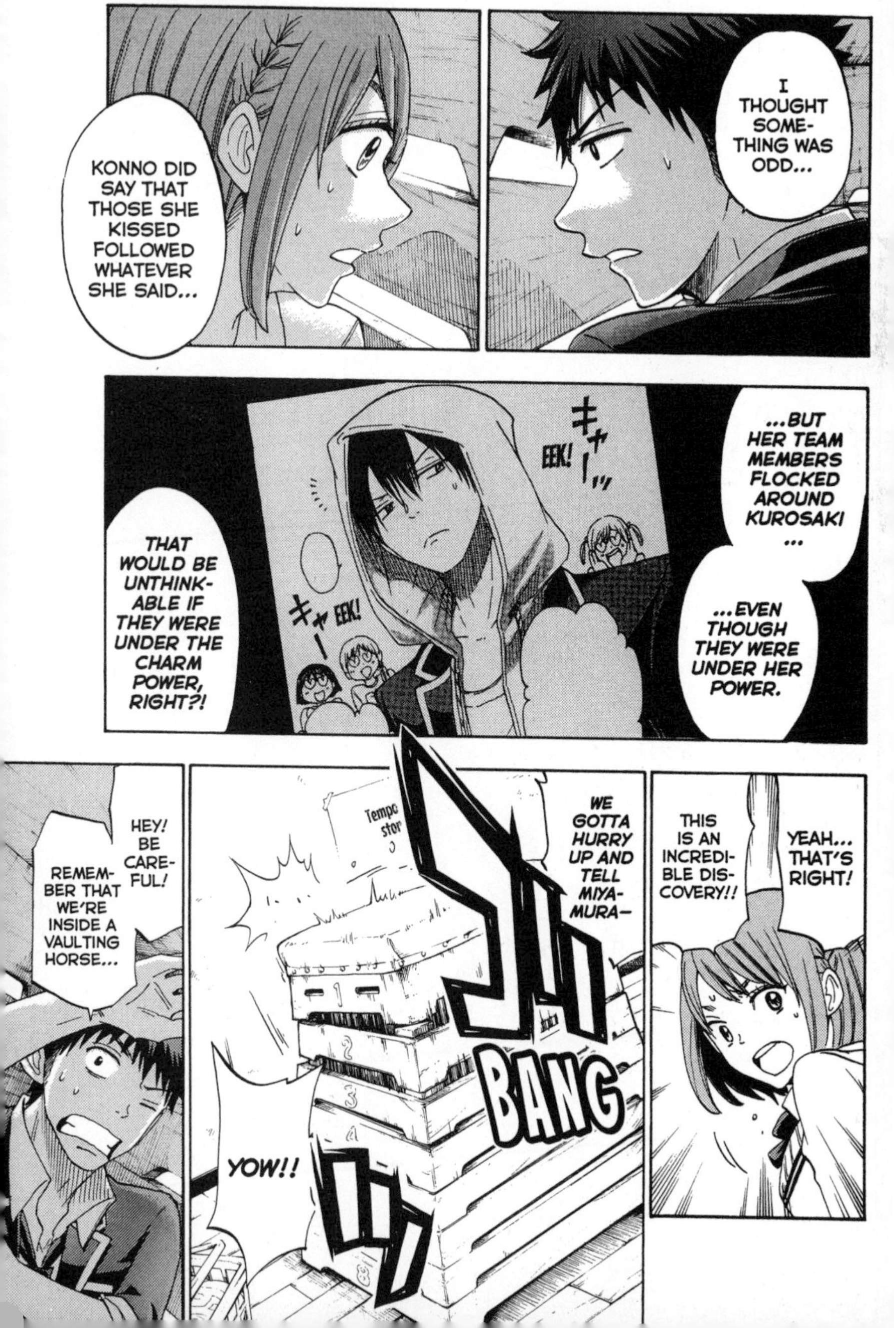
I THOUGHT SOMETHING WAS ODD...
KONNO DID SAY THAT THOSE SHE KISSED FOLLOWED WHATEVER SHE SAID...
...BUT HER TEAM MEMBERS FLOCKED AROUND KUROSAKI...
...EVEN THOUGH THEY WERE UNDER HER POWER.
EEK!
EEK!
THAT WOULD BE UNTHINKABLE IF THEY WERE UNDER THE CHARM POWER, RIGHT?!
YEAH... THAT'S RIGHT!
THIS IS AN INCREDIBLE DISCOVERY!!
WE GOTTA HURRY UP AND TELL MIYAMURA—
BANG
YOW!!
HEY! BE CAREFUL!
REMEMBER THAT WE'RE INSIDE A VAULTING HORSE...

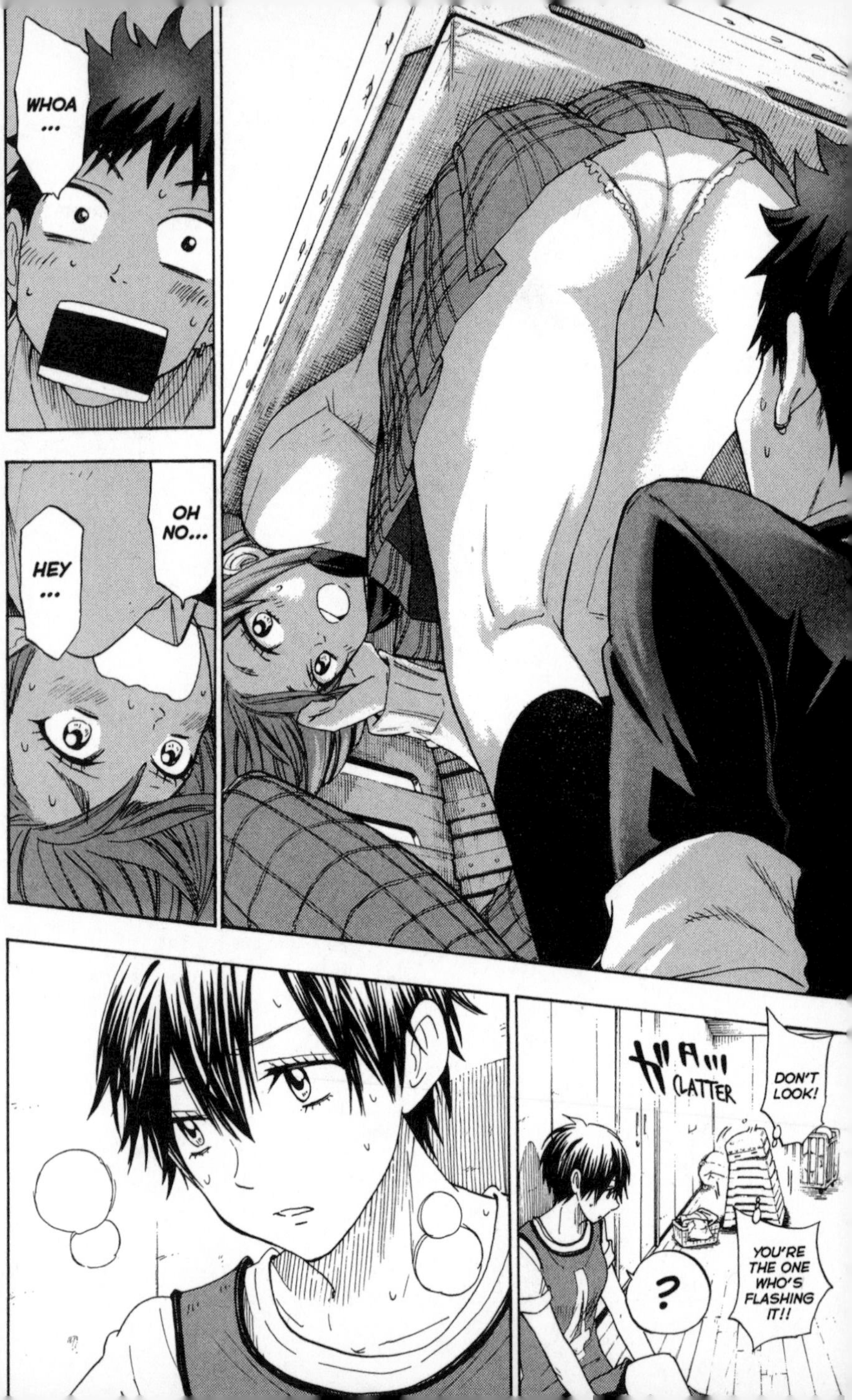
WHOA...
OH NO...
HEY...
DON'T LOOK!
CLATTER
YOU'RE THE ONE WHO'S FLASHING IT!!
?

CHAPTER 99: Care for a bean-jam bun?

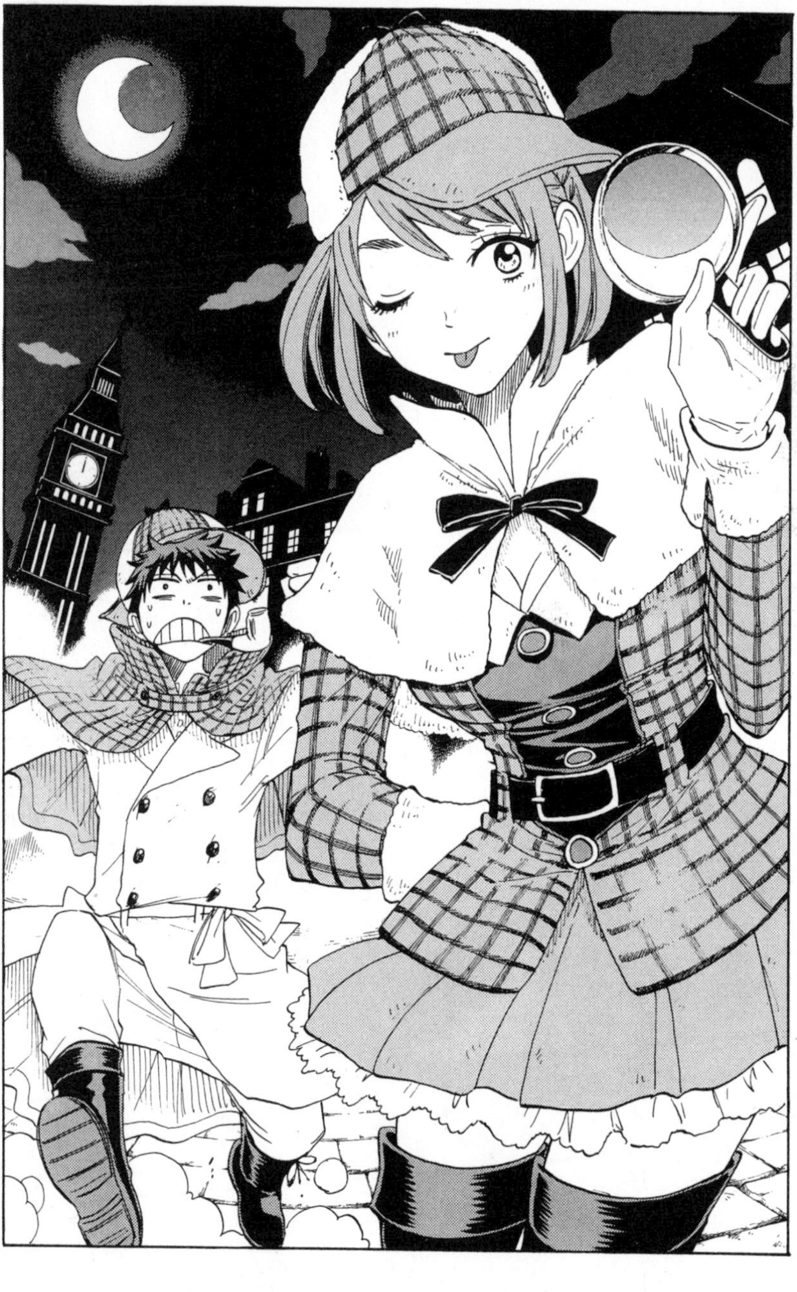

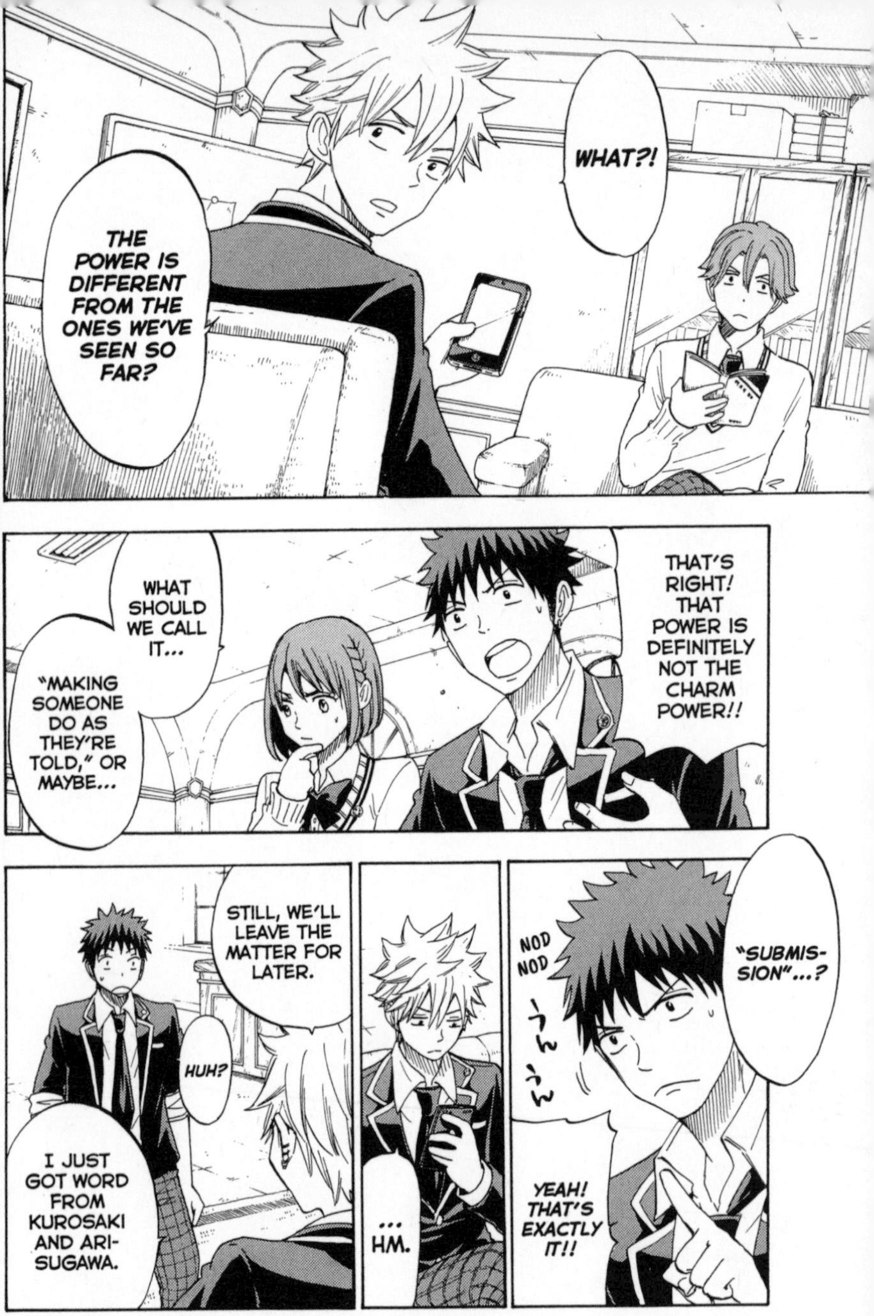
WHAT?!
THE POWER IS DIFFERENT FROM THE ONES WE'VE SEEN SO FAR?
THAT'S RIGHT! THAT POWER IS DEFINITELY NOT THE CHARM POWER!!
WHAT SHOULD WE CALL IT...
"MAKING SOMEONE DO AS THEY'RE TOLD," OR MAYBE...
"SUBMISSION"...?
NOD NOD
うん うん
YEAH! THAT'S EXACTLY IT!!
... HM.
STILL, WE'LL LEAVE THE MATTER FOR LATER.
HUH?
I JUST GOT WORD FROM KUROSAKI AND ARI-SUGAWA.

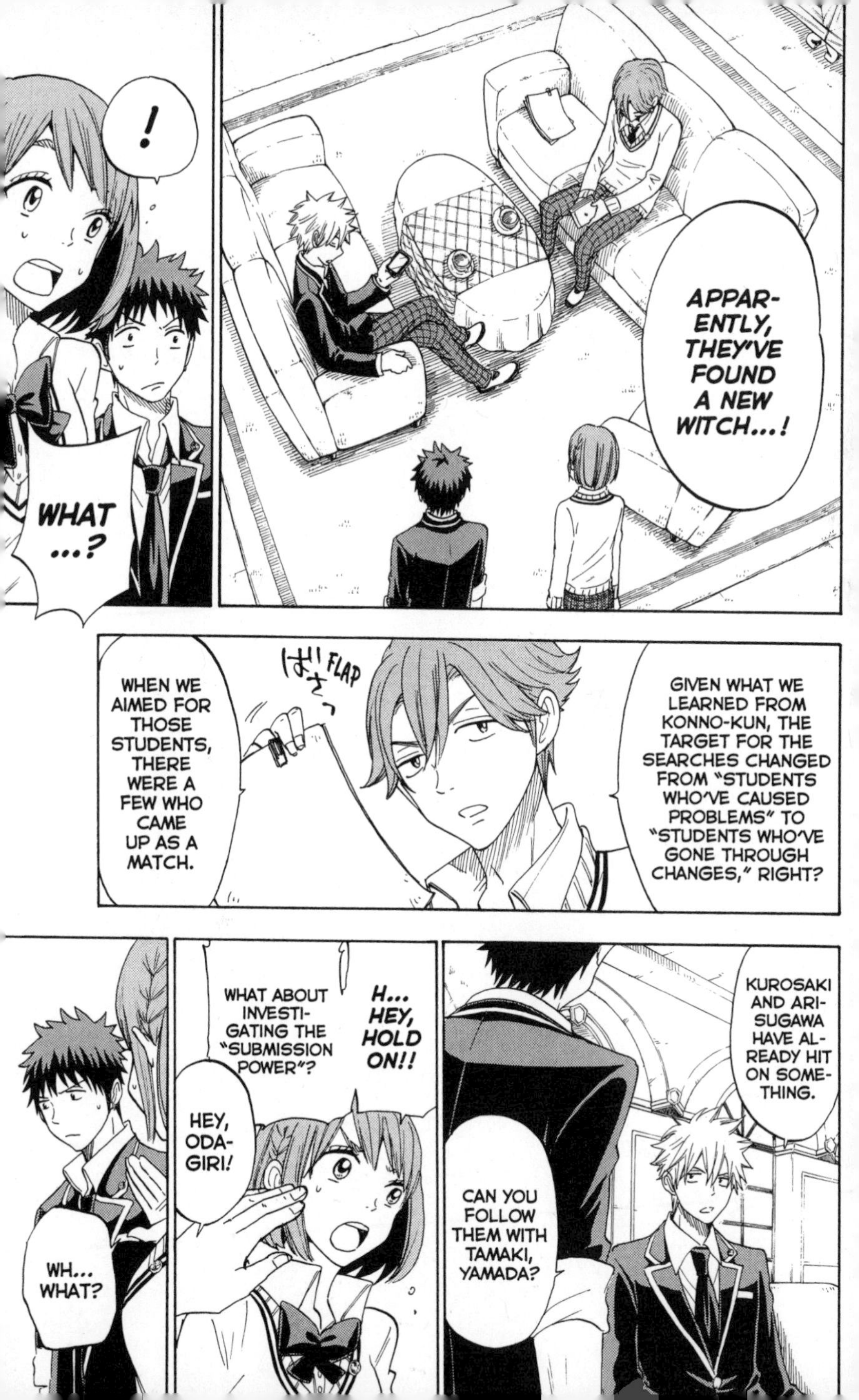
APPARENTLY, THEY'VE FOUND A NEW WITCH...!
!
WHAT...?
GIVEN WHAT WE LEARNED FROM KONNO-KUN, THE TARGET FOR THE SEARCHES CHANGED FROM "STUDENTS WHO'VE CAUSED PROBLEMS" TO "STUDENTS WHO'VE GONE THROUGH CHANGES," RIGHT?
ばさっ FLAP
WHEN WE AIMED FOR THOSE STUDENTS, THERE WERE A FEW WHO CAME UP AS A MATCH.
KUROSAKI AND ARISUGAWA HAVE ALREADY HIT ON SOMETHING.
CAN YOU FOLLOW THEM WITH TAMAKI, YAMADA?
H... HEY, HOLD ON!!
WHAT ABOUT INVESTIGATING THE "SUBMISSION POWER"?
HEY, ODAGIRI!
WH... WHAT?

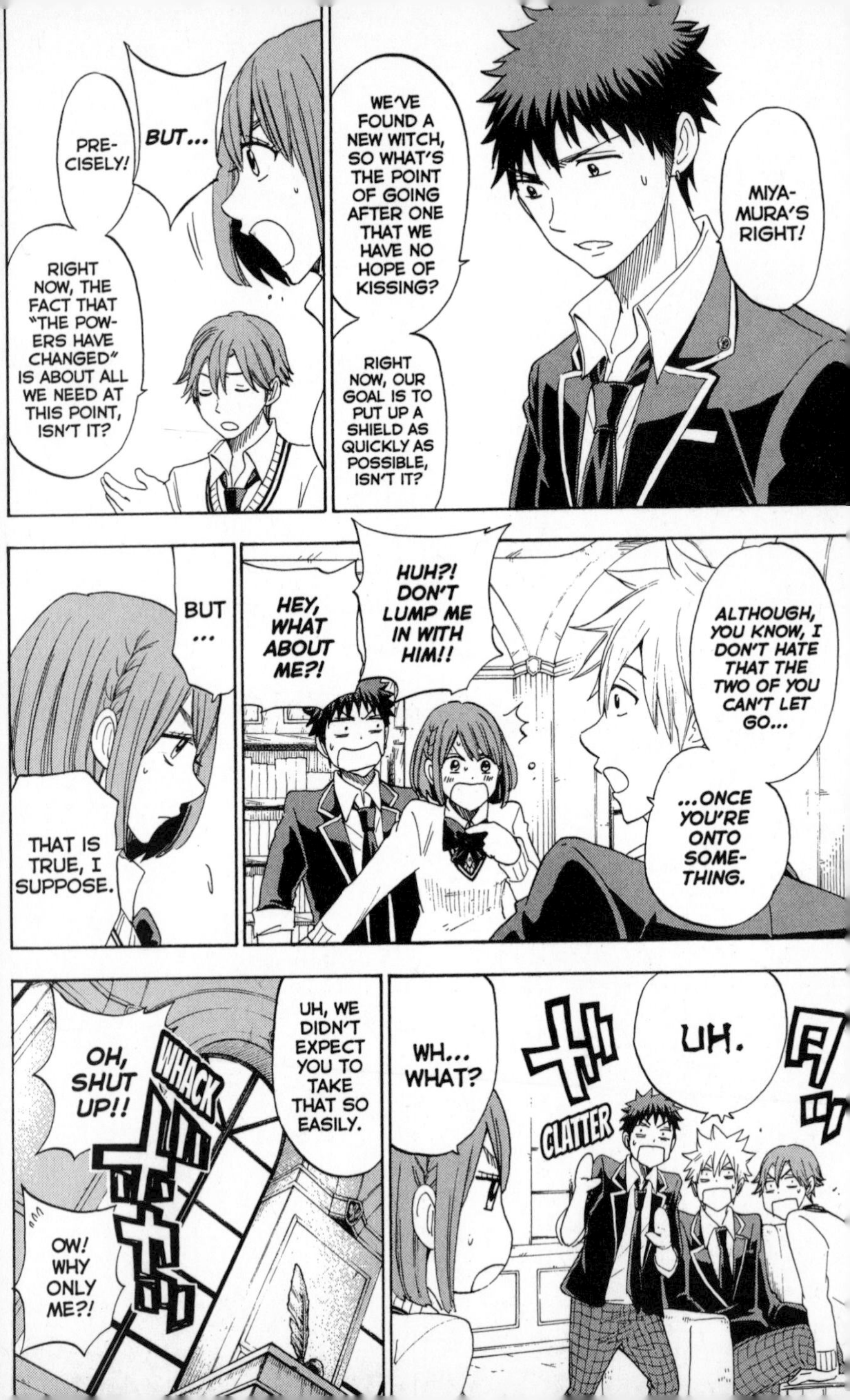
MIYAMURA'S RIGHT!
WE'VE FOUND A NEW WITCH, SO WHAT'S THE POINT OF GOING AFTER ONE THAT WE HAVE NO HOPE OF KISSING?
RIGHT NOW, OUR GOAL IS TO PUT UP A SHIELD AS QUICKLY AS POSSIBLE, ISN'T IT?
BUT...
PRECISELY!
RIGHT NOW, THE FACT THAT "THE POWERS HAVE CHANGED" IS ABOUT ALL WE NEED AT THIS POINT, ISN'T IT?
ALTHOUGH, YOU KNOW, I DON'T HATE THAT THE TWO OF YOU CAN'T LET GO...
...ONCE YOU'RE ONTO SOMETHING.
HUH?! DON'T LUMP ME IN WITH HIM!!
HEY, WHAT ABOUT ME?!
BUT...
THAT IS TRUE, I SUPPOSE.
UH.
CLATTER
WH... WHAT?
UH, WE DIDN'T EXPECT YOU TO TAKE THAT SO EASILY.
OH, SHUT UP!!
WHACK
OW! WHY ONLY ME?!

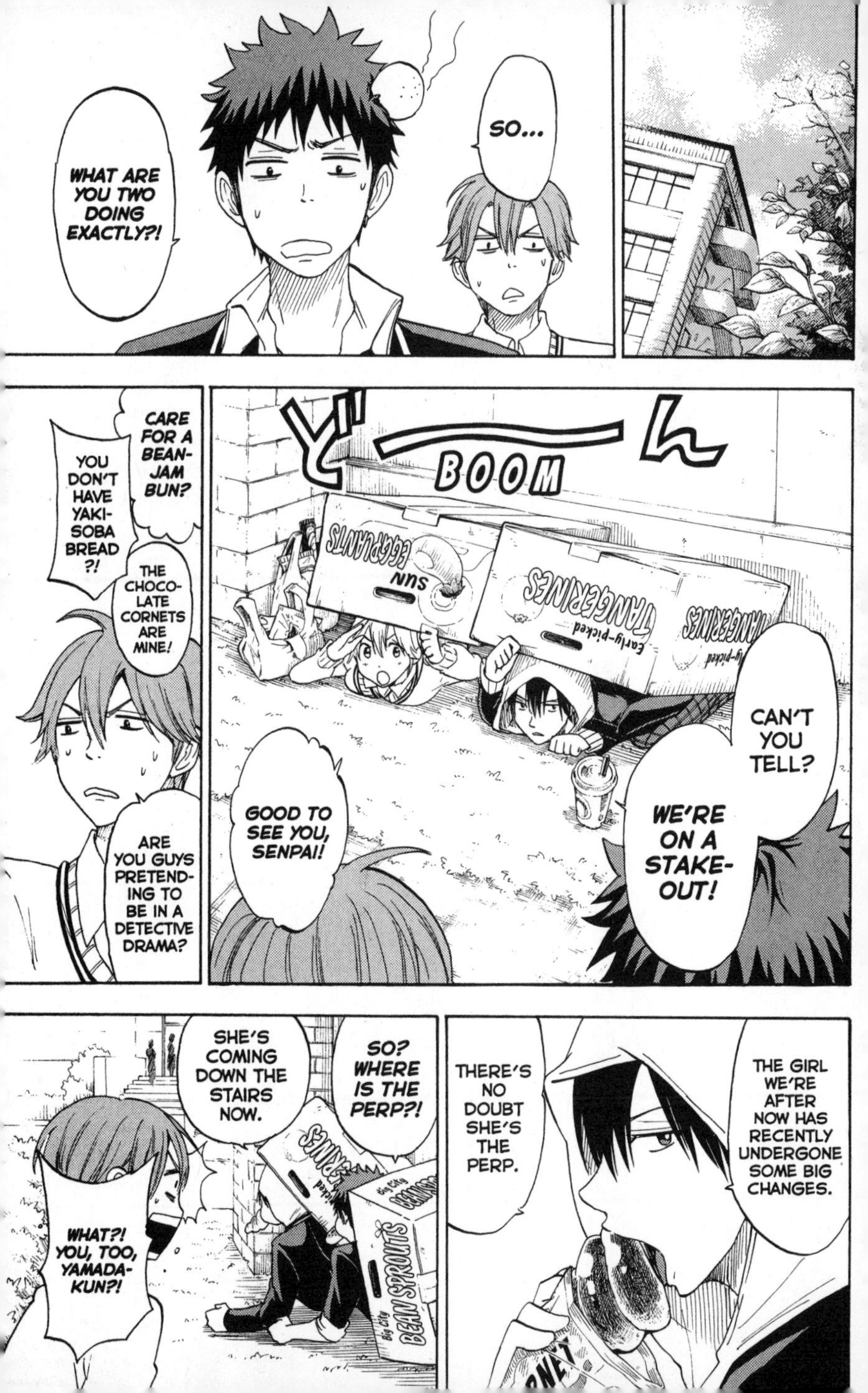
SO...
WHAT ARE YOU TWO DOING EXACTLY?!
BOOM
CAN'T YOU TELL?
WE'RE ON A STAKE-OUT!
SUN EGGPLANTS
Early-picked TANGERINES
GOOD TO SEE YOU, SENPAI!
CARE FOR A BEAN-JAM BUN?
YOU DON'T HAVE YAKI-SOBA BREAD?!
THE CHOCOLATE CORNETS ARE MINE!
ARE YOU GUYS PRETENDING TO BE IN A DETECTIVE DRAMA?
THE GIRL WE'RE AFTER NOW HAS RECENTLY UNDERGONE SOME BIG CHANGES.
THERE'S NO DOUBT SHE'S THE PERP.
SO? WHERE IS THE PERP?!
SHE'S COMING DOWN THE STAIRS NOW.
Big City BEAN SPROUTS
WHAT?! YOU, TOO, YAMADA-KUN?!

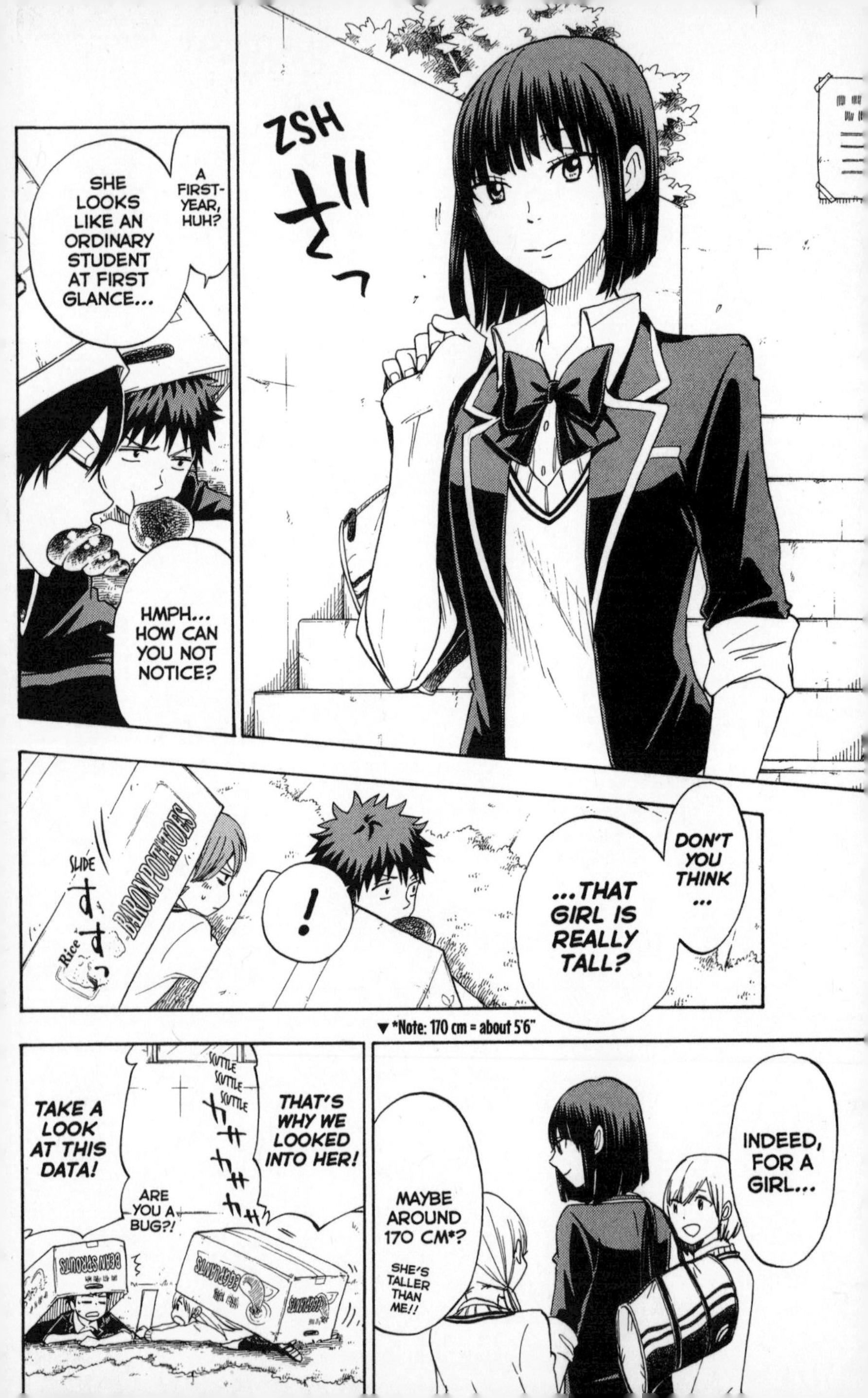
ZSH
ざっ
A FIRST-YEAR, HUH?
SHE LOOKS LIKE AN ORDINARY STUDENT AT FIRST GLANCE...
HMPH... HOW CAN YOU NOT NOTICE?
DON'T YOU THINK ...
...THAT GIRL IS REALLY TALL?
!
BARON POTATOES
SLIDE
すすっ
Rice
INDEED, FOR A GIRL...
MAYBE AROUND 170 CM*?
SHE'S TALLER THAN ME!!
THAT'S WHY WE LOOKED INTO HER!
SCUTTLE SCUTTLE SCUTTLE
TAKE A LOOK AT THIS DATA!
ARE YOU A BUG?!
EGGPLANTS
BEAN SPROUTS
▼ *Note: 170 cm = about 5'6"

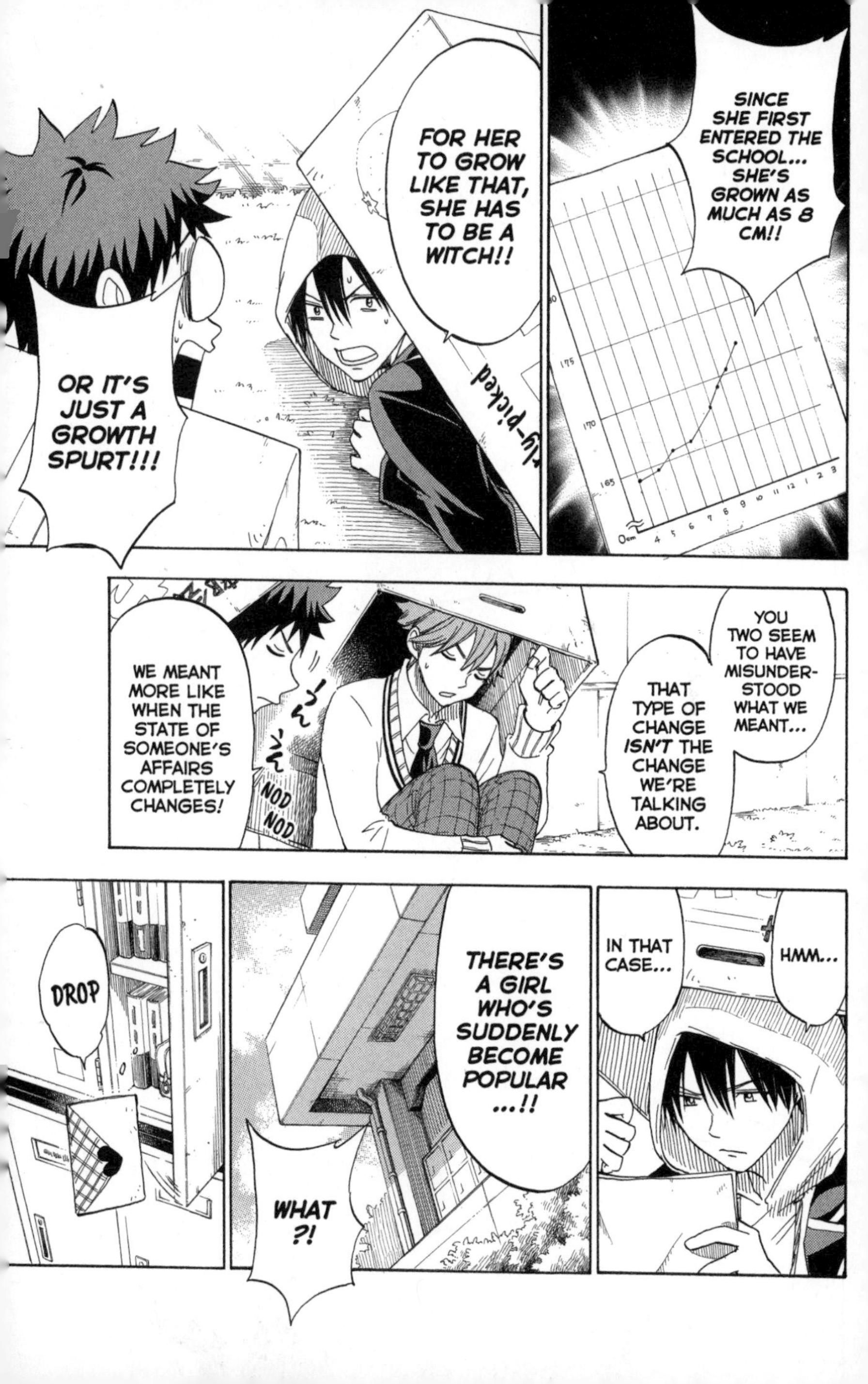
SINCE SHE FIRST ENTERED THE SCHOOL... SHE'S GROWN AS MUCH AS 8 CM!!
175
170
165
0cm
4 5 6 7 8 9 10 11 12 1 2 3
FOR HER TO GROW LIKE THAT, SHE HAS TO BE A WITCH!!
OR IT'S JUST A GROWTH SPURT!!!
YOU TWO SEEM TO HAVE MISUNDER-STOOD WHAT WE MEANT...
THAT TYPE OF CHANGE *ISN'T* THE CHANGE WE'RE TALKING ABOUT.
WE MEANT MORE LIKE WHEN THE STATE OF SOMEONE'S AFFAIRS COMPLETELY CHANGES!
NOD NOD
HMM...
IN THAT CASE...
THERE'S A GIRL WHO'S SUDDENLY BECOME POPULAR ...!!
WHAT ?!
DROP

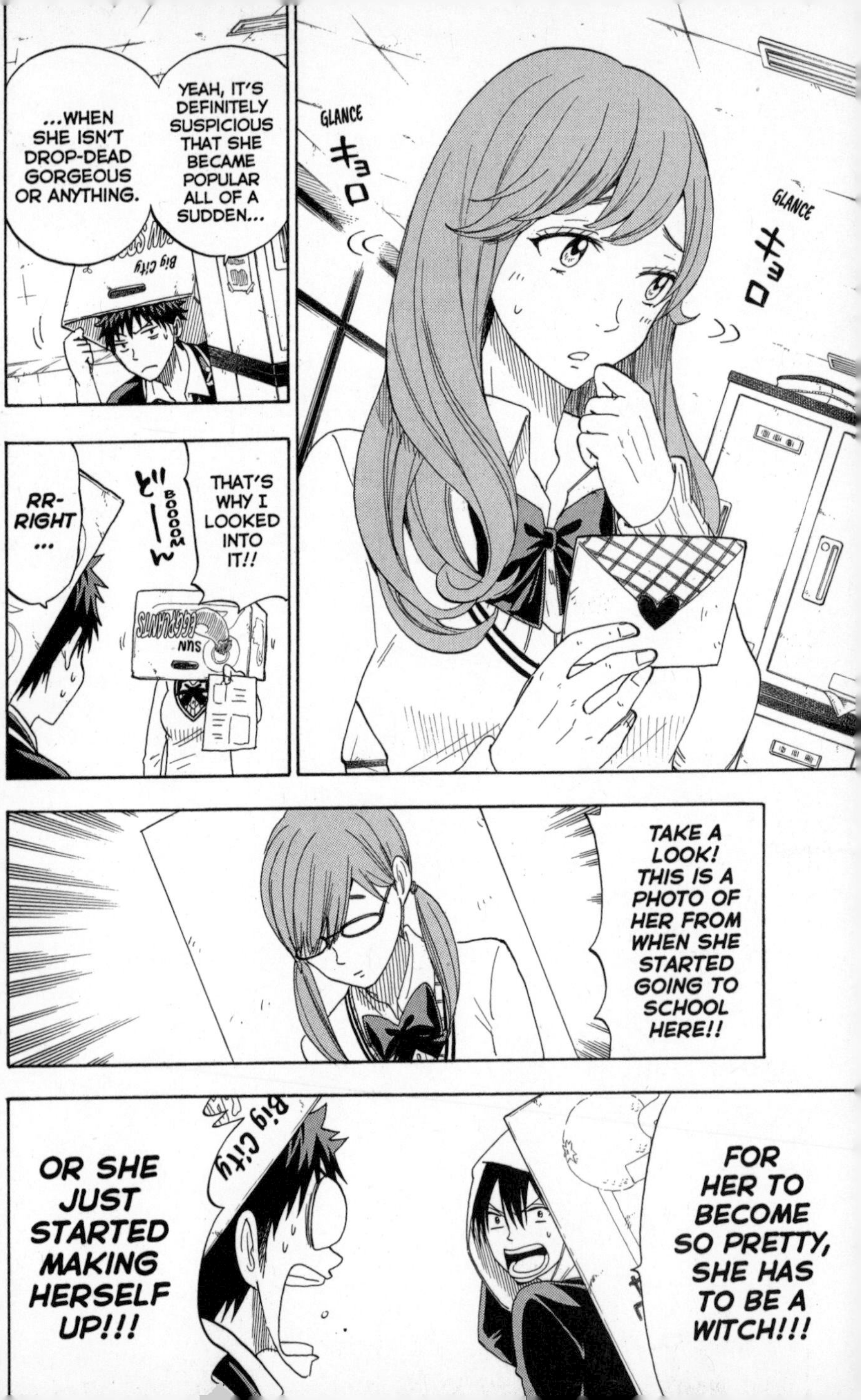

GLANCE
キョロ
GLANCE
キョロ
YEAH, IT'S DEFINITELY SUSPICIOUS THAT SHE BECAME POPULAR ALL OF A SUDDEN...
...WHEN SHE ISN'T DROP-DEAD GORGEOUS OR ANYTHING.
Big City
THAT'S WHY I LOOKED INTO IT!!
どーん
BOOOOOM
RR-RIGHT ...
SUN EGGPLANTS
TAKE A LOOK! THIS IS A PHOTO OF HER FROM WHEN SHE STARTED GOING TO SCHOOL HERE!!
FOR HER TO BECOME SO PRETTY, SHE HAS TO BE A WITCH!!!
Big City
OR SHE JUST STARTED MAKING HERSELF UP!!!

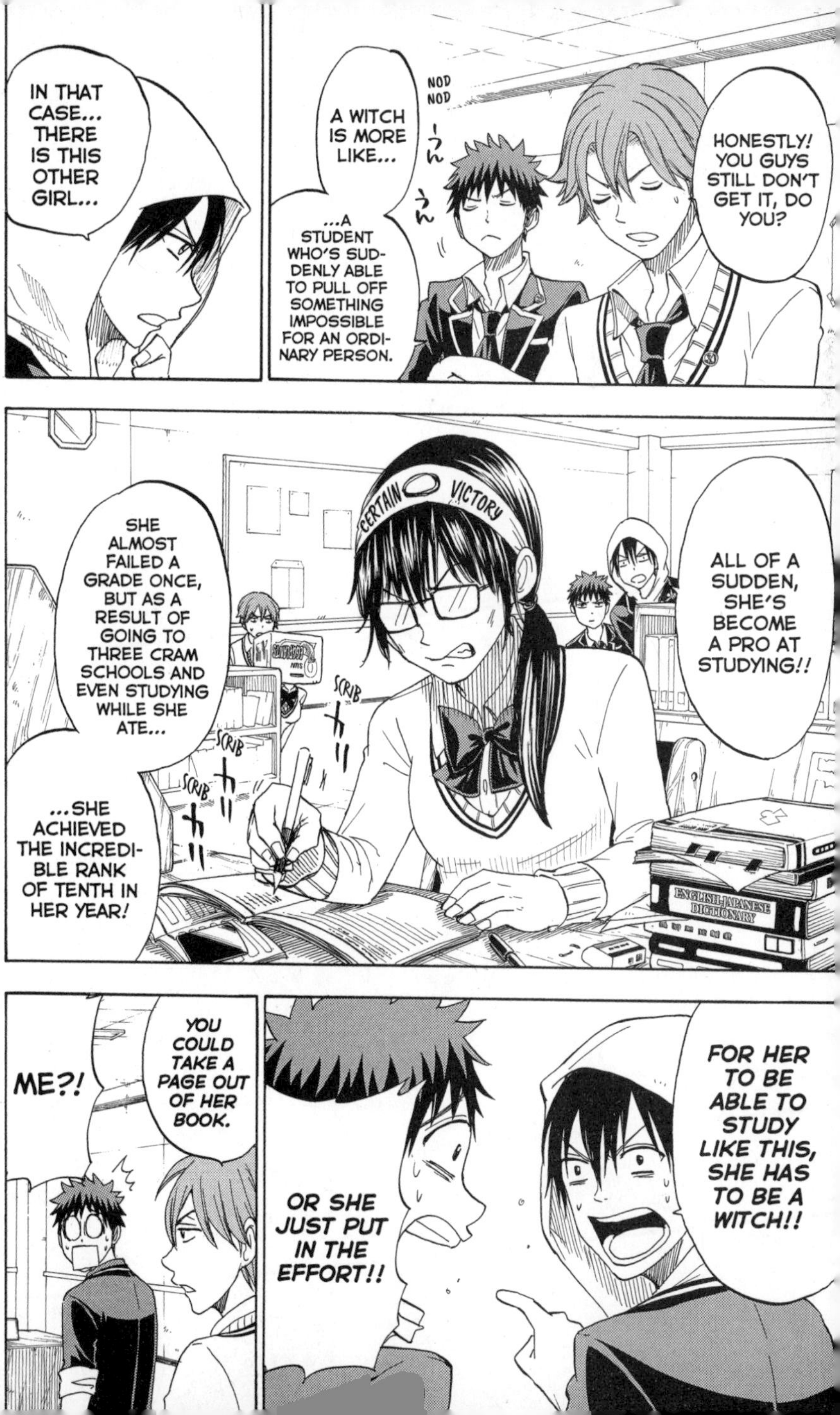

HONESTLY! YOU GUYS STILL DON'T GET IT, DO YOU?
A WITCH IS MORE LIKE...
NOD NOD
うん うん
...A STUDENT WHO'S SUDDENLY ABLE TO PULL OFF SOMETHING IMPOSSIBLE FOR AN ORDINARY PERSON.
IN THAT CASE... THERE IS THIS OTHER GIRL...
ALL OF A SUDDEN, SHE'S BECOME A PRO AT STUDYING!!
CERTAIN VICTORY
SHE ALMOST FAILED A GRADE ONCE, BUT AS A RESULT OF GOING TO THREE CRAM SCHOOLS AND EVEN STUDYING WHILE SHE ATE...
SCRIB
SCRIB
SCRIB
...SHE ACHIEVED THE INCREDIBLE RANK OF TENTH IN HER YEAR!
ENGLISH-JAPANESE DICTIONARY
FOR HER TO BE ABLE TO STUDY LIKE THIS, SHE HAS TO BE A WITCH!!
OR SHE JUST PUT IN THE EFFORT!!
YOU COULD TAKE A PAGE OUT OF HER BOOK.
ME?!

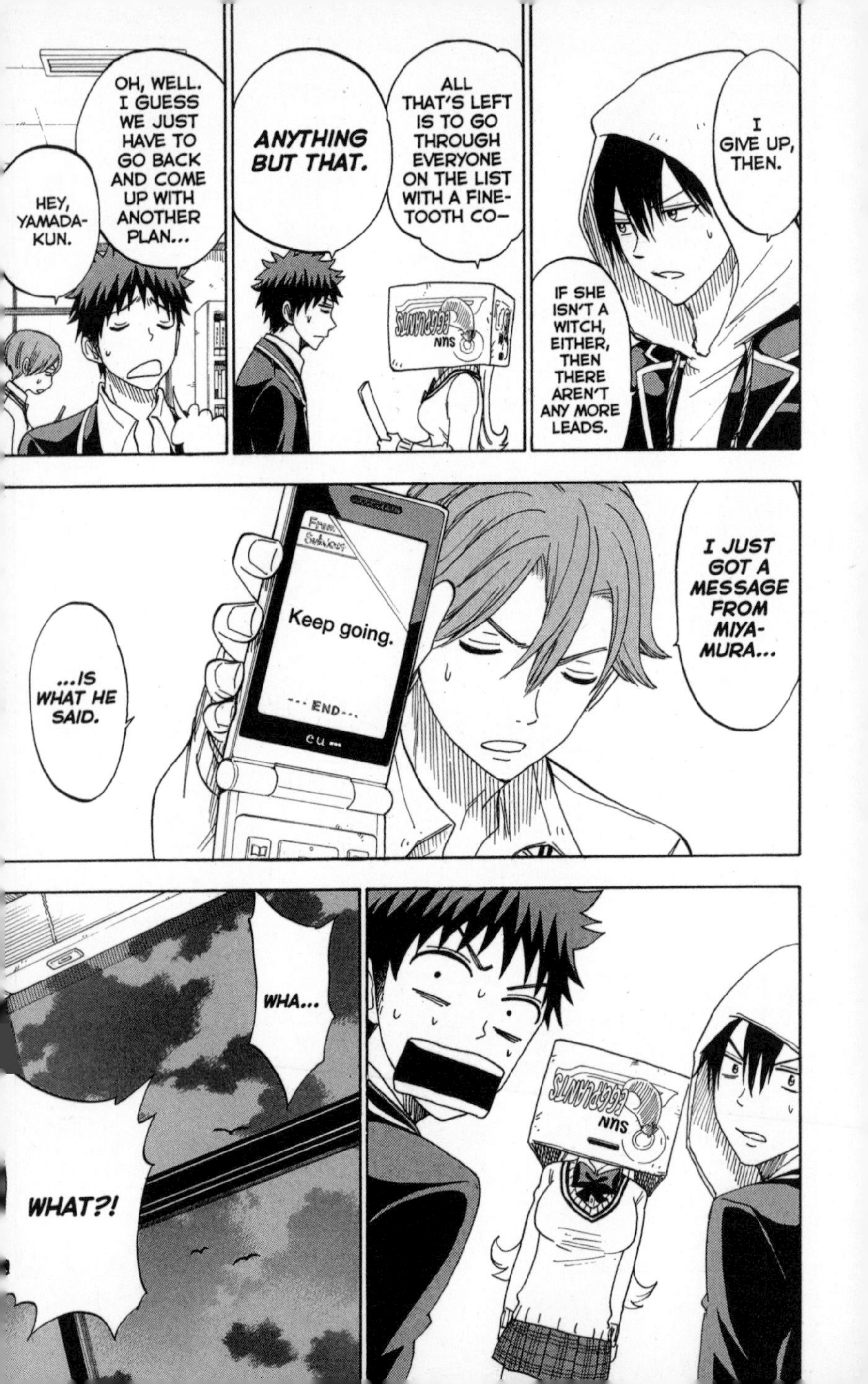

I GIVE UP, THEN.
IF SHE ISN'T A WITCH, EITHER, THEN THERE AREN'T ANY MORE LEADS.
ALL THAT'S LEFT IS TO GO THROUGH EVERYONE ON THE LIST WITH A FINE-TOOTH CO—
ANYTHING BUT THAT.
OH, WELL. I GUESS WE JUST HAVE TO GO BACK AND COME UP WITH ANOTHER PLAN...
HEY, YAMADA-KUN.
I JUST GOT A MESSAGE FROM MIYAMURA...
Keep going.
--- END ---
...IS WHAT HE SAID.
WHA...
WHAT?!

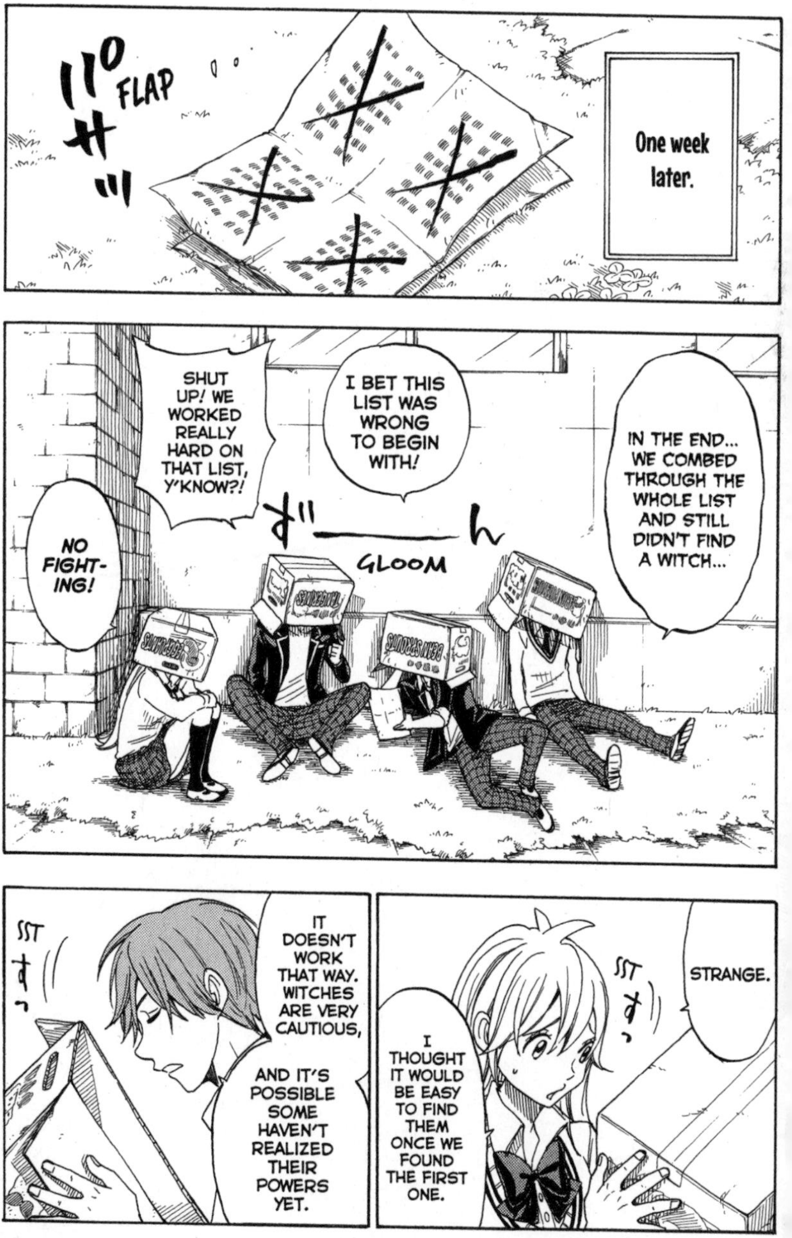
One week later.
FLAP
IN THE END... WE COMBED THROUGH THE WHOLE LIST AND STILL DIDN'T FIND A WITCH...
I BET THIS LIST WAS WRONG TO BEGIN WITH!
SHUT UP! WE WORKED REALLY HARD ON THAT LIST, Y'KNOW?!
GLOOM
NO FIGHT-ING!
STRANGE.
I THOUGHT IT WOULD BE EASY TO FIND THEM ONCE WE FOUND THE FIRST ONE.
SST
IT DOESN'T WORK THAT WAY. WITCHES ARE VERY CAUTIOUS,
AND IT'S POSSIBLE SOME HAVEN'T REALIZED THEIR POWERS YET.
SST

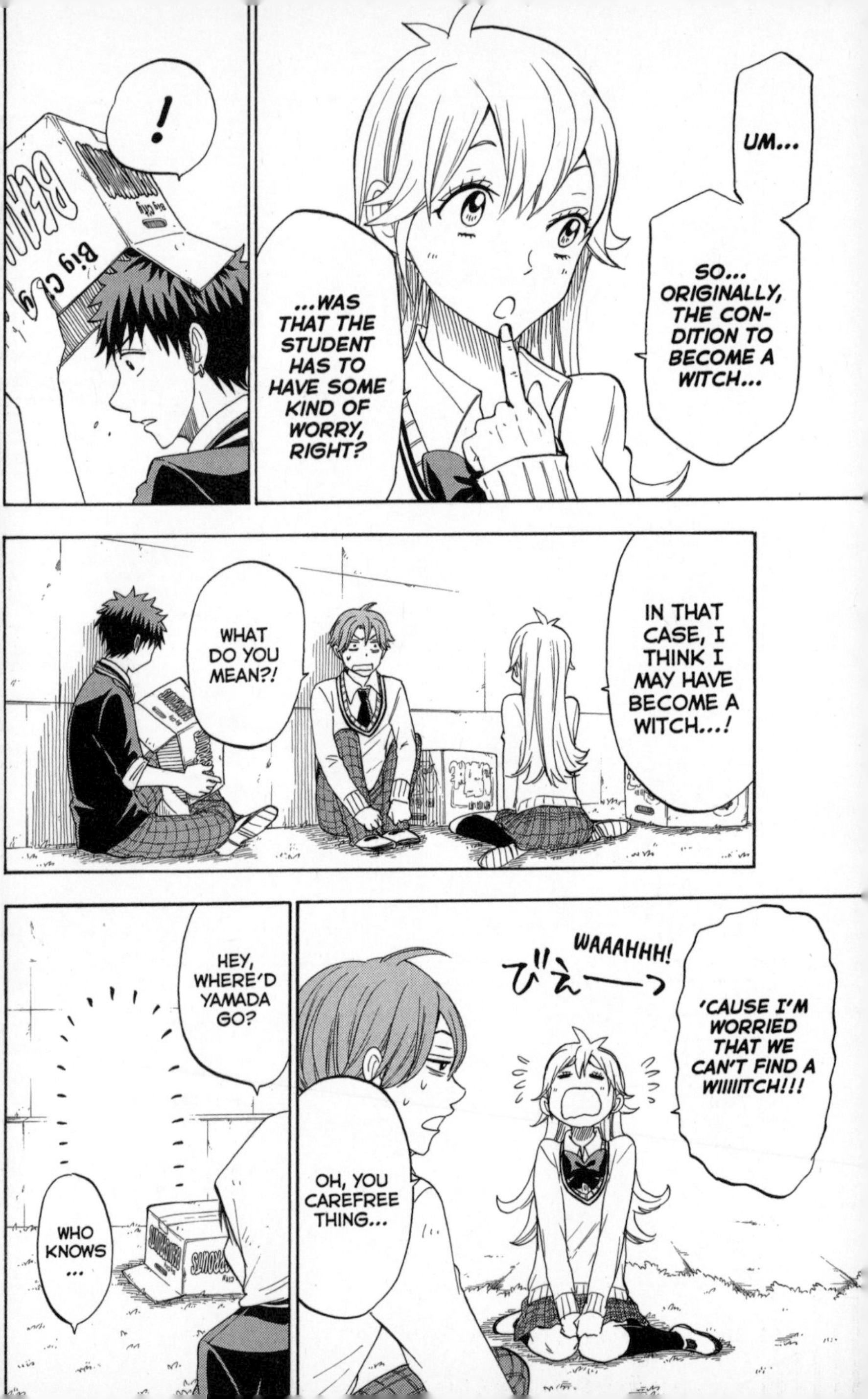
UM...
SO... ORIGINALLY, THE CON-DITION TO BECOME A WITCH...
...WAS THAT THE STUDENT HAS TO HAVE SOME KIND OF WORRY, RIGHT?
!
IN THAT CASE, I THINK I MAY HAVE BECOME A WITCH...!
WHAT DO YOU MEAN?!
WAAAHHH!
びえ〜っ
'CAUSE I'M WORRIED THAT WE CAN'T FIND A WIIIIITCH!!!
OH, YOU CAREFREE THING...
HEY, WHERE'D YAMADA GO?
WHO KNOWS...

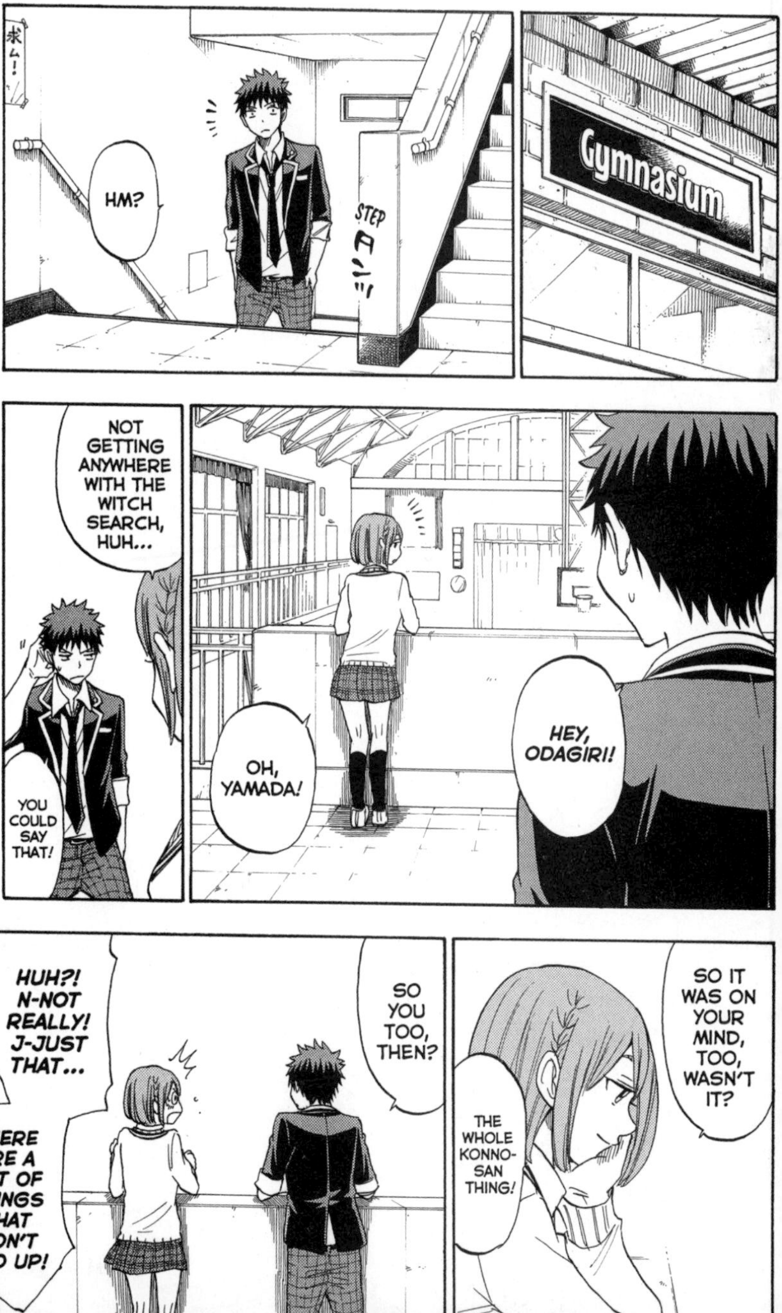

Gymnasium
HM?
STEP
HEY, ODAGIRI!
OH, YAMADA!
NOT GETTING ANYWHERE WITH THE WITCH SEARCH, HUH...
YOU COULD SAY THAT!
SO IT WAS ON YOUR MIND, TOO, WASN'T IT?
THE WHOLE KONNO-SAN THING!
SO YOU TOO, THEN?
HUH?! N-NOT REALLY! J-JUST THAT...
THERE ARE A LOT OF THINGS THAT DON'T ADD UP!

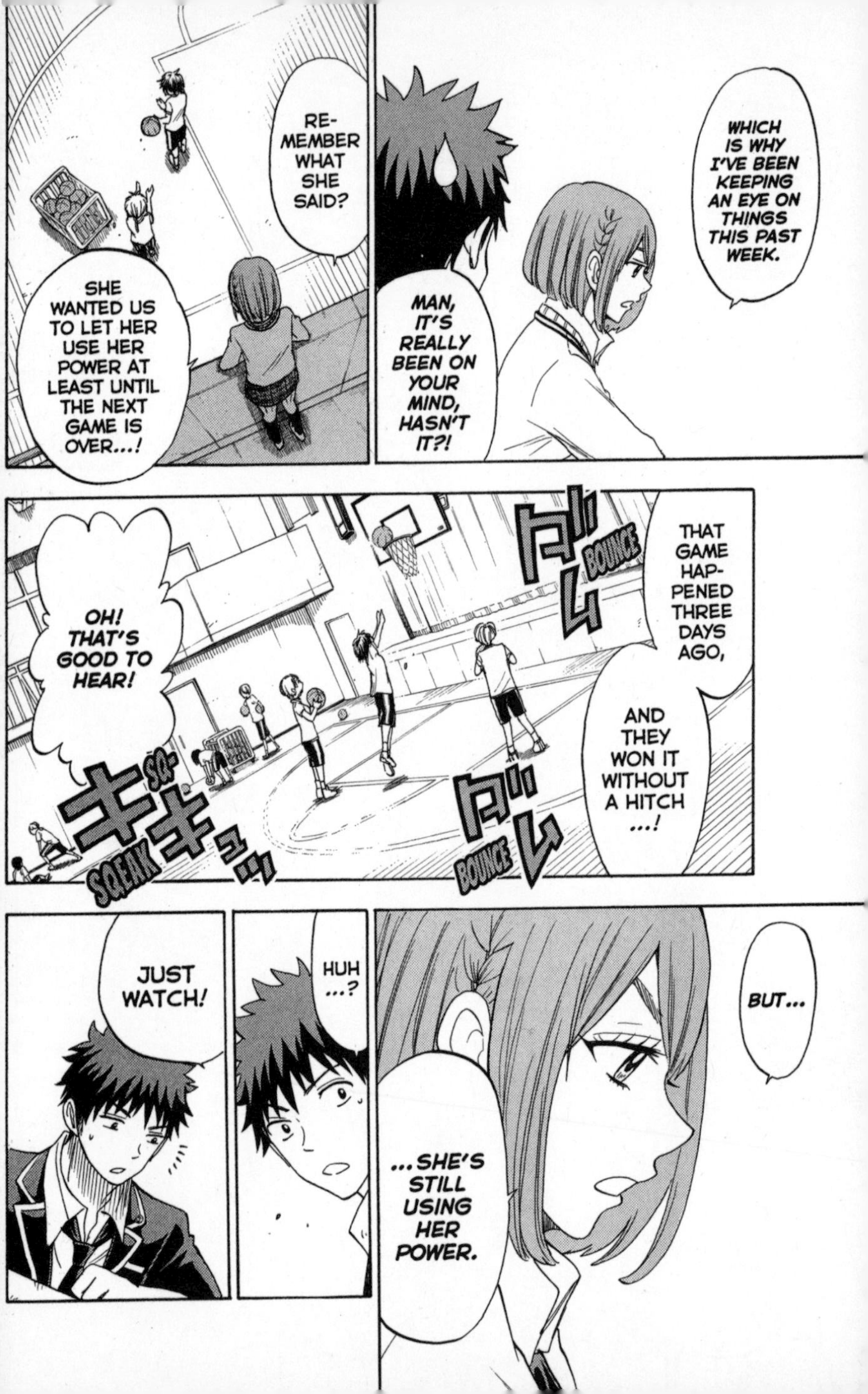
WHICH IS WHY I'VE BEEN KEEPING AN EYE ON THINGS THIS PAST WEEK.
MAN, IT'S REALLY BEEN ON YOUR MIND, HASN'T IT?!
RE-MEMBER WHAT SHE SAID?
SHE WANTED US TO LET HER USE HER POWER AT LEAST UNTIL THE NEXT GAME IS OVER...!
THAT GAME HAP-PENED THREE DAYS AGO,
AND THEY WON IT WITHOUT A HITCH ...!
BOUNCE
BOUNCE
OH! THAT'S GOOD TO HEAR!
SQ-SQEAK
BUT...
...SHE'S STILL USING HER POWER.
HUH ...?
JUST WATCH!

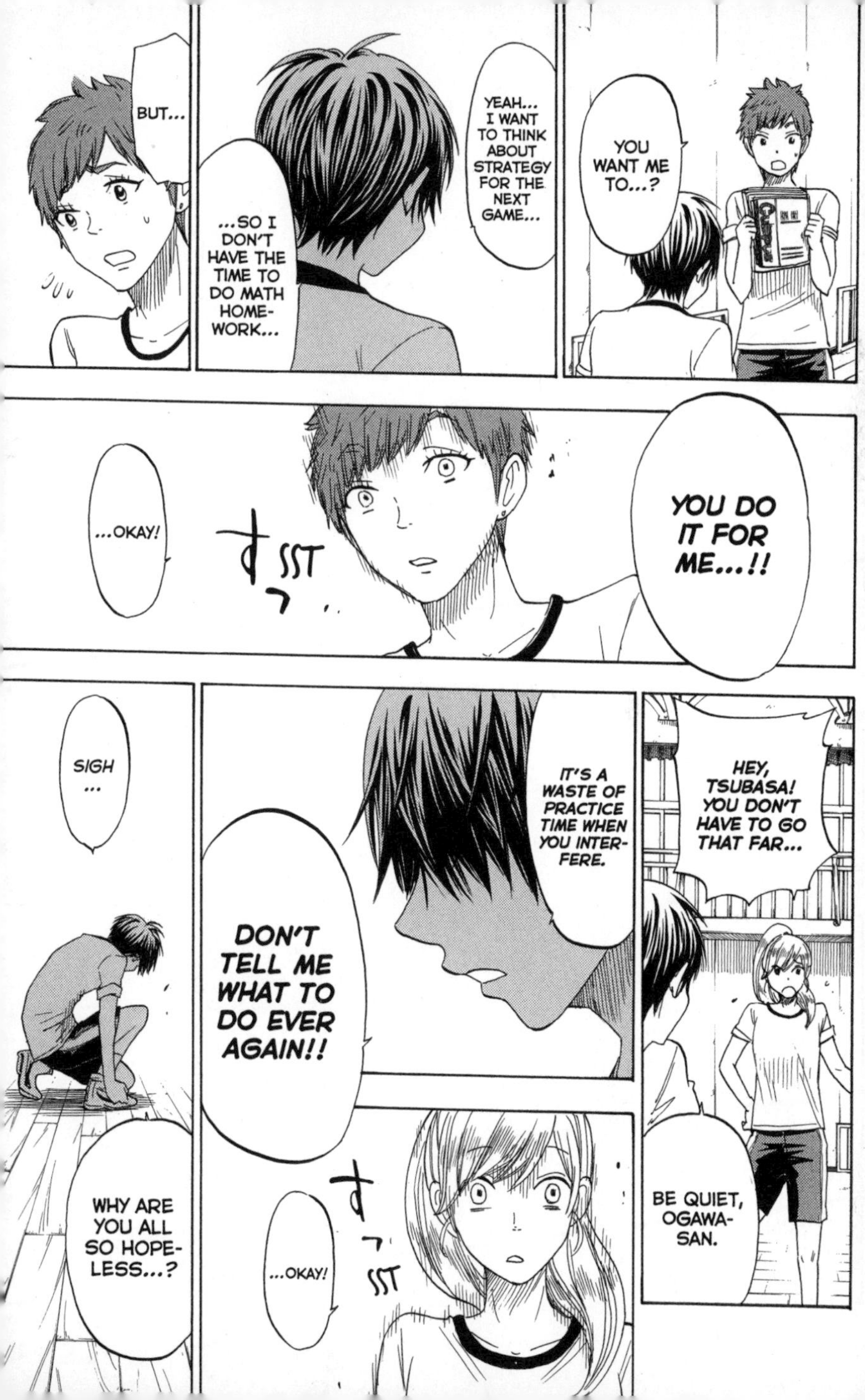
YOU WANT ME TO...?
YEAH... I WANT TO THINK ABOUT STRATEGY FOR THE NEXT GAME...
...SO I DON'T HAVE THE TIME TO DO MATH HOMEWORK...
BUT...
YOU DO IT FOR ME...!!
SST
...OKAY!
HEY, TSUBASA! YOU DON'T HAVE TO GO THAT FAR...
BE QUIET, OGAWA-SAN.
IT'S A WASTE OF PRACTICE TIME WHEN YOU INTERFERE.
DON'T TELL ME WHAT TO DO EVER AGAIN!!
SST
...OKAY!
SIGH...
WHY ARE YOU ALL SO HOPELESS...?

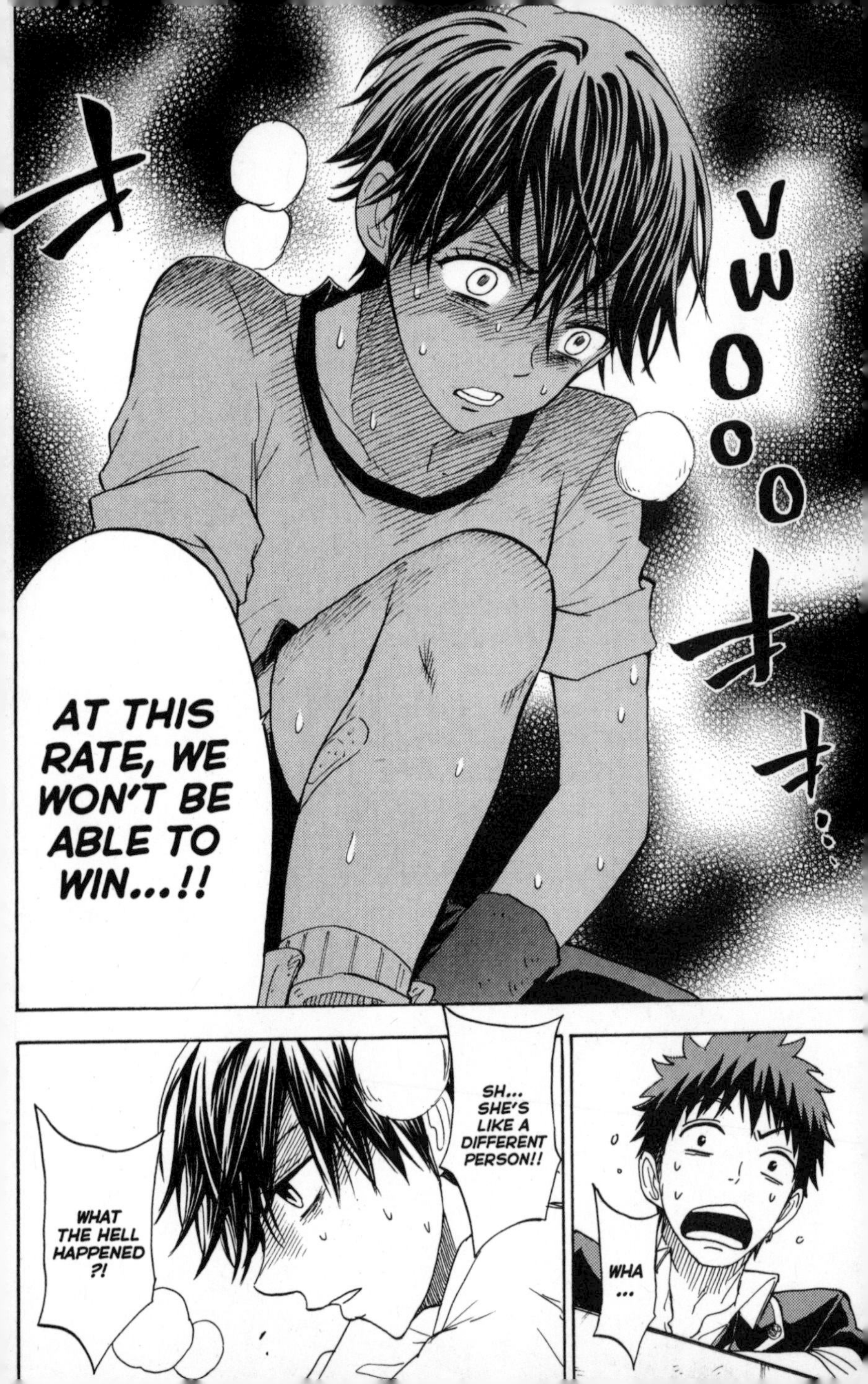
VWOOOO
AT THIS RATE, WE WON'T BE ABLE TO WIN...!!
WHA...
SH... SHE'S LIKE A DIFFERENT PERSON!!
WHAT THE HELL HAPPENED?!

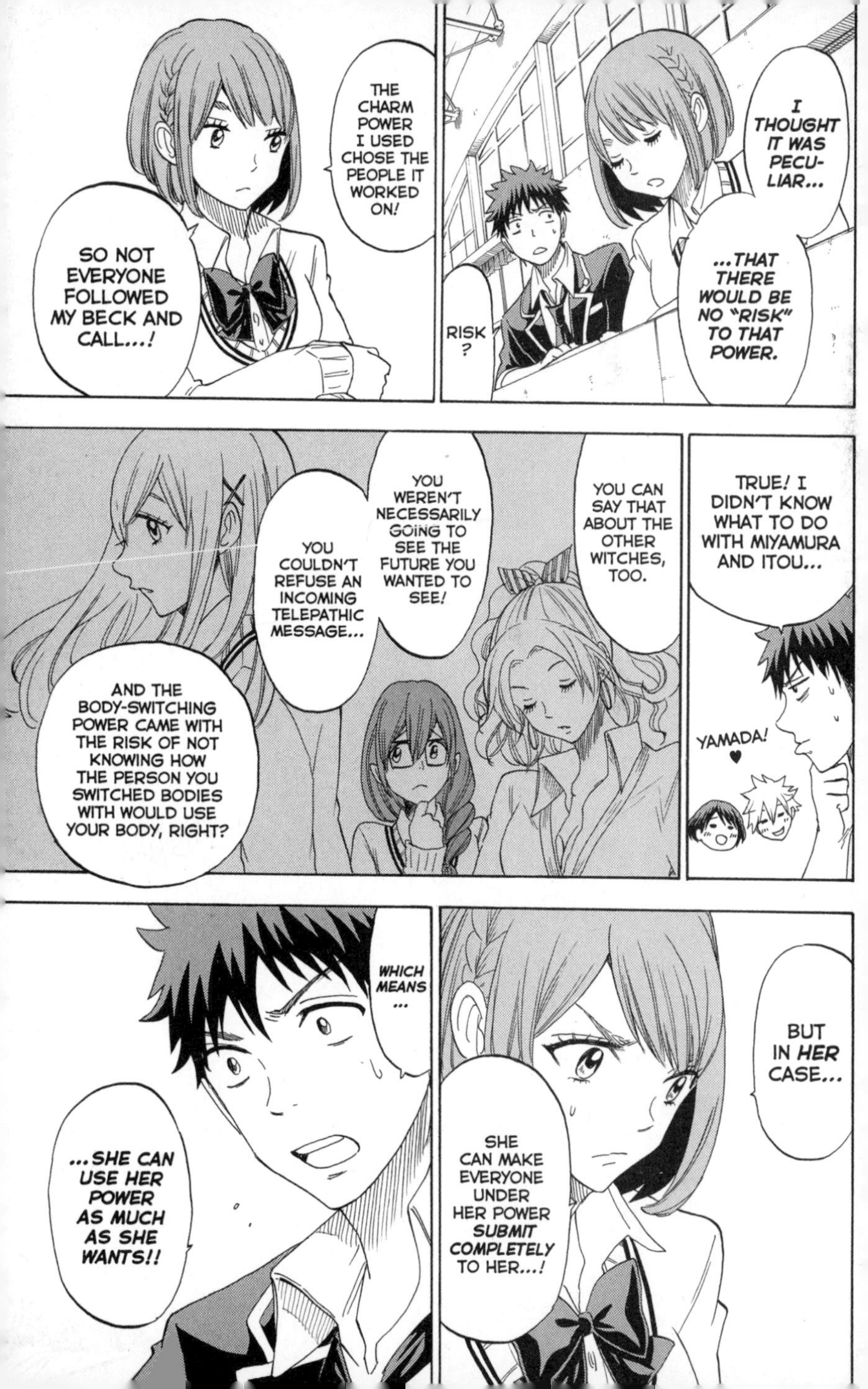

I THOUGHT IT WAS PECULIAR...
...THAT THERE WOULD BE NO "RISK" TO THAT POWER.
RISK?
THE CHARM POWER I USED CHOSE THE PEOPLE IT WORKED ON!
SO NOT EVERYONE FOLLOWED MY BECK AND CALL...!
TRUE! I DIDN'T KNOW WHAT TO DO WITH MIYAMURA AND ITOU...
YAMADA! ♥
YOU CAN SAY THAT ABOUT THE OTHER WITCHES, TOO.
YOU WEREN'T NECESSARILY GOING TO SEE THE FUTURE YOU WANTED TO SEE!
YOU COULDN'T REFUSE AN INCOMING TELEPATHIC MESSAGE...
AND THE BODY-SWITCHING POWER CAME WITH THE RISK OF NOT KNOWING HOW THE PERSON YOU SWITCHED BODIES WITH WOULD USE YOUR BODY, RIGHT?
BUT IN HER CASE...
SHE CAN MAKE EVERYONE UNDER HER POWER SUBMIT COMPLETELY TO HER...!
WHICH MEANS...
...SHE CAN USE HER POWER AS MUCH AS SHE WANTS!!

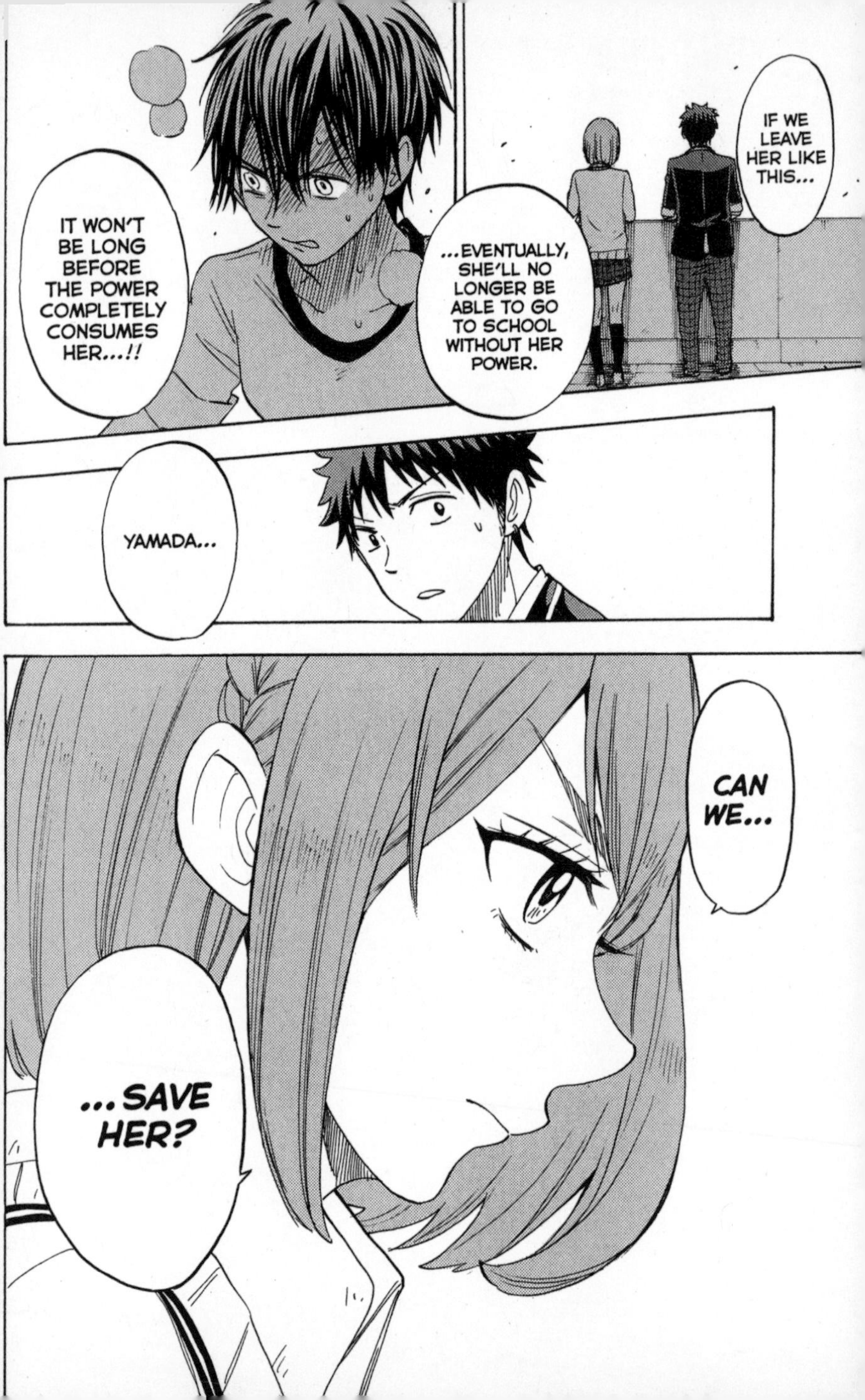
IF WE LEAVE HER LIKE THIS...
...EVENTUALLY, SHE'LL NO LONGER BE ABLE TO GO TO SCHOOL WITHOUT HER POWER.
IT WON'T BE LONG BEFORE THE POWER COMPLETELY CONSUMES HER...!!
YAMADA...
CAN WE...
...SAVE HER?

CHAPTER 100: Really pissed off.

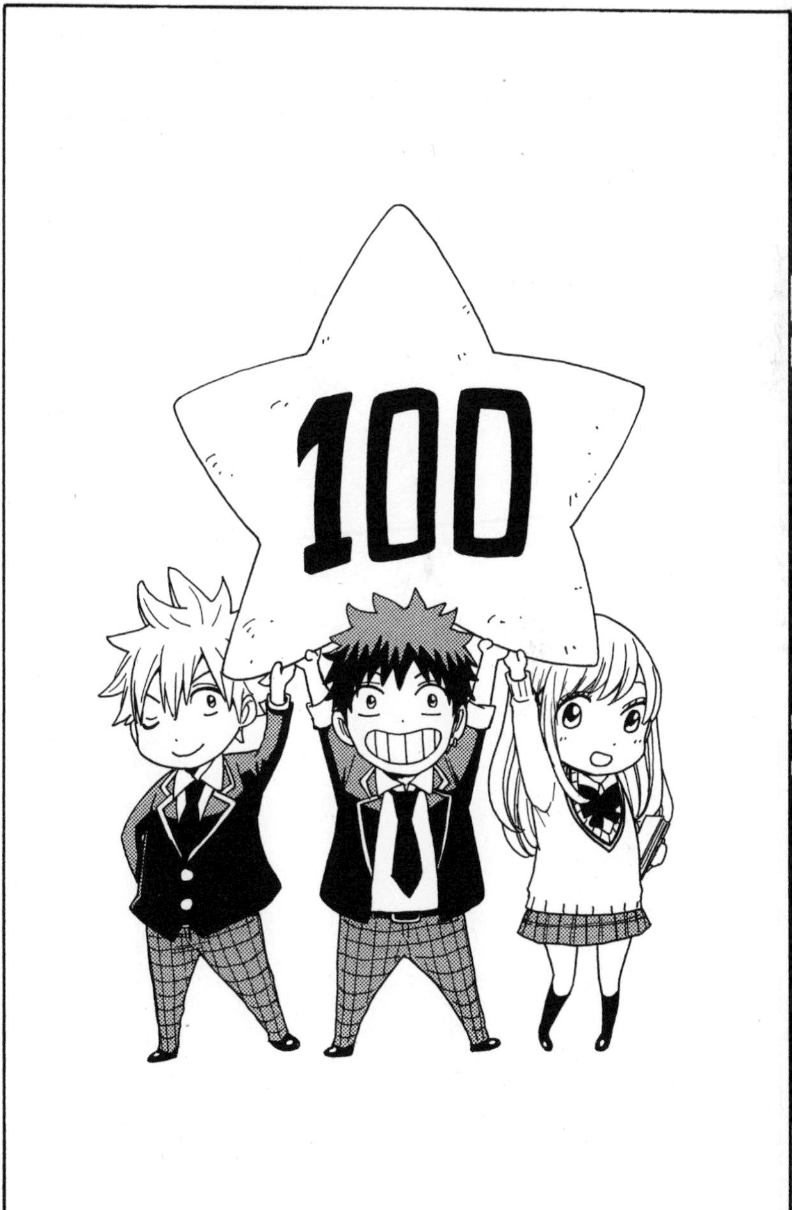

100

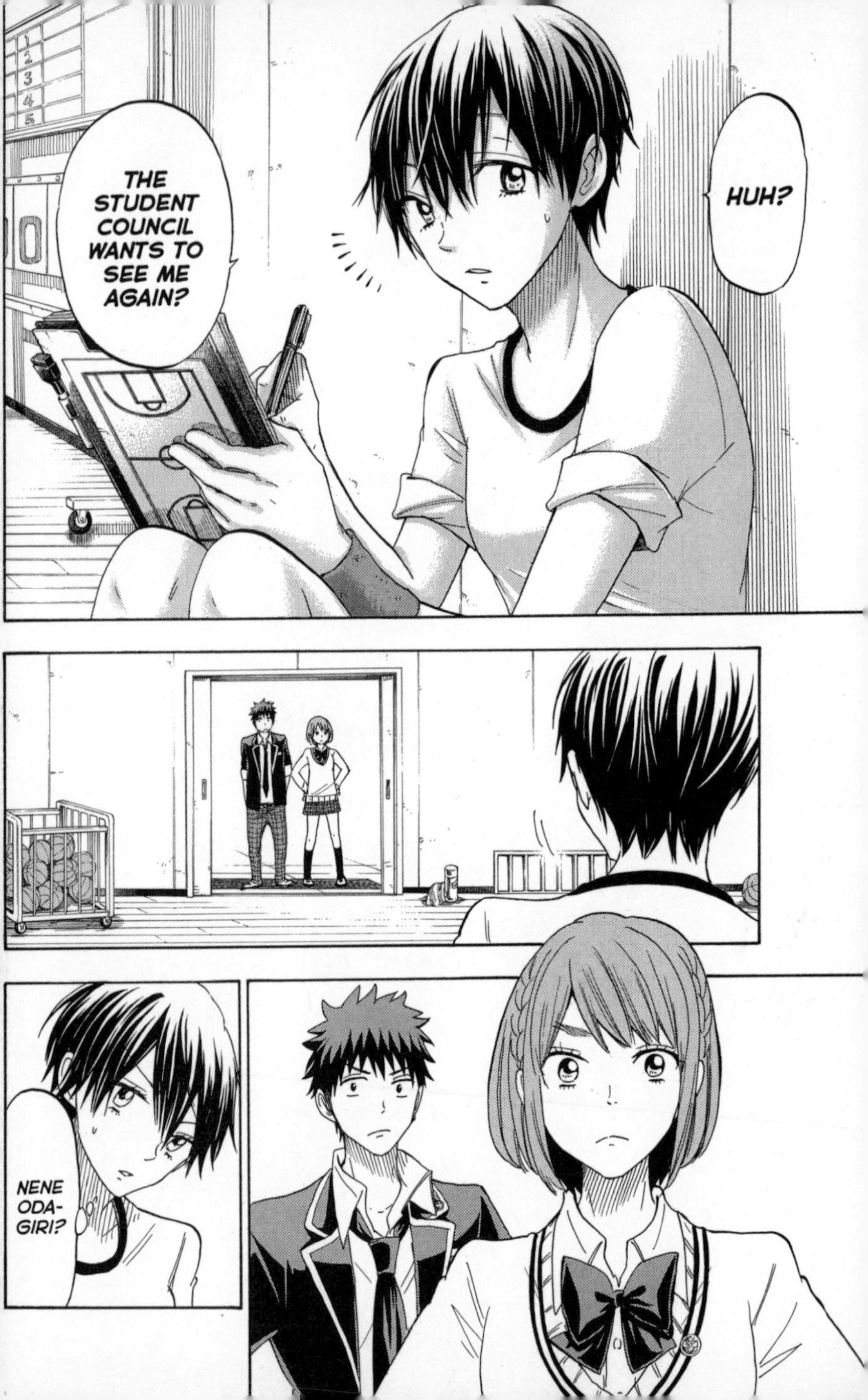
HUH?
THE STUDENT COUNCIL WANTS TO SEE ME AGAIN?
NENE ODA-GIRI?

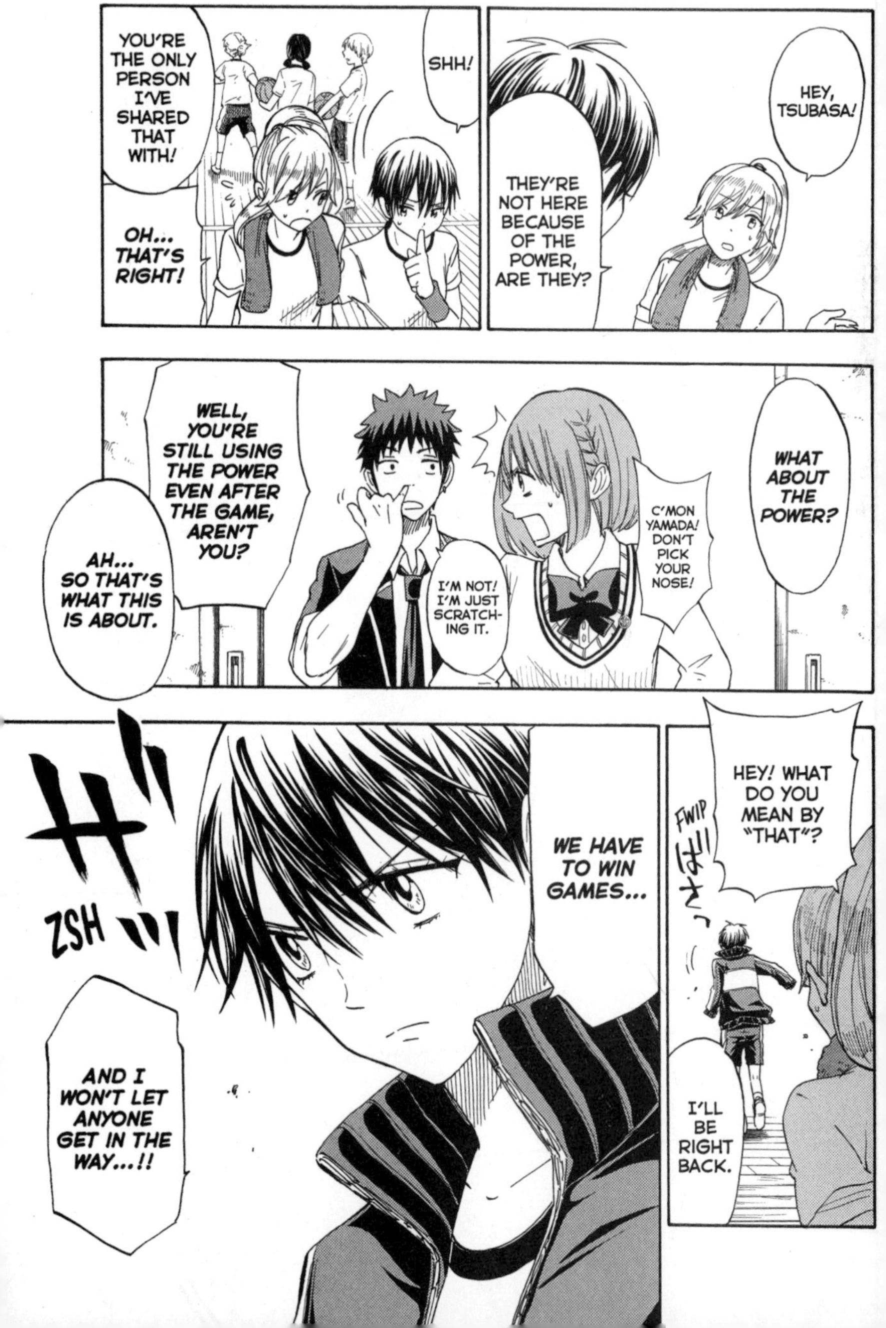
HEY, TSUBASA!
THEY'RE NOT HERE BECAUSE OF THE POWER, ARE THEY?
SHH!
YOU'RE THE ONLY PERSON I'VE SHARED THAT WITH!
OH... THAT'S RIGHT!
WHAT ABOUT THE POWER?
C'MON YAMADA! DON'T PICK YOUR NOSE!
I'M NOT! I'M JUST SCRATCHING IT.
WELL, YOU'RE STILL USING THE POWER EVEN AFTER THE GAME, AREN'T YOU?
AH... SO THAT'S WHAT THIS IS ABOUT.
HEY! WHAT DO YOU MEAN BY "THAT"?
FWIP
ばさっ
I'LL BE RIGHT BACK.
WE HAVE TO WIN GAMES...
ザッ
ZSH
AND I WON'T LET ANYONE GET IN THE WAY...!!

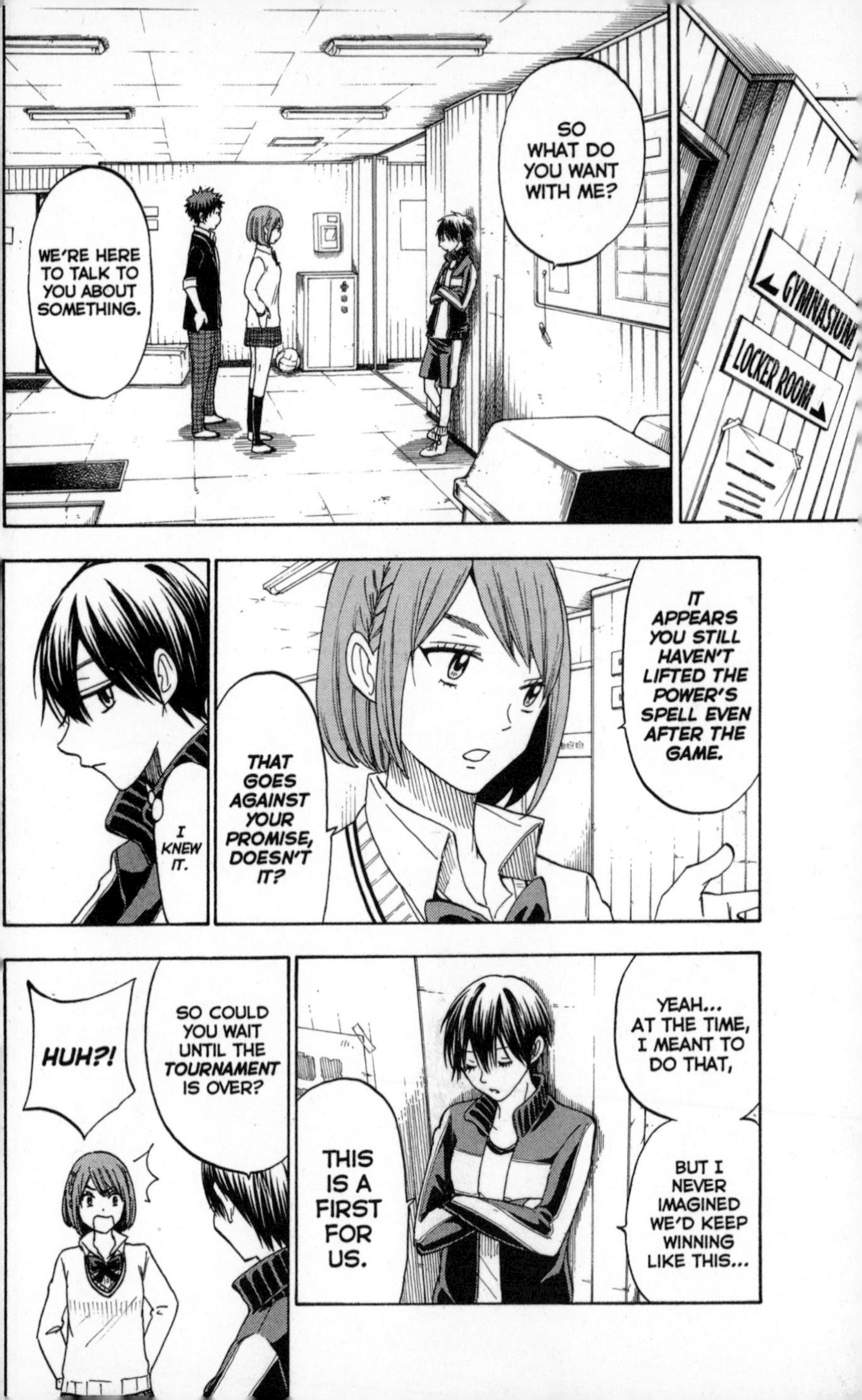
GYMNASIUM
LOCKER ROOM
SO WHAT DO YOU WANT WITH ME?
WE'RE HERE TO TALK TO YOU ABOUT SOMETHING.
IT APPEARS YOU STILL HAVEN'T LIFTED THE POWER'S SPELL EVEN AFTER THE GAME.
THAT GOES AGAINST YOUR PROMISE, DOESN'T IT?
I KNEW IT.
YEAH... AT THE TIME, I MEANT TO DO THAT,
BUT I NEVER IMAGINED WE'D KEEP WINNING LIKE THIS...
THIS IS A FIRST FOR US.
SO COULD YOU WAIT UNTIL THE TOURNAMENT IS OVER?
HUH?!

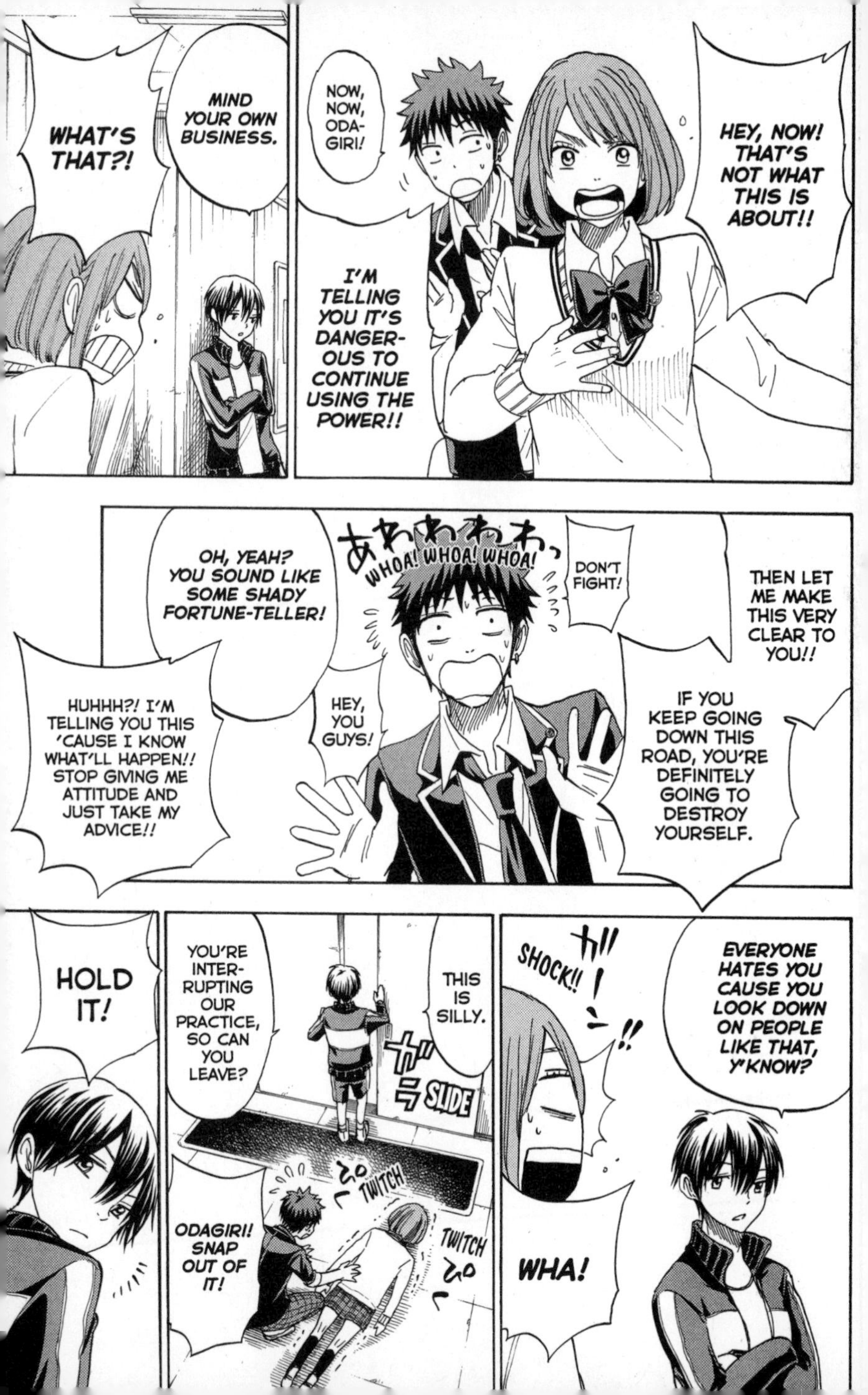
HEY, NOW! THAT'S NOT WHAT THIS IS ABOUT!!
NOW, NOW, ODA-GIRI!
I'M TELLING YOU IT'S DANGER-OUS TO CONTINUE USING THE POWER!!
MIND YOUR OWN BUSINESS.
WHAT'S THAT?!
THEN LET ME MAKE THIS VERY CLEAR TO YOU!!
IF YOU KEEP GOING DOWN THIS ROAD, YOU'RE DEFINITELY GOING TO DESTROY YOURSELF.
DON'T FIGHT!
あわわわわっ
WHOA! WHOA! WHOA!
OH, YEAH? YOU SOUND LIKE SOME SHADY FORTUNE-TELLER!
HEY, YOU GUYS!
HUHHH?! I'M TELLING YOU THIS 'CAUSE I KNOW WHAT'LL HAPPEN!! STOP GIVING ME ATTITUDE AND JUST TAKE MY ADVICE!!
EVERYONE HATES YOU CAUSE YOU LOOK DOWN ON PEOPLE LIKE THAT, Y'KNOW?
SHOCK!!
WHA!
THIS IS SILLY.
SLIDE
YOU'RE INTER-RUPTING OUR PRACTICE, SO CAN YOU LEAVE?
TWITCH
TWITCH
ODAGIRI! SNAP OUT OF IT!
HOLD IT!

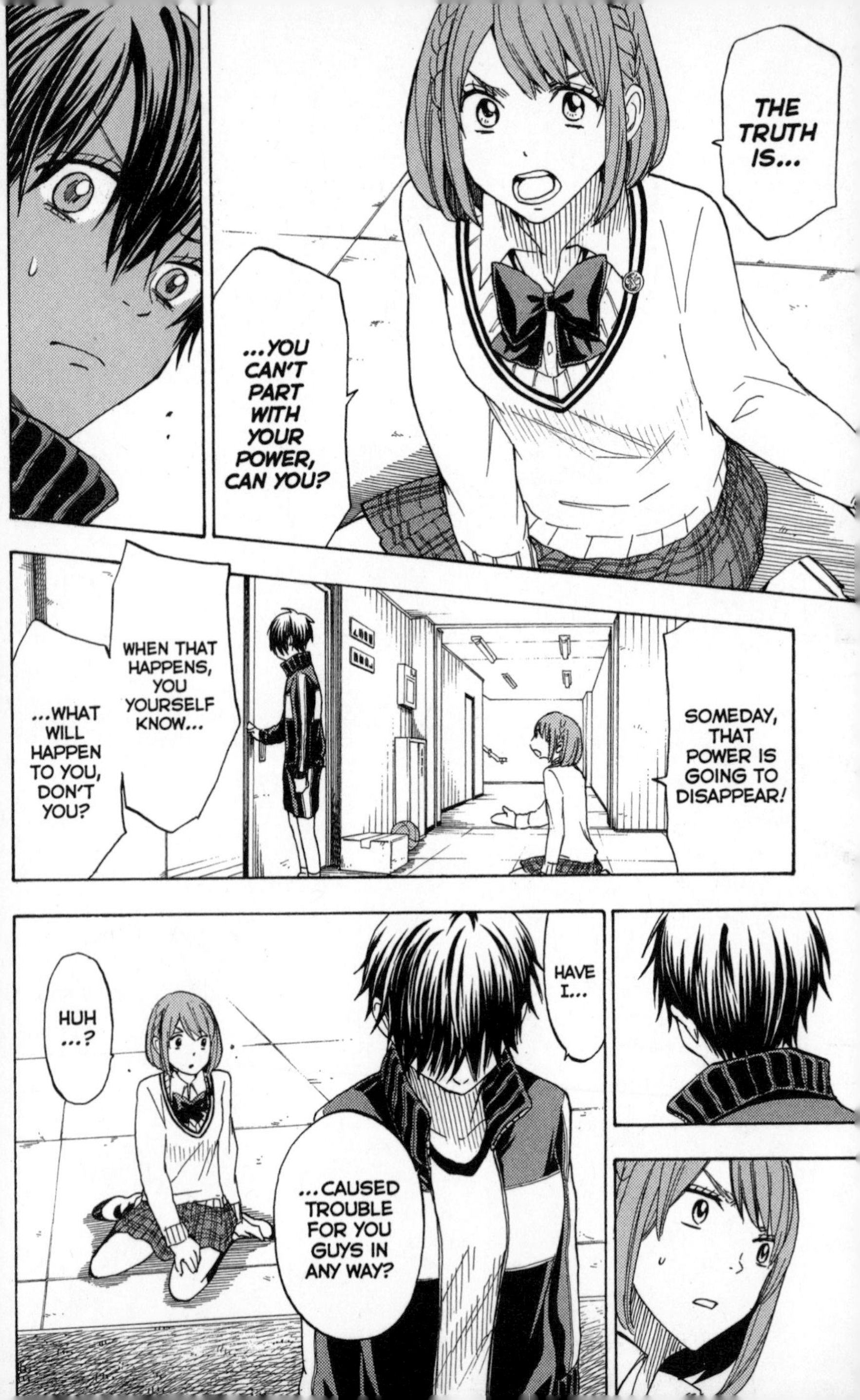
THE TRUTH IS...
...YOU CAN'T PART WITH YOUR POWER, CAN YOU?
SOMEDAY, THAT POWER IS GOING TO DISAPPEAR!
WHEN THAT HAPPENS, YOU YOURSELF KNOW...
...WHAT WILL HAPPEN TO YOU, DON'T YOU?
HAVE I...
...CAUSED TROUBLE FOR YOU GUYS IN ANY WAY?
HUH ...?

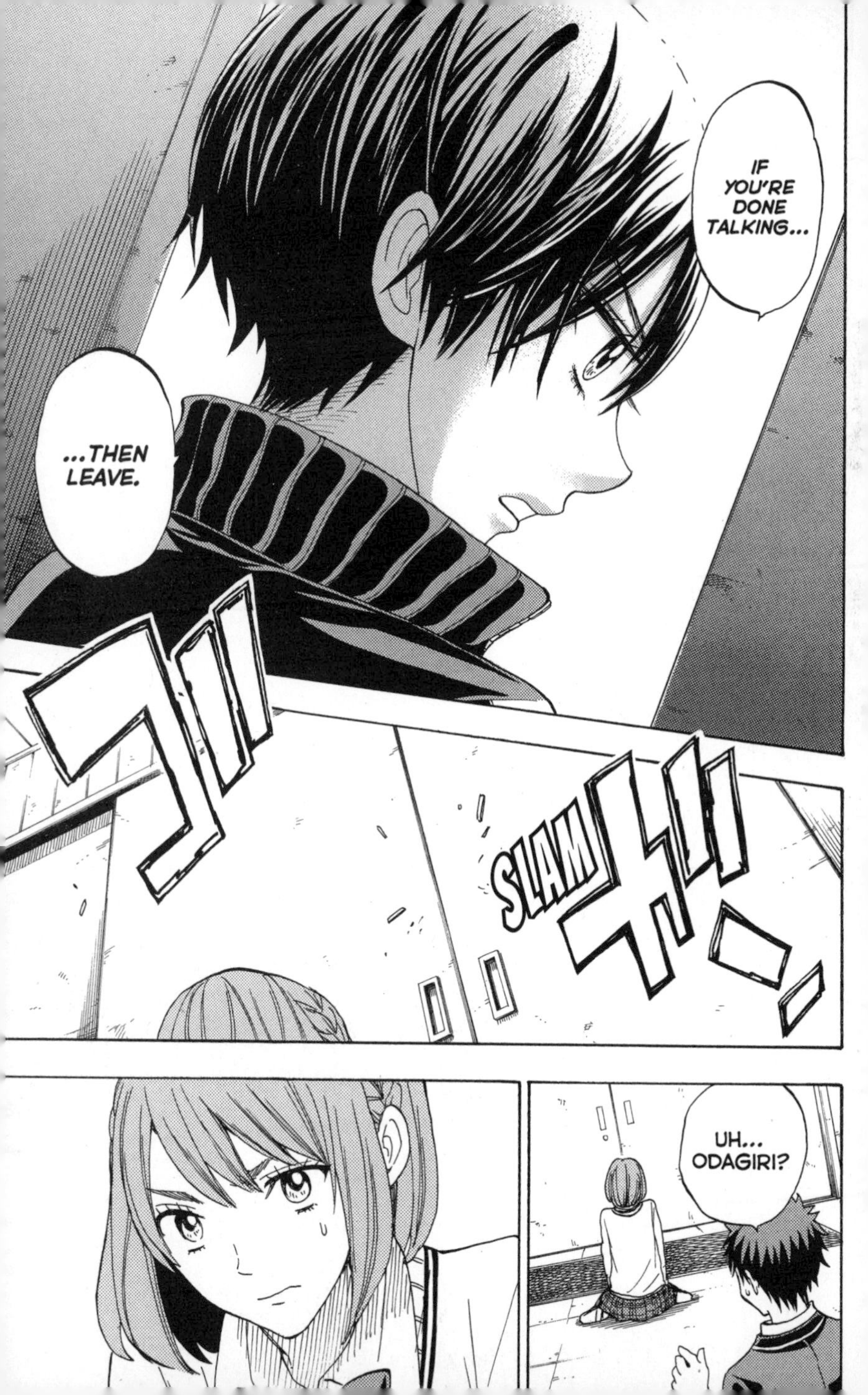
IF YOU'RE DONE TALKING...
...THEN LEAVE.
SLAM
UH... ODAGIRI?

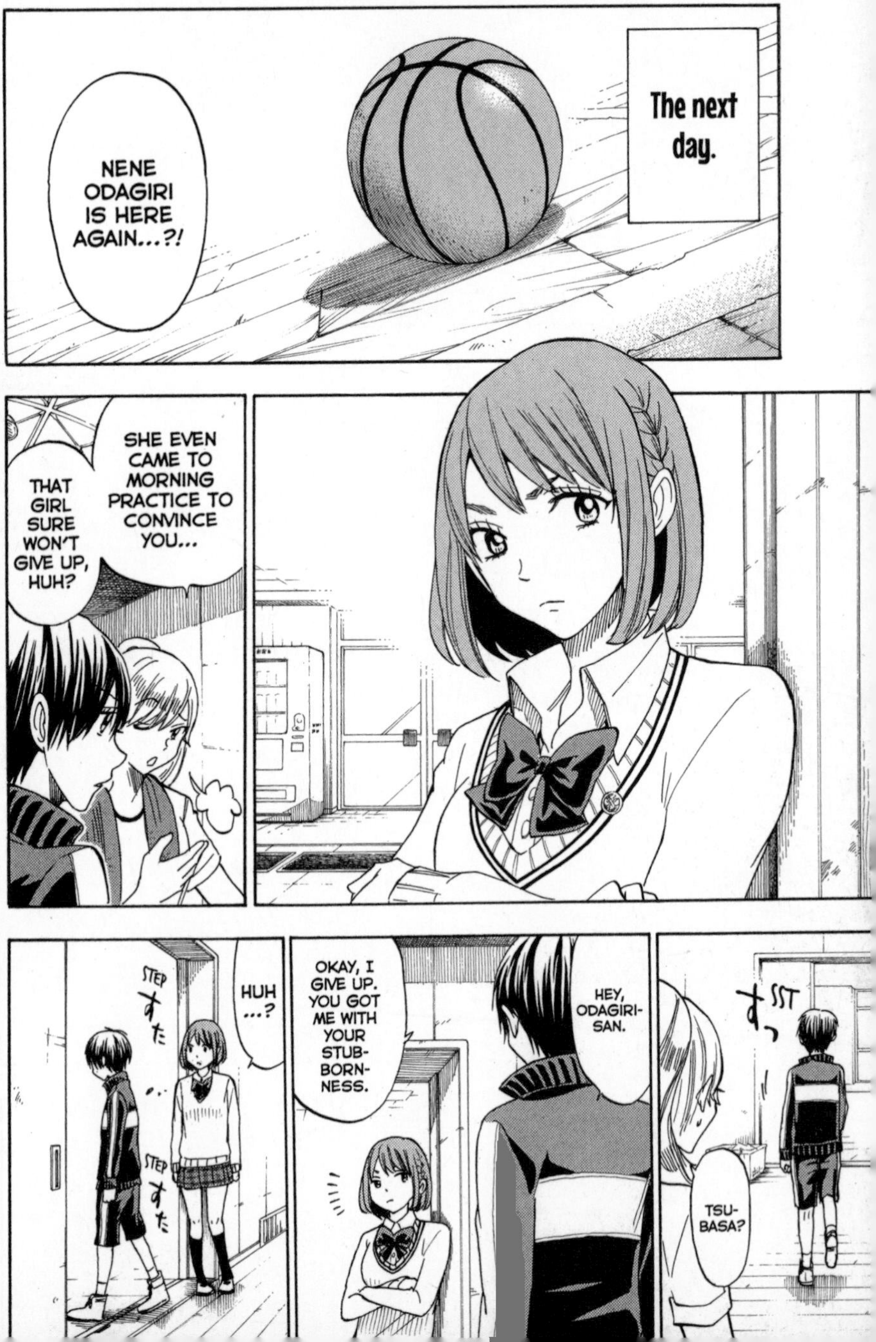
The next day.
NENE ODAGIRI IS HERE AGAIN...?!
SHE EVEN CAME TO MORNING PRACTICE TO CONVINCE YOU...
THAT GIRL SURE WON'T GIVE UP, HUH?
すっ SST
TSU-BASA?
HEY, ODAGIRI-SAN.
OKAY, I GIVE UP. YOU GOT ME WITH YOUR STUBBORNNESS.
HUH ...?
STEP すた
STEP すた

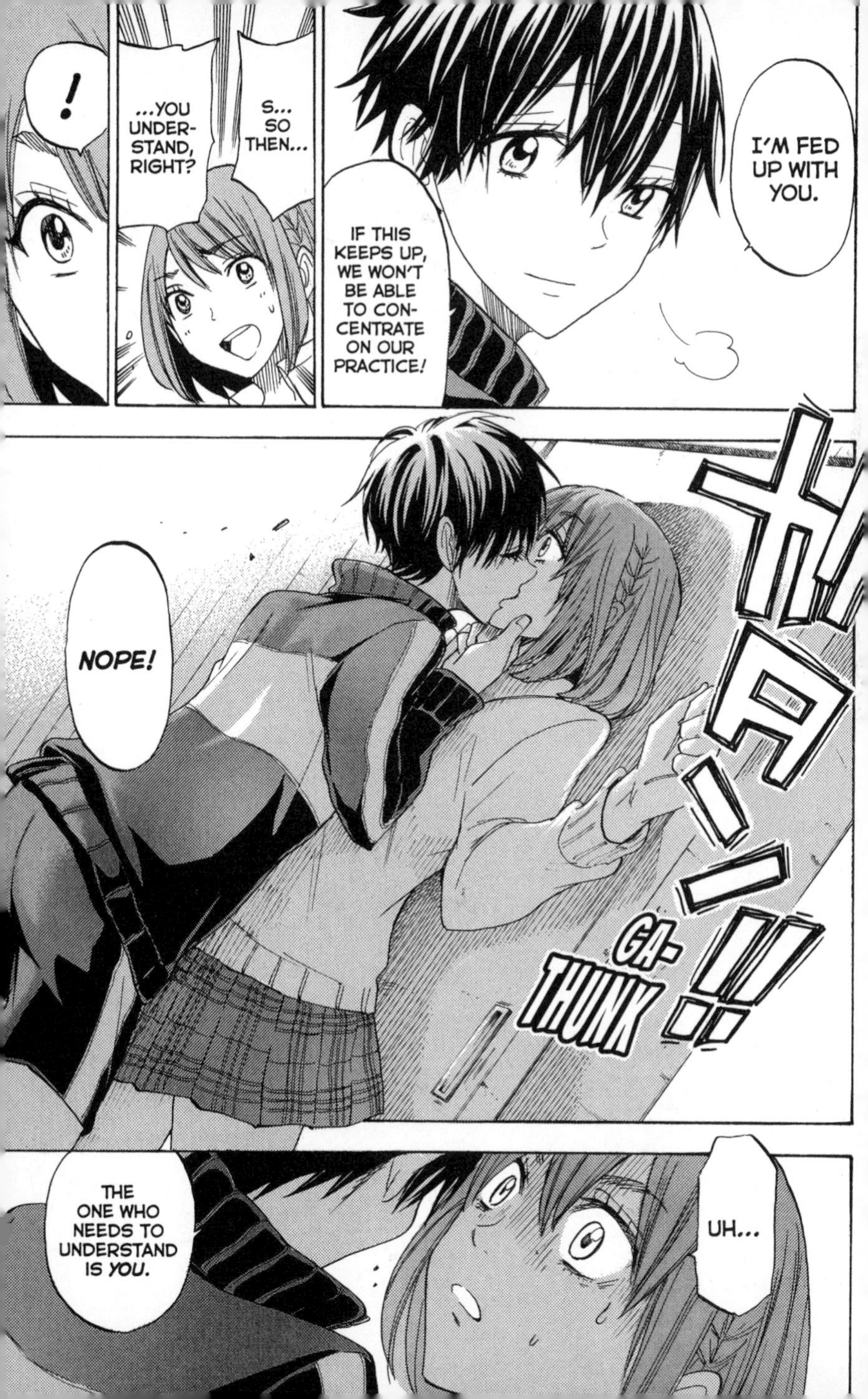
I'M FED UP WITH YOU.
IF THIS KEEPS UP, WE WON'T BE ABLE TO CONCENTRATE ON OUR PRACTICE!
S... SO THEN...
...YOU UNDERSTAND, RIGHT?
!
GA-THUNK
NOPE!
UH...
THE ONE WHO NEEDS TO UNDERSTAND IS *YOU*.

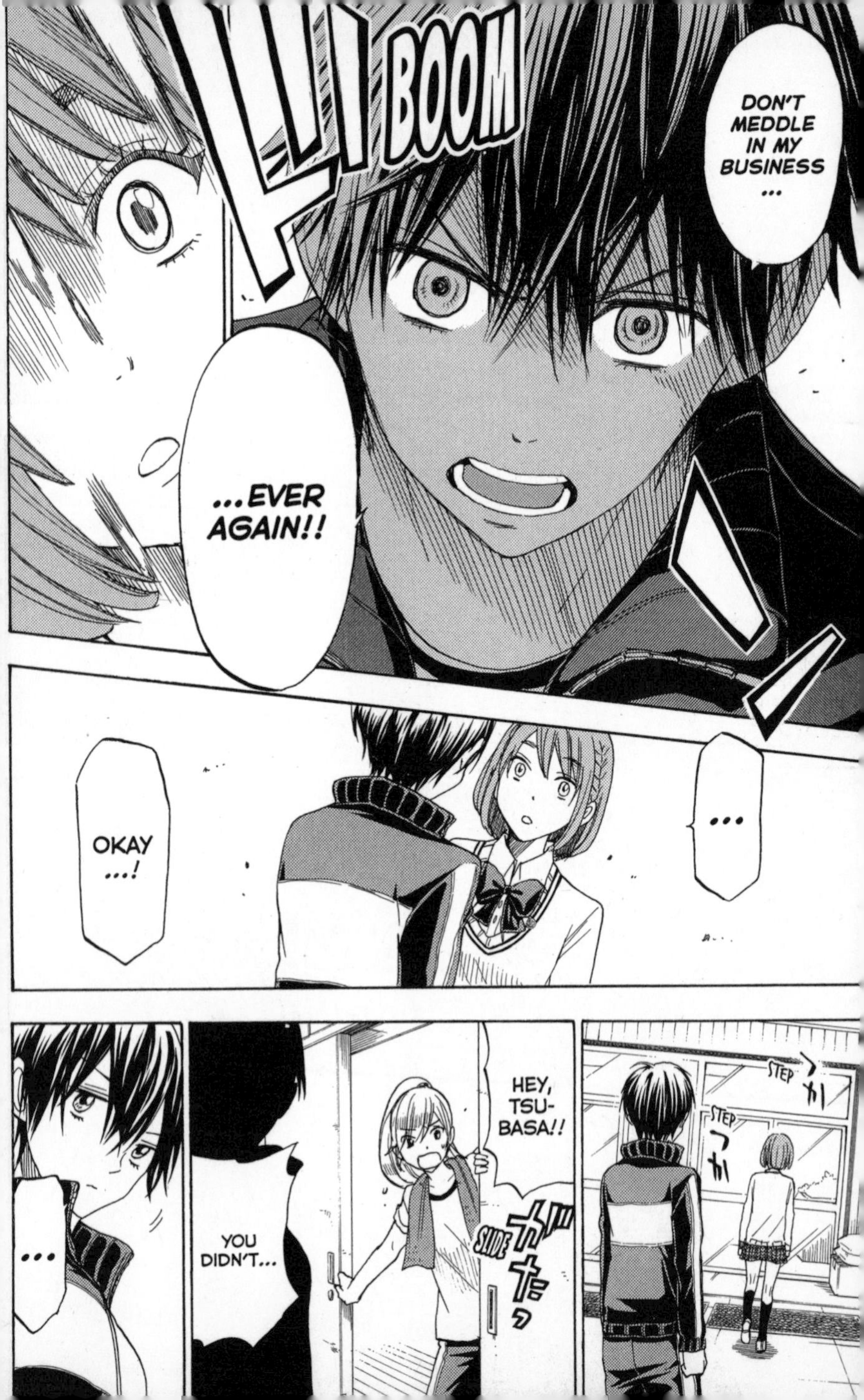
BOOM
DON'T MEDDLE IN MY BUSINESS ...
...EVER AGAIN!!
...
OKAY ...!
STEP
STEP
HEY, TSU-BASA!!
SLIDE
YOU DIDN'T...
...

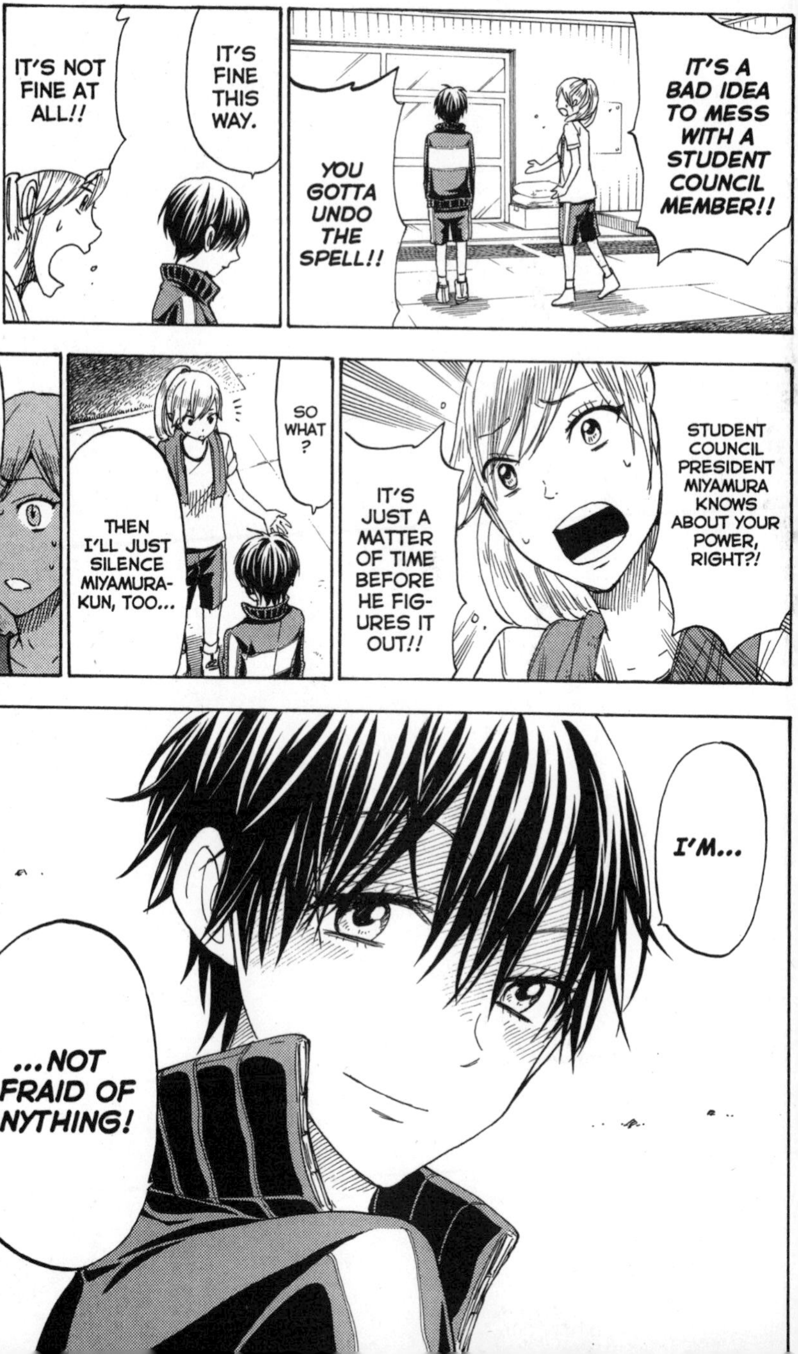
IT'S A BAD IDEA TO MESS WITH A STUDENT COUNCIL MEMBER!!
YOU GOTTA UNDO THE SPELL!!
IT'S FINE THIS WAY.
IT'S NOT FINE AT ALL!!
STUDENT COUNCIL PRESIDENT MIYAMURA KNOWS ABOUT YOUR POWER, RIGHT?!
IT'S JUST A MATTER OF TIME BEFORE HE FIGURES IT OUT!!
SO WHAT?
THEN I'LL JUST SILENCE MIYAMURA-KUN, TOO...
TSU-BASA...
I'M...
...NOT AFRAID OF ANYTHING!

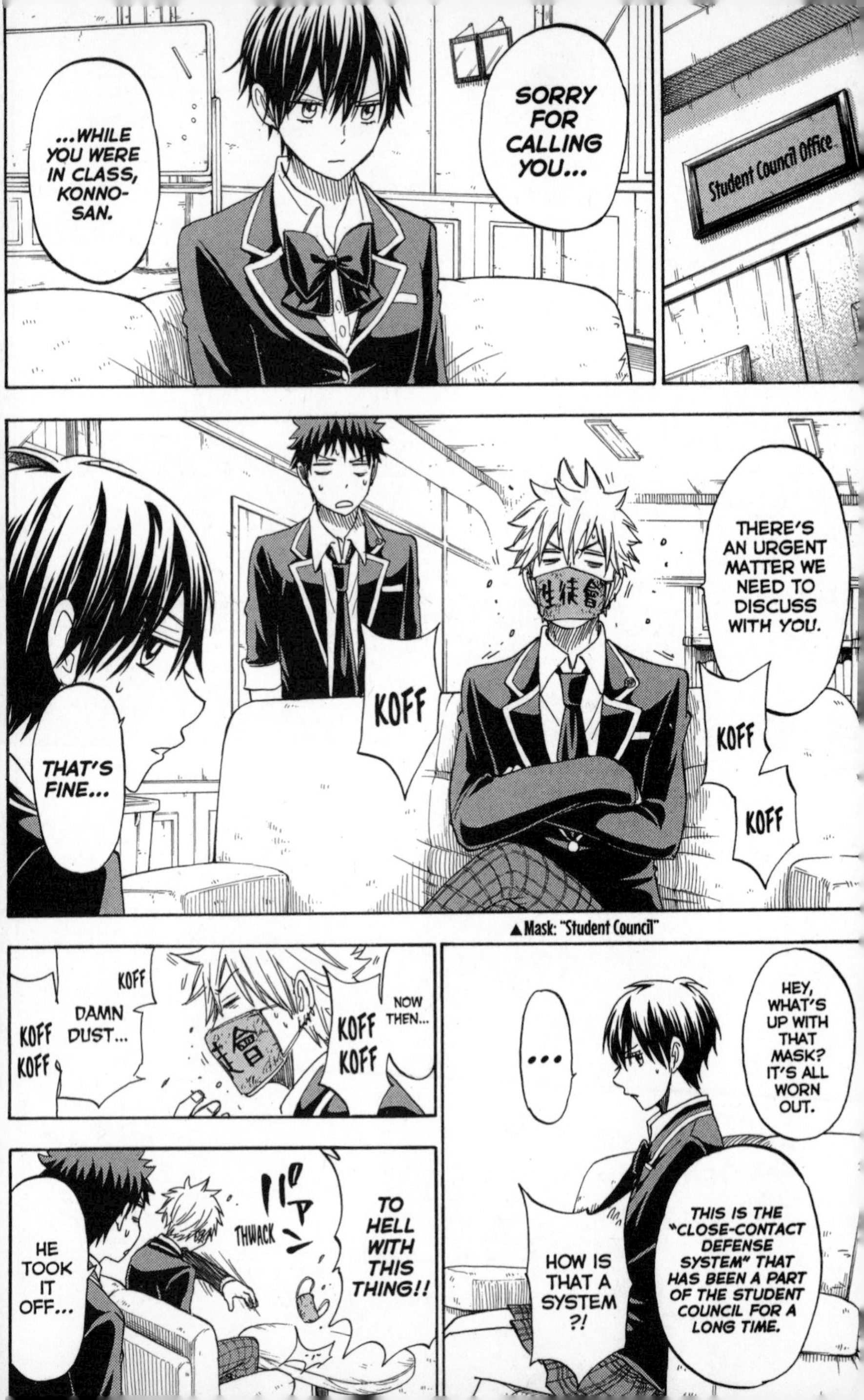
Student Council Office
SORRY FOR CALLING YOU...
...WHILE YOU WERE IN CLASS, KONNO-SAN.
THERE'S AN URGENT MATTER WE NEED TO DISCUSS WITH YOU.
KOFF
KOFF
生徒會
KOFF
THAT'S FINE...
▲Mask: "Student Council"
HEY, WHAT'S UP WITH THAT MASK? IT'S ALL WORN OUT.
...
NOW THEN...
KOFF KOFF
KOFF
DAMN DUST...
KOFF KOFF
THIS IS THE "CLOSE-CONTACT DEFENSE SYSTEM" THAT HAS BEEN A PART OF THE STUDENT COUNCIL FOR A LONG TIME.
HOW IS THAT A SYSTEM?!
TO HELL WITH THIS THING!!
パァン
THWACK
HE TOOK IT OFF...

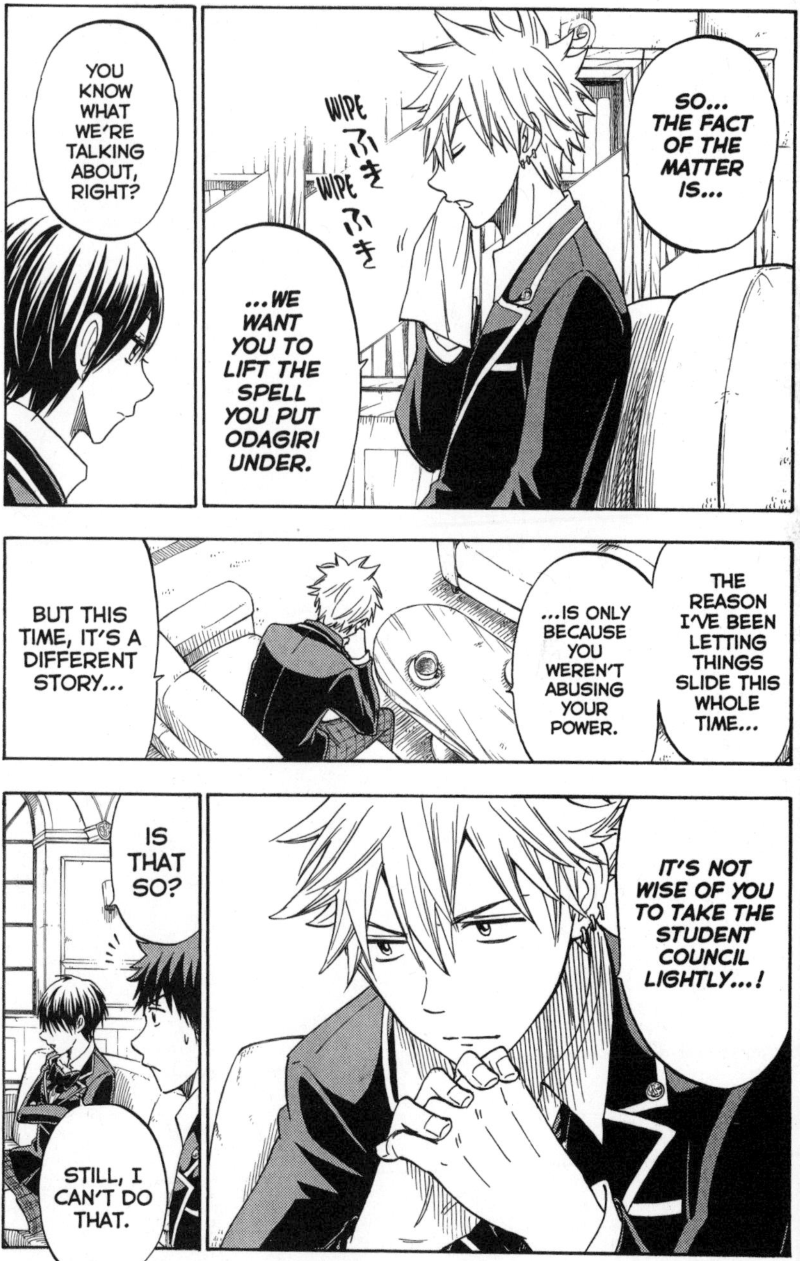
SO... THE FACT OF THE MATTER IS...
WIPE ふき
WIPE ふき
...WE WANT YOU TO LIFT THE SPELL YOU PUT ODAGIRI UNDER.
YOU KNOW WHAT WE'RE TALKING ABOUT, RIGHT?
THE REASON I'VE BEEN LETTING THINGS SLIDE THIS WHOLE TIME...
...IS ONLY BECAUSE YOU WEREN'T ABUSING YOUR POWER.
BUT THIS TIME, IT'S A DIFFERENT STORY...
IT'S NOT WISE OF YOU TO TAKE THE STUDENT COUNCIL LIGHTLY...!
IS THAT SO?
STILL, I CAN'T DO THAT.

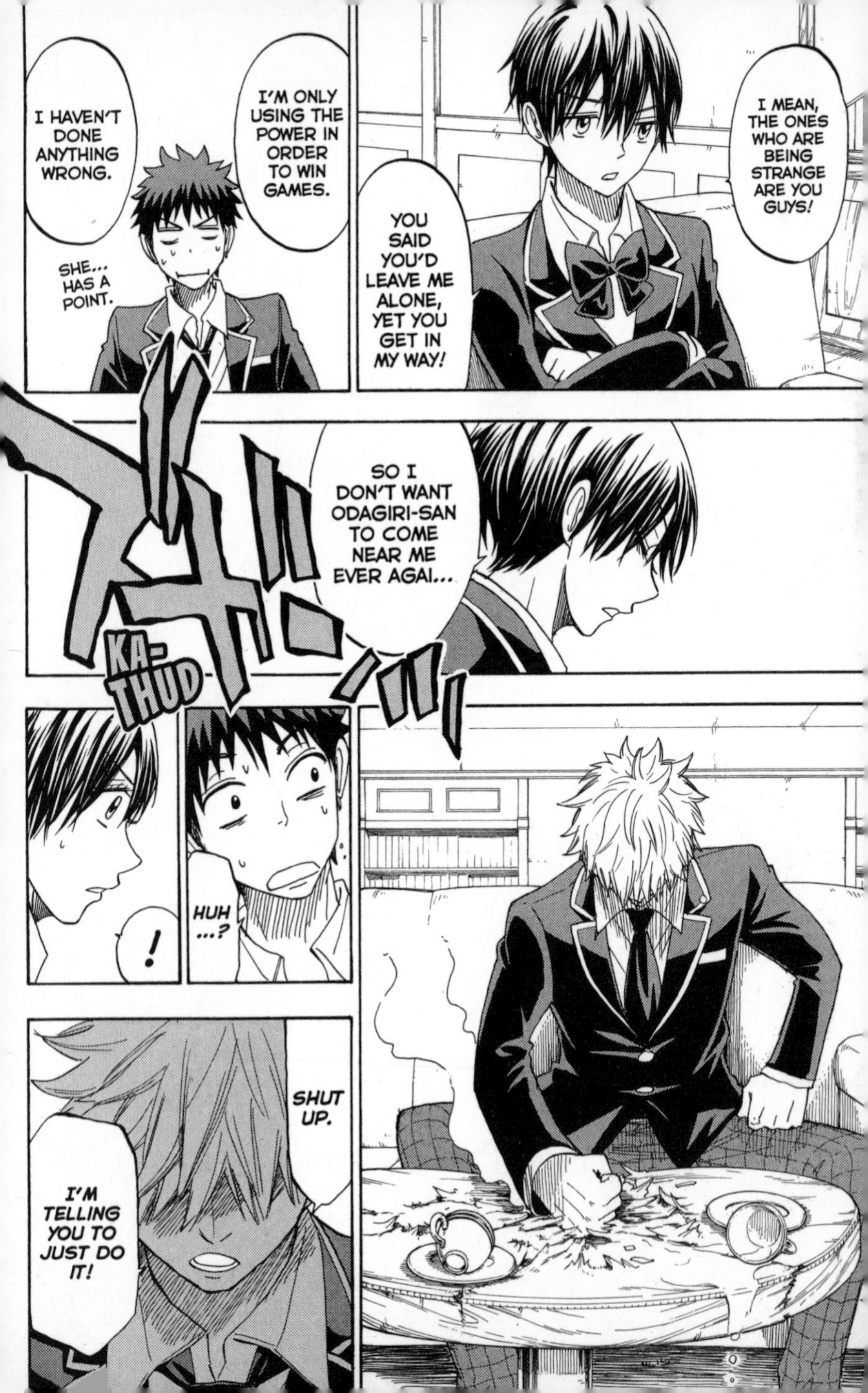
I MEAN, THE ONES WHO ARE BEING STRANGE ARE YOU GUYS!
YOU SAID YOU'D LEAVE ME ALONE, YET YOU GET IN MY WAY!
I'M ONLY USING THE POWER IN ORDER TO WIN GAMES.
I HAVEN'T DONE ANYTHING WRONG.
SHE... HAS A POINT.
SO I DON'T WANT ODAGIRI-SAN TO COME NEAR ME EVER AGAI...
KA-THUD
!
HUH ...?
SHUT UP.
I'M TELLING YOU TO JUST DO IT!

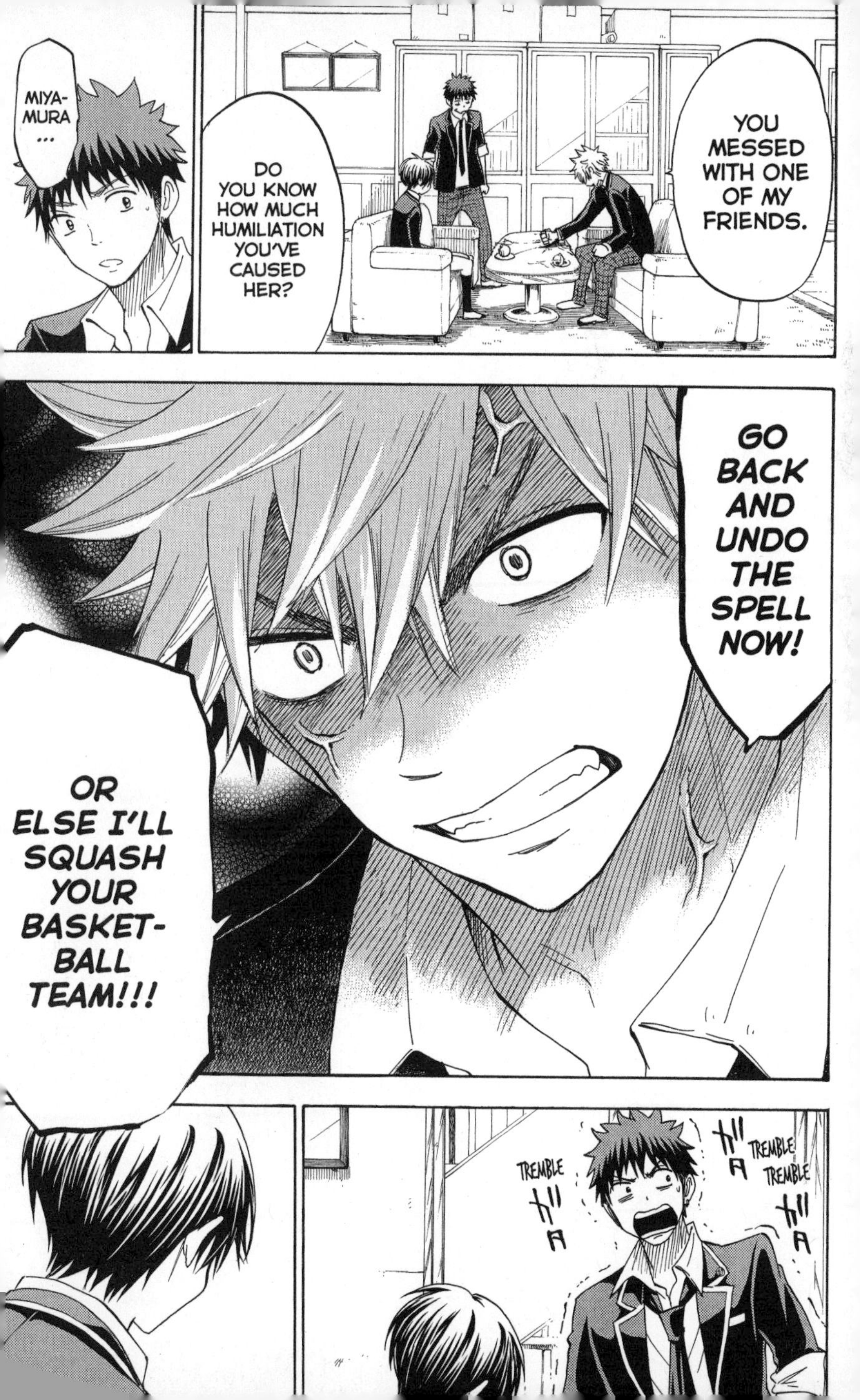
YOU MESSED WITH ONE OF MY FRIENDS.
DO YOU KNOW HOW MUCH HUMILIATION YOU'VE CAUSED HER?
MIYA-MURA ...
GO BACK AND UNDO THE SPELL NOW!
OR ELSE I'LL SQUASH YOUR BASKET-BALL TEAM!!!
TREMBLE TREMBLE
TREMBLE

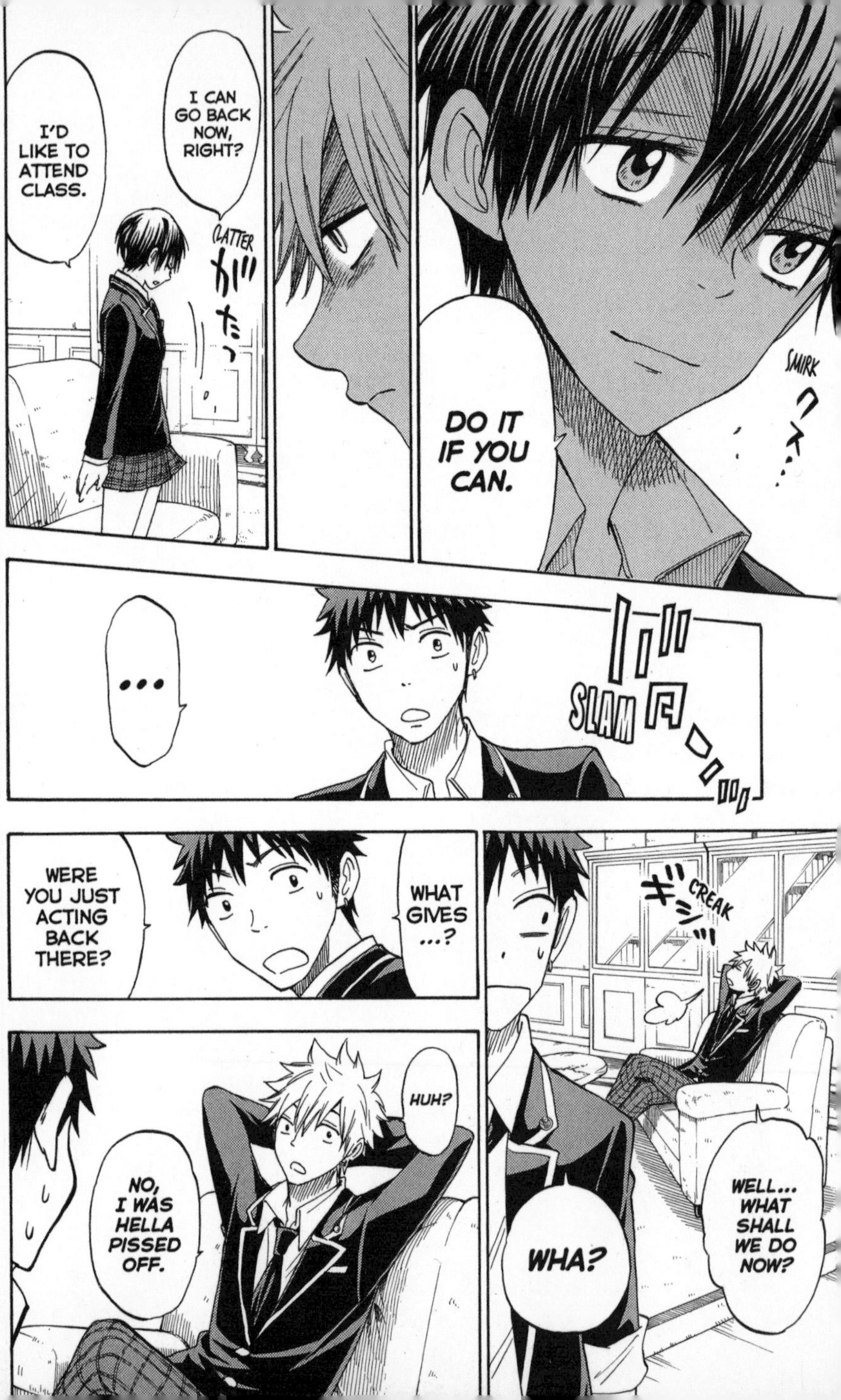

SMIRK
クスッ…
DO IT IF YOU CAN.
I CAN GO BACK NOW, RIGHT?
CLATTER
がたっ
I'D LIKE TO ATTEND CLASS.
SLAM
バタン
...
CREAK
ギシッ
WELL... WHAT SHALL WE DO NOW?
WHA?
WHAT GIVES ...?
WERE YOU JUST ACTING BACK THERE?
HUH?
NO, I WAS HELLA PISSED OFF.

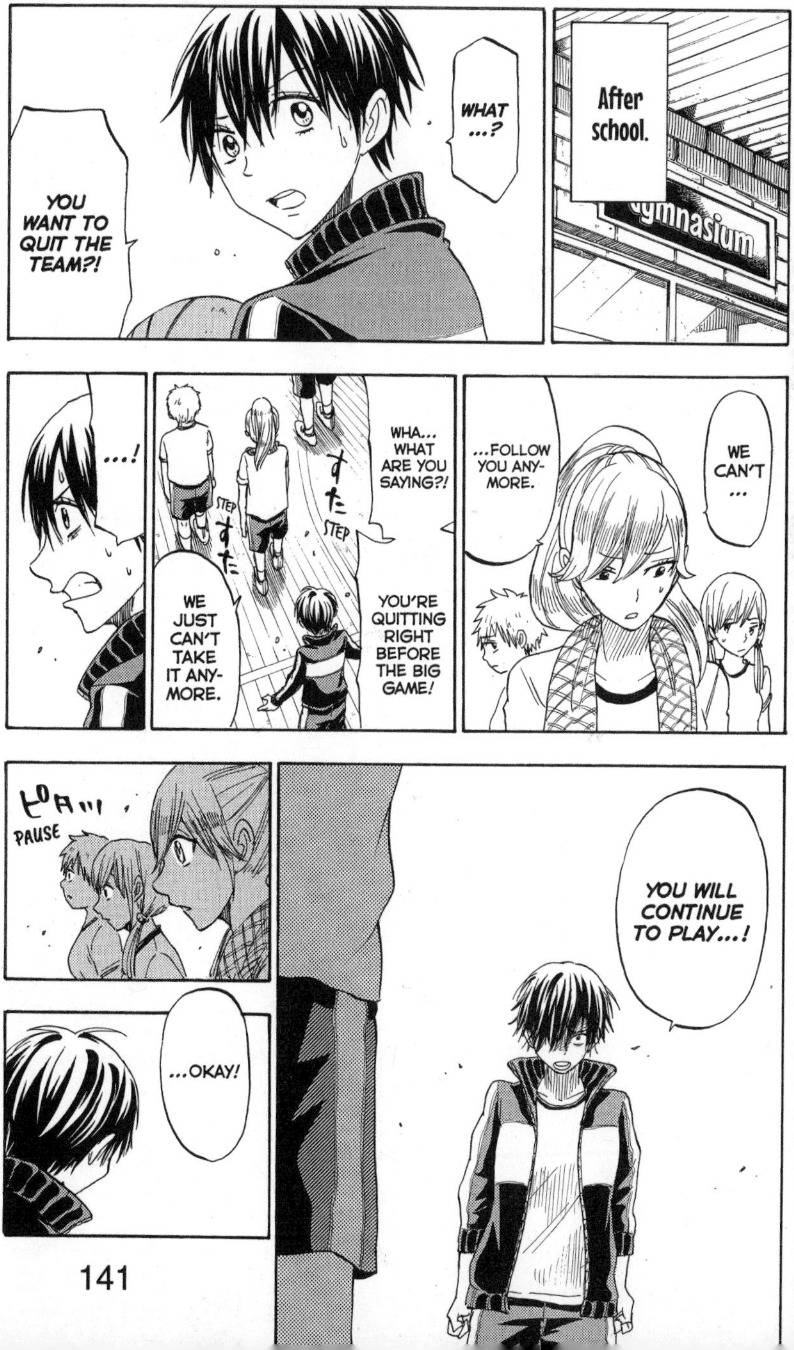
After school.
WHAT ...?
YOU WANT TO QUIT THE TEAM?!
WE CAN'T ...
...FOLLOW YOU ANY-MORE.
WHA... WHAT ARE YOU SAYING?!
YOU'RE QUITTING RIGHT BEFORE THE BIG GAME!
すた
STEP
すた
STEP
WE JUST CAN'T TAKE IT ANY-MORE.
...!
YOU WILL CONTINUE TO PLAY...!
ピタッ
PAUSE
...OKAY!

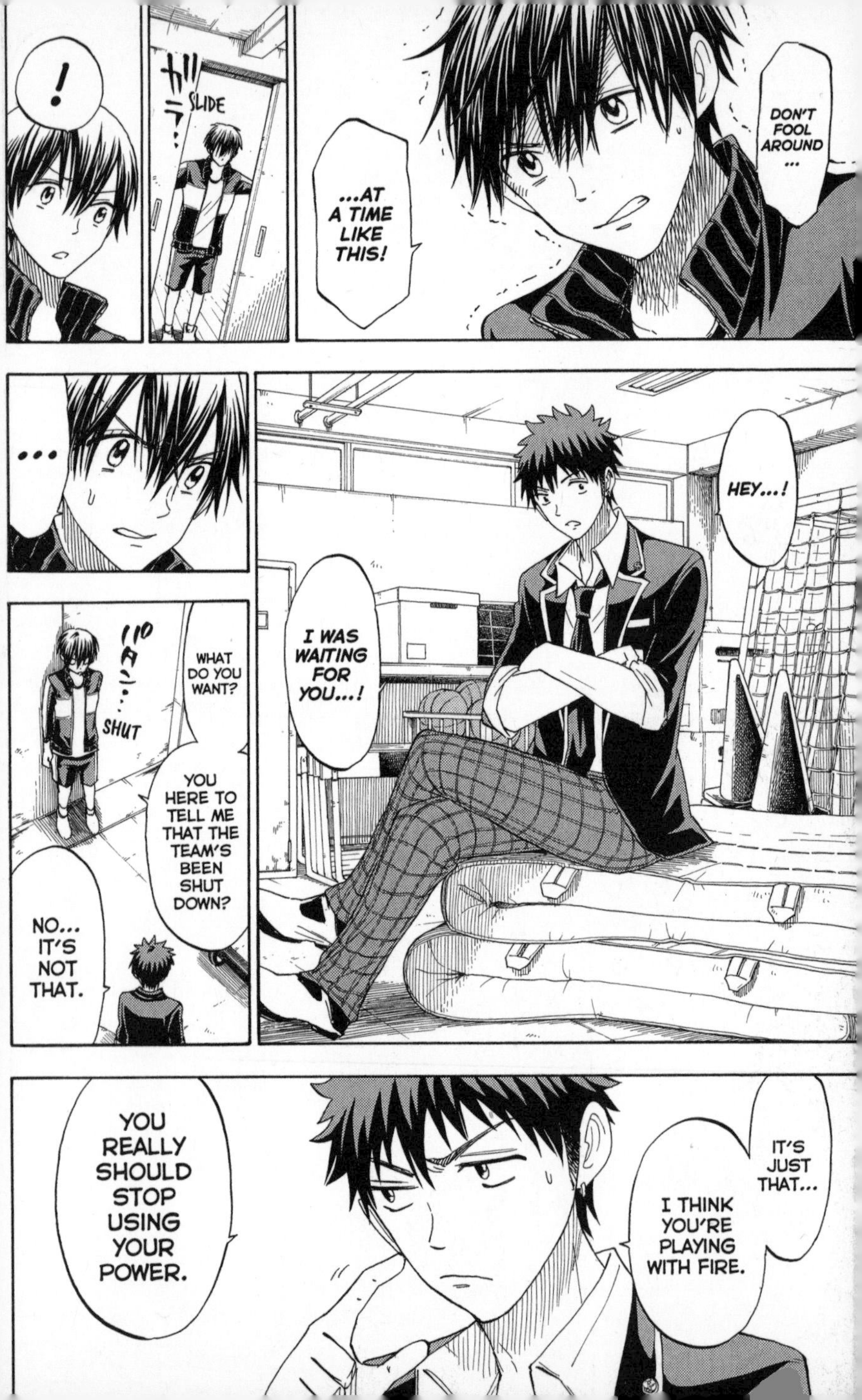
DON'T FOOL AROUND...
...AT A TIME LIKE THIS!
SLIDE
!
HEY...!
I WAS WAITING FOR YOU...!
...
SHUT
WHAT DO YOU WANT?
YOU HERE TO TELL ME THAT THE TEAM'S BEEN SHUT DOWN?
NO... IT'S NOT THAT.
IT'S JUST THAT...
I THINK YOU'RE PLAYING WITH FIRE.
YOU REALLY SHOULD STOP USING YOUR POWER.

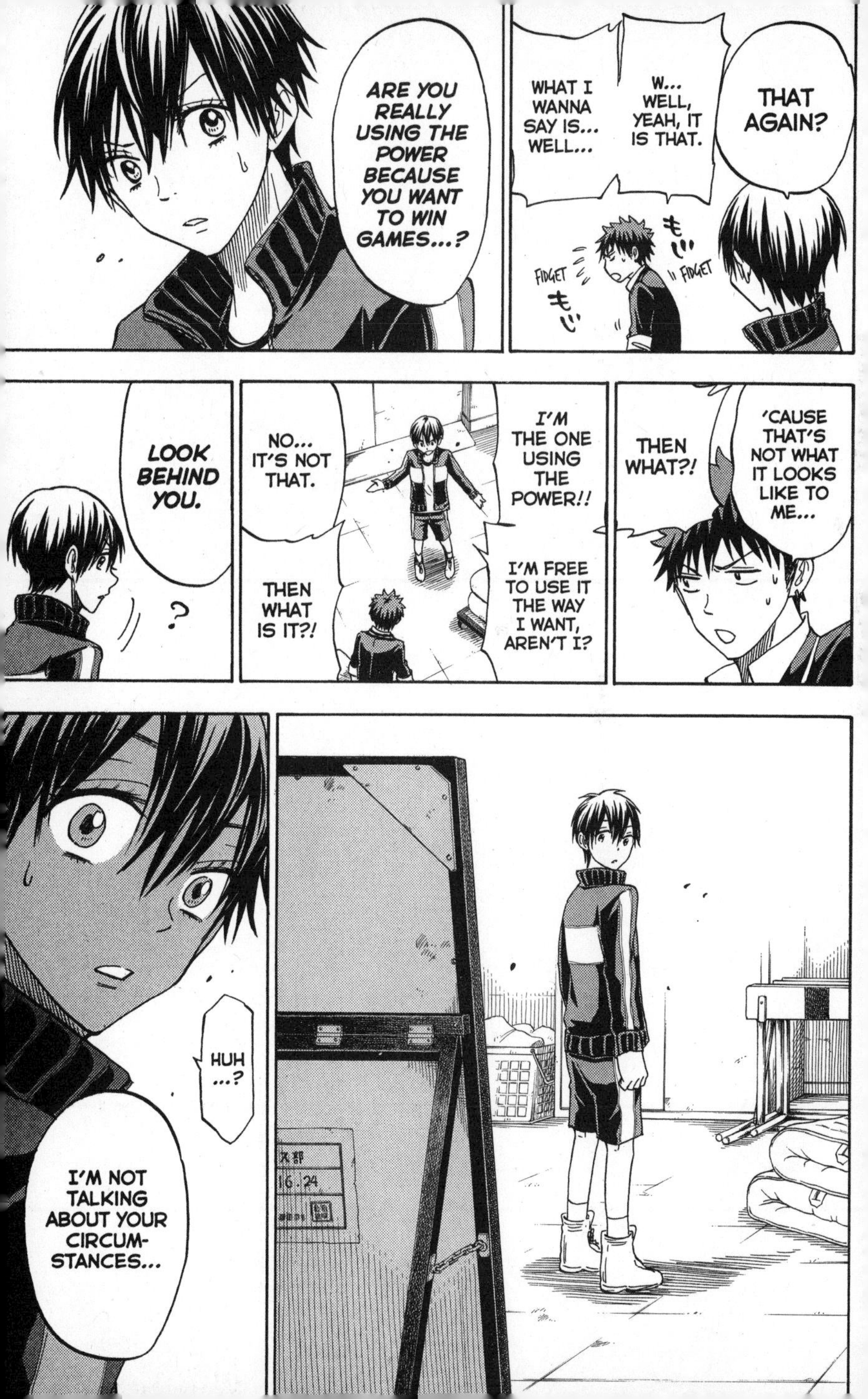
THAT AGAIN?
W... WELL, YEAH, IT IS THAT.
WHAT I WANNA SAY IS... WELL...
もじ
FIDGET
もじ
FIDGET
ARE YOU REALLY USING THE POWER BECAUSE YOU WANT TO WIN GAMES...?
'CAUSE THAT'S NOT WHAT IT LOOKS LIKE TO ME...
THEN WHAT?!
I'M THE ONE USING THE POWER!!
I'M FREE TO USE IT THE WAY I WANT, AREN'T I?
NO... IT'S NOT THAT.
THEN WHAT IS IT?!
LOOK BEHIND YOU.
?
HUH...?
I'M NOT TALKING ABOUT YOUR CIRCUM-STANCES...

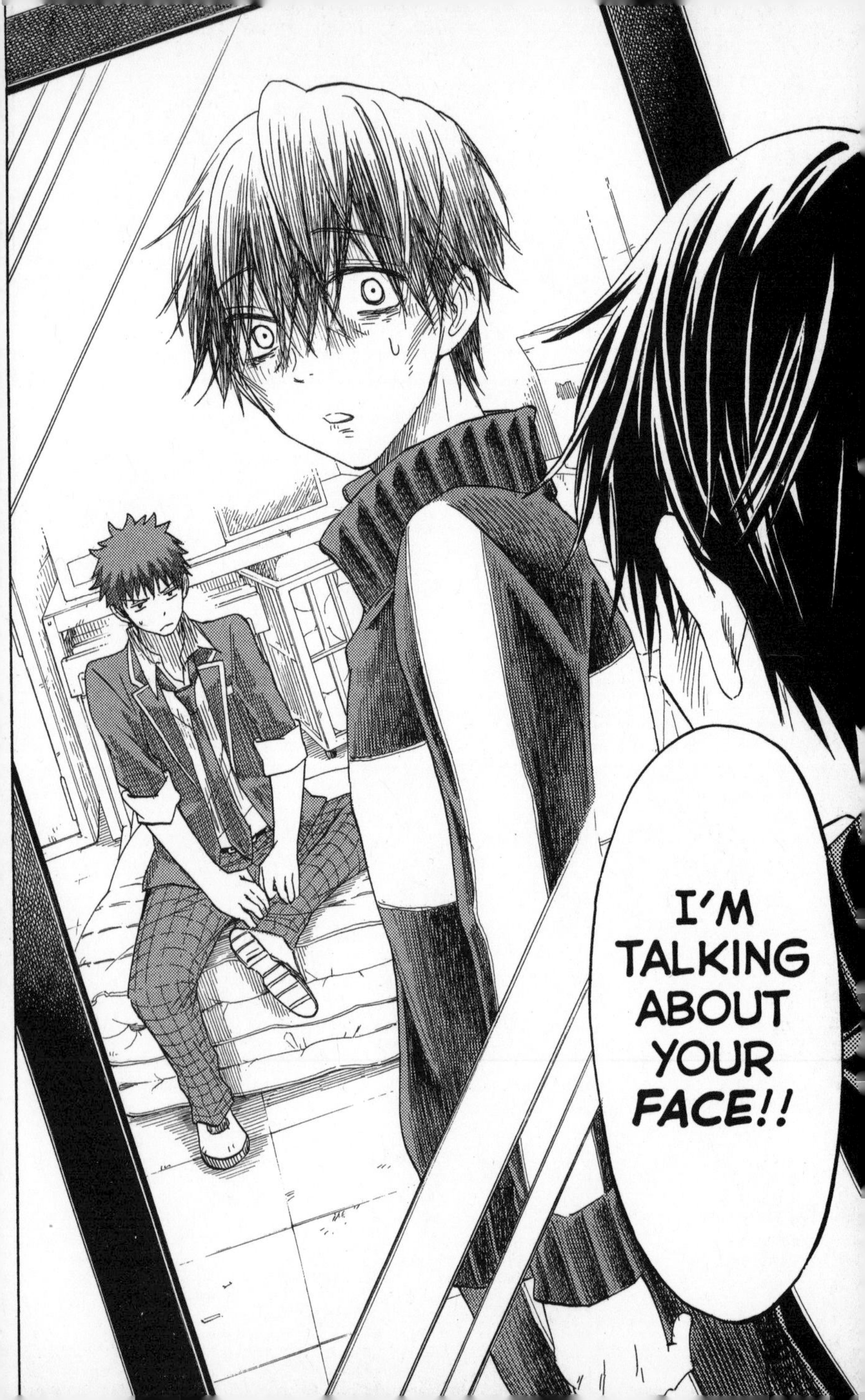
I'M TALKING ABOUT YOUR *FACE!!*

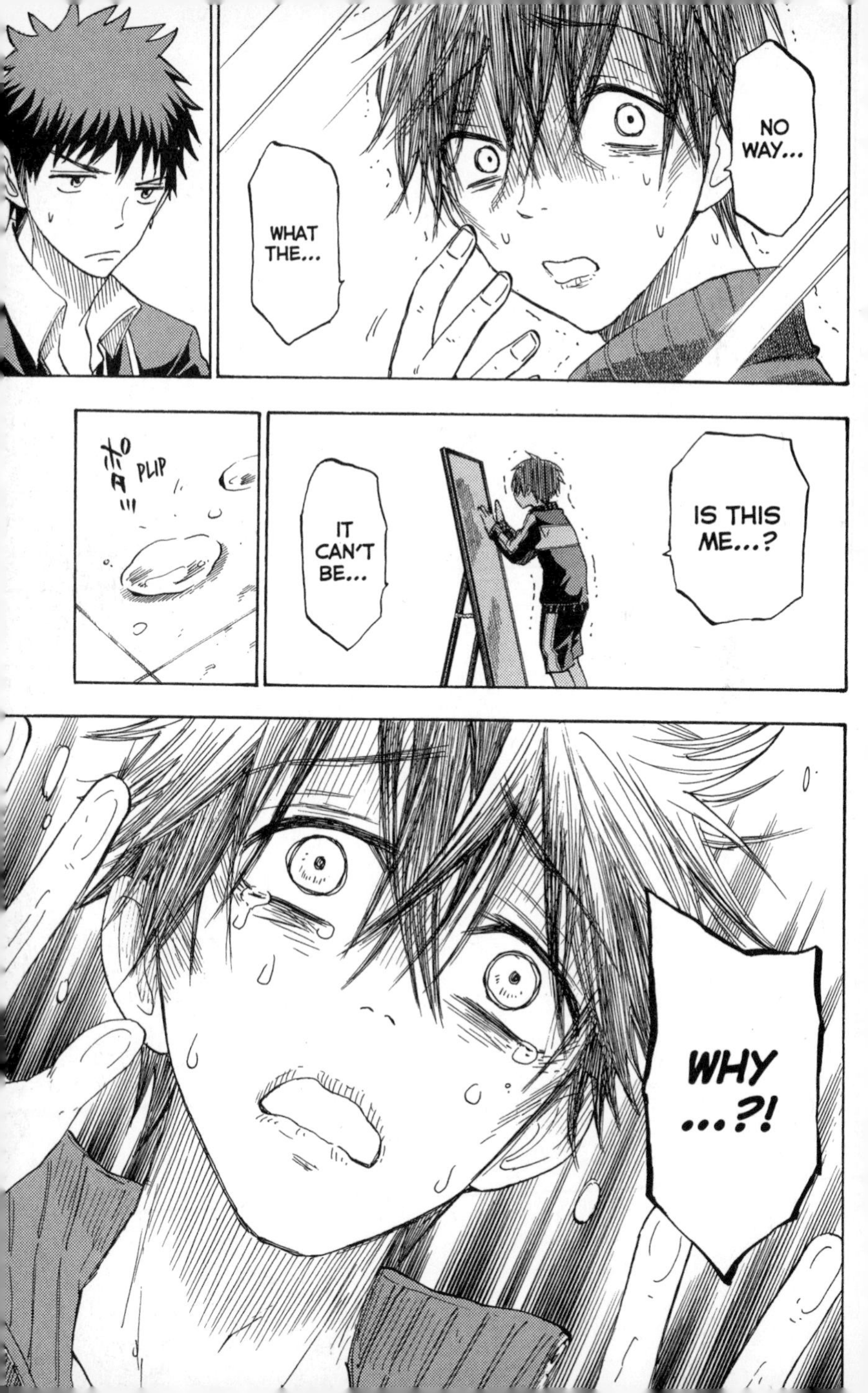
NO WAY...
WHAT THE...
IS THIS ME...?
IT CAN'T BE...
ポタ
PLIP
WHY ...?!

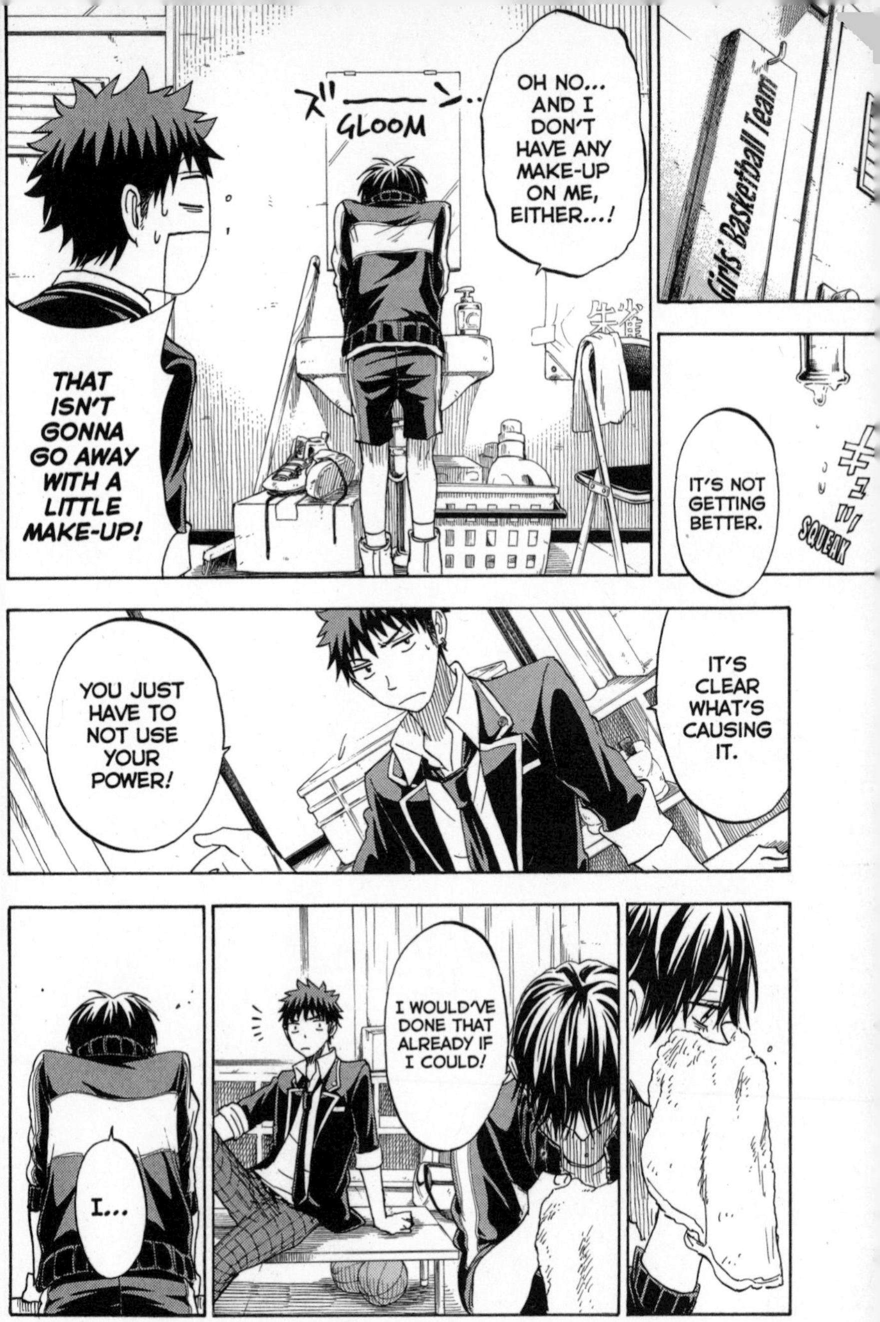
Girls' Basketball Team
IT'S NOT GETTING BETTER.
SQUEAK
GLOOM
OH NO... AND I DON'T HAVE ANY MAKE-UP ON ME, EITHER...!
THAT ISN'T GONNA GO AWAY WITH A LITTLE MAKE-UP!
IT'S CLEAR WHAT'S CAUSING IT.
YOU JUST HAVE TO NOT USE YOUR POWER!
I WOULD'VE DONE THAT ALREADY IF I COULD!
I...

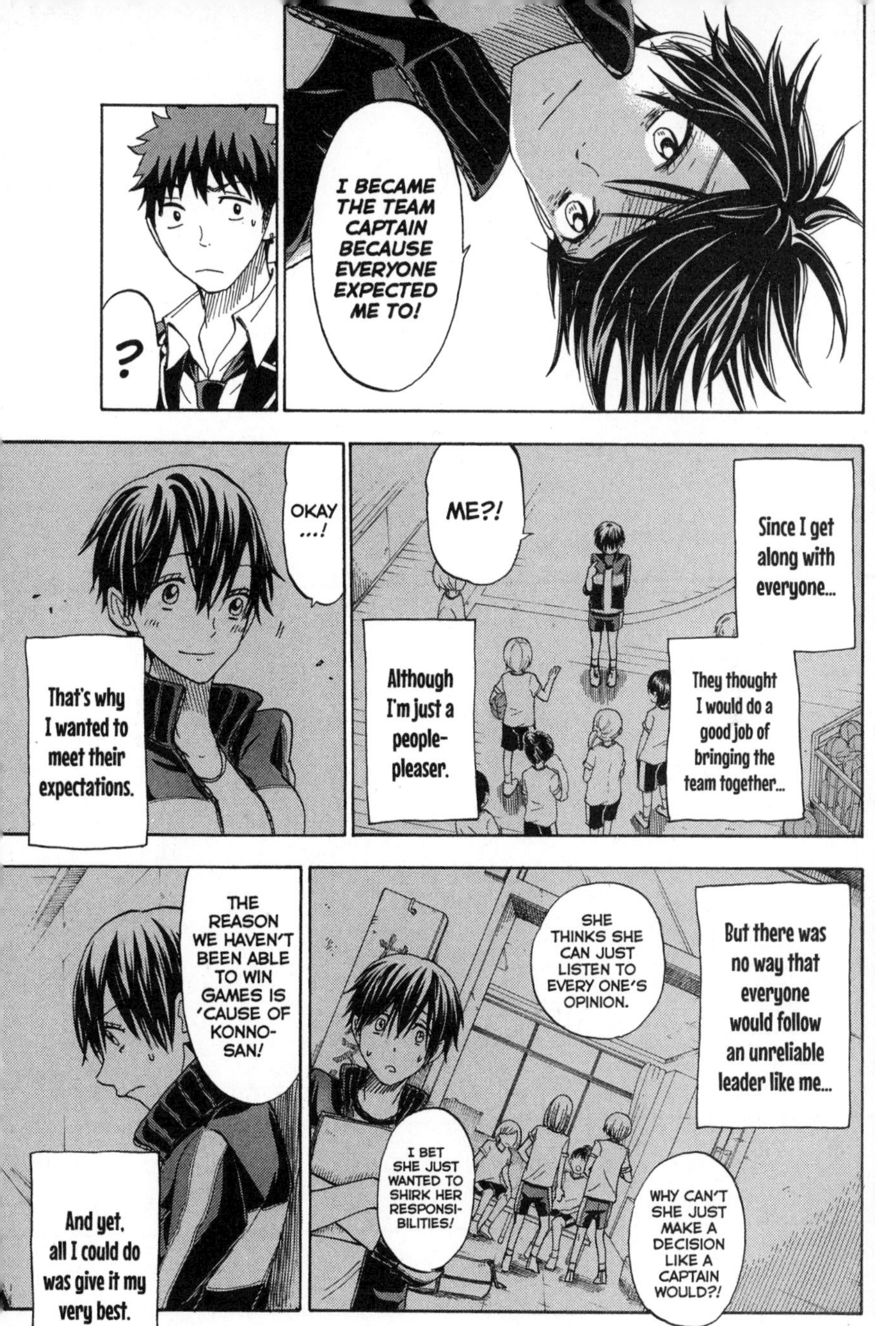
I BECAME THE TEAM CAPTAIN BECAUSE EVERYONE EXPECTED ME TO!
?
Since I get along with everyone...
ME?!
They thought I would do a good job of bringing the team together...
Although I'm just a people-pleaser.
OKAY ...!
That's why I wanted to meet their expectations.
But there was no way that everyone would follow an unreliable leader like me...
SHE THINKS SHE CAN JUST LISTEN TO EVERY ONE'S OPINION.
WHY CAN'T SHE JUST MAKE A DECISION LIKE A CAPTAIN WOULD?!
I BET SHE JUST WANTED TO SHIRK HER RESPONSI-BILITIES!
THE REASON WE HAVEN'T BEEN ABLE TO WIN GAMES IS 'CAUSE OF KONNO-SAN!
And yet, all I could do was give it my very best.

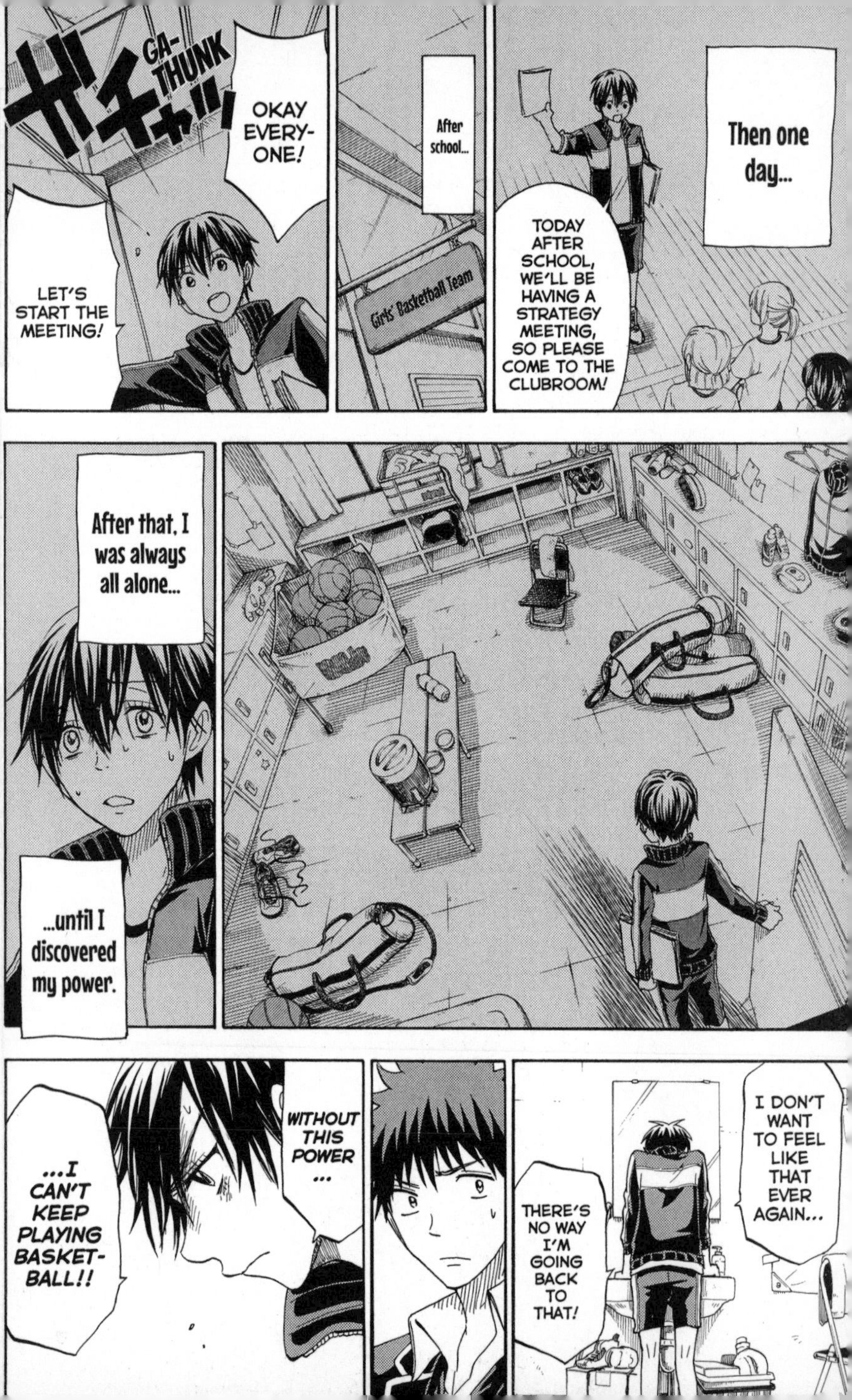

Then one day...
TODAY AFTER SCHOOL, WE'LL BE HAVING A STRATEGY MEETING, SO PLEASE COME TO THE CLUBROOM!
After school...
Girls' Basketball Team
OKAY EVERY-ONE!
GA-THUNK
LET'S START THE MEETING!
After that, I was always all alone...
...until I discovered my power.
I DON'T WANT TO FEEL LIKE THAT EVER AGAIN...
THERE'S NO WAY I'M GOING BACK TO THAT!
WITHOUT THIS POWER...
...I CAN'T KEEP PLAYING BASKET-BALL!!

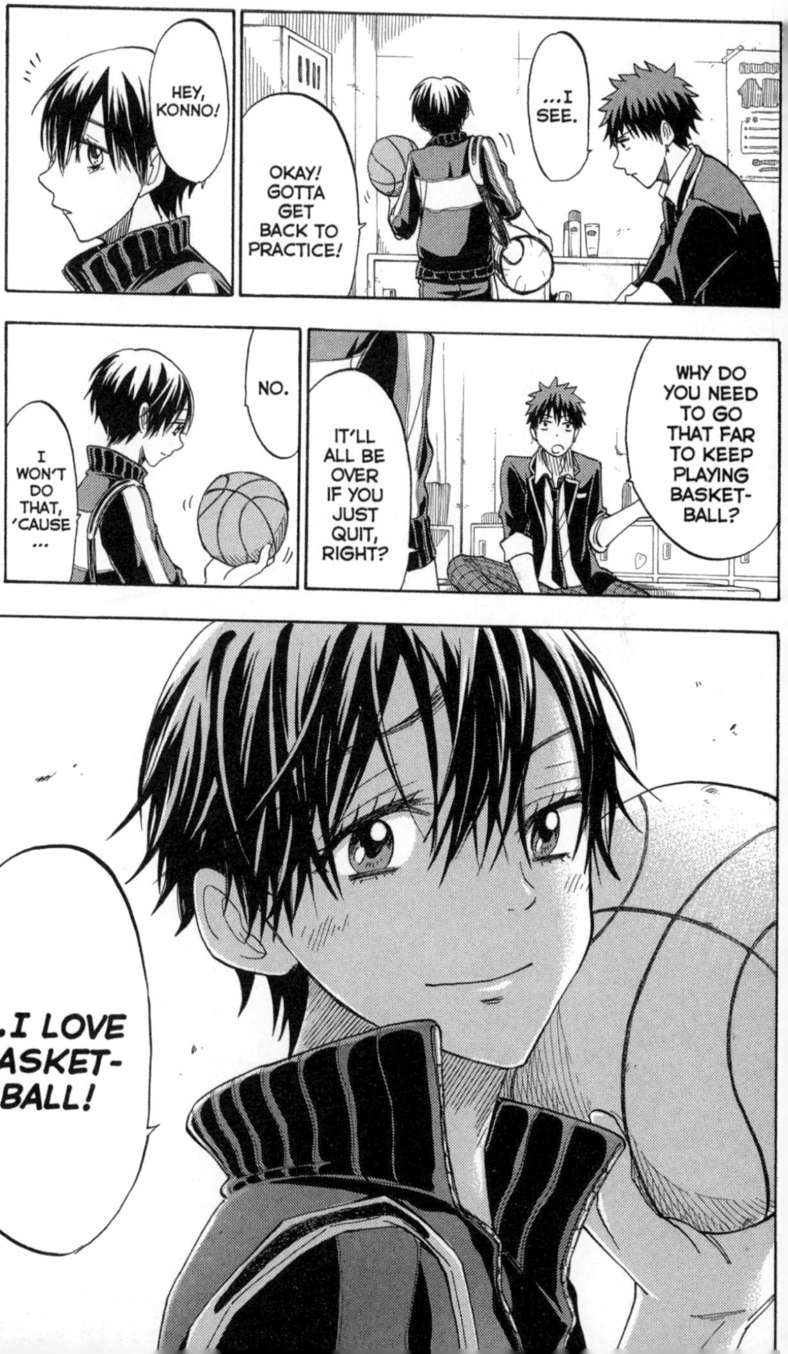
...I SEE.
OKAY! GOTTA GET BACK TO PRACTICE!
HEY, KONNO!
WHY DO YOU NEED TO GO THAT FAR TO KEEP PLAYING BASKET-BALL?
IT'LL ALL BE OVER IF YOU JUST QUIT, RIGHT?
NO.
I WON'T DO THAT, 'CAUSE ...
...I LOVE BASKET-BALL!

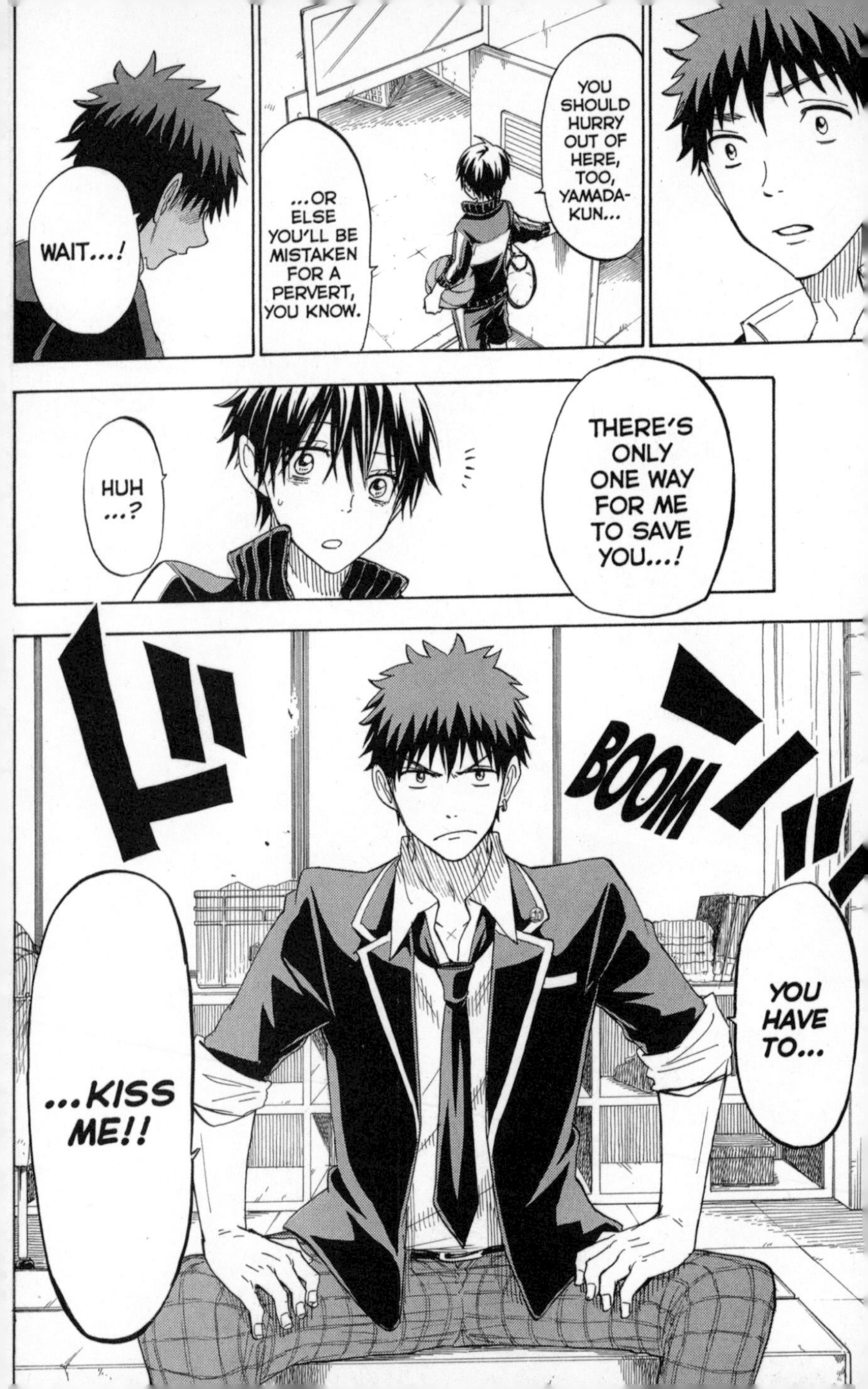
YOU SHOULD HURRY OUT OF HERE, TOO, YAMADA-KUN...
...OR ELSE YOU'LL BE MISTAKEN FOR A PERVERT, YOU KNOW.
WAIT...!
THERE'S ONLY ONE WAY FOR ME TO SAVE YOU...!
HUH...?
ド
BOOM
YOU HAVE TO...
...KISS ME!!

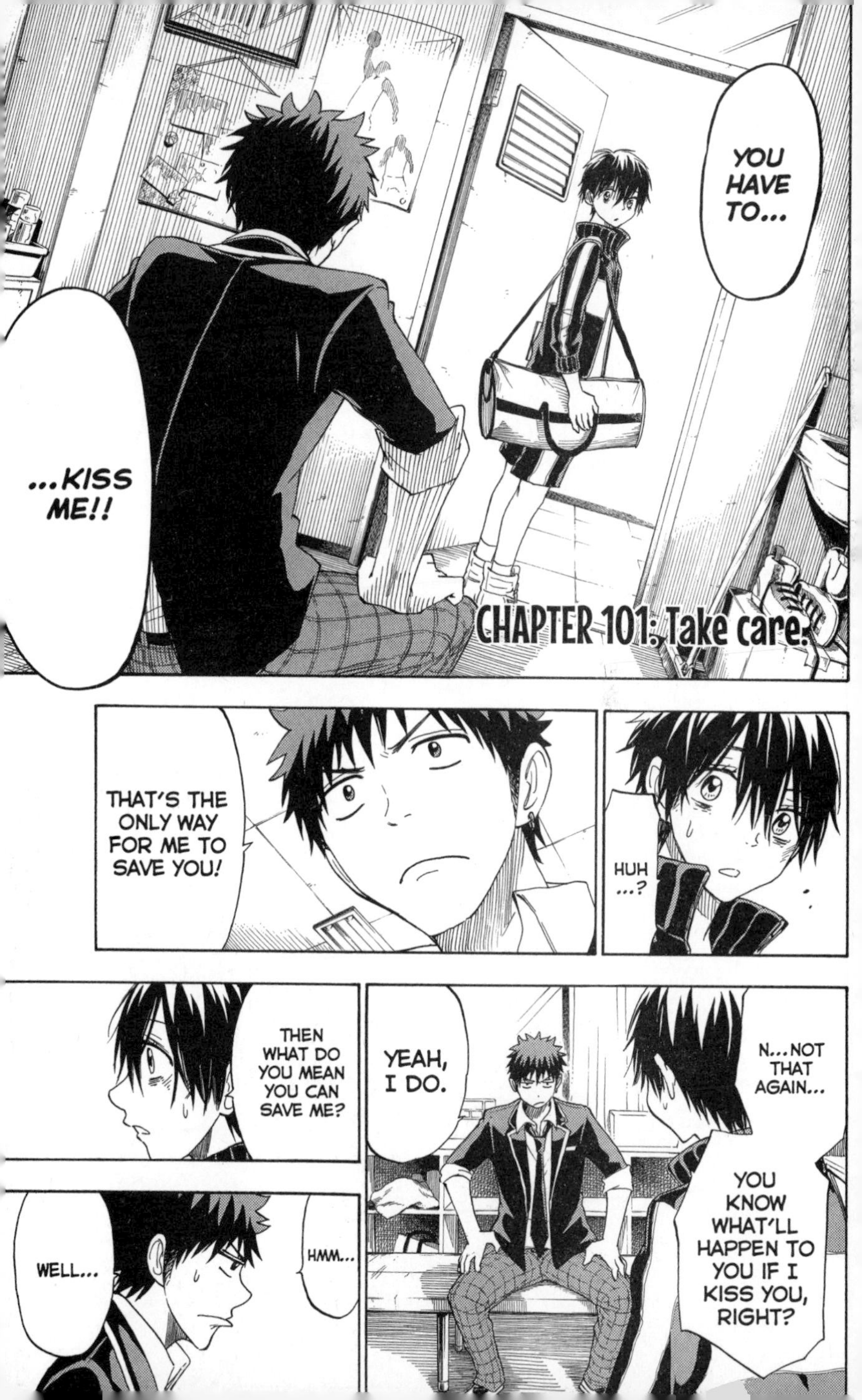
YOU HAVE TO...
...KISS ME!!
CHAPTER 101: Take care.
HUH ...?
THAT'S THE ONLY WAY FOR ME TO SAVE YOU!
N...NOT THAT AGAIN...
YEAH, I DO.
YOU KNOW WHAT'LL HAPPEN TO YOU IF I KISS YOU, RIGHT?
THEN WHAT DO YOU MEAN YOU CAN SAVE ME?
HMM...
WELL...

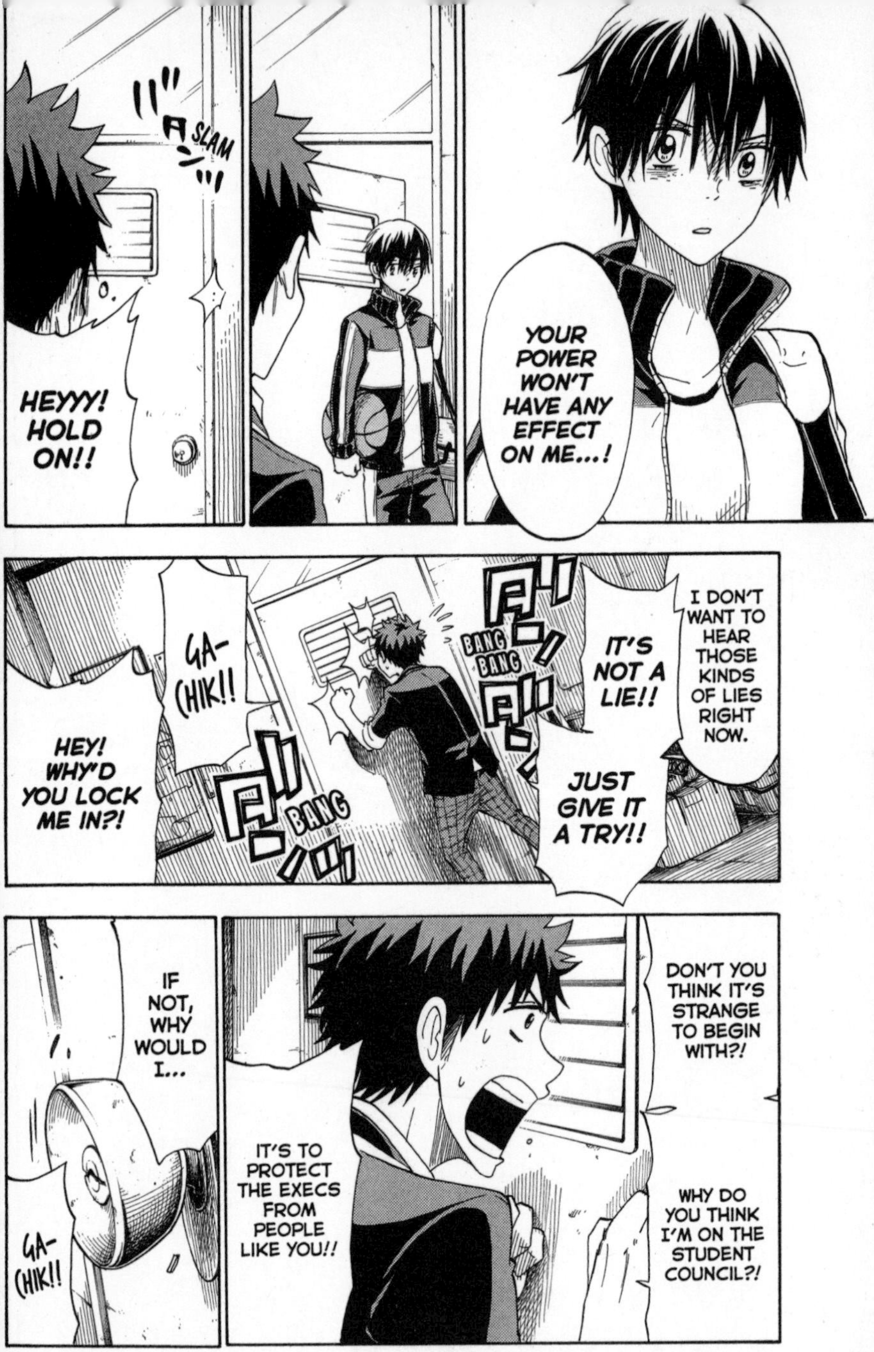
YOUR POWER WON'T HAVE ANY EFFECT ON ME...!
SLAM
HEYYY! HOLD ON!!
I DON'T WANT TO HEAR THOSE KINDS OF LIES RIGHT NOW.
IT'S NOT A LIE!!
JUST GIVE IT A TRY!!
BANG BANG
BANG
GA-CHIK!!
HEY! WHY'D YOU LOCK ME IN?!
DON'T YOU THINK IT'S STRANGE TO BEGIN WITH?!
WHY DO YOU THINK I'M ON THE STUDENT COUNCIL?!
IT'S TO PROTECT THE EXECS FROM PEOPLE LIKE YOU!!
IF NOT, WHY WOULD I...
GA-CHIK!!

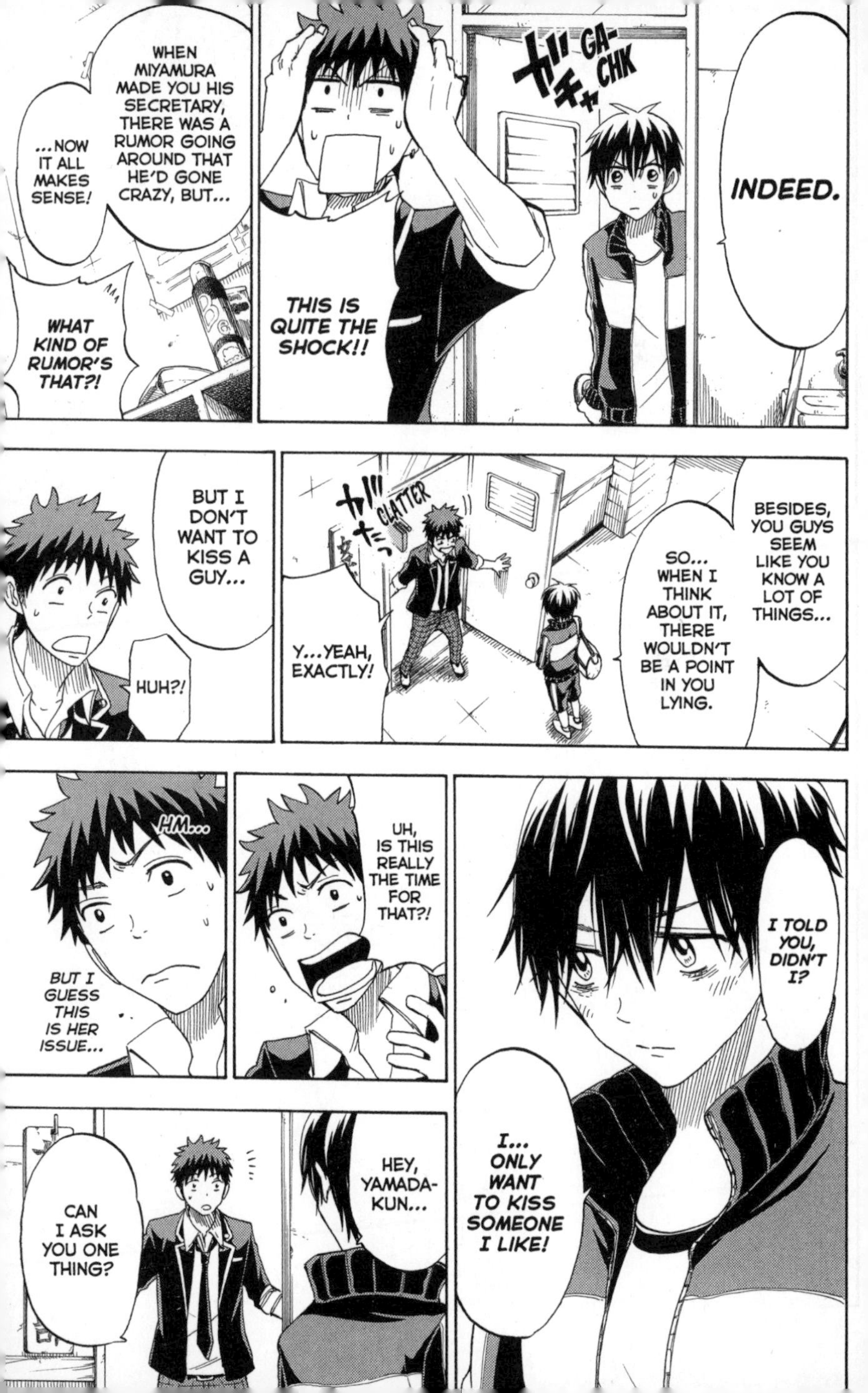
GA-CHK
INDEED.
THIS IS QUITE THE SHOCK!!
WHEN MIYAMURA MADE YOU HIS SECRETARY, THERE WAS A RUMOR GOING AROUND THAT HE'D GONE CRAZY, BUT...
...NOW IT ALL MAKES SENSE!
WHAT KIND OF RUMOR'S THAT?!
BESIDES, YOU GUYS SEEM LIKE YOU KNOW A LOT OF THINGS...
SO... WHEN I THINK ABOUT IT, THERE WOULDN'T BE A POINT IN YOU LYING.
CLATTER
Y...YEAH, EXACTLY!
BUT I DON'T WANT TO KISS A GUY...
HUH?!
I TOLD YOU, DIDN'T I?
I... ONLY WANT TO KISS SOMEONE I LIKE!
UH, IS THIS REALLY THE TIME FOR THAT?!
HM...
BUT I GUESS THIS IS HER ISSUE...
HEY, YAMADA-KUN...
CAN I ASK YOU ONE THING?

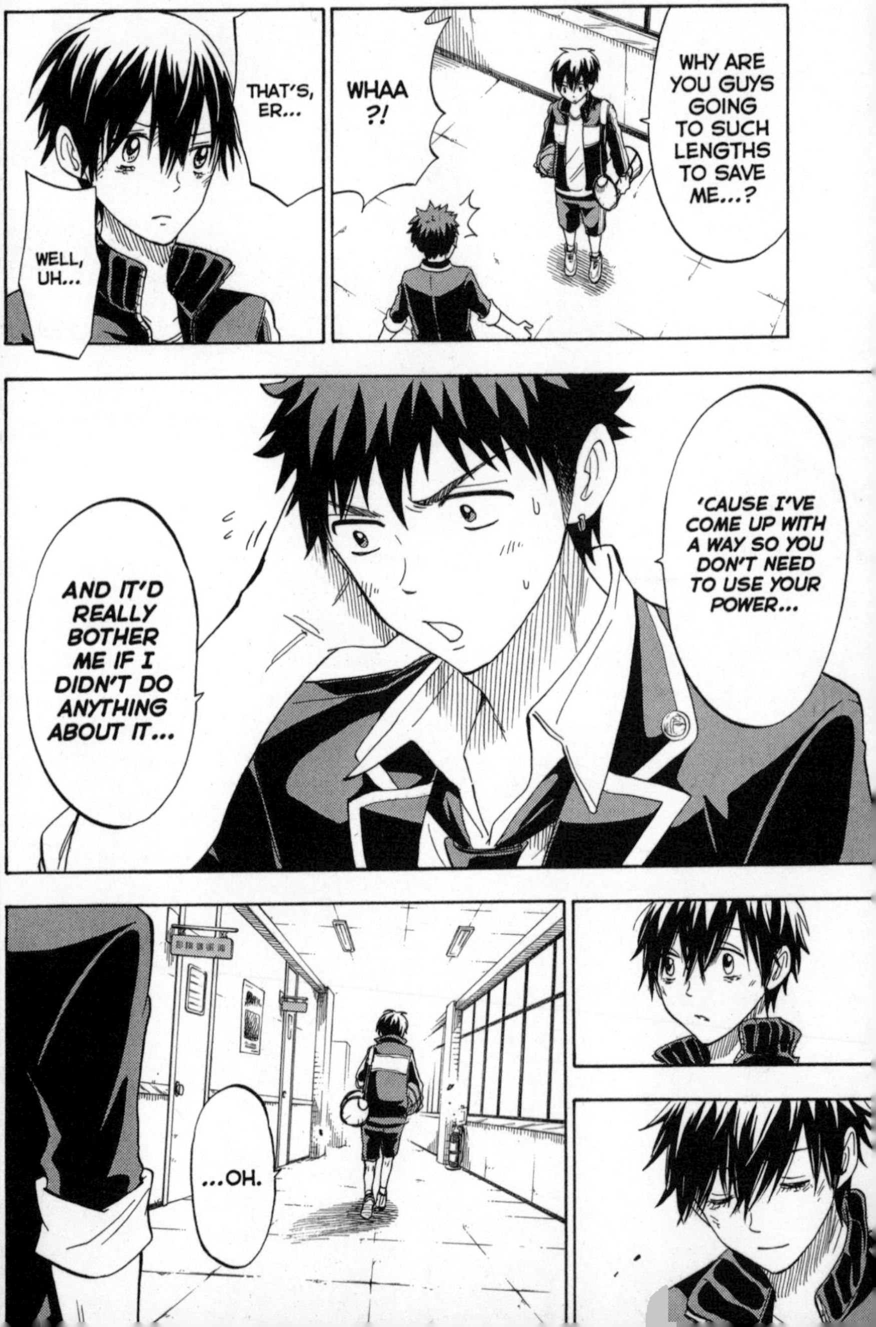
WHY ARE YOU GUYS GOING TO SUCH LENGTHS TO SAVE ME...?
WHAA ?!
THAT'S, ER...
WELL, UH...
'CAUSE I'VE COME UP WITH A WAY SO YOU DON'T NEED TO USE YOUR POWER...
AND IT'D REALLY BOTHER ME IF I DIDN'T DO ANYTHING ABOUT IT...
...OH.

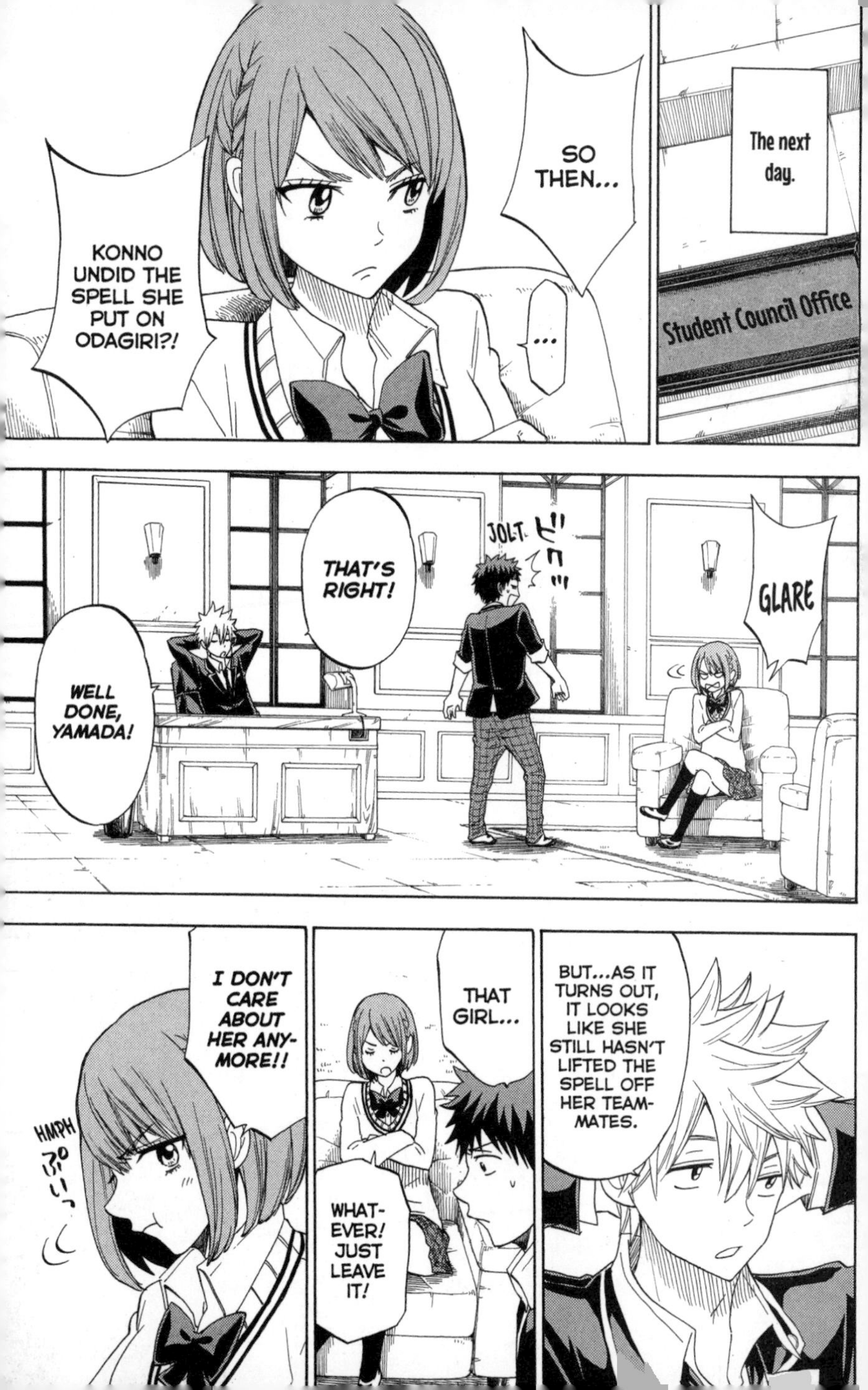

The next day.
Student Council Office
SO THEN...
...
KONNO UNDID THE SPELL SHE PUT ON ODAGIRI?!
GLARE
JOLT ビクッ
THAT'S RIGHT!
WELL DONE, YAMADA!
BUT...AS IT TURNS OUT, IT LOOKS LIKE SHE STILL HASN'T LIFTED THE SPELL OFF HER TEAM-MATES.
THAT GIRL...
WHAT-EVER! JUST LEAVE IT!
I DON'T CARE ABOUT HER ANY-MORE!!
HMPH ぷいっ

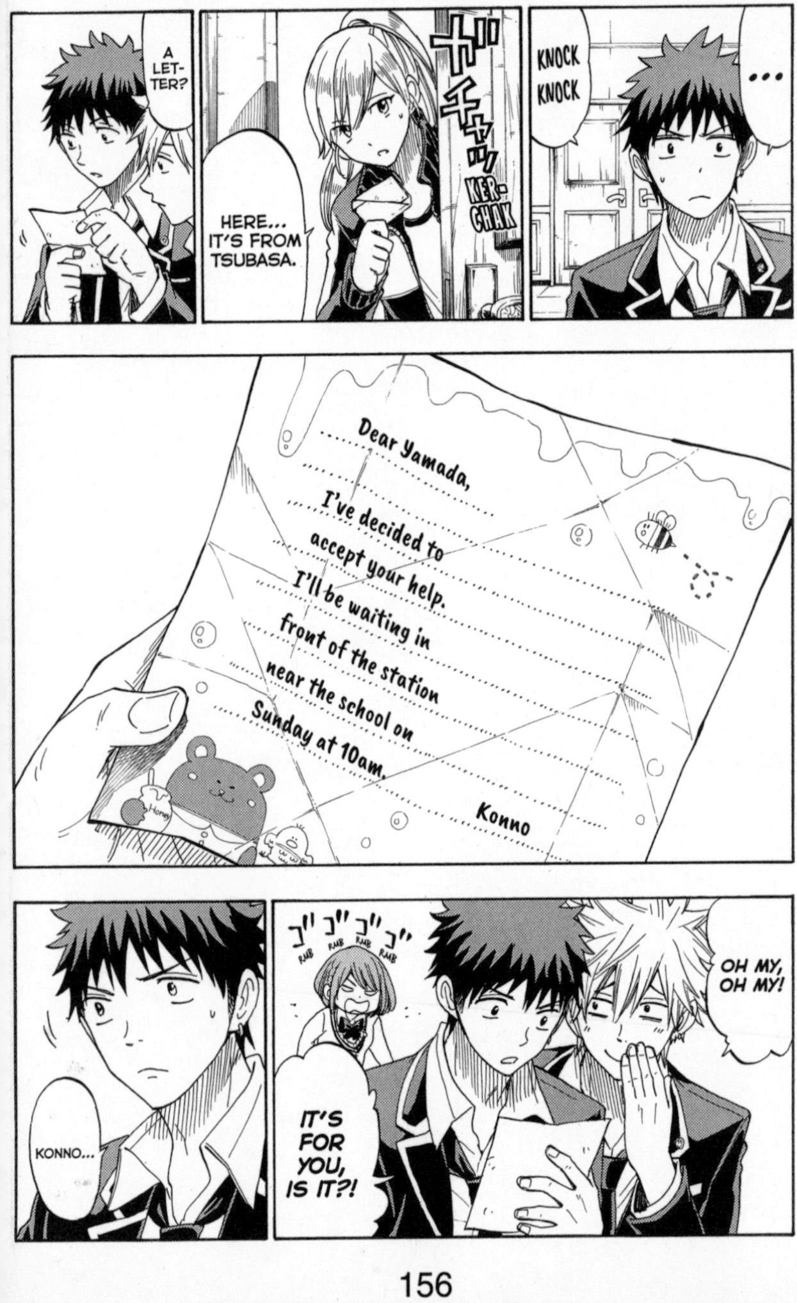
...
KNOCK KNOCK
ガチャッ
KER-CHAK
HERE... IT'S FROM TSUBASA.
A LETTER?
Dear Yamada,
I've decided to accept your help.
I'll be waiting in front of the station near the school on Sunday at 10am.
Konno
Honey
OH MY, OH MY!
ゴゴゴゴ
RMB RMB RMB RMB
IT'S FOR YOU, IS IT?!
KONNO...

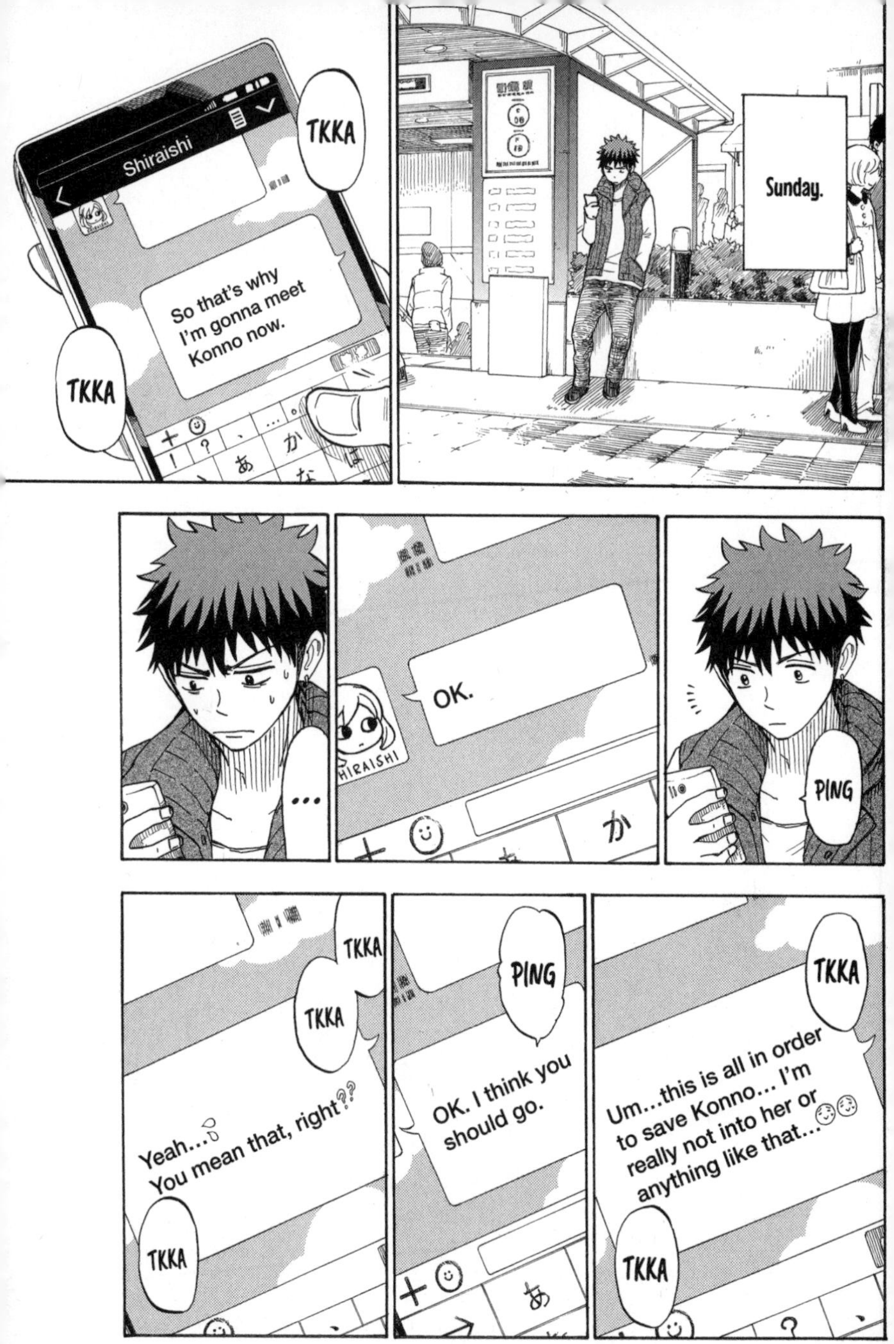
Sunday.
TKKA
Shiraishi
So that's why I'm gonna meet Konno now.
TKKA
PING
OK.
...
TKKA
Um...this is all in order to save Konno... I'm really not into her or anything like that...
TKKA
PING
OK. I think you should go.
TKKA
TKKA
Yeah...
You mean that, right??
TKKA

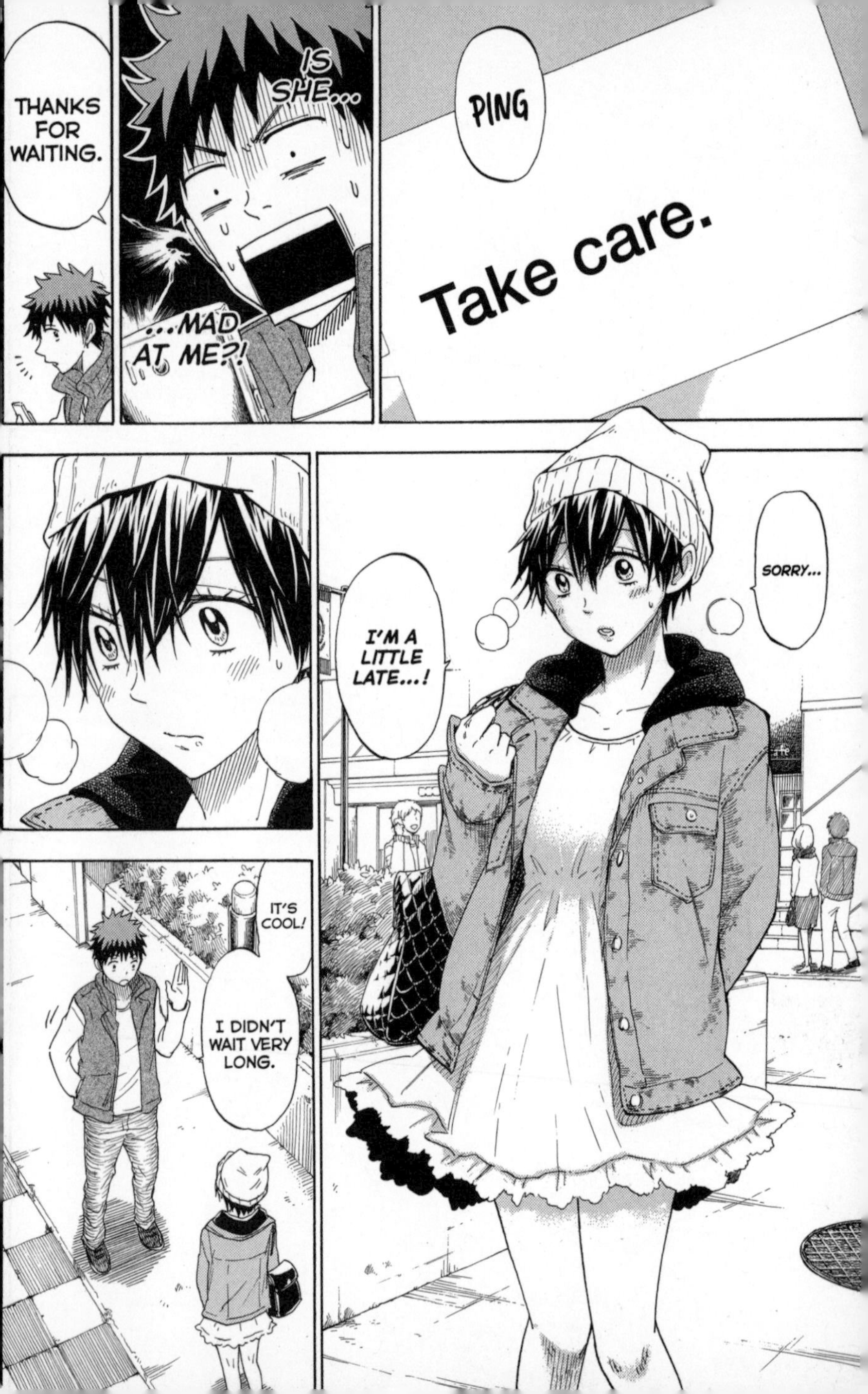
PING
Take care.
IS SHE...
...MAD AT ME?!
THANKS FOR WAITING.
SORRY...
I'M A LITTLE LATE...!
IT'S COOL!
I DIDN'T WAIT VERY LONG.

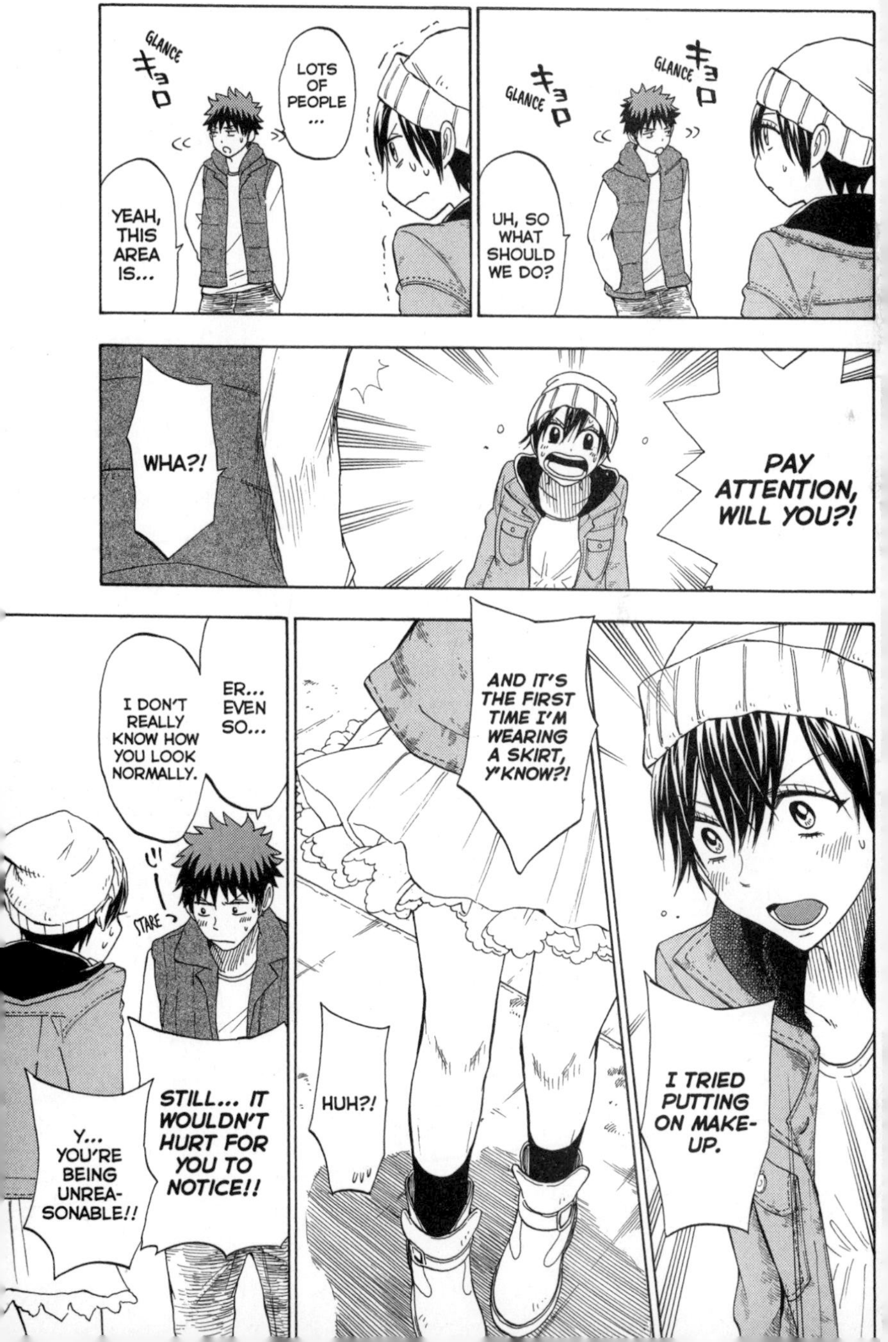
GLANCE
キョロ
GLANCE
キョロ
UH, SO WHAT SHOULD WE DO?
LOTS OF PEOPLE ...
GLANCE
キョロ
YEAH, THIS AREA IS...
PAY ATTENTION, WILL YOU?!
WHA?!
I TRIED PUTTING ON MAKE-UP.
AND IT'S THE FIRST TIME I'M WEARING A SKIRT, Y'KNOW?!
HUH?!
ER... EVEN SO...
I DON'T REALLY KNOW HOW YOU LOOK NORMALLY.
STARE
STILL... IT WOULDN'T HURT FOR YOU TO NOTICE!!
Y... YOU'RE BEING UNREA-SONABLE!!

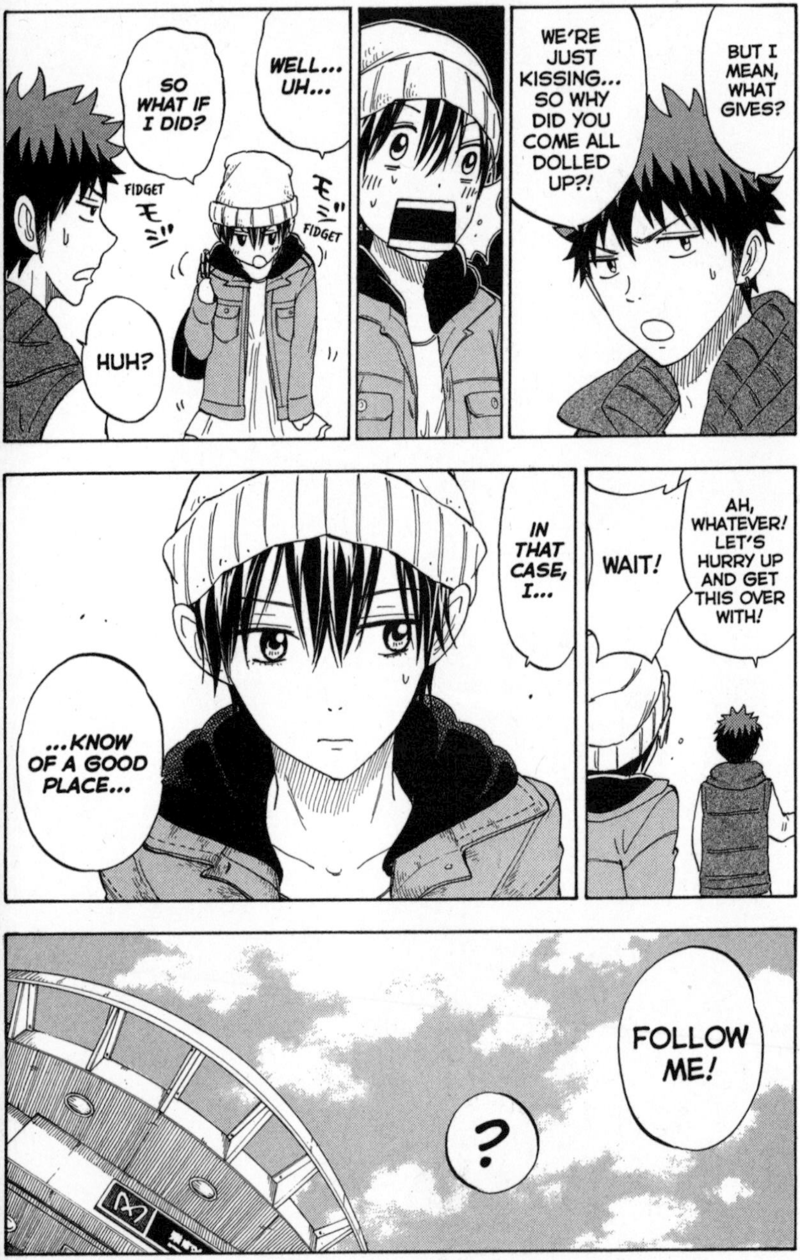
BUT I MEAN, WHAT GIVES?
WE'RE JUST KISSING... SO WHY DID YOU COME ALL DOLLED UP?!
WELL... UH...
SO WHAT IF I DID?
FIDGET
FIDGET
HUH?
AH, WHATEVER! LET'S HURRY UP AND GET THIS OVER WITH!
WAIT!
IN THAT CASE, I...
...KNOW OF A GOOD PLACE...
FOLLOW ME!
?

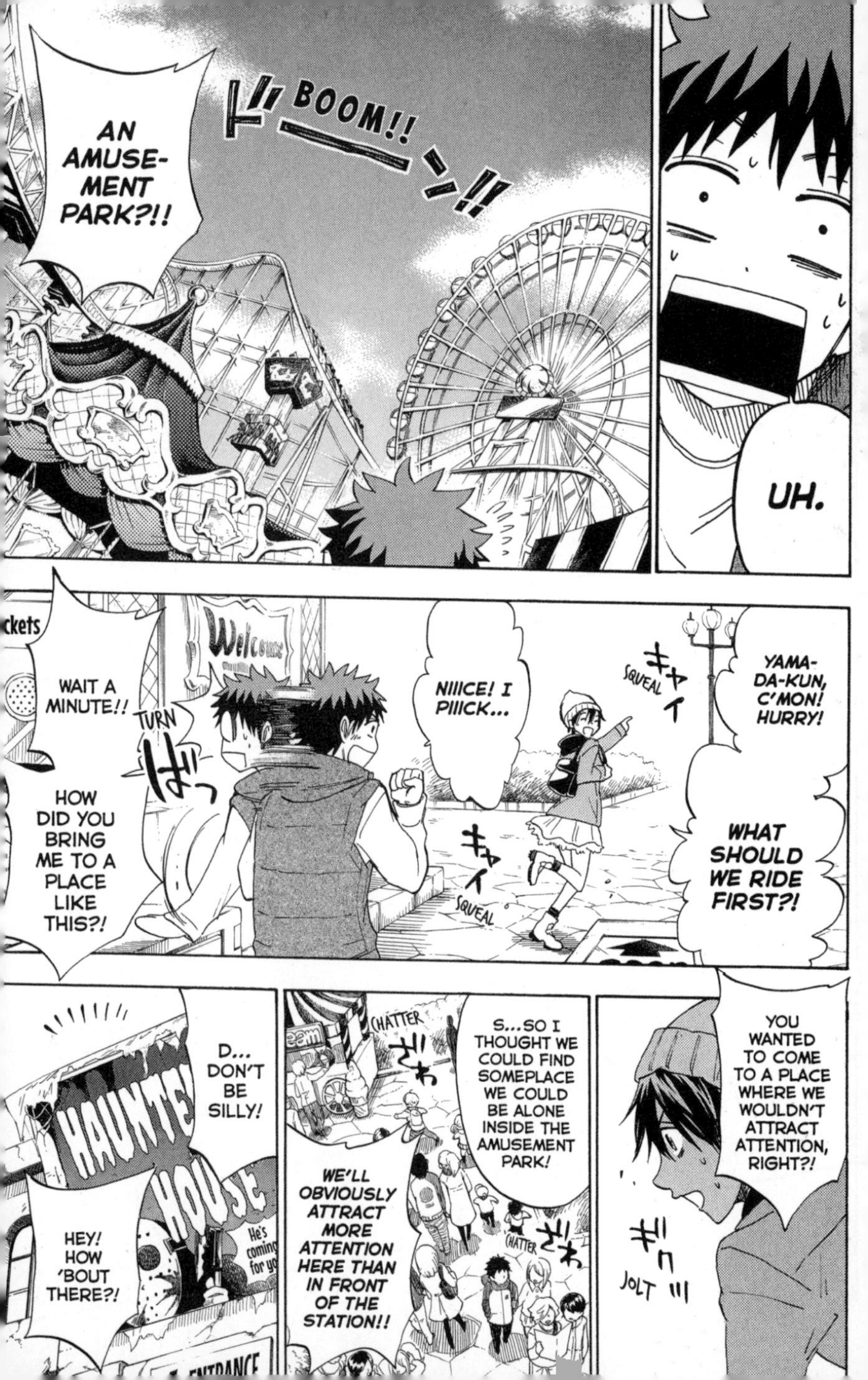
UH.
BOOM!!
AN AMUSE-MENT PARK?!!
YAMA-DA-KUN, C'MON! HURRY!
SQUEAL
WHAT SHOULD WE RIDE FIRST?!
SQUEAL
NIIICE! I PIIICK...
Welcome
WAIT A MINUTE!!
TURN
HOW DID YOU BRING ME TO A PLACE LIKE THIS?!
YOU WANTED TO COME TO A PLACE WHERE WE WOULDN'T ATTRACT ATTENTION, RIGHT?!
JOLT
S...SO I THOUGHT WE COULD FIND SOMEPLACE WE COULD BE ALONE INSIDE THE AMUSEMENT PARK!
CHATTER
WE'LL OBVIOUSLY ATTRACT MORE ATTENTION HERE THAN IN FRONT OF THE STATION!!
CHATTER
D... DON'T BE SILLY!
HOUSE
HEY! HOW 'BOUT THERE?!
ENTRANCE

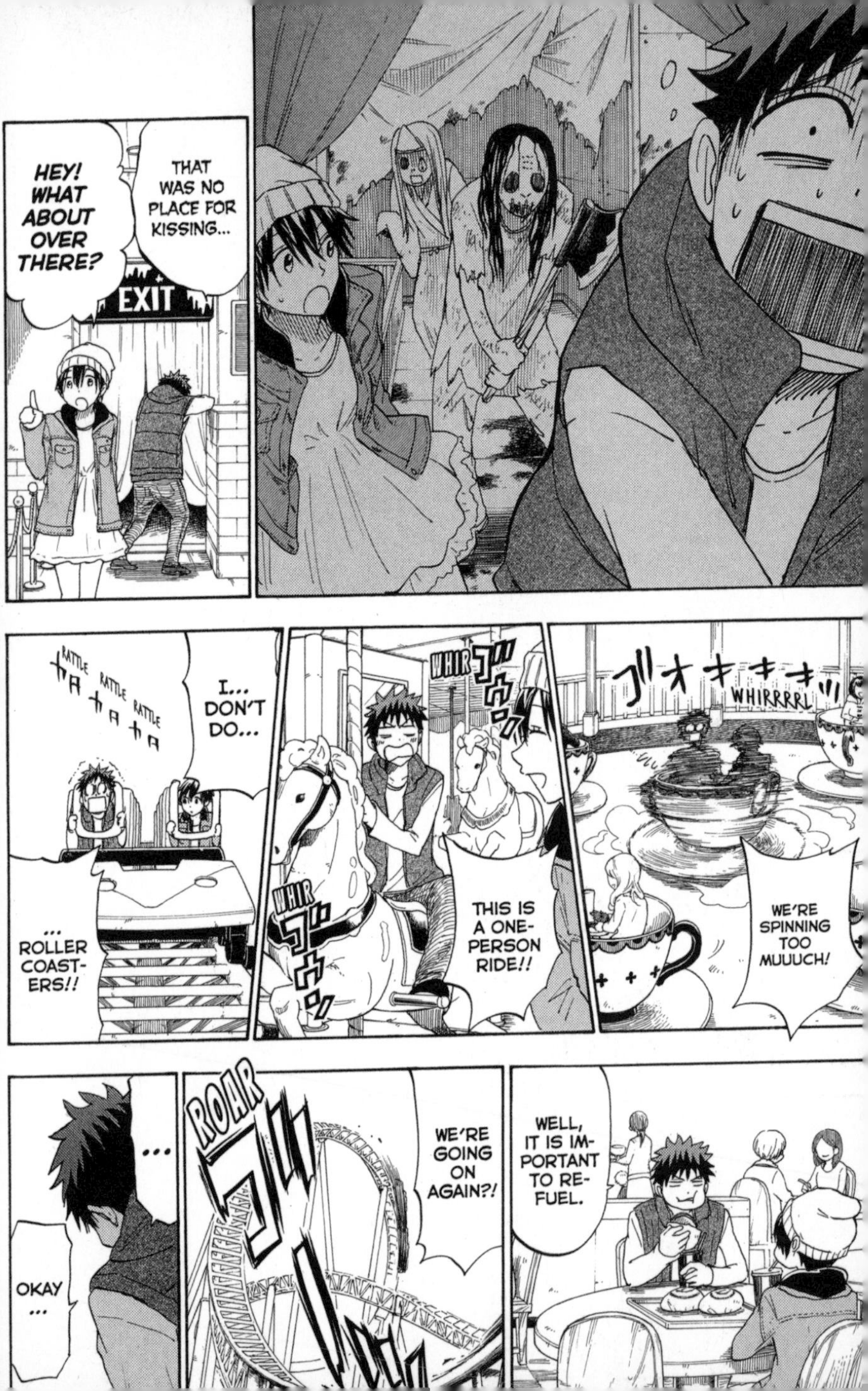
THAT WAS NO PLACE FOR KISSING...
HEY! WHAT ABOUT OVER THERE?
EXIT
WHIRRRRL
WE'RE SPINNING TOO MUUUCH!
WHIR
THIS IS A ONE-PERSON RIDE!!
WHIR
I... DON'T DO...
RATTLE RATTLE RATTLE
... ROLLER COASTERS!!
WELL, IT IS IMPORTANT TO REFUEL.
WE'RE GOING ON AGAIN?!
ROAR
...
OKAY ...

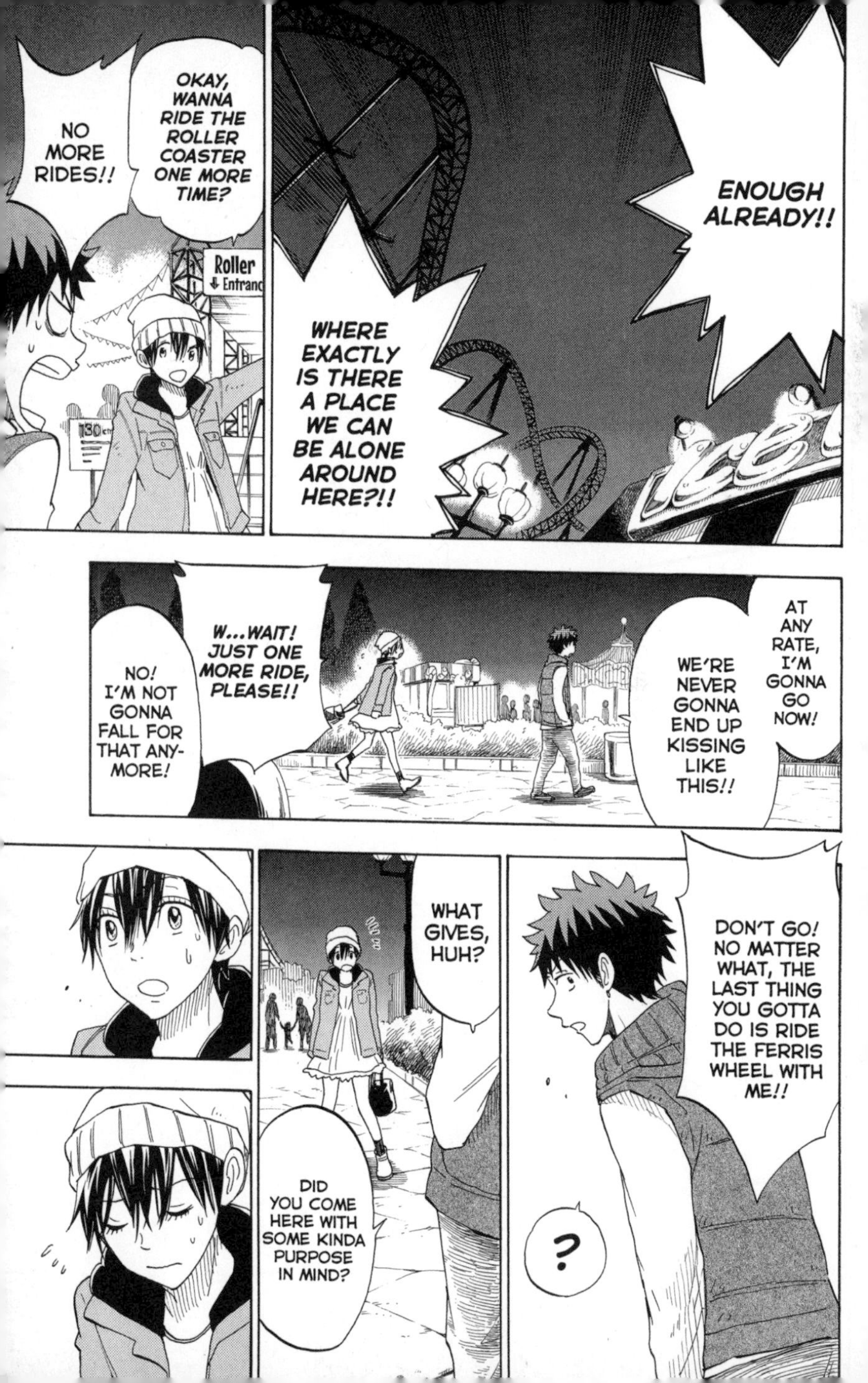
ENOUGH ALREADY!!
WHERE EXACTLY IS THERE A PLACE WE CAN BE ALONE AROUND HERE?!!
OKAY, WANNA RIDE THE ROLLER COASTER ONE MORE TIME?
NO MORE RIDES!!
Roller
⇓ Entranc
AT ANY RATE, I'M GONNA GO NOW!
WE'RE NEVER GONNA END UP KISSING LIKE THIS!!
W...WAIT! JUST ONE MORE RIDE, PLEASE!!
NO! I'M NOT GONNA FALL FOR THAT ANY-MORE!
DON'T GO! NO MATTER WHAT, THE LAST THING YOU GOTTA DO IS RIDE THE FERRIS WHEEL WITH ME!!
?
WHAT GIVES, HUH?
DID YOU COME HERE WITH SOME KINDA PURPOSE IN MIND?

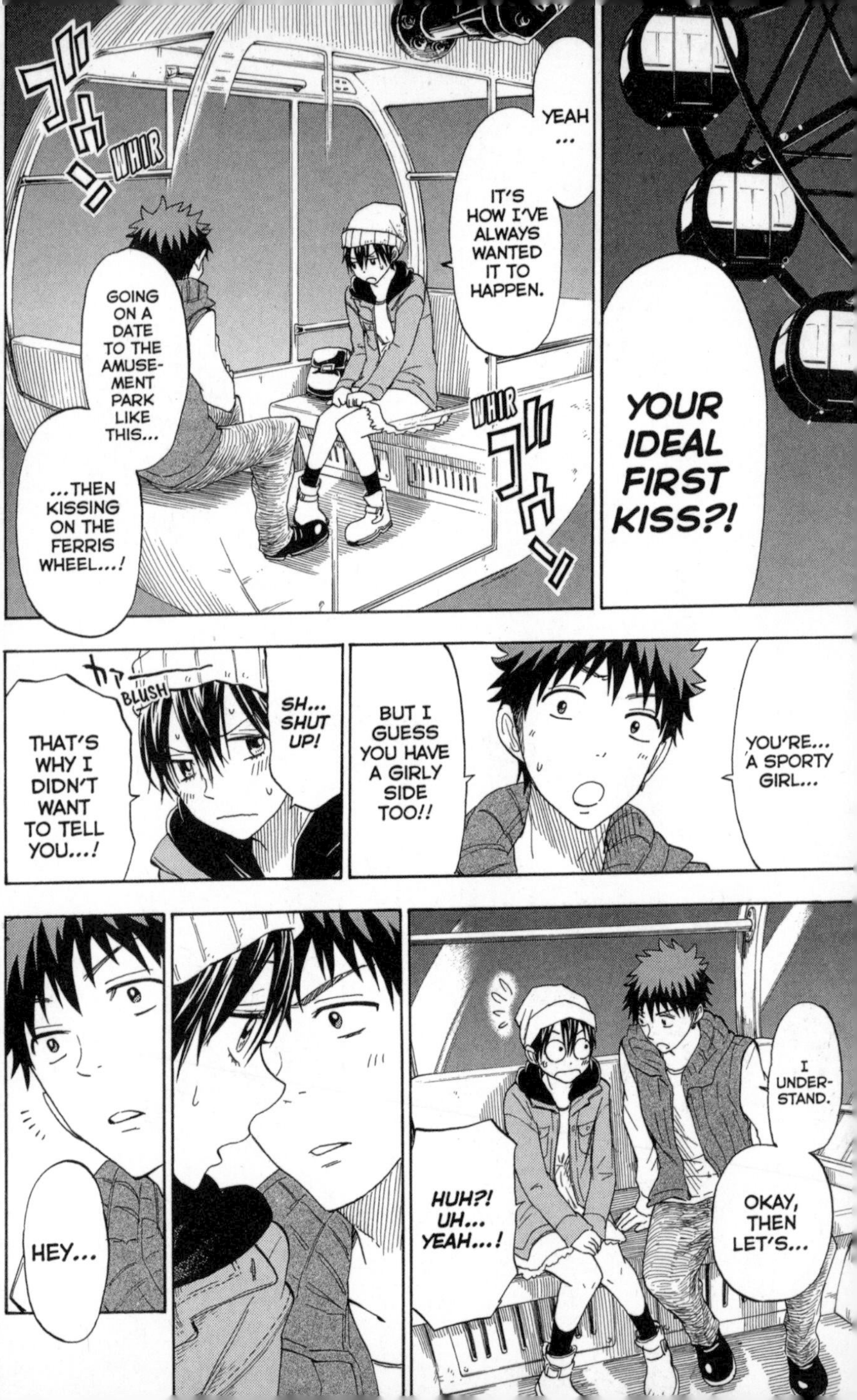
YOUR IDEAL FIRST KISS?!
YEAH...
IT'S HOW I'VE ALWAYS WANTED IT TO HAPPEN.
WHIR
WHIR
GOING ON A DATE TO THE AMUSEMENT PARK LIKE THIS...
...THEN KISSING ON THE FERRIS WHEEL...!
YOU'RE... A SPORTY GIRL...
BUT I GUESS YOU HAVE A GIRLY SIDE TOO!!
SH... SHUT UP!
BLUSH
THAT'S WHY I DIDN'T WANT TO TELL YOU...!
I UNDERSTAND.
OKAY, THEN LET'S...
HUH?! UH... YEAH...!
HEY...

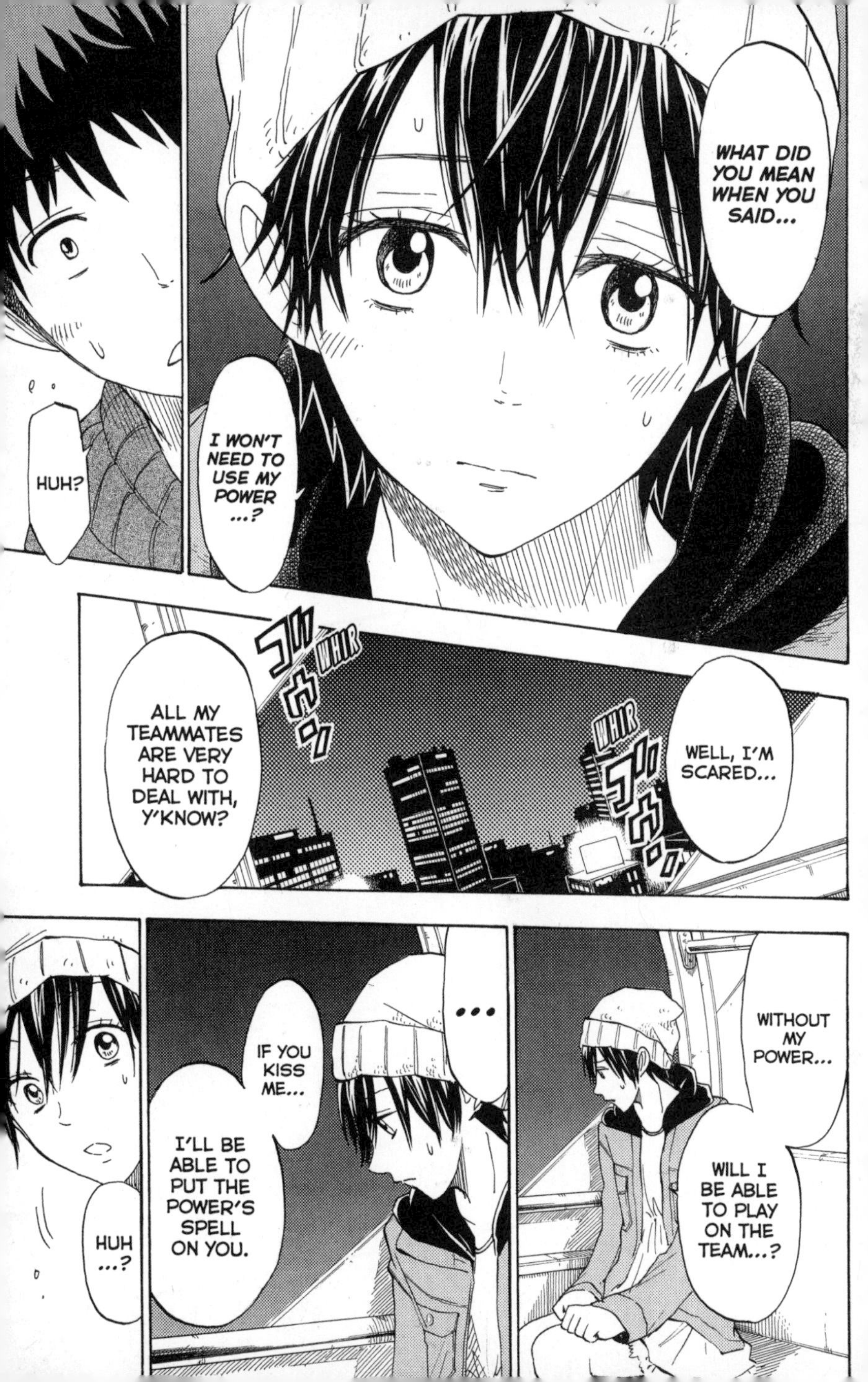
WHAT DID YOU MEAN WHEN YOU SAID...
I WON'T NEED TO USE MY POWER ...?
HUH?
WHIR
WELL, I'M SCARED...
WHIR
ALL MY TEAMMATES ARE VERY HARD TO DEAL WITH, Y'KNOW?
WITHOUT MY POWER...
WILL I BE ABLE TO PLAY ON THE TEAM...?
...
IF YOU KISS ME...
I'LL BE ABLE TO PUT THE POWER'S SPELL ON YOU.
HUH ...?

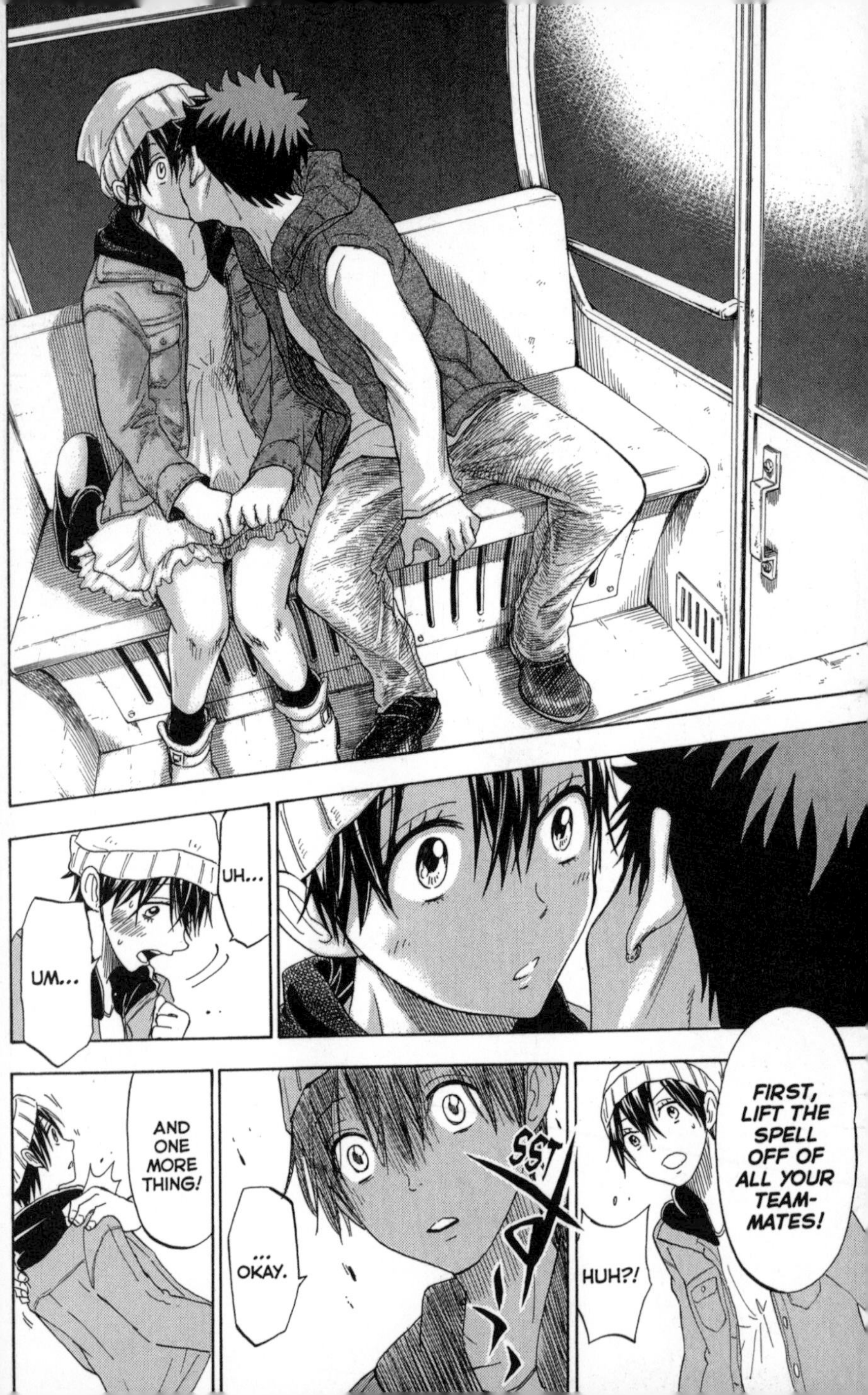
UH...
UM...
FIRST, LIFT THE SPELL OFF OF ALL YOUR TEAM-MATES!
HUH?!
SST
...OKAY.
AND ONE MORE THING!

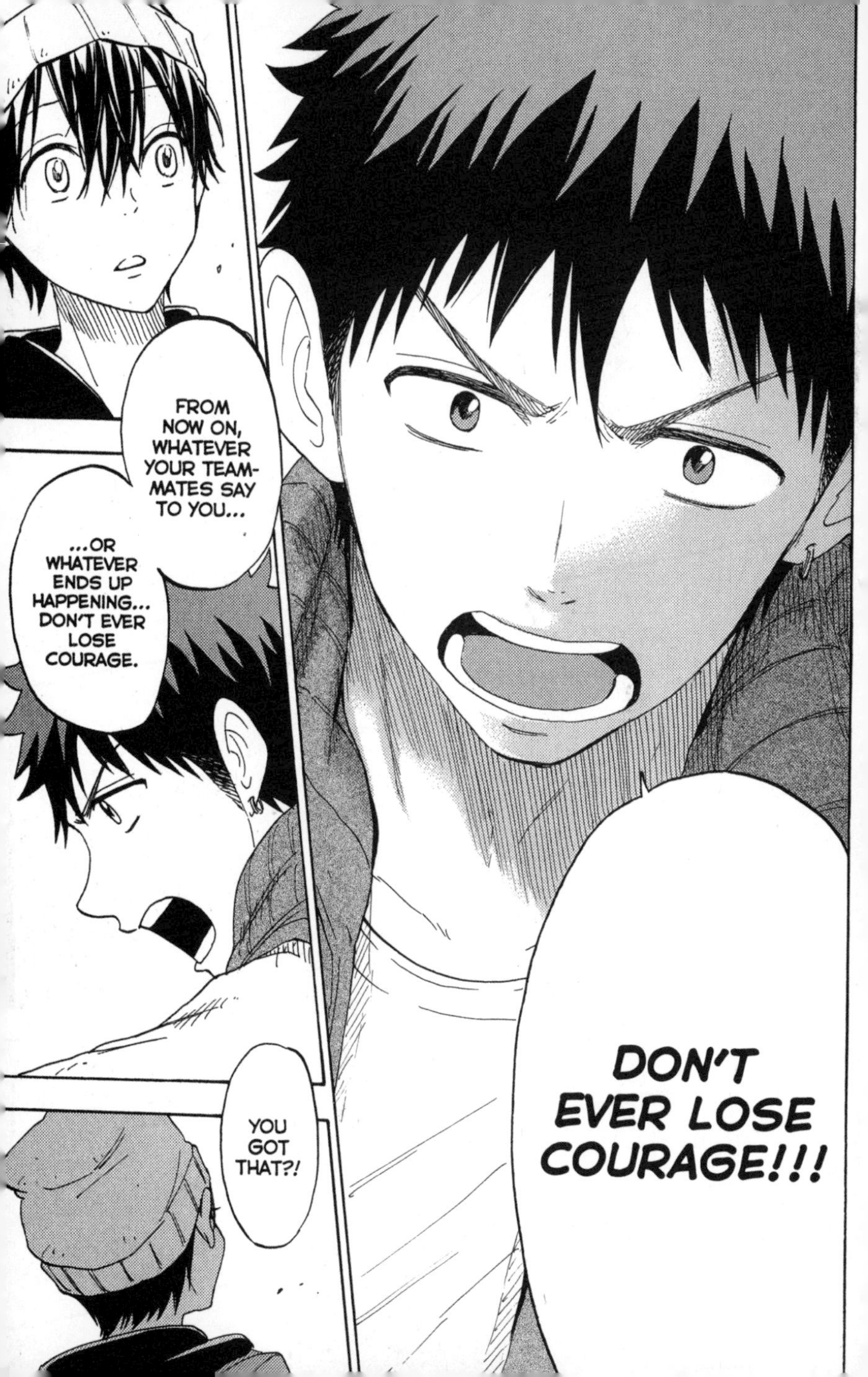
DON'T EVER LOSE COURAGE!!!
FROM NOW ON, WHATEVER YOUR TEAM-MATES SAY TO YOU...
...OR WHATEVER ENDS UP HAPPENING... DON'T EVER LOSE COURAGE.
YOU GOT THAT?!

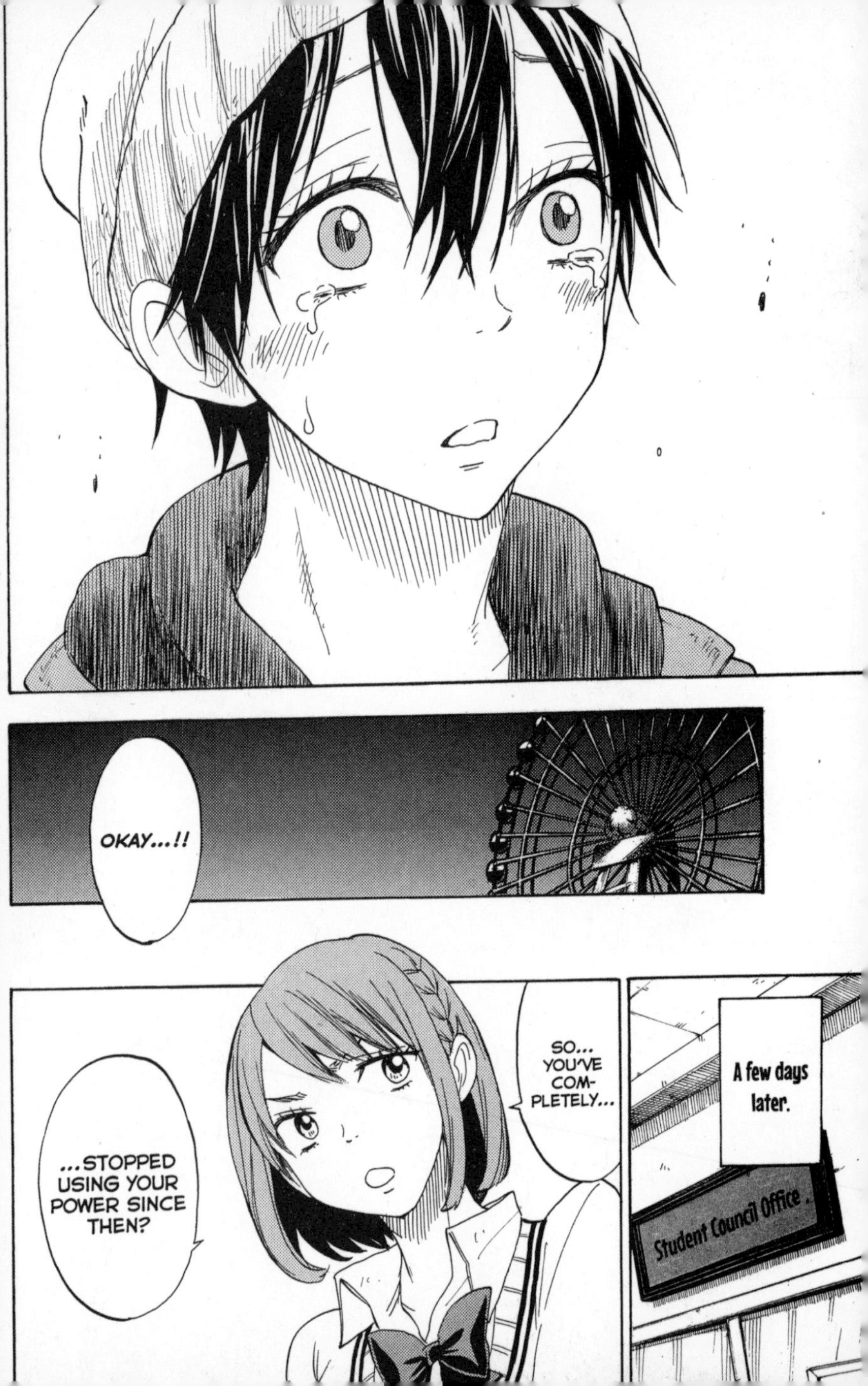
OKAY...!!
A few days later.
Student Council Office
SO... YOU'VE COM-PLETELY...
...STOPPED USING YOUR POWER SINCE THEN?

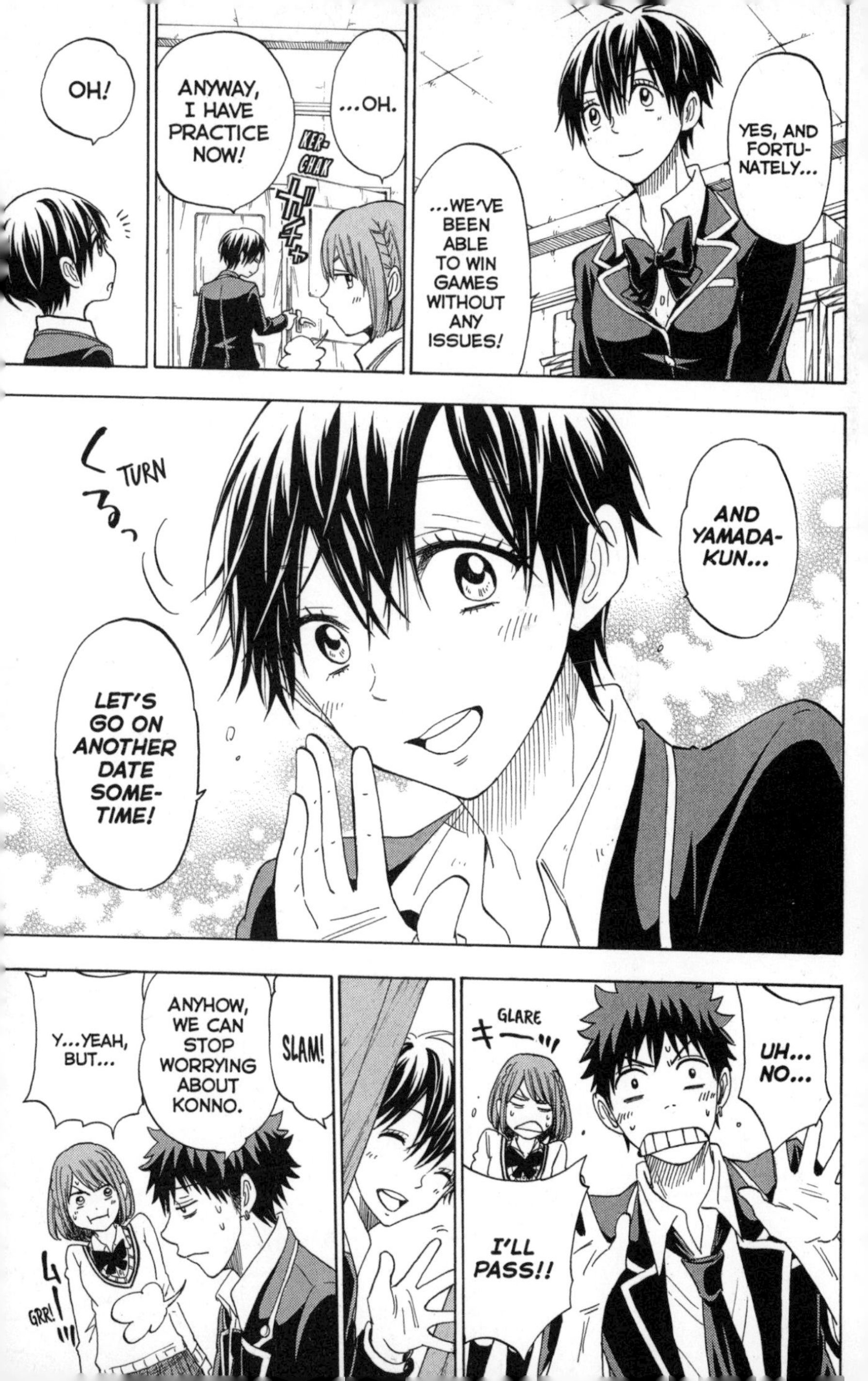
YES, AND FORTUNATELY...
...WE'VE BEEN ABLE TO WIN GAMES WITHOUT ANY ISSUES!
...OH.
ANYWAY, I HAVE PRACTICE NOW!
KER-CHAK
OH!
AND YAMADA-KUN...
TURN
LET'S GO ON ANOTHER DATE SOMETIME!
UH... NO...
GLARE
I'LL PASS!!
SLAM!
ANYHOW, WE CAN STOP WORRYING ABOUT KONNO.
Y...YEAH, BUT...
GRR!

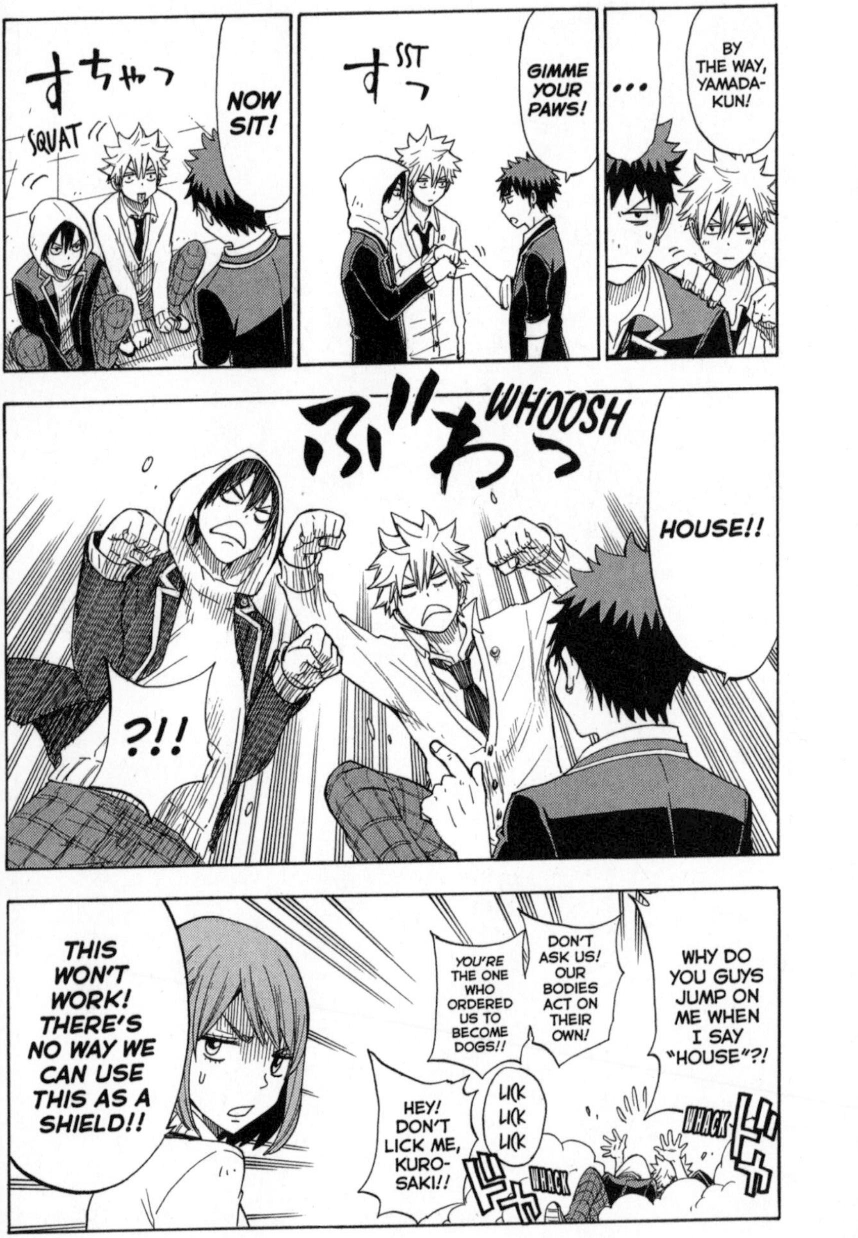
BY THE WAY, YAMADA-KUN!
...
GIMME YOUR PAWS!
すっ
SST
NOW SIT!
すちゃっ
SQUAT
HOUSE!!
ぶわっ
WHOOSH
?!!
WHY DO YOU GUYS JUMP ON ME WHEN I SAY "HOUSE"?!
DON'T ASK US! OUR BODIES ACT ON THEIR OWN!
YOU'RE THE ONE WHO ORDERED US TO BECOME DOGS!!
WHACK
LICK LICK LICK
HEY! DON'T LICK ME, KURO-SAKI!!
WHACK
THIS WON'T WORK! THERE'S NO WAY WE CAN USE THIS AS A SHIELD!!

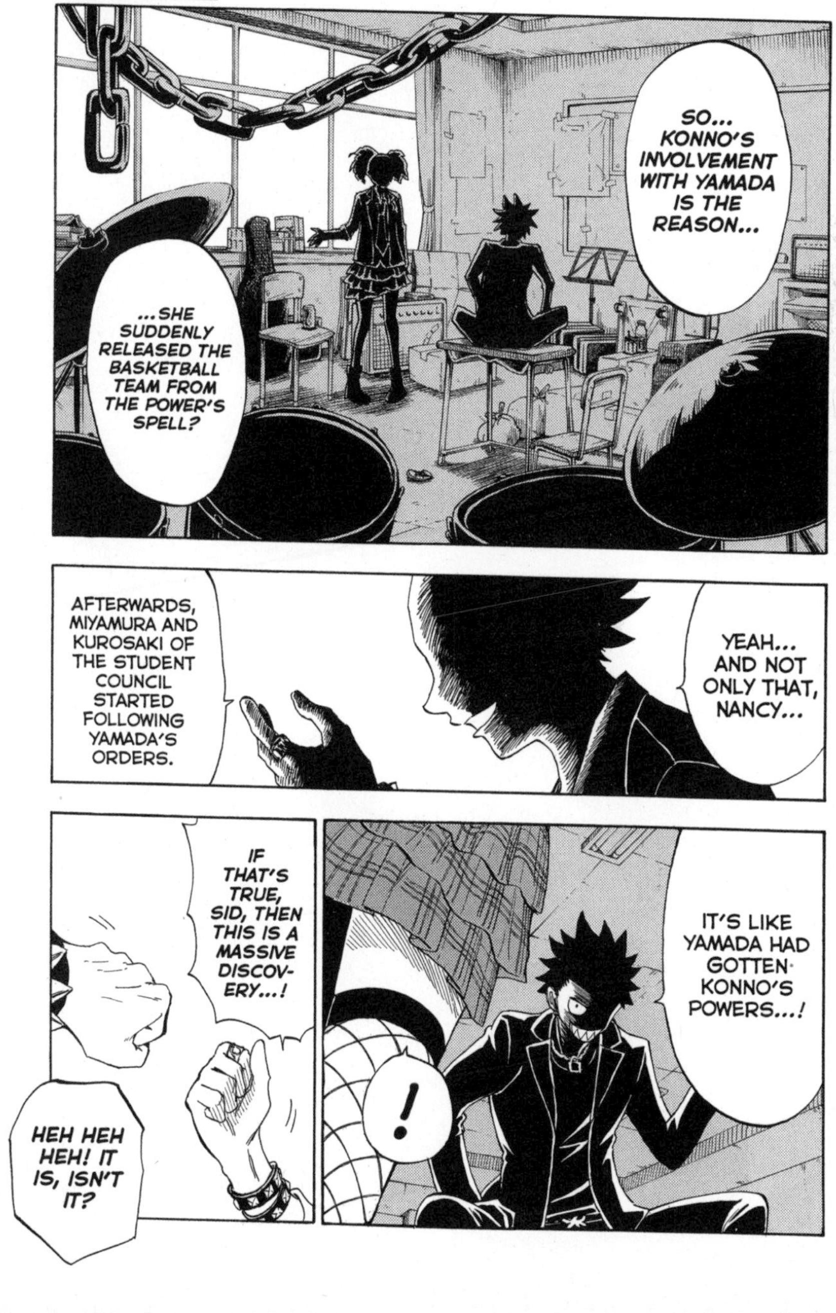
SO... KONNO'S INVOLVEMENT WITH YAMADA IS THE REASON...
...SHE SUDDENLY RELEASED THE BASKETBALL TEAM FROM THE POWER'S SPELL?
YEAH... AND NOT ONLY THAT, NANCY...
AFTERWARDS, MIYAMURA AND KUROSAKI OF THE STUDENT COUNCIL STARTED FOLLOWING YAMADA'S ORDERS.
IT'S LIKE YAMADA HAD GOTTEN KONNO'S POWERS...!
!
IF THAT'S TRUE, SID, THEN THIS IS A MASSIVE DISCOVERY...!
HEH HEH HEH! IT IS, ISN'T IT?

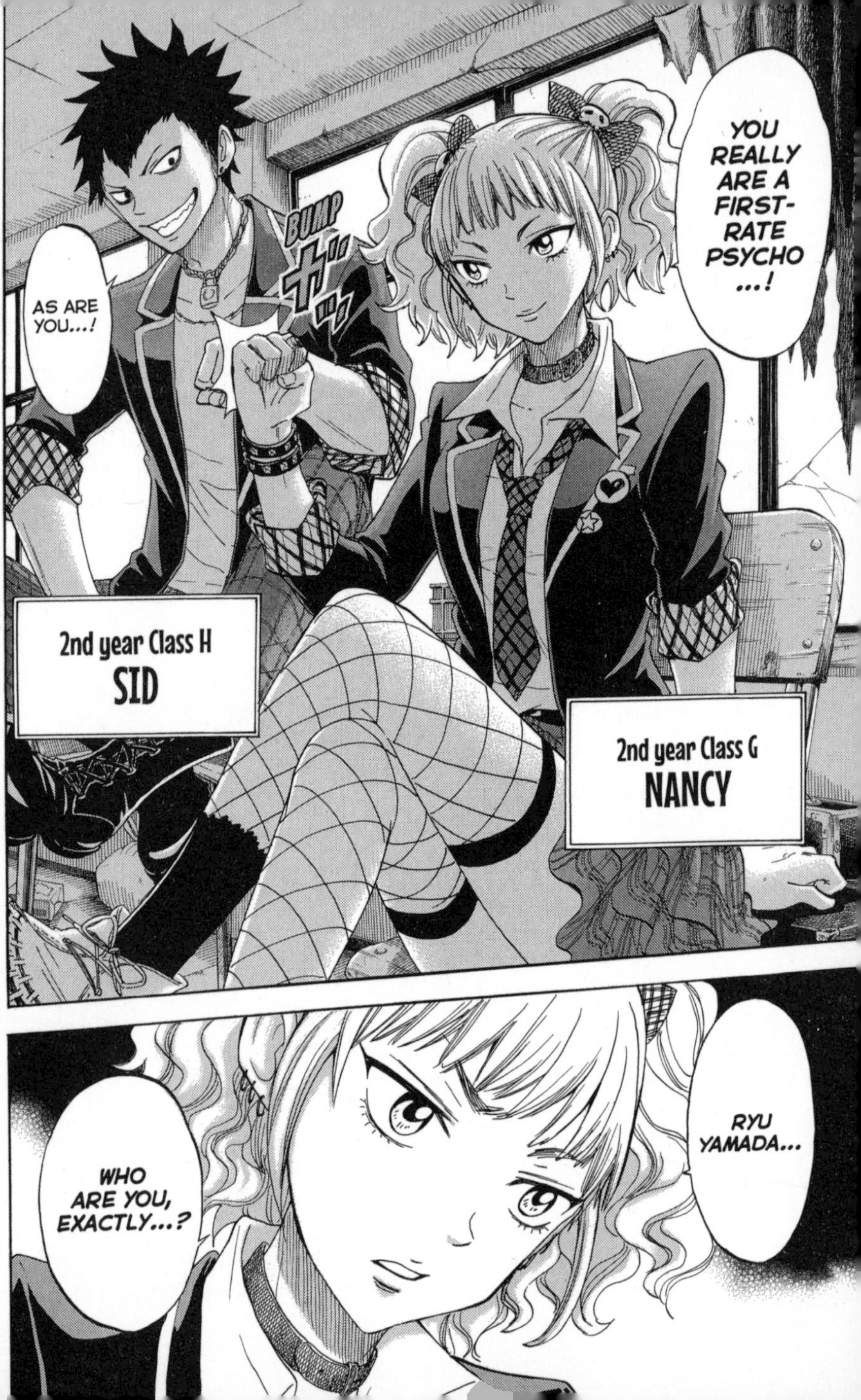
YOU REALLY ARE A FIRST-RATE PSYCHO ...!
BUMP
AS ARE YOU...!
2nd year Class G NANCY
2nd year Class H SID
RYU YAMADA...
WHO ARE YOU, EXACTLY...?

CHAPTER 102: You can see what his real intentions are.

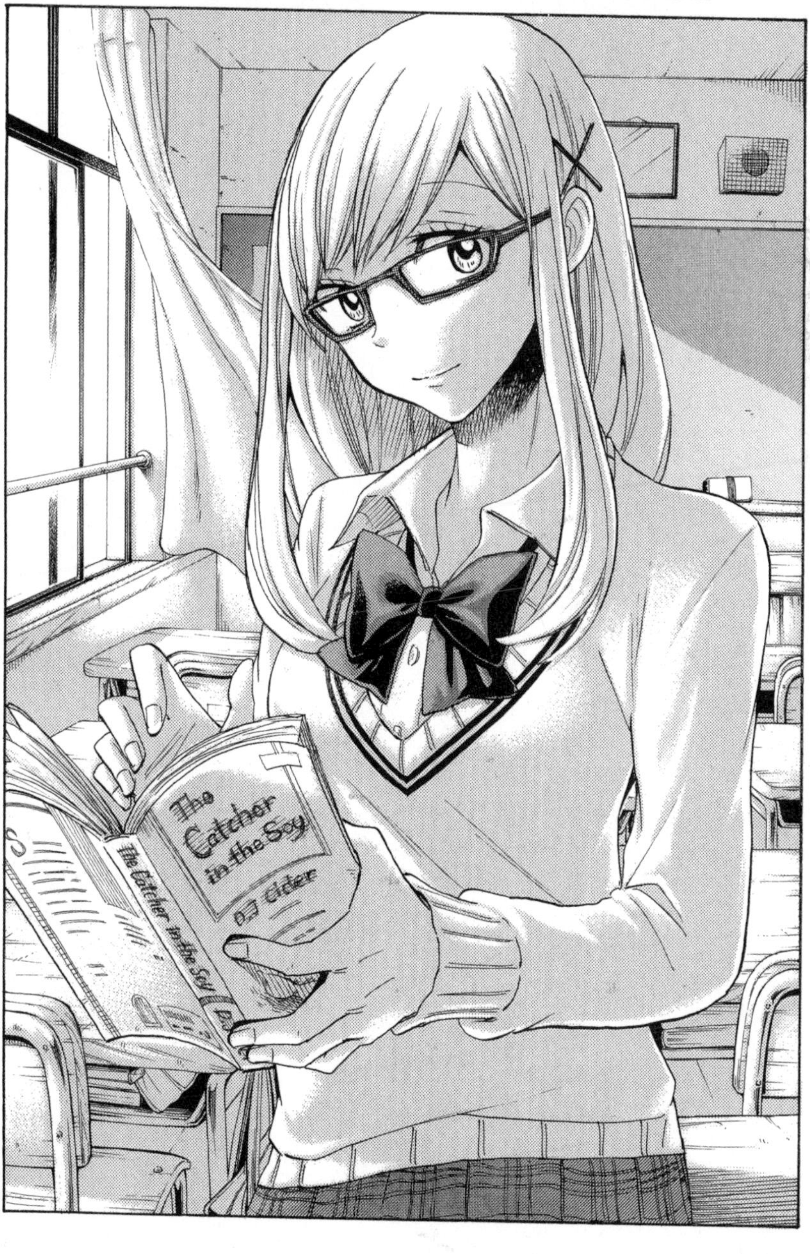
The Catcher in the Soy
O.J Cider
The Catcher in the Soy

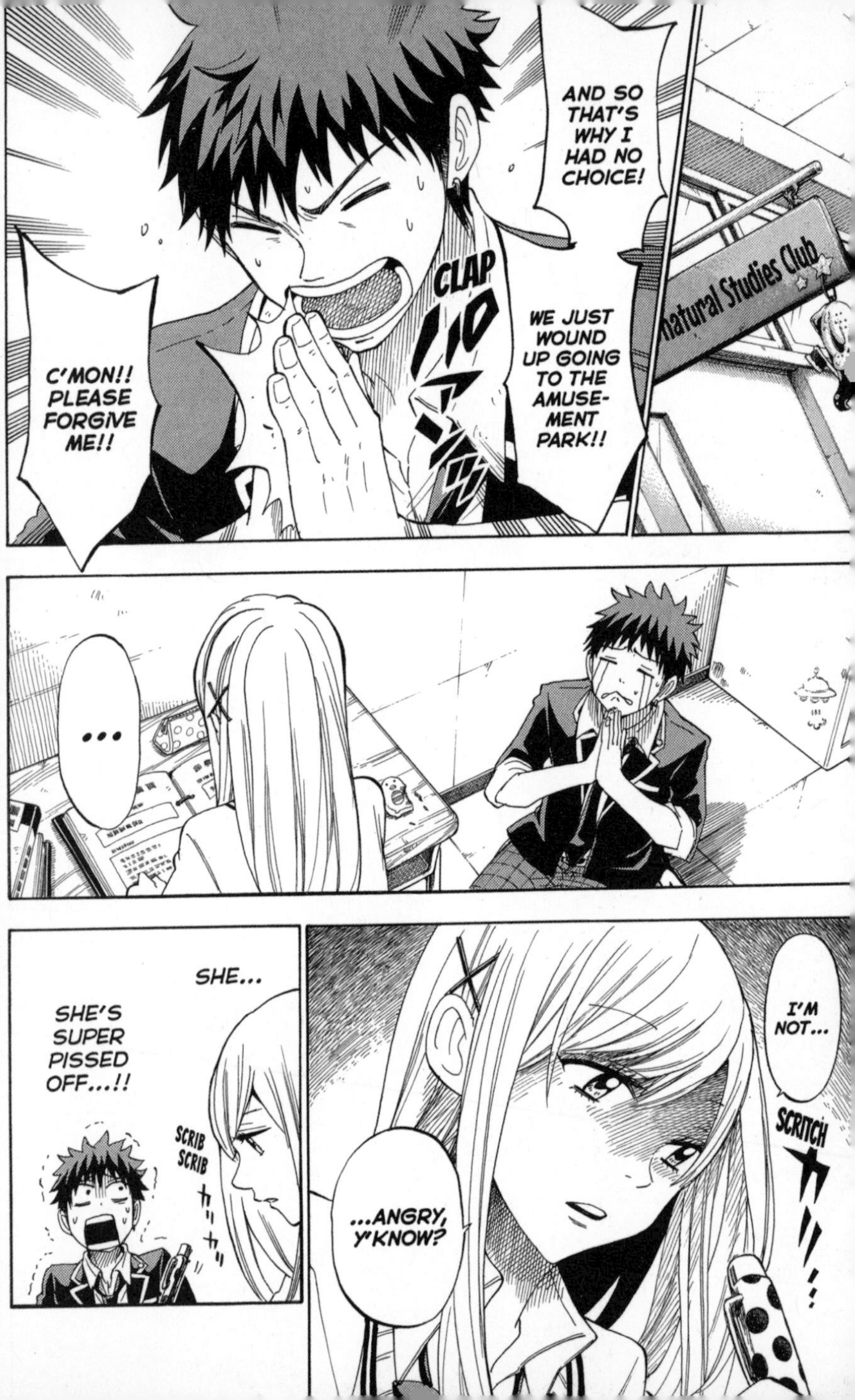
AND SO THAT'S WHY I HAD NO CHOICE!
Natural Studies Club
WE JUST WOUND UP GOING TO THE AMUSEMENT PARK!!
CLAP
C'MON!! PLEASE FORGIVE ME!!
...
I'M NOT...
SCRITCH
...ANGRY, Y'KNOW?
SHE...
SHE'S SUPER PISSED OFF...!!
SCRIB SCRIB

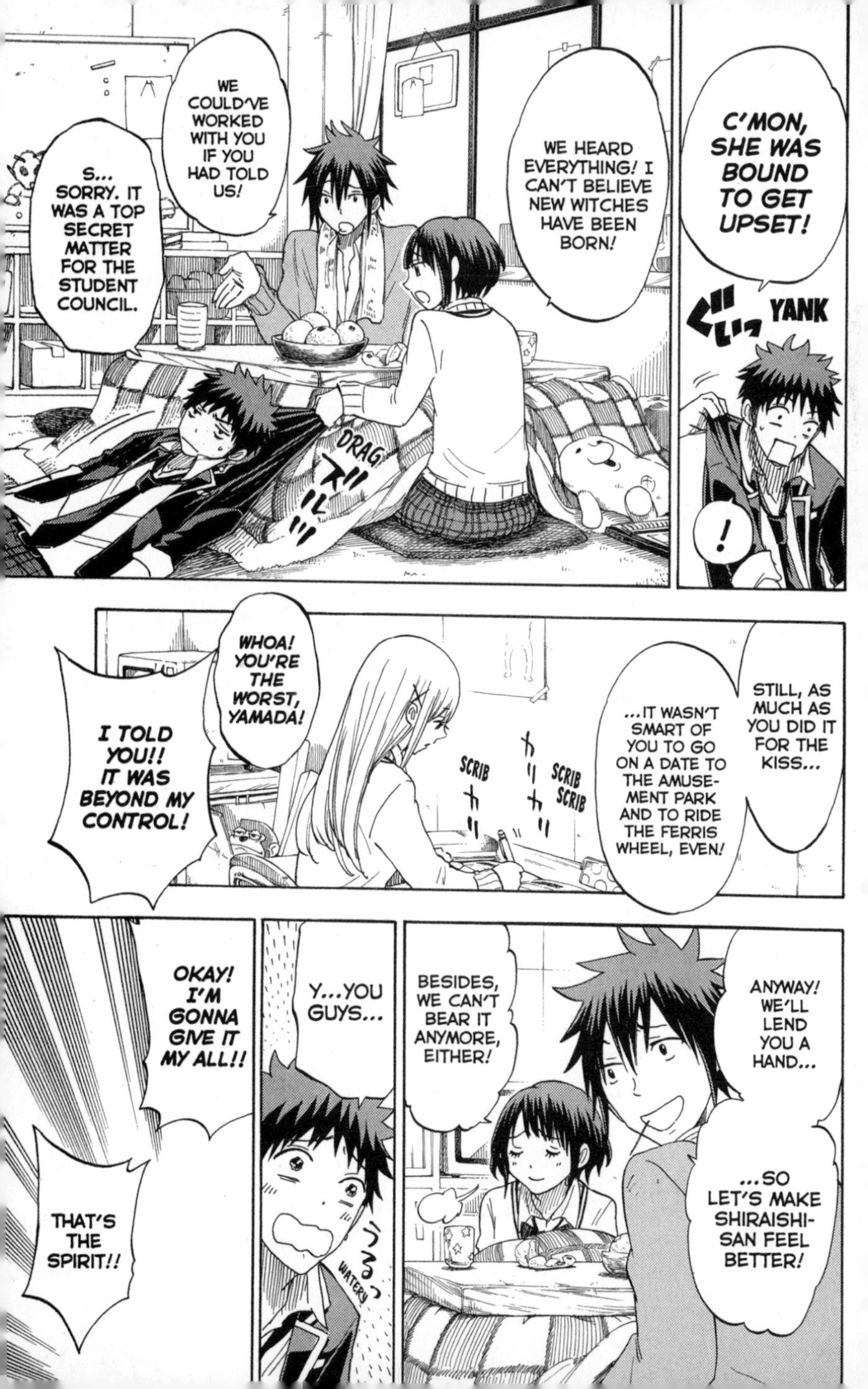
C'MON, SHE WAS BOUND TO GET UPSET!
YANK
!
WE HEARD EVERYTHING! I CAN'T BELIEVE NEW WITCHES HAVE BEEN BORN!
WE COULD'VE WORKED WITH YOU IF YOU HAD TOLD US!
S... SORRY. IT WAS A TOP SECRET MATTER FOR THE STUDENT COUNCIL.
DRAG
STILL, AS MUCH AS YOU DID IT FOR THE KISS...
...IT WASN'T SMART OF YOU TO GO ON A DATE TO THE AMUSEMENT PARK AND TO RIDE THE FERRIS WHEEL, EVEN!
SCRIB SCRIB
SCRIB
WHOA! YOU'RE THE WORST, YAMADA!
I TOLD YOU!! IT WAS BEYOND MY CONTROL!
ANYWAY! WE'LL LEND YOU A HAND...
...SO LET'S MAKE SHIRAISHI-SAN FEEL BETTER!
BESIDES, WE CAN'T BEAR IT ANYMORE, EITHER!
Y...YOU GUYS...
WATERY
OKAY! I'M GONNA GIVE IT MY ALL!!
THAT'S THE SPIRIT!!

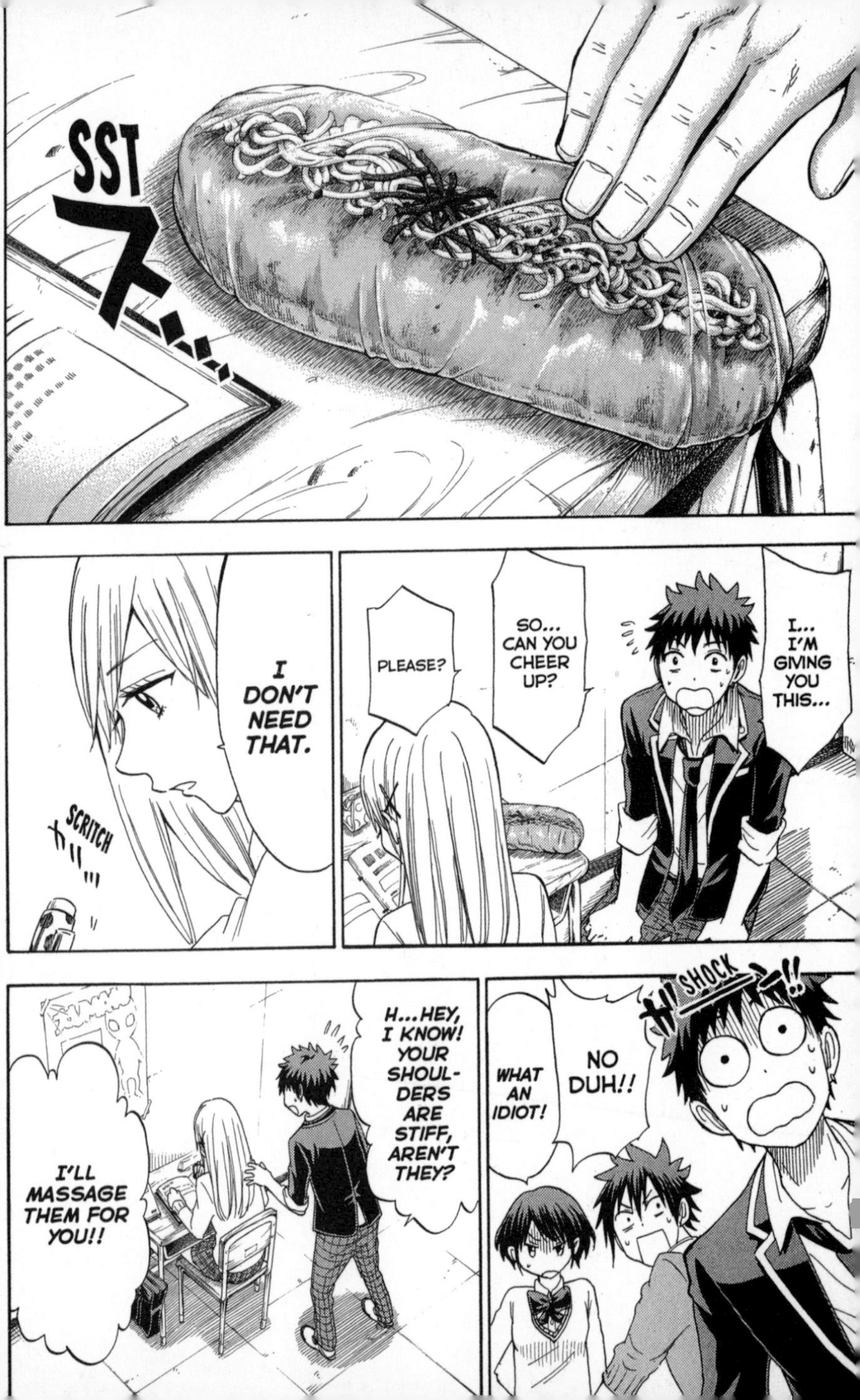
SST
I... I'M GIVING YOU THIS...
SO... CAN YOU CHEER UP?
PLEASE?
I DON'T NEED THAT.
SCRITCH
SHOCK
NO DUH!!
WHAT AN IDIOT!
H...HEY, I KNOW! YOUR SHOUL-DERS ARE STIFF, AREN'T THEY?
I'LL MASSAGE THEM FOR YOU!!

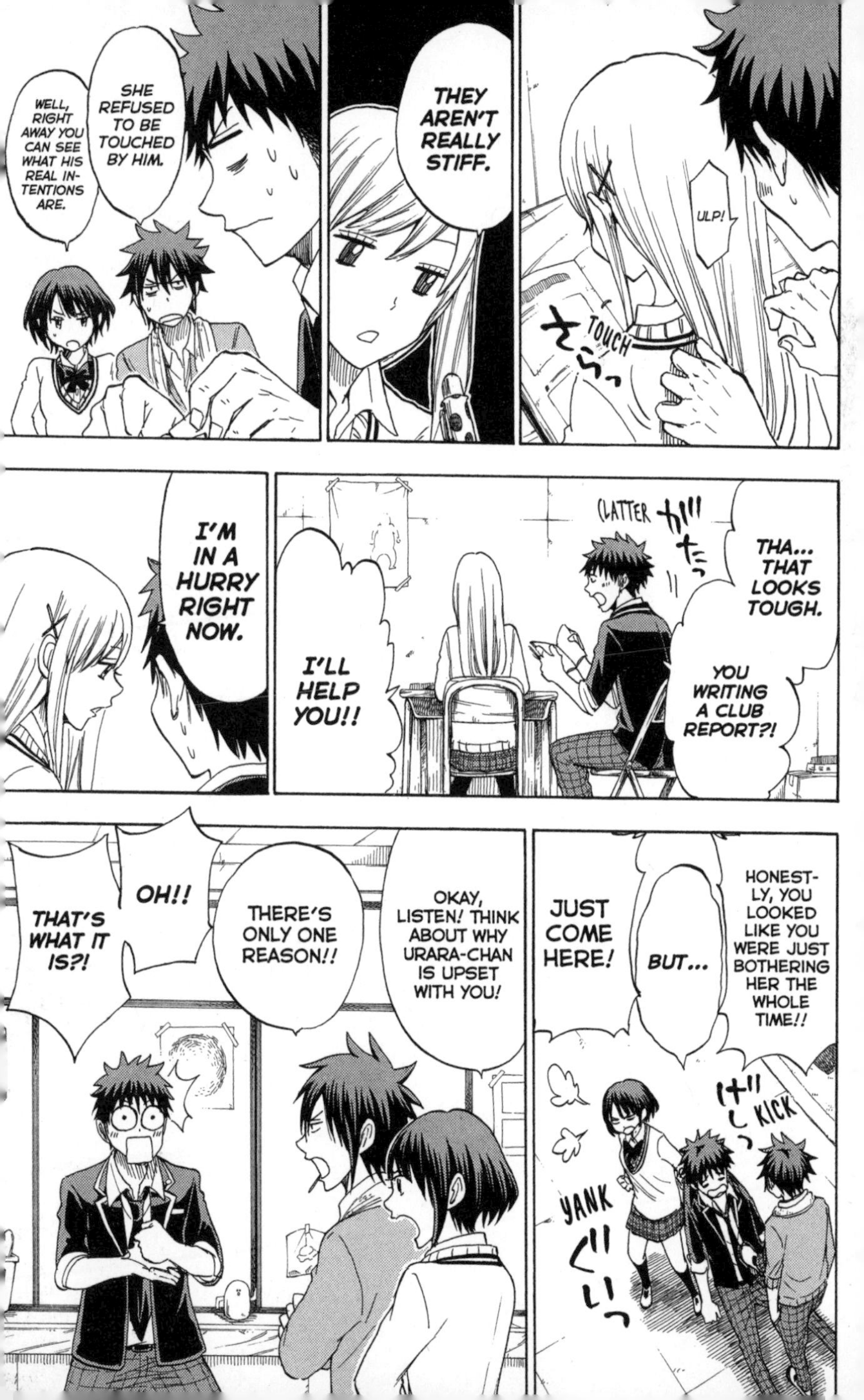
ULP!
TOUCH
THEY AREN'T REALLY STIFF.
SHE REFUSED TO BE TOUCHED BY HIM.
WELL, RIGHT AWAY YOU CAN SEE WHAT HIS REAL IN-TENTIONS ARE.
CLATTER
THA... THAT LOOKS TOUGH.
YOU WRITING A CLUB REPORT?!
I'LL HELP YOU!!
I'M IN A HURRY RIGHT NOW.
HONEST-LY, YOU LOOKED LIKE YOU WERE JUST BOTHERING HER THE WHOLE TIME!!
BUT...
JUST COME HERE!
KICK
YANK
OKAY, LISTEN! THINK ABOUT WHY URARA-CHAN IS UPSET WITH YOU!
THERE'S ONLY ONE REASON!!
OH!!
THAT'S WHAT IT IS?!

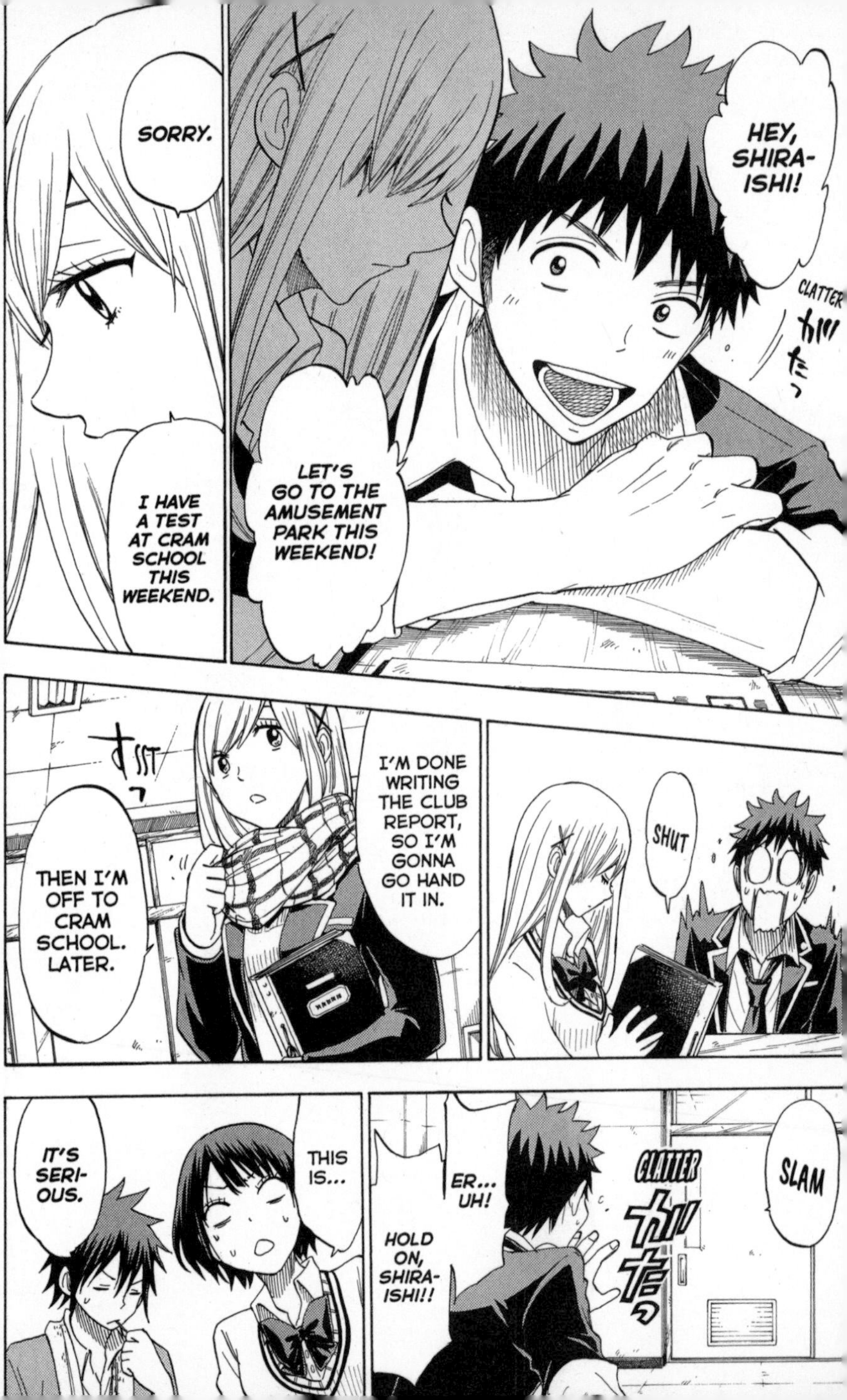
HEY, SHIRA-ISHI!
CLATTER
LET'S GO TO THE AMUSEMENT PARK THIS WEEKEND!
SORRY.
I HAVE A TEST AT CRAM SCHOOL THIS WEEKEND.
SHUT
I'M DONE WRITING THE CLUB REPORT, SO I'M GONNA GO HAND IT IN.
SSST
THEN I'M OFF TO CRAM SCHOOL. LATER.
SLAM
CLATTER
ER... UH!
HOLD ON, SHIRA-ISHI!!
THIS IS...
IT'S SERI-OUS.

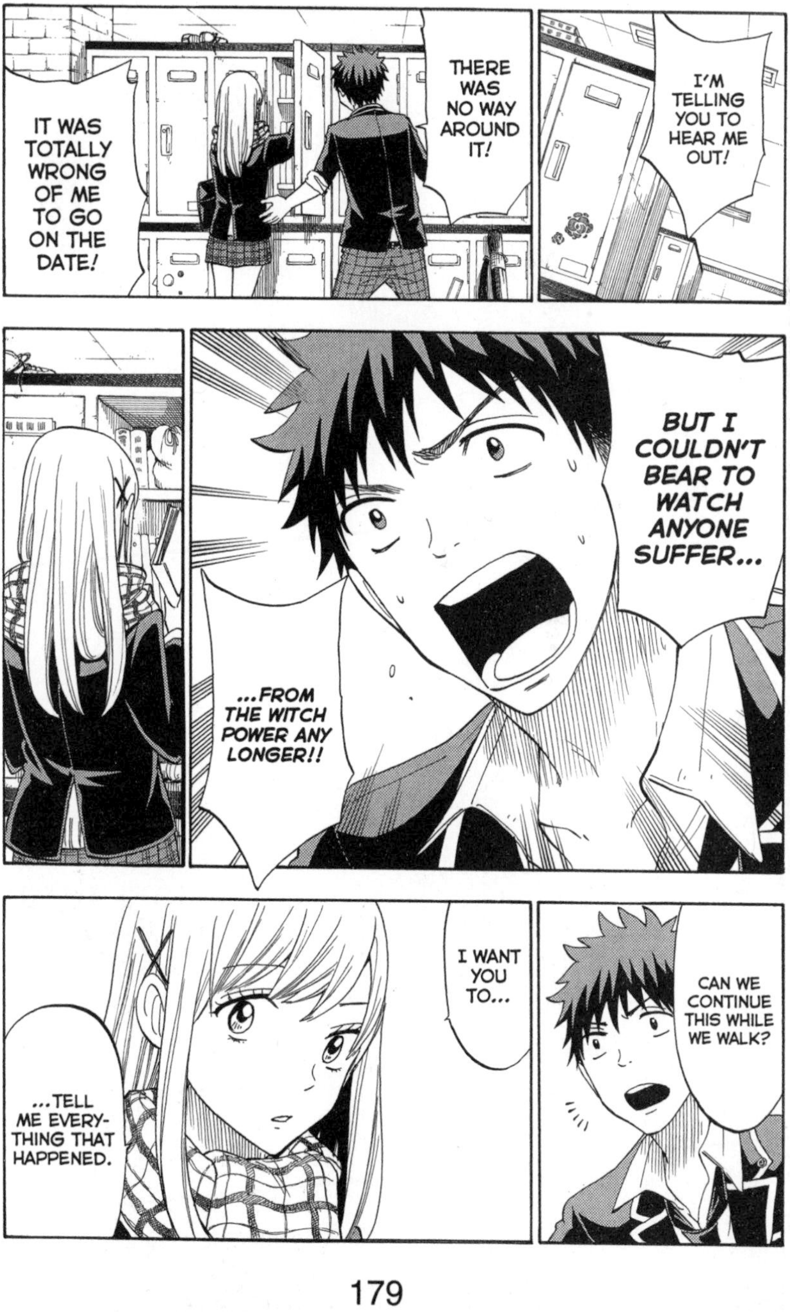
I'M TELLING YOU TO HEAR ME OUT!
THERE WAS NO WAY AROUND IT!
IT WAS TOTALLY WRONG OF ME TO GO ON THE DATE!
BUT I COULDN'T BEAR TO WATCH ANYONE SUFFER...
...FROM THE WITCH POWER ANY LONGER!!
CAN WE CONTINUE THIS WHILE WE WALK?
I WANT YOU TO...
...TELL ME EVERY-THING THAT HAPPENED.

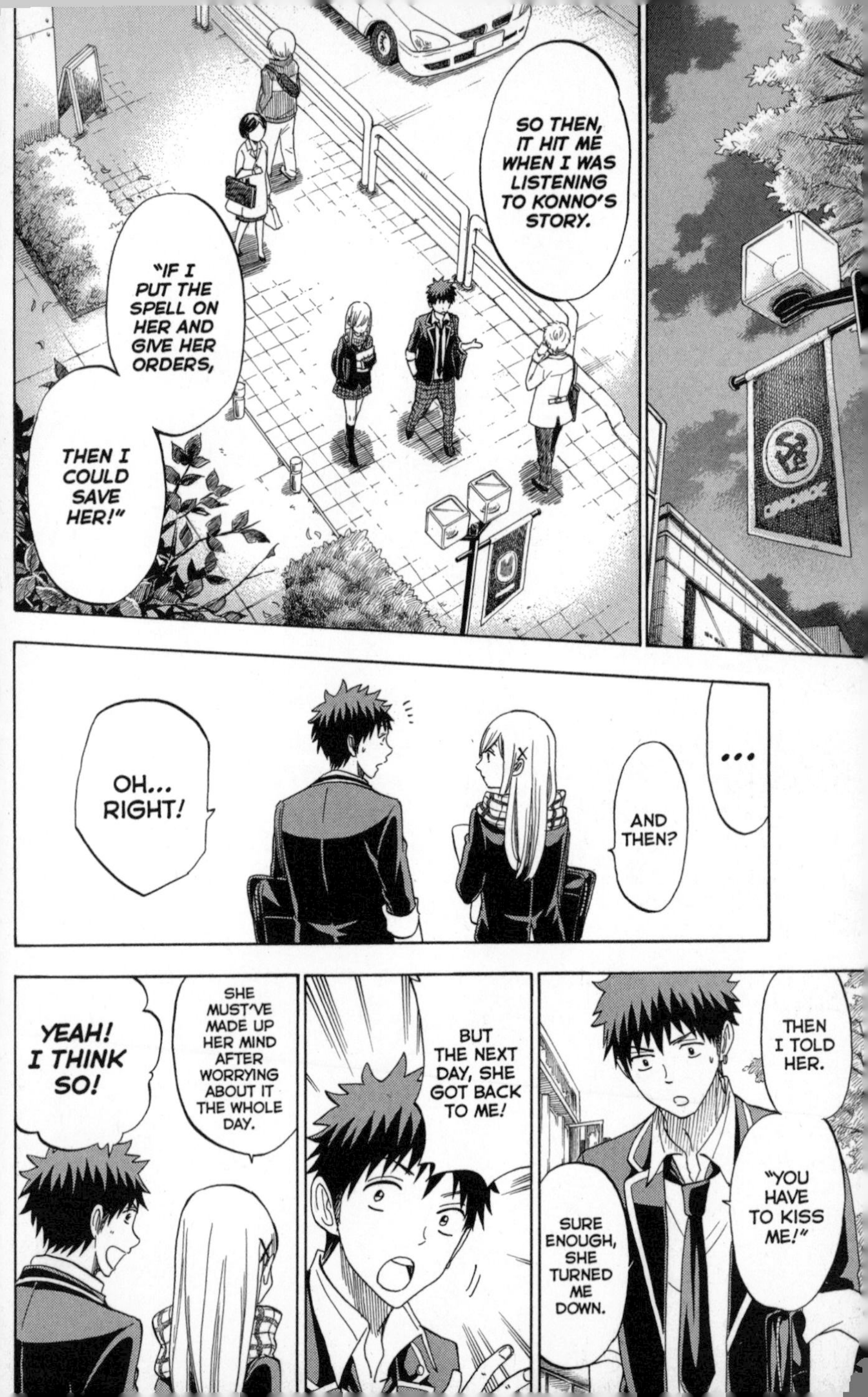
SO THEN, IT HIT ME WHEN I WAS LISTENING TO KONNO'S STORY.
"IF I PUT THE SPELL ON HER AND GIVE HER ORDERS,
THEN I COULD SAVE HER!"
...
AND THEN?
OH... RIGHT!
THEN I TOLD HER.
"YOU HAVE TO KISS ME!"
SURE ENOUGH, SHE TURNED ME DOWN.
BUT THE NEXT DAY, SHE GOT BACK TO ME!
SHE MUST'VE MADE UP HER MIND AFTER WORRYING ABOUT IT THE WHOLE DAY.
YEAH! I THINK SO!

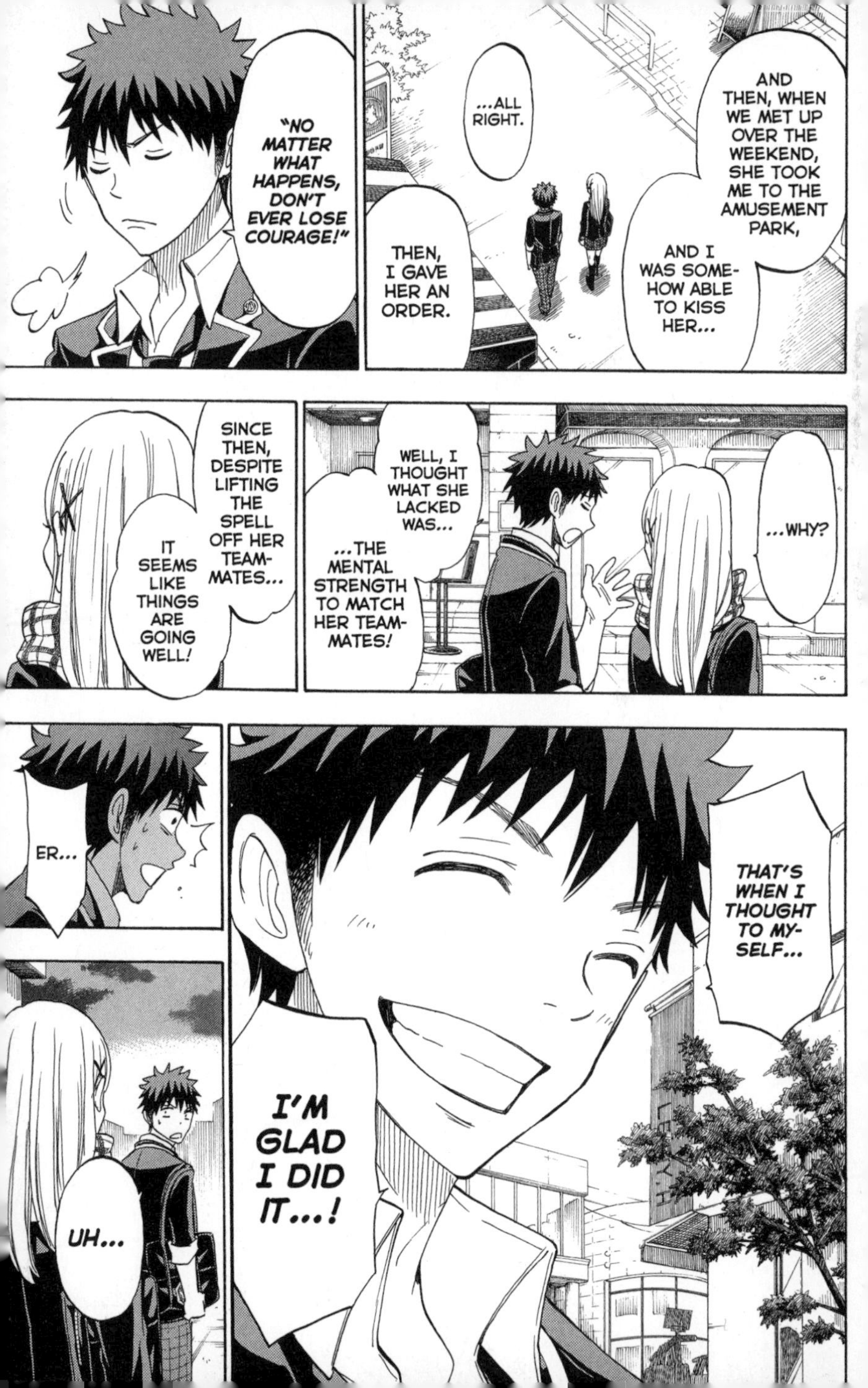
AND THEN, WHEN WE MET UP OVER THE WEEKEND, SHE TOOK ME TO THE AMUSEMENT PARK,
AND I WAS SOMEHOW ABLE TO KISS HER...
...ALL RIGHT.
THEN, I GAVE HER AN ORDER.
"NO MATTER WHAT HAPPENS, DON'T EVER LOSE COURAGE!"
...WHY?
WELL, I THOUGHT WHAT SHE LACKED WAS...
...THE MENTAL STRENGTH TO MATCH HER TEAMMATES!
SINCE THEN, DESPITE LIFTING THE SPELL OFF HER TEAMMATES...
IT SEEMS LIKE THINGS ARE GOING WELL!
THAT'S WHEN I THOUGHT TO MYSELF...
I'M GLAD I DID IT...!
ER...
UH...

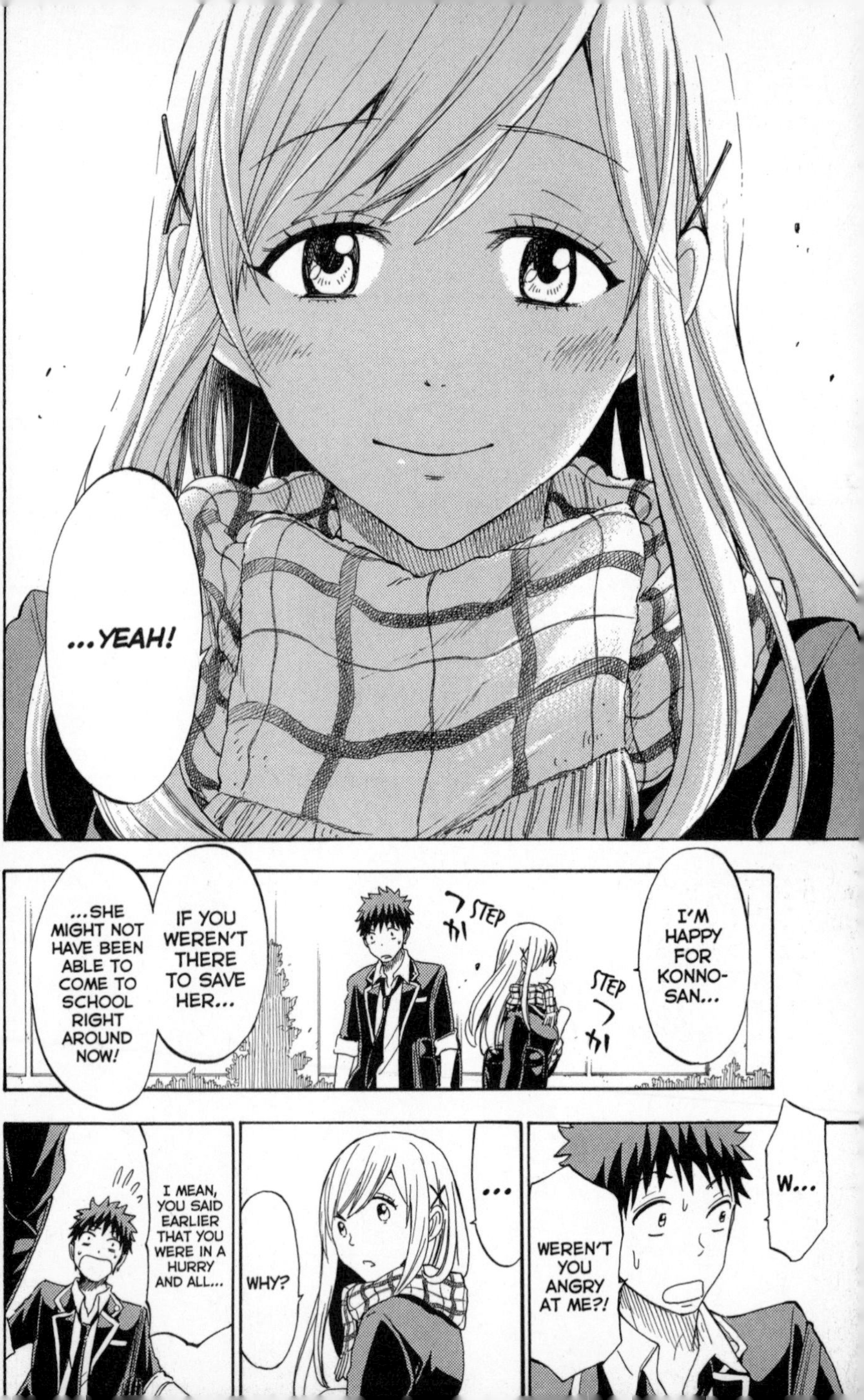
...YEAH!
I'M HAPPY FOR KONNO-SAN...
STEP
STEP
IF YOU WEREN'T THERE TO SAVE HER...
...SHE MIGHT NOT HAVE BEEN ABLE TO COME TO SCHOOL RIGHT AROUND NOW!
W...
WEREN'T YOU ANGRY AT ME?!
...
WHY?
I MEAN, YOU SAID EARLIER THAT YOU WERE IN A HURRY AND ALL...

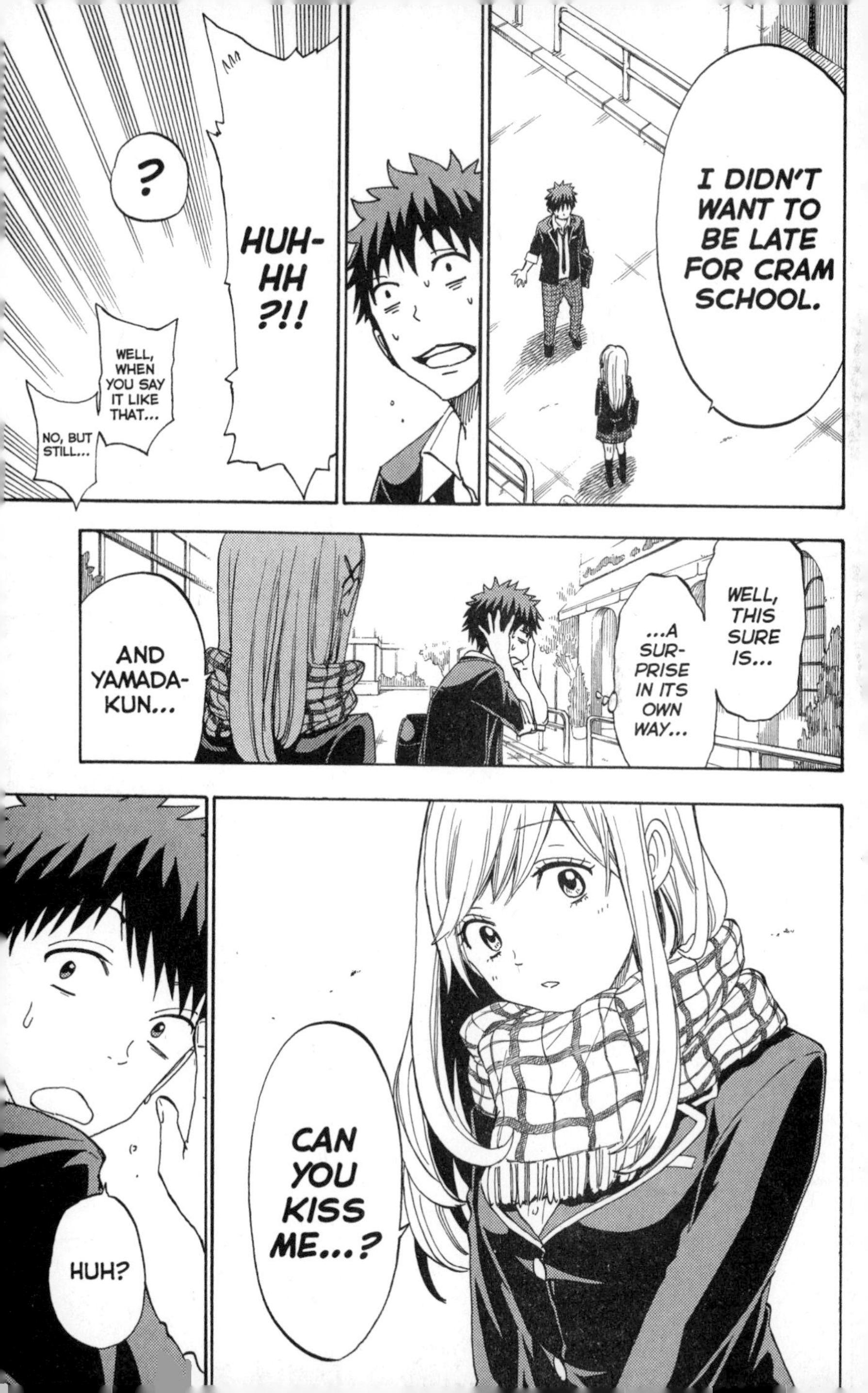
I DIDN'T WANT TO BE LATE FOR CRAM SCHOOL.
HUH-HH?!!
?
WELL, WHEN YOU SAY IT LIKE THAT...
NO, BUT STILL...
WELL, THIS SURE IS...
...A SURPRISE IN ITS OWN WAY...
AND YAMADA-KUN...
CAN YOU KISS ME...?
HUH?

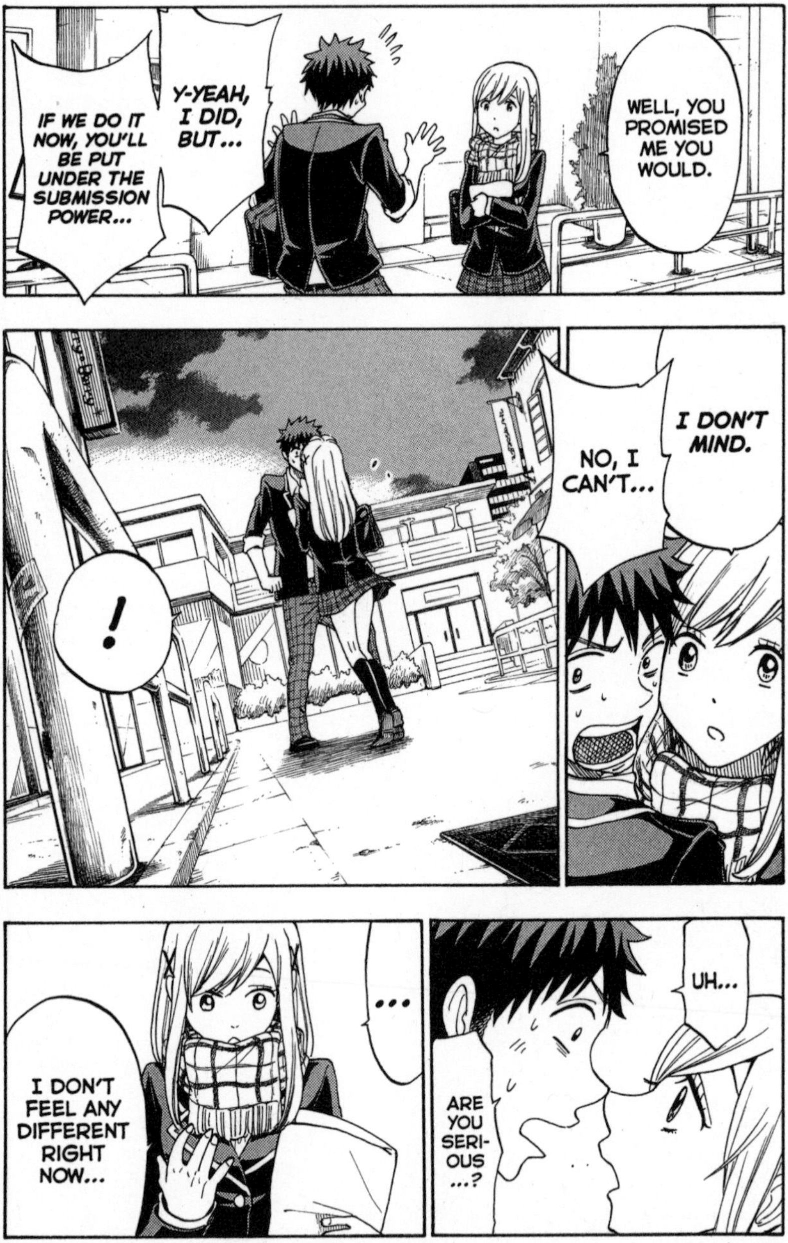
WELL, YOU PROMISED ME YOU WOULD.
Y-YEAH, I DID, BUT...
IF WE DO IT NOW, YOU'LL BE PUT UNDER THE SUBMISSION POWER...
I DON'T MIND.
NO, I CAN'T...
!
UH...
ARE YOU SERI-OUS ...?
...
I DON'T FEEL ANY DIFFERENT RIGHT NOW...

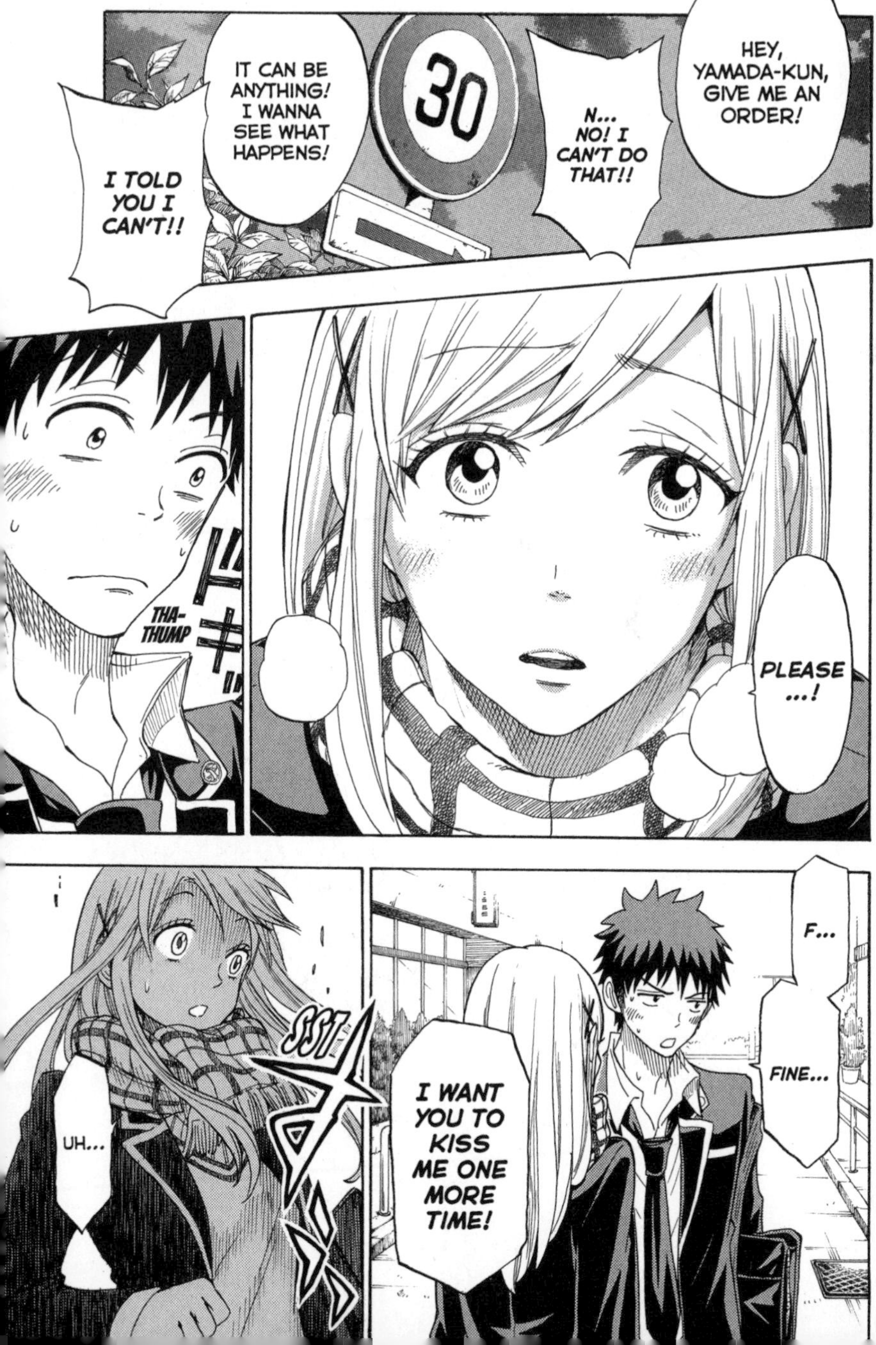
HEY, YAMADA-KUN, GIVE ME AN ORDER!
N... NO! I CAN'T DO THAT!!
IT CAN BE ANYTHING! I WANNA SEE WHAT HAPPENS!
I TOLD YOU I CAN'T!!
PLEASE ...!
THA-THUMP
F...
FINE...
I WANT YOU TO KISS ME ONE MORE TIME!
SSST
UH...

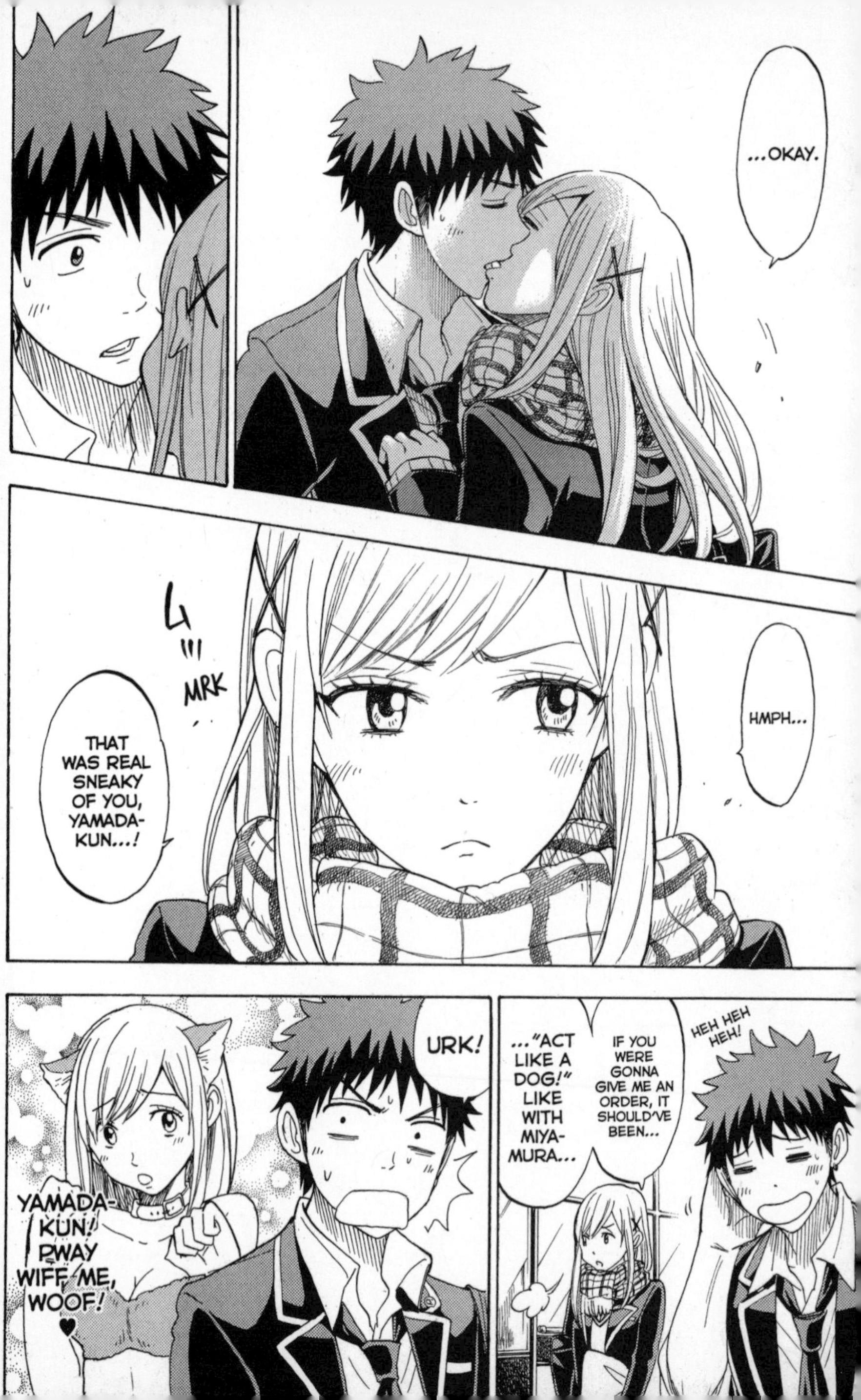
...OKAY.
HMPH...
MRK
THAT WAS REAL SNEAKY OF YOU, YAMADA-KUN...!
HEH HEH HEH!
IF YOU WERE GONNA GIVE ME AN ORDER, IT SHOULD'VE BEEN...
..."ACT LIKE A DOG!" LIKE WITH MIYAMURA...
URK!
YAMADA-KUN! PWAY WIFF ME, WOOF! ♥

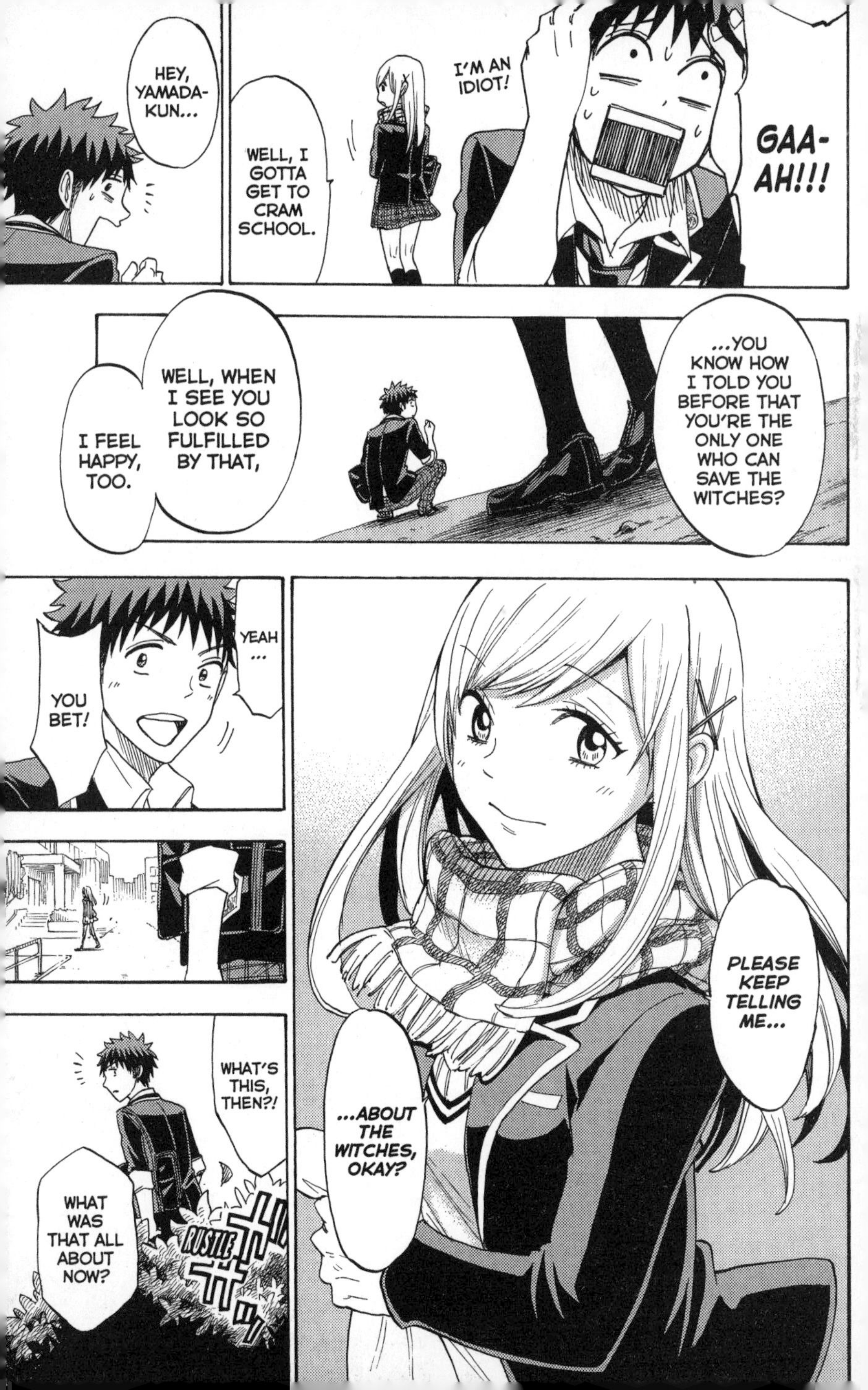
GAA-AH!!!
I'M AN IDIOT!
WELL, I GOTTA GET TO CRAM SCHOOL.
HEY, YAMADA-KUN...
...YOU KNOW HOW I TOLD YOU BEFORE THAT YOU'RE THE ONLY ONE WHO CAN SAVE THE WITCHES?
WELL, WHEN I SEE YOU LOOK SO FULFILLED BY THAT,
I FEEL HAPPY, TOO.
PLEASE KEEP TELLING ME...
...ABOUT THE WITCHES, OKAY?
YEAH...
YOU BET!
WHAT'S THIS, THEN?!
WHAT WAS THAT ALL ABOUT NOW?
RUSTLE

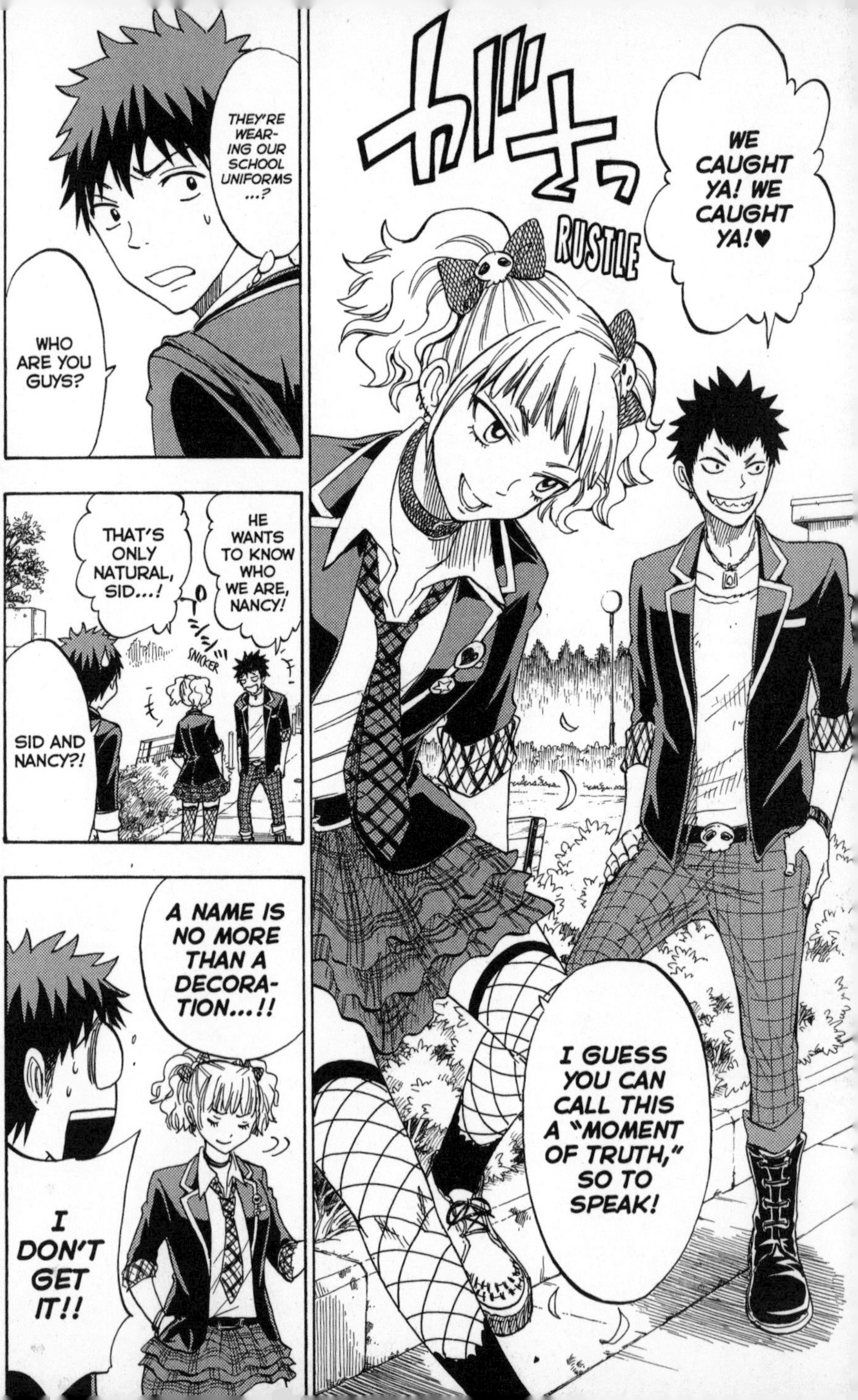
RUSTLE
WE CAUGHT YA! WE CAUGHT YA!♥
I GUESS YOU CAN CALL THIS A "MOMENT OF TRUTH," SO TO SPEAK!
THEY'RE WEAR-ING OUR SCHOOL UNIFORMS ...?
WHO ARE YOU GUYS?
HE WANTS TO KNOW WHO WE ARE, NANCY!
THAT'S ONLY NATURAL, SID...!
SNICKER
SID AND NANCY?!
A NAME IS NO MORE THAN A DECORA-TION...!!
I DON'T GET IT!!

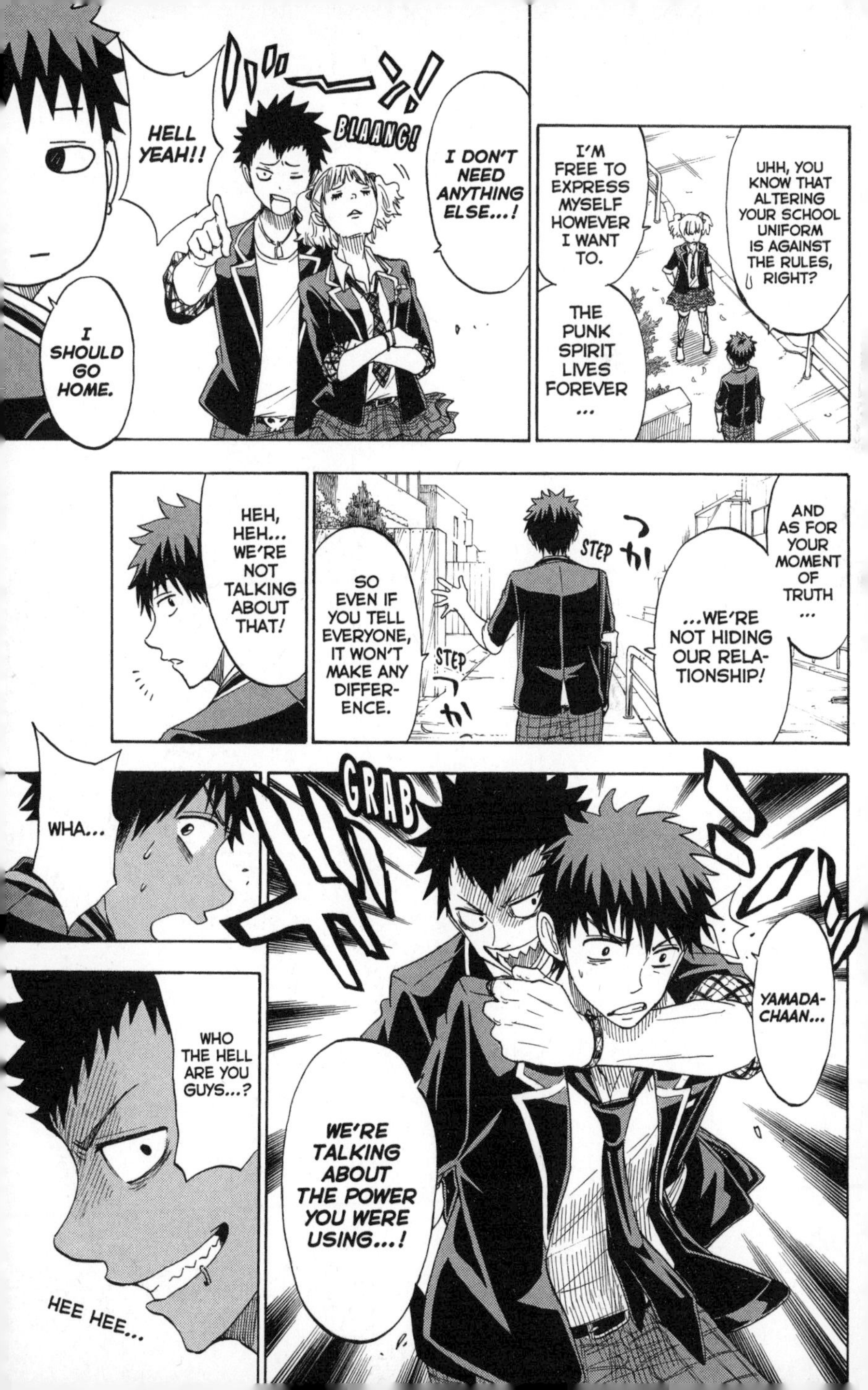
UHH, YOU KNOW THAT ALTERING YOUR SCHOOL UNIFORM IS AGAINST THE RULES, RIGHT?
I'M FREE TO EXPRESS MYSELF HOWEVER I WANT TO.
THE PUNK SPIRIT LIVES FOREVER...
BLAAANG!
I DON'T NEED ANYTHING ELSE...!
HELL YEAH!!
I SHOULD GO HOME.
AND AS FOR YOUR MOMENT OF TRUTH...
...WE'RE NOT HIDING OUR RELATIONSHIP!
STEP
STEP
SO EVEN IF YOU TELL EVERYONE, IT WON'T MAKE ANY DIFFERENCE.
HEH, HEH... WE'RE NOT TALKING ABOUT THAT!
GRAB
YAMADA-CHAAN...
WE'RE TALKING ABOUT THE POWER YOU WERE USING...!
WHA...
WHO THE HELL ARE YOU GUYS...?
HEE HEE...

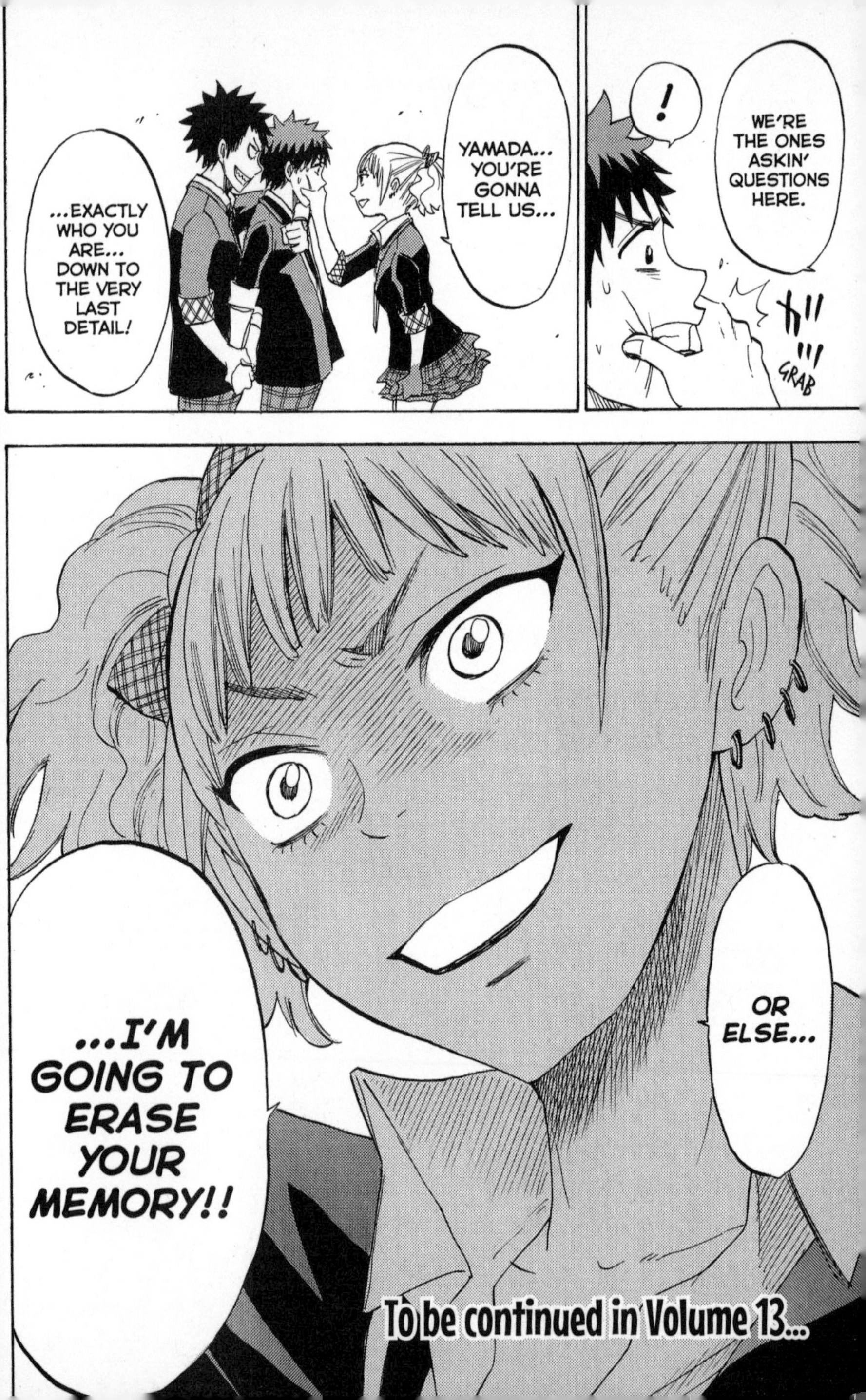
!
WE'RE THE ONES ASKIN' QUESTIONS HERE.
GRAB
YAMADA... YOU'RE GONNA TELL US...
...EXACTLY WHO YOU ARE... DOWN TO THE VERY LAST DETAIL!
OR ELSE...
...I'M GOING TO ERASE YOUR MEMORY!!
To be continued in Volume 13...

Translation Notes

Susshi, page 69

If it's not obvious, this is Suzaku High's own version of Nessie (commonly known as the Loch Ness Monster).

Bean-jam bun and chocolate cornets, page 111

Bean-jam buns (JP: manju) are pastries that have been filled with a paste made of boiled azuki beans and sugar and are a fairly common treat in Japan. Chocolate cornets are also a common pastry that consists of a chocolate-filled brioche. The actual pastry resembles a horn, which is the root meaning of the name "cornet."

Close-Contact Defense System, page 136

The Chinese character used here for "council" in "student council" is an old form of that character. When Miyamura mentions that the Close-Contact Defense System has been a part of the Student Council for a long time, it's obvious from the use of that particular character. This is because characters like that haven't been used regularly in Japan since at least the 1950s.

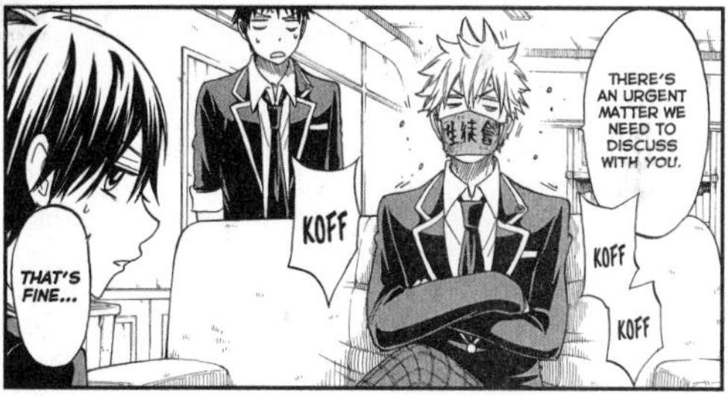

THERE'S AN URGENT MATTER WE NEED TO DISCUSS WITH YOU.
KOFF
KOFF
KOFF
THAT'S FINE...

House, page 170

In Japan, "house" is a relatively common command for a dog to return to or go into their dog house or cage.

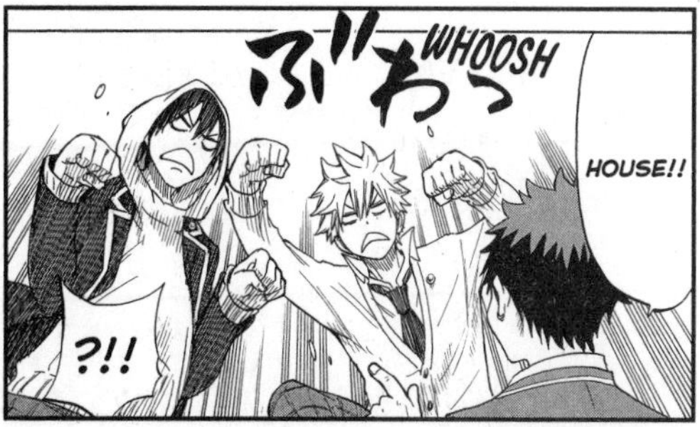

HOUSE!!
ぶわっ
WHOOSH
?!!

Yamada-kun and the Seven Witches volume 12 is a work of fiction.
Names, characters, places, and incidents are the products of the author's
imagination or are used fictitiously. Any resemblance to actual events,
locales, or persons, living or dead, is entirely coincidental.

A Kodansha Comics Trade Paperback Original.

Yamada-kun and the Seven Witches volume 12 copyright © 2014 Miki
Yoshikawa
English translation copyright © 2016 Miki Yoshikawa

All rights reserved.

Published in the United States by Kodansha Comics,
an imprint of Kodansha USA Publishing, LLC, New York.

Publication rights for this English edition arranged through Kodansha Ltd.,
Tokyo.

First published in Japan in 2014 by Kodansha Ltd., Tokyo, as Yamada-
kun to Nananin no Majo volume 12.

ISBN 978-1-63236-141-7

Printed in the United States of America.

www.kodanshacomics.com

9 8 7 6 5 4 3 2 1

Translation: David Rhie
Lettering: Sara Linsley
Editing: Ajani Oloye
Kodansha Comics edition cover design: Phil Balsman